TRANSFORMATIONAL
PREACHING:
THE BASICS

David M. Brown

"Transformational Preaching: The Basics," by David M. Brown. ISBN 978-1-60264-672-8 (softcover) and ISBN 978-1-60264-673-5 (ebook).

Published 2010 by Virtualbookworm.com Publishing Inc., P.O. Box 9949, College Station, TX, 77842, US. ©2010 David M. Brown. All rights reserved. No part of this publication may be reproduced, stored in a retrieval system, or transmitted in any form or by any means, electronic, mechanical, recording or otherwise, without the prior written permission of David M. Brown.

Manufactured in the United States of America.

I dedicate this book to
present and future preachers around the world
who seek to understand and apply the principles herein.

Contents

Preface

This book is an edited version of my much larger work that was first published in 2003 and revised in 2007. That book, *Transformational preaching: Theory and practice,* is an examination of the preaching task from an all-encompassing view of preaching's primary "contexts." That work included the contexts of evangelical Christianity, corporate worship, and pastoral ministry. There are also chapters on rhetorical action in preaching, the prophetic ministry of preaching, the "word of God" as *message* rather than the static language of the written Scriptures, biblical inspiration, narrative truth, metaphor, and persuasion theory. These subjects are relevant to understanding what happens when we preach, but are not necessary for a "basic" understating of the theory and practice of putting a sermon together and proclaiming that word from the Lord with authority. If any of these subjects are of interest to you, you might consider taking a look at that longer version.

In this work, however, I have trimmed those 12 chapters, primarily to make these theoretical underpinnings of preaching more accessible to those who are not attracted by such a thick book, but also to allow a more manageable translation of the work for international exposure. I initially wrote *Transformational Preaching* to teach preaching teachers in Russia, and this shorter version, without the North American contextualization and some of the non-essential theory, will, hopefully, make the book more easily "translatable" and, thus, accessible to non-English speakers, particularly should I have the privilege of teaching internationally again.

I have also reorganized the material for this work into three hopefully-clearer sections that conform to the three primary influences on the preaching event: 1.) the *transaction* of *preaching,* and 2.) the *content* and 3.) *structure* of the *sermon.* This, I believe, makes the material more understandable, particularly for an international audience.

To further shorten the number of pages, I have also removed introductory and ending materials in each chapter, as well as most of the footnotes and all of the endnotes and source citations. Most of these works are not readily available to students in other countries or in different language groups. Their inclusion in the longer version provides research possibilities for English-speaking students, but seemed unnecessary for an international audience.

At the same time, I have lengthened the current project. At the suggestion of my Russian interpreter, I've added an Appendix with five "sample sermons" in it. He felt this would help the reader get a better idea of the kind of sermons I'm talking about. I have also re-worked the subject Index.

Finally, I have carefully combed through the text for this version of *Transformational Preaching* with an eye to minor editing, by changing a word or phrase here or there. Thus, if you compare this text with the original of my longer work, you will find, from time to time, slightly different wording or phrasing. In my view, these changes make the text more readable, but in no way change the intent of, or add additional information to, the original version.

I give thanks to those who have supported the larger work and who have responded to the impulse to purchase, study, and apply it. While this shorter version will also be published in English (as well as in an electronic format), its primary purpose is to give the international community the opportunity to understand these theoretical foundations of preaching and apply those theoretical insights to preaching in their own contexts.

To those of you who study and apply these principles, I pray the Lord's richest blessings on your most holy task of confidently and passionately proclaiming the eternal, loving, and powerful gospel of our Lord Jesus Christ.

So, with understanding and vigor, I encourage you to "preach the word, ready in season and out of season" (2 Timothy 4:2). May our Lord be honored!

David M. Brown
Pickerington, Ohio
08 September 2010

PROLOGUE:
An introduction to
the preaching ministry

In my own country of America, I have observed that in almost every church, preaching is poorly practiced because it is poorly understood. Preachers, for the most part, are inadequately prepared to preach, perhaps because most of our seminaries offer preaching *courses* but, because of time and financial constraints, spend little time in the actual *training* of preachers. Thus, if we could step back from our exposure to *usual preaching practices* and try to understand what really constitutes *the act of preaching,* we might be surprised at would we would discover.

This book attempts to do that. It is my sincere prayer that, if your preaching education has been inadequate, these chapters will cause you to think seriously about your *approach to* and *understanding of* preaching and, most especially, how you actually *practice* it. I do this not to dissuade you from the holy task of preaching, but so that you will, with intelligence and reason, approach this biblical task in a way that will more clearly communicate the good news of Jesus to those with whom you have the opportunity to minister. By being ready "in season and out," may it challenge and improve your own practice of preaching.

In this introductory section, we'll take a look at the act of preaching from the perspective of an external observer. These three chapters prepare the way for the rest of the book: the first is an Introduction to preaching that might cause you some discomfort. Chapter 1, then, will help us think about a definition of preaching, followed by Chapter 2 (again, an uncomfortable study) that raises the important distinction between preaching and teaching.

The intention of these chapters is to prepare you, the reader, for the rest of the book. As we go along, we will explore significant theory as well as practical, hands-on examples that will, hopefully, lead you toward the intentional (and intensive) effort required to become a transformational preacher!

Introduction

ONE AMONG MANY?

This book, in a way, is just *one more* preaching text in a market that is already flooded with such books. In a daze, you sift through them, pick up an interesting title, glance at the back cover, and if stimulated to read further, you turn to the flyleaf. But there are so many of them, and, as you have learned, most say pretty much the same thing. You may well be asking, "why another one?" In a way, this *is* just another preaching text, with theoretical and practical guidelines for the practice of preaching.

But I hope you will find that this book is also different. While it *is* theory-informed practice (with a strong connection between principle and discipline), it also presents a *different* model of preaching than you may find elsewhere. This text is a comprehensive examination of many facets of preaching, but it also marks a departure from much of the "standard wisdom" of many other preaching books. As an almost radical approach to the preaching ministry, it treats preaching as an oral *event* rather than a scripted *tradition*. That is, I won't argue for preaching just because it's something we *should* do or something that *should* happen in a particular way. Preaching is much more than *content* and *form* and the clever reading of a well-prepared manuscript. It is a highly significant *oral* experience that happens between people, a surprisingly holy act through which lives are changed. I will be talking about *what actually happens* in preaching, and, in that way, this book attempts a different perspective on the preaching ministry. Let me explain what I mean.

A DIFFERENT PERSPECTIVE

In a new day, we need to *think in a new way* about the discipline of preaching, and in a way that radically reorients theory. That's the task of this book. In some respects, the approach here identifies a new *paradigm,* though one that is already practiced from many pulpits and platforms around the world. But the old lingers, because any change from one form to another takes a long time. Thomas Kuhn (1962), in his seminal work on paradigm shifts, tells us that new paradigms emerge slowly as old structures are replaced by new. It takes time, but it also requires a radical rethinking of the old. So if we want to *change* our preaching, we must *think about* it in a new way.

To begin that, how many squares do you see in Figure I.1?

Figure I.1

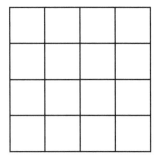

When I first attempted this problem, my inclination was to say "16." But when I was challenged to think more strategically, I realized that there's also one big square that surrounds them all (a 4 x 4 configuration). And then I noticed 2 x 2 squares (there are nine of them). Following logical progression, 3 x 3 squares gave me four more. That's 30 squares all together. The solution to the puzzle depends on how you "see" it. Taking notice of all the parts of the full image provides a more complete picture of what's there.

In the same way, we can perceive the preaching ministry from several different perspectives: the authority of Scripture, the role of the preacher, his or her engagement with listeners, the sermon's content and structure, the *relationship* between the preacher and people that influences the experience, various environmental factors, the needs and dreams of the listeners, the preaching contexts, hermeneutical principles, the quality of the preacher's sleep last night (or lack thereof)—all play a part in the event. There is nothing simple about preaching, and the more of these elements that are taken into consideration (like the more squares in the box), the more we can learn about what happens when we preach. That is, preaching is *not* just about biblical principles and expository rules. This book is an attempt to pinpoint some of the significant elements of this human action of "preaching" that engages both divine and community dialog.

Here's another little exercise: try to cover all nine dots in Figure 1.2 with four straight lines without taking your pencil off the paper:

Figure I.2

.　　　　.　　　　.

.　　　　.　　　　.

.　　　　.　　　　.

If you're frustrated with this problem, that's o.k. The trick can't be done unless you think "outside" the natural boundaries created by the dots. That is, to "get the picture," you have to look beyond the *ordinary* framework of the dots. When you do that, the puzzle is fairly easy to solve, as in Figure I.3 (on top of the next page).

In order to adopt a new way of preaching, we must learn to look "outside the box." In a radically changing social and Christian milieu around the world, the proclamation of biblical truth has also been changing. When we think about "seeker sensitive" approaches and the new "generations" that have been identified, and recognize a global interest in renewal of worship, it is important that we understand what is happening in the pulpits of our churches and auditoriums. When we do that, we will discover a rich reorientation of our understanding of what makes preaching *preaching*.

I hope you'll be able to do that with me as I attempt to "frame" preaching in a new way. As with every preacher, your understanding is limited by what you *already* think, and if your *perception* about preaching changes, chances are that your *practice* will also change. That's what leads to a paradigm shift.

A CHANGE OF PARADIGMS

During the past several decades, I believe we have been witnessing the emergence of a new paradigm for preaching. But in order to understand this new approach, we first must understand the old one. It isn't hard to recognize—it has been evident in two forms in homiletical circles for many, many decades, and has been the model of choice for generations of preachers.

Figure I.3

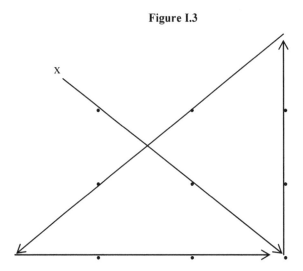

THE FORMER PARADIGM

Today's most popular and practiced homiletical orientation is one that merges teaching with preaching. The pulpit has become the location from which the Bible is *taught*. After all, it is said, people are biblically illiterate, and, because corporate worship is the only public gathering of the congregation, it is important to take the opportunity to *teach* the Bible to them, chapter by chapter, verse by verse. The preacher's goal, then, is to offer significant reflections on the text to help today's Christians *understand* the theology behind a text. It often leads to what the scholars say about each verse, Greek word, or theological issue, and which views are right and which are wrong. The approach, it is supposed, develops a more biblically-literate, sophisticated laity. Because it encourages biblical exposition, it is generally known as the *expository* model.

This approach to "preaching as teaching" is a natural development from an earlier model that had the same basic orientation. It was satirized as the "three points and a poem" method, suggesting that every good sermon usually included three reflections on a theological issue or biblical text and then closed with a poem. The purpose of these sermons was to provide valuable *insights* on doctrine, the Bible, or Christian theology, often with alliterative words or phrases so people could remember them. So we still hear informational sermons that proclaim the word of God as "Active, Alive, and Amazing!" or instructions that Christians are to "Pray, Preach, and Persevere!" Most of these sermons are carefully crafted documents that are read from the pulpit. They create *reflective* listeners who are supposed to be interested in *explanations* of Scripture, presuming that by *thinking about* spiritual matters, or by having the right kind of biblical *insight* or *knowledge,* they will know how to live out their faith. My father was one of the finest preachers of this style, with meaty, thoughtful sermons that made a significant difference to many of his listeners. It was the acceptable style of preaching in his day, and the one in which he was taught.

However, this approach to preaching, for the most part, is based on at least two faulty assumptions. The first is that people listen to preaching to *study* and *learn.* This posture implies that the most important approach to the Christian faith is *cerebral* or *rational,* and the best way to satisfy that intellectual hunger of these avid listeners is to *teach* them.

The second assumption is that the purpose of listening is to *remember.* And because listeners can remember no more than three points, alliteration (used as a mnemonic device) was introduced. More recently, note-taking has been encouraged, where worshipers either bring notebooks to worship or the preacher provides a blank sermon outline in the printed order of worship. In this way, more "points" are allowed, since the information can be written down and taken home for further study and reflection. Sometimes an overhead projector is used in this "worship/classroom" setting, and sometimes, even, the preacher will provide a printed copy of the full sermon text to be taken home afterward. In any case, the *effect* of preaching is basically left until later.

Unfortunately, when the main goal of preaching is the dissemination of information, the Christian faith tends to become an *intellectual* pursuit that is *passionless* and *uneventful,* and the Church not only loses her spokespersons but also the confrontational power that is necessary for the transformation of people's lives. Indeed, when *teaching* replaces preaching, both of these important ministries suffer. *Preaching* is lost altogether, and the most significant *teaching* in the Church comes through the *lecture* method, which is absolutely the worst form of pedagogy.

THE EMERGING PARADIGM

At the same time that this "cerebral" approach to preaching has been almost universally practiced, a different kind of voice has been surfacing. It is what I am identifying as a *new paradigm.* In contrast to the preaching-as-teaching model, this new approach understands preaching as *persuasive* discourse; it is *convicting, motivational,* and/or *inspirational.* It does not merely pass along important information or the brilliant insights of the preacher. Preaching, when it is *preaching,* confronts its listeners with a truth-driven biblical challenge that has the purpose of changing an *attitude or action.* This is what I call *transactional* discourse, and it has the power to *transform* the heart and will of its listeners.

The idea of *transaction* also suggests that the real work of preaching happens *during* the preaching event. The power of the Holy Spirit transforms the mind, heart, attitude, and life-orientation of the listener, *as meaning emerges* through the preaching event, *at the time of* the proclamation, not by remembering it later. This, again, separates this new paradigm from the old.

If you are practicing the old paradigm and want to think about issues related to the preaching ministry, I encourage you to do so. But you might have to set aside your prior assumptions and come at the preaching ministry in a fresh way. If you reflect on what *really* happens in the preaching event rather than what you think *should* happen, your preaching may well become transformational. That's my hope in offering this book.

UNDERSTANDING THE THEORY

You will notice that there is a lot of theory in this book, and you may wonder why you need it. Indeed, you may be tempted to skip over the theory and go right to the practical recommendations. I encourage you not to do that, since my approach is what is called *theory-driven practice.* You won't find tricks or short cuts to your preaching, because practical advice is important only when it *follows* theory. *Theory* provides a general philosophy of preaching. It not only helps us examine pertinent information and relevant issues, but it explains what happens in the preaching event.

So what you will find here is a whole *way* of understanding preaching: the practical matters won't necessarily be of help if you don't grasp the *philosophy* of preaching that accompanies it. So *chew on* and *digest* what is theoretical here. Only then should you *put it into practice,* because *practice* only makes sense when it is derived from a particular *theoretical* perspective.

Actually, *all* preaching is based on some kind of theory, but often the theory is either not known or is inaccurate, or it is based on incorrect assumptions. There is good and bad theory behind all preaching. But without adequate or well-grounded theory, practice often goes awry. If you preach without understanding its theoretical base, there is then only one acceptable method for preaching—that of following a *model.* Then you are forced into the rules and regulations of a form or system where your creativity and uniqueness are severely restricted. That's why it is critical that you understand theory. Its practical application then comes not by following *rules,* but by applying *principles* that are derived from that sound *theory.* So I am arguing that if you get the *theory right,* the *right practice* will follow. Only then can your preaching keep improving.

Second, the theory you will find here, for the most part, emerges from the academy. I will be calling upon some of the current scholarly disciplines that influence the preaching experience, but always with an eye toward its *practical effect* on preaching. In the past several years, exciting thinking has been done in the fields of human communications, rhetoric, sociology and anthropology, the structure of discourse, orality, and performance theory. I have been studying and reflecting on these disciplines, and have "baptized" many of their insights for preaching. Coupled with strong biblical studies and an awareness of a quickly-changing secular culture, these perspectives on the preaching ministry help us understand what happens when *preaching* happens, and how best to carry out this critical ministry of the Church. As you will see, these disciplines have led me to some rather startling convictions about what preaching is and how it should be practiced.

Finally, theory means that this is a "principled" rather than a "how-to" approach (though you will find plenty of "how to" information here). In my experience, principles can lead to very *different* practices, and the issues and principles I present here are designed with that in mind. I do not intend that you mimic the practical advice you find here, but I do want to provide examples of how the principle can be applied. I strongly encourage your own freedom to develop and emerge as your own kind of preacher. Keep that in mind: the *theory* will help you *understand* preaching, but it should also help you practice the art and discipline of preaching *in your own way.* Ultimately, I hope you will "recontextualize" these principles in your own culture and local situation and according to your own personality.

Here's an interesting phenomenon that I learned from Dick Francis, that internationally-known mystery writer *(Flying Finish* [1966], NY: Pocket Books, p. 73). Horse breeding can be a very lucrative business, both for those who own champion racing stallions and those who breed mares for the purpose of selling the offspring. Mares are bred with different stallions to increase the likelihood of new champions being born. Typically, the stallion stays in his own stable and the mare is brought to him (she travels from stable to stable). However, because a new foal cannot travel for a month after it is born, and so as not to lose precious time, the pregnant mare is taken to the place where she will be bred next. Her foal is thus born in a new stable, and, while the mare is still suckling her newborn, she is re-inseminated by the resident stallion. The foal, then, which was conceived in one place, is birthed in that new stable. That is, *what is conceived and has gestated in one environment is given birth in another.*

That's what I'm talking about here. A "principled" approach should have the ability to contextualize preaching in a different environment than that in which it gestated. In other words, the theoretical foundation and practical principles that developed in my own study and practice of preaching can be given birth in your unique context; what emerged from my pulpit can be reborn in your own experience; what has been conceived in America can be birthed in Russia. A "model" approach does not have this flexibility. But *theory,* on the other hand, has many applications: the "there and then" can be practiced in the "here and now" in a different way.

But I also hope the theory and principles will help you reflect on preaching for the rest of your life. Your preaching ministry will be different all along the way as you mature in ministry and as your environment of ministry changes through the years. For this reason, I encourage you to stay on a "growing edge" as long as you are able to preach. My hope is that this book will help you continue to emerge as your own kind of "preacher artist" for the rest of your life, and that you will find the theory helpful through the years. From time to time, I hope that you will re-examine the book either in a disciplined way or as you become aware of struggles with particular aspects of your preaching.

THE DESIGN OF THE BOOK

The book is structured in such a way that it identifies particular characteristics of preaching. You may already have noticed from the Table of

Contents that the book is divided into three sections (plus a Prologue and Epilogue). In this Introductory chapter and two subsequent chapters in the Prologue, I will define preaching as *transactional, incarnational, biblical, influential,* and *intentional,* as *integrated* aspects of a single preaching event. Look at them as different ways of perceiving the *same* experience, like five microscopes fixed on a single "preaching slide."

Once we complete the Introduction and two chapters of the Prologue, Section I begins our understanding of preaching by examining human communication theory (in five chapters). It sets preaching within the framework of *oral communication.* I identify preaching as *transactional,* as the primary way in which humans *communicate.* We are able to understand preaching only after we adequately understand human communication, particularly public monological communication. Thus, the *active experience of preaching* concerns this book, as an "event" in which a single transaction happens between preacher and congregation. Preaching is not the "delivery" of a sermon that has been carefully packaged in the study (though preaching requires adequate preparation). Rather, it is the *emergence of biblical meaning* that comes through the unique interactive experience between a particular preacher and a particular congregation at a particular moment.

Included in Part B of this section will be two short chapters on the role of the preacher in the preaching event. This is what I identify as the *incarnational* role of the preacher, that every preacher is unique, as God intends. We will then examine the important distinction between the two "languages" that every literate society knows: written and oral. Each has its own structure, and, as we will see, this distinction offers a more accurate understanding of *oral* human communication. With it, we will move away from both the "three points and a poem" and "expository" models, because those approaches tend to exchange oral language for written. The old paradigm generally reflects an underlying bias that preaching is *doctrinal,* and that doctrinal information is *a-contextual.* Orality, however, demands a *transactional* view of human communication, one that is also *relational* and *contextual.*

In Sections II and III, then, we will turn our attention to the sermon itself. Section II is an examination of the *content* of the sermon. The six chapters of Part A will focus on what I mean by "biblical preaching" and how the biblical text should be handled in your sermon. If we are serious about *biblical preaching,* we must recognize that Scripture informs and constrains the preaching ministry. That is, the Bible offers the very foundation for and content of preaching, and it is the authority of Scripture that lends confidence to the authority of the preacher who speaks on behalf of our Lord.

Part B of Section II, then, includes two chapters on the narrative content of the sermon, which is essential in oral communication if we really want to reach our listeners. Orality implies that the content and form of preaching must reach *hearts,* not just minds. And this, in turn, implies the use of story. However, unlike other textbooks that identify stories or personal examples as *support materials* or *illustrations,* I call them "actualizing resources," because they help bring about (or *actualize)* the biblical truth, which is the transformative word of God that emerges in the preaching event.

In Section III, we will examine the *structure* of a sermon. Structure helps us understand how to construct an *intentional* sermon. This section will look at how the gathered materials are put together so the listener is most effectively confronted with the living word of God. That is, a sermon is coherently structured for *listening.*

Finally, the Epilogue contains four chapters that will help you before and after the preaching event: where you get ideas for sermons, how to develop your own short and long-range routines for preparing sermons and planning ahead of time, and a few recommendations for what to do after you've preached this week.

Together, these chapters contain the essence of my much longer work that includes other influences on the preaching ministry, but these chapters are the "basics" that converge on the single experience that I call *transformational preaching.*

WHAT *NOT* TO EXPECT

If that is what you *will* encounter in these pages, what, then, should you *not* expect?

First, don't look for an explanation of different *models* of preaching. This book will not present an assortment of *approaches* to preaching from which to pick and choose, nor will it demonstrate different styles of preaching or the way various preachers practice their craft. It is very singularly oriented toward the method I call *transformational preaching.* Yes, the *theory* and *principles* will lead to certain "advice," but the whole approach also encourages you to develop your own unique style of preaching.

Nor is this a survey of different *methods* of preaching. In the 1960s and later, different preaching *forms* were encouraged: mime, dialogue, music, drama, and narrative, to name a few. These creative approaches to preaching can be effective, but we won't deal with them here. Instead, we'll be talking exclusively about *monological* preaching (as I will define it in Chapter 1). This is not to *discount* the importance of other preaching forms (including that of the teaching paradigm), but my concern is to argue persuasively for *this* approach to preaching.

Finally, this book will not present a "Bible approach" to preaching, as a survey of everything the Bible says about preachers and their craft. The Bible is not a sourcebook for how preaching ought to be done, in spite of those "Bibliolotrists" who would like to believe that the Bible is an all-sufficient guide for *everything* we think or do as Christians. The Bible certainly includes a host of preachers from whom we can learn many things about the business of preaching. The Bible *inspires* our preaching and *provides authoritative content* for our preaching. But it is not a practical handbook with simplistic rules for *how* to preach. That's why there are so many textbooks that tell us how to do it. It's the reason why I have "baptized" several academic disciplines for this study, because the insights we glean from those sources are invaluable in helping us understand the preaching ministry.

PERSONAL HISTORY AND BIASES

We are now at a place where it might be helpful for you to know a bit more about me. I offer this information so that you will understand more fully what you will encounter in this book.

A PERSONAL PILGRIMAGE

As I've already intimated, this book departs from the "standard wisdom" that you will find in many preaching texts. It's an approach that arises from a long practice of preaching that began consistently in 1973, as pastor, but then included interim pastor, missionary, educator, and "pulpit supply" preacher. I've not always got it right. I experimented and struggled with preaching forms early in my ministry. I read about and studied preaching, attended seminars, and earned a Master's degree in Homiletics and a Ph.D. in Rhetoric and Communication. My style, and the approach to preaching that you find here, have developed over time.

In all but the first four years of my preaching ministry, I have preached without notes. My preaching has developed and matured as I have conscientiously reflected on the art and discipline of preaching, and I have experienced both the exuberance and disappointment of an active preaching ministry. I taught public speaking courses at secular universities for six years. I've conducted several small group training experiences and led a host of seminars. I have taught preaching courses in different settings, including four multi-cultural international seminaries and schools, and three non-English speaking national seminaries in Europe. My five years of teaching, preaching, and consultation work in non-degree theological education throughout Europe has introduced me to extraordinary people and extraordinary preachers and extraordinary preaching environments. I have now been preaching consistently for over 37 years. In that time, I have grown in my understanding and practice of the preaching ministry.

I cite my training and experience not to suggest that I have a special dispensation for or expertise in preaching. I do so merely to suggest that I have preached, contemplated preaching, and adapted my style throughout my life. I still learn every time I preach and every time I engage in conversation about preaching. But I have not always preached well. That's why I encourage you to *keep practicing* and *changing* your own ministry of preaching. The theory and principles you learn here should help you discover something new about your own *practice* of preaching, but they will only be useful if you adapt them and *practice* them. My prayer is that this book will drive you to become an even better preacher than you are now.

PERSONAL PERSPECTIVES

There are three additional biases that you will find reflected in this text. I state them here so you will understand my personal culture, context, traditions, and orientation. I am not suggesting that you *adopt* these convictions without processing them in and through your own experience and context—I offer them only so that you will understand more fully what is to come in the chapters that follow.

God as "Father"

First, I unapologetically refer to God as "He." While this may be considered politically incorrect, I do not believe this practice to be *exclusivism*. Language *always* has limitations. In the past, I have tried to talk about God without using personal pronouns ("God gave God's own Son"), but that, for me, leads to a highly impersonal God Who is devoid of warmth and with Whom it is difficult to maintain a relationship. Because references to God are more commonly accepted using masculine pronouns, and because Jesus, using the social and linguistic conventions of his own time, referred to God as his "heavenly Father," I, too, use masculine pronouns to talk about God. (It is also my practice to use the Upper Case form "He" or "Him" to refer to God, but the lower case "he" or "him" to identify Jesus or the Holy Spirit.)

This is *not* to suggest that God is somehow more "masculine" than "feminine" or "neuter." All three designations, by necessity, are *metaphoric* understandings of the God Who reveals Himself in and through nature, Scripture, the prophets, and Jesus. I fully appreciate God's revelation in *masculine* terms, as the strong *male warrior* (Exodus 15:3), the *Father* of Jesus (Luke 23:46), and when John depicts Jesus as the *husband* of the Church (Revelation 19:7). I also fully recognize the *female* characteristics of God, when, for instance, Jesus identifies God as a *woman* searching for her lost coin (Luke 15:8-10), when he refers to himself as a *mother hen* (Matthew 23:37), and when Paul identifies Jesus as the "wisdom *(sophia)* of God" (1 Corinthians 1:24). But God is also referred to in genderless (neutral) terms, as πνευμα ("Spirit") in John 4:24. I have settled on the masculine forms simply for convenience and social norm, so that my discussion of preaching will not get lost in issues of gender conflict.

However, it is also my prayer that this will not become an obstacle for those for whom a *masculine* identity for God is problematic. I am simply using what is for me an accessible and understandable designation of God, but without attempting to make that metaphor an all-encompassing identity of God.

At the same time, I reject the usage of "man" or "mankind" as a way to talk about *people* who are both masculine and feminine. In these cases, I have tried to use inclusive terms like "humanity" or "individuals."

Men and women preachers

You will discover that I refer to preachers using both masculine and feminine pronouns. According to Peter's quotation of Joel 2:28 in his Pentecost sermon (Acts 2:17-18), we are living in the "last days," and in these last days, both *sons and daughters* are engaged in the prophetic preaching ministry. I believe strongly that God experientially calls both men and women to preach today. There are a host of books and other resources that examine a full biblical perspective on the role of women in the church, including pulpit ministry. Where possible, I have tried to substitute inclusive language in older quotations that limit preaching to males. But when making these changes has created awkward wording, I have retained the original language.

First and Second Testaments

Finally, I refer to what are traditionally designated "Old" and "New" Testaments as "First" and "Second" Testaments. I hope this doesn't cause confusion. "Old," to me, implies *out-moded* or *out-dated.* And sometimes the "New" revelation of God in Jesus Christ is perceived as a *replacement* of the "Older" Covenant, thus suggesting that the New Testament is "more inspired" than the Old. By using the terms "First" and "Second" Testaments, I hope to avoid this tendency.

At the same time, of course, I realize that "Second Testament" might also imply the existence of a "Third" or "Fourth Testament," but this is an idea that I fully reject. The Bible, as we have it today, for theological and practical purposes, is its "final edition." In my evangelical Christian view, both First and Second Testaments are equally inspired and both equally important for what I call "gospel preaching."

FOR THE LIFE-LONG STUDENT

Finally, let me offer some personal words to those of you who are using this book to study preaching.

If you are a beginning student of preaching, my prayer is that this text will help you get started. But you will only *start* your study here. You will then grow and develop into your own kind of preacher in the future. That will happen once you start to preach consistently. The issues and information contained in this book should be helpful as you engage these ideas throughout your preaching ministry. Indeed, it will be most helpful if you see this approach as a *framework* from which you can develop your own style.

For most of you, though, this book will be a *developmental step* in your preaching pilgrimage. Whether you have had the privilege of preaching only a few times or are a seasoned veteran of the pulpit, you are still a *student* of preaching. If you've been at it a long time, you might notice that your old textbook doesn't really reflect what you've been *practicing* or how you now understand your craft. That indicates growth.

But perhaps your preaching hasn't really changed much through the years. If that is the case, you are likely to find a lot of the material in this book disturbing and challenging. That's only natural, since this approach in some ways presents a new view of preaching. But that's the stuff of which learning is made. New information will only disturb you if you take it *seriously.* That's why I ask that you read and reflect on what you find here, so you might discover how this approach plays against the reality of preaching as you have come to know it *in actual practice.* As you take this approach seriously, it is likely that you will have to *unlearn* some of your prior assumptions about preaching or what you have been told about it, or how you have thought about it in your many years of practice.

Here's another way to look at it: like your physician, you only have a license to *practice* preaching, not a license to *preach.* And as with your physician who must maintain her education, you, too, need to keep *learning.* So I encourage you to read and absorb *all* the information you can find about preaching—especially *other* textbooks and materials and discussions that present a different approach and other perspectives. Experiment with your own art form as you go along. My prayer is that this approach will challenge you to grow in your own pilgrimage of *continually becoming* a preacher.

Indeed, the strategy you find here may refocus your entire preaching ministry, and, if you take it seriously, it may even radically transform your preaching. But this is not a "fix-it" book for those who are looking for quick or easy solutions to improve lacklustre preaching. Rather, this book is designed to force you to *re-evaluate* your preaching ministry. If your current preaching isn't theoretically sound, you can't just tinker with it and hope that things will change, because your theoretical grounding must also change. If you find this book to be an offensive critique of your preaching, I make no apology, particularly if it leads you to discovery, which, in turn, helps you discard some of your ineffective practices and encourages your preaching to become even more relevant and life-changing for your listeners. You might not agree with much of what I have to say, but the theory, information, and implications are sound, and they should raise searching questions for you. Actually, as I've already said, the best education happens when you read or hear something that is new to you, that *stretches* you, that is *uncomfortable* for you. If you only read things that you already know, little learning or growing happens. So don't be afraid of being stretched. Don't be afraid to wrestle with these ideas, because even if you ultimately reject them, the wrestling will bear fruit.

At the same time, don't believe everything you hear or read! I wholeheartedly accept and practice what I have written here, and I hope you will take this approach seriously. But I also hope you will glean from this book what makes sense *to you,* and that you will process the information in ways that will be most helpful for your own context, culture, and traditions. I ask you to *engage* the ideas you find here.

In the chapters that follow, I have borrowed from many preaching texts and homileticians who have informed my own emerging approach to preaching. Thus, this text, in many ways, encapsulates information that has been identified by others as foundational to the preaching ministry. There are many books that include useful *principles* that support this new paradigm of preaching, even though these valuable principles may be nested within the old paradigm.

But in other ways, this book sheds new light on the discipline of preaching. Even so, I recognize that the information here is inadequate, and I apologize to scholars who are already more learned in these particular disciplines than I. Indeed, there may be incorrect information or wrong assumptions on my part. But the nature of academic work is such that more significant thinking emerges from the foundations laid by others. In many ways, I am merely standing on the shoulders of giants, but I also realize that by the time this book is published, it is likely that there will be new information in these disciplines that will be of significant value to the preaching ministry. I welcome this new thinking.

Finally, don't expect to learn how to preach from this book! You will only learn how to preach once you start to *preach consistently*. It doesn't mean getting up once in a while and trying your hand at it. It means having to preach regularly, week after week, in relationship with an authentic, engaged congregation. And that's something that never grows old. I learn something about preaching every time I preach—and I have much to learn from others who preach, too.

THE CONTINUING CHALLENGE

The Apostle Paul writes in Romans 1:15-16 that preaching is the *power* of the gospel. Paul couldn't think of any more significant ministry that displays the power of God than that of preaching. We see him demonstrating that power all through the stories of the *Acts,* practicing the kind of preaching through which people's lives are absolutely and eternally changed by the gospel of Jesus Christ. Paul recognized that when all the complex elements of the preaching event are brought together by the Holy Spirit, when the system "works" as it should, then lives and communities are transformed.

The biblical challenge is clear. It continues for our preaching today. Oh that we could grasp such power in our own pulpits! The Church is crying for preachers today, for those who are willing to stand up and unashamedly announce, "This is what the Lord demands of us today! How will we respond?"

Indeed, as we see from Paul's own practice, a powerful preaching ministry is not something to be taken lightly. The contemporary worshiping congregation needs to hear a preacher more than a teacher, a single voice that unashamedly rings clear with gospel power, that calls its hearers to respond to the will of a holy God. When that kind of preaching resounds from our pulpits, the Church will be transformed into a strong and relevant biblical community, and new disciples will be added to the kingdom.

Let me say again as strongly and excitedly as I can: *through good preaching, the Holy Spirit can transform the lives of individuals and local congregations—indeed, entire communities!*

It is my most profound prayer that we will find an energetic renewal in our pulpits throughout the 21st century.

May it be so in your own preaching!

CHAPTER 1
Preaching, for a Change

A *PUNNY* TITLE

The title of this chapter is a play on words. Its first meaning is probably more evident without the punctuation: *"Preaching for a change."* It indicates my belief that good preaching can bring about *change,* that it has the possibility of transforming the life of your local church and the lives of your listeners. Good preaching shouldn't settle for merely passing on interesting information or creative insights from or about a biblical text. Rather, preaching that is *transformational* will enable the Holy Spirit to bring about *change* in your listeners.

The second meaning of the title suggests that, in my experience, there isn't a lot of *preaching* happening in many of our pulpits today, particularly when it is so popularly practiced as *teaching.* That's one reason why I've written this book, to encourage preaching, as a *change* from the way it is often understood and practiced. At the beginning of our pilgrimage together, my prayer is that what you find here will be challenging and encouraging for your preaching, for a change!

PREACHING IN THE CATALYTIC MODE

The National Historic Site of Hopewell, Pennsylvania, is a restored 18th century industrial village that had been built around a blast furnace. When I first walked into the building that houses the furnace, I was overwhelmed by the large brick chimney that stretches up into the top of the tall, barn-like building. I learned later that this was not a chimney, but the actual furnace. Echoing through the building is the constant creak of an old water wheel pumping a pair of large bellows in the rear of the building. The air puffs its way through large ducts that force oxygen into the furnace.

From 1771 to 1883, when the furnace was in operation, it generated molten iron for cast iron stoves. The iron was produced when charcoal, limestone, and iron ore were dropped in layers in the top of the furnace. The intense heat fused these ingredients together through a catalytic reaction, as the carbon from the charcoal reduced the iron oxides to molten iron. Through a little trap door in the bottom of the furnace the iron workers removed the molten metal, which was then poured into sand castings.

This same kind of process happens in preaching. It is, in every way, a *synergetic* experience, where the result of the interaction is greater than the individual components can produce by themselves. It is Paul Scott Wilson's (1995) approach, that *content, form*, and *function* are fused in preaching. Everything comes together, and all work at the same time. The Holy Spirit creates this catalytic fusion from the human efforts of the preacher, the power and authority of Scripture, and the attitudes and circumstances of each listener. All are merged in a spiritually-heated environment. Something *happens* in the preaching event that is greater than the individual components.

So preaching is a fusion of several distinct facets of a common, shared experience. All of its various elements merge together and interact with each other. Sermon envisioning and construction adheres to particular principles, but the real "sermon" emerges from a unique mix of elements that ultimately come together in the pulpit. This is what I mean when I say that preaching is *transformational.* It is an event in which preacher, text, and listener are brought together by the Holy Spirit to create a holy, relevant, *life-transforming experience.* As I hope you will see, this kind of preaching, when understood as an *experience,* is far different from that of *reporting* interesting biblical information from the pulpit.

"SERMON" VS. "PREACHING"

What happens in Sunday morning discourse? If we listen in on the preaching in different worshiping communities, we might find, in one, the *lecture* format, where listeners are expected to take notes; in another, a step-on-your-toes, fully prophetic, confrontational proclamation. In one, a fully-anticipated and boring rendition of trite and meaningless theological jargon; in another, an *insightful* sermon in which the preacher has plucked sometimes-brilliant ideas from a particular biblical text. In one, an *expository explanation* of a particular text of Scripture in a verse-by-verse guided tour; in another, a topical discussion that hardly mentions the Bible. In one, a rapid Bible-hopping, Bible-flipping, Bible-thumping passion; in another, a monotonal monologue that doesn't move beyond a single word in a particular text. In one, a *"three points and a poem"* sermon read from the pulpit; in another, a *dialogue* sermon that leads directly to congregational discussion. In one, an *inductive* presentation; in another, *deductive* reasoning. In one, a *historical/biblical study;* in another, an inspirational message that has no relationship to the context in which it is proclaimed. In one, a short discourse for seeker-sensitive ears; in another, an intricately-developed biblical dissertation for the theologically numb.

The list could go on. But no matter what its style, preaching today happens in a secularized, post-modern world, one in which myriad distractions determine the mental orientation of listeners and alters not only their attention span but their focus as well. These 21st century listeners have learned to receive information in condensed pieces, a natural development from the Sesame Street generation and the 45-second political "sound bites" of the evening news. Today's preacher needs to know how to orient a biblical message in ways that the contemporary listener will be able to comprehend.

This brings us, then, to the difference between "sermon" and "preaching," two words that, for me, identify different orientations to the study of pulpit discourse.

SERMON AND HOMILETICS

The first term is "sermon," which I associate with the formal study of "homiletics." That is, it is preaching that is concerned with the content, argument, and structure of *sermons.* It has to do with pulpit rhetoric that can be *remembered* later in the week, where congregations are expected to *recall* the insights the preacher gained as he or she thought about the biblical text beforehand. Its focus is on the preacher's ability to *pass along information* in a memorable fashion. "Sermon," in this way, is *preacher-oriented.* While all preaching must be concerned with content, when we talk about "sermon," the emphasis is on the *text* rather than the *experience.*

"Sermons" are good and bad. They come in all sorts, forms, and styles, and those who teach from a "sermon" orientation focus on the *forms* that sermons take. This is what I mean when I say that "sermon" is the *text* of pulpit discourse.

This is also how I understand the word *homiletics,* as a discipline that studies sermons and preachers and the biblical and historic development of preaching. It might be considered the *science* side of the coin. Will homiletics be engaged in this book? Certainly! *Homiletics* helps us understand and put together a legitimate "sermon." *Homiletics* is important in so far as biblical exegesis and sermon construction and the hours of preparation prepare one for the *act of preaching,* which is the other side of the coin.

PREACHING

Let's look, then, at what I mean by "preaching," and see how it differs from my understanding of "sermon."

AN EVENT

Preaching is an *event.* It is that experience of stepping into the pulpit and *engaging* your listeners. It is preaching that brings about change in their hearts and lives. *Preaching,* rather than *homiletics,* is the engine that drives this approach. Preaching, as *an experience* rather than a "sermon," is *performative,* and, thus, *event* oriented. This event is not about a text, its content, or its printed form. In fact, a preaching perspective suggests that preaching is *not* meant to be *memorable,* except as the by-product of an engaging *experience.*

Life transformation comes about as the listener is engaged in the preaching event, *as it happens.* The Holy Spirit changes lives *through* the spoken word, *during* the experience of preaching. With this approach, the emphasis is on *hearing* and *message* rather than *written text* and *form.* Thus, preaching is listener-centered.

So when I talk about *preaching,* I'm referring to something more than just *sermon construction.* While there are different types of sermons, *preaching* describes the event in which these sermons are engaged. Another way to say this is that preaching always involves a *sermon* (its content), but not all sermons are preaching. The distinction I'm making is that preaching is *rhetorical discourse that seeks a response.* It is *a call to action.* It refuses to let the listener merely hear or learn a biblical truth or insight. It takes its responsibility one step further. The preacher intends for the listener to *respond* in some way to the biblical truth.

AN ART FORM

Preaching is also an *art form.* When you visit your neighborhood bookshop, you may notice piles of art reproduction books on the "sale" tables. There are a great number of these art books on the market (almost as many as there are preaching texts!). Let's suppose you are interested in oil painting rather than sculpture, water color, or chalk drawing, so you begin to sort through the volumes. You note that there are a host of oil painters (Rembrandt, Picasso, and Bob Ross) and great differences in style (impressionism, cubism, and Early Renaissance). If you were going to try your hand at oil painting, you might want to examine several of these artists, think about them, and study their different techniques. But the time would come when you would have to buy your own materials and start practicing on your own canvases until you find your own style. If you were to stick with it, you might even "perfect" that unique style, as one that is all your own.

It's the same with preaching. Different scholars have different approaches to it. There are no rights or wrongs about it. Nor are there any hard and fast rules that make it a "sure thing." That's why there are so many different styles and methods of preaching, and so many different books on the subject. (It doesn't mean that the information in these books necessarily leads you to *good* preaching, but it is to say that there are different styles because there aren't any universal laws about preaching.) The bottom line is that there are no *rules* for preaching that will insure a perfect sermon every time.

PRINCIPLES AND PRACTICE

The approach you will find in this book presents theory-driven *principles.* Often, these principles lead to particular practices, but not with the idea that there is only one way to do it or that there is such a thing as a perfect sermon. My hope is that the theory and practices of preaching, as presented here, will keep challenging you toward excellence, as you improve your own critically important preaching style.

Ultimately, you will come to understand and appreciate preaching only as you *think about preaching* and *practice preaching.* No artist was perfect the first time he or she put brush to canvas (or whatever other medium was used). It took years of discipline and observation, study, and practice. In the same way, preaching as an art form means that you are an artist in the pulpit. You will continue to improve your skills for the rest of your life, but only if you keep evaluating and learning. That's the purpose of this book. I want to help you to step back, examine, reflect, draw conclusions, and change things about how you preach, every time you try it.

This is also to suggest that you keep experimenting with your preaching, at least for the first five or ten years. David Kolb (1991) offers a model of experiential learning. It's a spiral form, which says that we have an experience, reflect on it, draw principles from it, and apply those new principles to the next experience. So you try something new in your preaching and decide that it didn't work out right. You think about it, decide that you didn't use enough stories, and try it a new way next time. That works well in this new experience, but then the *structure* of your ideas didn't flow as well as you expected. So you try something else the next time. In this way, your style grows through experimentation, trial and error, and continual reflection and improvement. That's what I mean by continuing to practice your art form.

SEEKING A DEFINITION

Now comes an important question. I've just been talking about *many* genres of art, and many *forms* within each genre. Why, then, do I dare write a book about a *distinct* approach? Why would I dare to suggest that the transformational preaching model is the *best* way to preach? It's a good question, and I want to answer it by attempting to define what I mean by preaching. As you will see, preaching is an experience that must be grounded in good theory. But when we attempt a definition, certain issues emerge that force us to think about the preaching ministry, perhaps in a different way than we've considered it before.

There are many ways homileticians define preaching. Some seek to include the centrality of Jesus and the Bible, such as William Thompson's (1966) definition. A sermon, he writes, is "the Word of God (Jesus Christ) who has been revealed in the pages of the written Word (the Bible) coming to the hearing of people by the proclamation of the Word (preaching)." Other definitions are more complex (and gender-exclusive). Haddon Robinson (1980), for instance, says that "(expository) preaching is the communication of a biblical concept, derived from and transmitted through a historical, grammatical, and literary study of a passage in its context, which the Holy Spirit first applies to the personality and experience of the preacher, then through him to his hearers." Other definitions are fairly simple, as Robert L. Thomas' (1992), who writes that a sermon is "a discourse setting forth the meaning of a passage in a popular form." In actuality, it could be argued that there are almost as many definitions of preaching as there are teachers of preaching (or, even, preachers).

However, let's look at the subject of definitions more broadly. One of my graduate school professors used to argue from what he called the *meta level.* It's a philosophical "higher plane" that is one step up in the system of thinking about things. That is, he would get us to consider the theory above (or behind) a particular theory. When we apply this principle to definitions, for instance, we find that they can usually be assigned to one of the following *meta* categories.

PRESCRIPTIVE

Some definitions we could call *prescriptive.* Prescriptive simply means what these objects, ideas, or events *should be like.* They are *theoretical* definitions. When preaching is defined prescriptively, it helps us understand what preaching is in its *ideal* form. A prescriptive definition is basically acontextual: it doesn't matter where preaching is done or how it is done. This kind of definition helps us understand what happens when *any* type of preaching occurs.

So, for instance, Al Fasol (1989) defines preaching as "orally communicating truth as found in the Bible in a way that applies God's Word to life today." My prior definition (1981) is also prescriptive: "a sermon is a call to action on some point of the biblical message." Both of these attempts suggest that preaching may be understood *theoretically,* as something that the preacher *comprehends* before stepping into the pulpit. These kinds of definitions are applicable no matter what particular *form* or *method* the sermon may take. They simply *prescribe* what takes place (or should take place) when preaching takes place.

EXPRESSIVE

A second category is *expressive* or explanatory. Expressive definitions understand objects, ideas, or events as they are *described* by *practitioners.* It is an *experiential* way of defining something. Social scientists say these definitions come from *insiders* who define practices in their own terms. In the discipline of preaching, for instance, preachers *explain* what happens when preaching happens. Generally, these definitions focus on *results.* For instance, Paul Scott Wilson (1995) defines preaching as "an event of encounter with God that leaves the congregation with stronger faith and deeper commitment to doing God's work." Likewise, Ilion T. Jones (1956) defines preaching as "God's saving approach to the souls of men and women." These definitions express what the preacher *intends* to accomplish in the sermon and what should happen with the listeners.

DESCRIPTIVE

The third approach to defining something is called *descriptive.* When an object, idea, or event is defined *descriptively,* it is presented so that it could be *observed* by an *outsider.* This is a *functional* or *instrumental* approach. It is the type of definition that appeals to social scientists, because it allows them to study a particular social phenomenon using scientific methodology and statistical analysis. If we follow a descriptive definition for preaching, then, we will be able to say, "When I see or experience this event, I know that preaching has happened."

For instance, we might arbitrarily say that by preaching we mean that "a religious leader stands before a religious gathering and orally presents a monological argument." We would know preaching, then, if we saw a specially-robed (or otherwise identifiable) person standing before a group of people in the context of a religious ceremony arguing a particular point of view. In this case, the "presenter" would have to be standing rather than sitting, and there would have to be speaking involved (thus ruling out mime). The trick of doing a descriptive definition is being able to narrow it sufficiently to include only that which you want to study. The prior definition, for instance, could also include the pastor leading a group Bible Study or the president of the local Promise Keepers instructing a group of men about auto repair. It might also include the activities of a Unitarian leader or a Buddhist monk or children at play, so it wouldn't work very well as a definition of preaching. This is simply to say that this kind of definition provides a way to define an observable *activity.*

Most definitions aren't as blatant as the one above, but we do find certain definitions about preaching that follow this approach. For instance, Richard Mayhue (1992) defines preaching as "(explaining) Scripture by laying open the text to public view in order to set forth its meaning, explain what is difficult to understand and make appropriate application." While Mayhue's definition leads to a *teaching* ministry, it does attempt to offer a *prescriptive* definition. That is, if there is a public gathering where Scripture is explained and applied, we can call it "preaching." (Of course, this also would apply to a Bible Study setting, so the definition doesn't "limit" itself to preaching as closely as it could.)

DEFINING BOUNDARIES FOR PREACHING

Given the complexities of this approach, it is this third way of understanding preaching that is most interesting and helpful. However, I'm not going to attempt to put a definition in one sentence that can be memorized or written down on an examination—it would be too long and complicated. But I do want to follow the descriptive model to help clarify what I'm talking about in this book. So I offer the following six characteristics as central to what I mean when I refer to preaching. They are *elements* or *influences* that inform or describe the preaching event. In my view, when *all* six elements of this definition are present, we will have a good understanding of preaching.

Actually, it could be said that this whole *book* is an attempt to define preaching. In that sense, what follows is a summation of what's to come, and will help you understand this particular approach to preaching. These six points are not listed in terms of importance, but are different *facets* or *elements* of the same experience.

1. EXPERIENTIAL

Preaching is an interactive *event,* a human *experience.* Thus, when I talk about preaching, I am not referring to a manuscript, "sermon," or the "delivery" of a message. Preaching is, at its heart, something that *happens* between human beings.

2. CONGREGATIONAL

Second, preaching is *congregational.* That is, it happens in a ritualistic event in the context of a gathered community of believers. Even most evangelistic preaching happens in the "congregational" setting of a local church, whether there are believers present or not. For this reason, most of the discussion in this book will be directed to preaching within the local congregation, even though the information and instruction will be relevant to preaching in other settings.

However, it is important to clarify what I mean by "congregational," because some preaching occurs outside the corporate worship environment (as it *should).* In these instances, even preaching that happens where there are no believers can be "congregational," if the listeners are *expecting* a certain kind of religious presentation. It is the *anticipation* of something "religious" that makes the experience "congregational." Without this element of expectation (even in a worshiping congregation of believers), preaching will not be preaching. It's why evangelistic preaching in a neighborhood park or Saturday-night tavern can be powerful and effective. "Congregational," at its heart, means *expectational.*

3. MONOLOGICAL

Preaching, as I am defining it, is a *monological* presentation that comes in a single, coherent discourse. Dialogue, drama, and music are worthy forms of proclamation, and I am not discounting their value (I've attempted some creative forms of preaching myself). But this book is about *monological* preaching. A gathered community hears a *single* voice proclaiming biblical truth. This means that preaching is a function of *a prepared preacher,* and is fully *incarnational.*

4. ORAL

Fourth, preaching is *oral proclamation* in an oral *transaction.* It is not read from a manuscript, because the oral word is aurally-received discourse, and, as we will see, the structure of oral language is quite different from that of written language. The congregation *listens* to preaching; they don't *read* the sermon (which is a different experience entirely). Yes, a lot of sermons are read from the pulpit (some better than others), but, for the most part, this is more the public reading of a Christian essay than it is *preaching.* This book is about preaching as an *oral* event, where preachers are engaged in communicating with oral language (the language of *conversation)* in a transactional experience with their listeners.

5. BIBLICAL

Fifth, preaching is *biblical*. This is a *content* issue. Preaching is established on, drawn from, and focused by a particular passage of Scripture. As we will see, a lot of sermons are not biblical in this sense. Many preachers gather biblical material from as many biblical "sites" as they can find to support their own theological perspective (it's what I will later categorize as a "theological" sermon). Rather, I am suggesting that preaching that is biblical proclaims a *single* biblical truth from a *single* biblical text.

6. PERSUASIVE

Finally, preaching is *persuasive* or *inspirational.* It is *not* the mere sharing of information or valuable insights that the preacher has gleaned in her or his study. Rather, persuasive discourse is the standard for preaching. Preaching always includes information, but the *purpose* of that information is to convict, persuade, motivate, or inspire its listeners. It moves beyond the presentation of information. Rather than merely transmitting good insights, preaching *uses* that information for persuasive purposes. It is what separates pulpit rhetoric from the classroom lecture.

A FUSION OF SIX

If we combine these characteristics, we'll arrive at an experience that I would define as "preaching." If any of these six elements is missing, it constitutes a different kind of experience than what I will be talking about in this book. Of course, there are other forms of public discourse that *could* be identified as preaching (and are by various homileticians), and other *forms* that can be equally transformative. But these six traits define the approach to preaching you will find here.

Finally, let me remind you that this definition is descriptive, not prescriptive. It isn't centered on what is *supposed* to happen. That is, when all these elements are brought together, transformation won't necessarily happen. Nor will good preaching happen. But the principles and practices that emerge from this definition will help you understand and work with issues, concepts, and information that should encourage and mature your own practice of preaching.

Altogether, it is my prayer that the chapters and the information that follow will help you understand and excite you to practice what I identify as *transformational preaching.*

CHAPTER 2
Lectern or Pulpit?:
The Role of Information

THE PREACHER-TEACHER

A significant perspective of this "new paradigm" of preaching is its distinction between teaching and preaching. I have already suggested that the current "three points and a poem" and "expository" models, as reflected in most of today's North American pulpits are based on *teaching;* the new paradigm of *proclamation.* It is my contention that when these two ministries are confused, the church loses out on both of these critical gifts to its ministries. That's why I feel it important to separate these two disciplines of pastoral ministry.

One of the latest titles in the Second Testament for the local church leader seems to have been a hyphenated word: "pastor-teacher" (Ephesians 4:11). However, as I've studied the role of the pastor in the Second Testament, I've discovered that teaching is just *one* of six biblical responsibilities of pastoral ministry, even though this verse has led some to suggest that teaching is the *primary* function of the pastor. For instance, Robert Thomas writes that "the central purpose of the sermon (is) a *teaching* device." And John MacArthur says, "The expositor's primary goal is to *teach* the Word accurately and completely." Unfortunately, this narrow restriction of the function of preaching to a *teaching* ministry leads to the abandonment of preaching as well as to the subsequent disempowerment of the teaching ministry, a move which, in my estimation, has resulted in the loss of "gospel power" in the church today *and* a poor approach to the church's call to disciple-making.

Clearly, the pastor's responsibility involves *both* teaching and preaching. Jesus commands us to love God with heart, soul, mind, and strength (Mark

12:30), and the totality of the Church's ministry needs to reflect this whole gospel for whole persons. It includes both preaching and teaching. But because teaching seems to be the primary thrust of pulpit ministry today, I want to examine these two important ministries of the Church. This will help us make a clearer distinction between preaching and teaching so that our understanding of preaching will be more focused and disciplined.

What's the difference? Generally, *teaching's* purpose is "here is what you should *know;* here's how you should *practice* your faith." It is informational. It imparts knowledge that leads to loving God with your *mind.*

The purpose of *preaching,* on the other hand, is "here is what you must *do,* how you must *respond* to biblical truth." It is a ministry of persuasion, inspiration, and/or motivation. Rather than providing listeners with an *understanding* of biblical truth (as happens in teaching), preaching's desire is to get listeners to *believe* and/or *act on* that biblical truth, where the listener is confronted with a decision. Preaching leads to loving God with your *heart* (will), *body* (action), and *strength* (resolve).

This suggests that transformational preaching is not as much *informational* as it is *motivational.* It is not the presentation of good ideas or insights *about* a biblical text or doctrinal issue. It takes its task one step further by wanting its listeners to *respond* to that biblical information. It is, in this way, *persuasive discourse.* When the pulpit is used for teaching, the Christian faith becomes cerebral and rationalistic—a religious discipline, if you will— rather than a *confrontational* one in which the listener is brought face to face with biblical truth and is called to respond to it.

In the Second Testament, the Greek word for teaching is διδαχη (didache) and the most commonly-used word for preaching is κερυγμα (kerygma). Unfortunately, the two disciplines are not easily separated: all preaching includes teaching, and teaching, to be effective, needs persuasive intent. *Both* information and persuasion are usually evident in each ministry. But when we think through the distinctions between teaching and preaching, the ultimate *intent* becomes critical: what is the purpose for practicing this ministry in the life of the local church?

I am not minimizing the importance of the teaching ministry. Indeed, I am a teacher myself. But teaching must find its proper place in the life of the church. What I *am* arguing for is a recognition that *preaching is a different ministry from teaching.* I believe that those who use the pulpit for teaching have a holy motivation for doing so. What I am convinced of, though, is that if the contemporary Church is to regain power from her pulpits, we must *separate* these two important ministries into their proper domains. When we do that, when teaching is provided elsewhere in the Church's life than from the pulpit, preaching is then able to reclaim its powerful, life-transforming, *rhetorical* ministry that is so much needed today.

The purpose of this chapter, then, is to examine the teaching ministry so we will better understand preaching.

A BIBLICAL STUDY

As we turn our attention to teaching, we begin with a brief overview of what the term "teaching" means in the Bible.

A BIBLICAL EXAMINATION OF TEACHING

In one form or another, nouns and verbs for teaching, instruction, or doctrine are used 330 times in Scripture, and almost half of them are derivatives of the Greek word, διδασκω (didasko: to teach). In those references, we see three "types" of teachers:

First, *God* is recognized as a Teacher. This includes all three "persons" of the Trinity: *Father/Creator* (as, for example, in the Septuagint's version of Job 36:22, Exodus 4:12, 15; Judges 3:2; many of the Psalms; and Isaiah 2:3). There are also 42 occasions in which *Jesus* is called "Teacher," along with 49 other references to his *teaching* ministry. And the *Holy Spirit* is also recognized as Teacher (in Luke 12:12, John 14:26, and 1 John 2:27).

Second, the *people of God* are teachers. This includes *ordinary people*, such as *parents* (Deuteronomy 4:9), *repentant sinners* (Psalm 51:13), and *women* (Jeremiah 9:20; Titus 2:3-4). But it also includes *priests, prophets, and leaders* (as in Exodus 35:34; Deuteronomy 5-6; 2 Chronicles 15:3; Ezra 7:6; and Ezekiel 44:23), and, of course, the *pastor-teacher* (Ephesians 4:12).

Third, the *Bible* is identified as a teacher (see Romans 15:4 and 2 Timothy 3:16).

Further, we find that the *ministry* of "teaching" is understood in different ways, too. Teaching is an *ability or gift* given to individuals (Romans 12:7), but also a *responsibility* of all Christians (Colossians 3:16; Hebrews 5:12). It is a *gift of leadership* given to build up the church (1 Corinthians 12:28, Ephesians 4:11), and a *role* responsibility in the church, as a *particular calling* (see Titus 2:3-4 and 1 Timothy 2:12). In every way, teaching is perceived as an *important* ministry, particularly as it combats false teachers and heresy (1 Timothy 6:2-5; Titus 1:10-14; and James 3:1).

PREACHING AND TEACHING IN THE MINISTRY OF JESUS

When the Gospel writers talk about the *proclamatory* ministry of Jesus, he is identified as both *preacher* and *teacher*. There are ten references to Jesus' *preaching* ministry and, as previously mentioned, 49 references to his *teaching*. In six of the verses where he *preaches* (Matthew 4:17; Mark 1:38; Mark 1:39, 2:2; Luke 4:43; and Luke 4:44), that word is mentioned by itself, without reference to teaching. Further, when Jesus practices the ministry of preaching, no discourses are transcribed that could be identified as "sermons": the Synoptic writers simply *identify* Jesus as a preacher. We have the unfortunate problem today that many discourses associated with Jesus' *teaching* are popularly identified as *preaching* discourses, as when parables are called "short sermons" or when Jesus' first compilation of sayings in Matthew 5, 6, and 7 is identified by contemporary editors as the *"Sermon on the Mount,"* when, according to Matthew 5:2, it is clearly *teaching* rather than *preaching.*

Of course, when the text refers to Jesus as *either* a preacher *or* teacher, it could be argued that preaching and teaching are *synonyms* in the minds of the Gospel writers. But there are four references in which Jesus is referred to as *both* teacher and preacher (Matthew 4:23, 9:35, 11:1; and Luke 20:1). Thus, at least Matthew and Luke make a distinction between preaching and teaching, and they recognize that Jesus did both.

Interestingly, in Mark, Jesus is either seen as a preacher *or* teacher. And there is no reference in John's Gospel to Jesus as a *preacher,* perhaps because, for John, Jesus is the "Word," the *embodiment* of the "message" of God, an incarnate, living *preachment.*

BIBLICAL DISTINCTIONS

Along with this perceived distinction between preaching and teaching among the Gospel writers, we also note this same differentiation in the rest of the Second Testament. There, we see several different Greek words for an orally-communicated message. Among them are the following:

1. Διδασκω *(didasko)*

As already indicated, this is a word that is sometimes mistaken for preaching. Actually, it means *to teach* or *instruct. Διδαχη* is the noun form that is typically translated as a *teaching* or, in many instances, *doctrine.*

This is a unique term. The next five seem to fall into a different category altogether, one that moves *beyond* an information posture.

2. Κηρυσσω *(kerysso)*

This Greek verb is most often translated *preach* or *proclaim. Κηρυγμα* (kerygma) is the noun form, the "sermon," "message," or "proclamation." This word appears 60 times in the Second Testament (as in Mark 1:38, Acts 10:42, and 1 Corinthians 1:21 and 23), and is the most common word for preaching. It refers to the spoken word of a herald (as in Acts 8:5 and 9:20), as the messenger who comes to proclaim the words of the king to the people. (In 1 Timothy 2:7, Paul uses the noun form, *κηρυξ [kyrux]* for "preacher" or "herald," drawn from the same root.) The proclamation, in this case, is not the messenger's word, but that of the king. The herald is simply the channel by which the words are conveyed.

When this word is used for proclamation, it suggests that preaching carries a direct or exact communication from the Lord, and implies the negation of the important role of the *preacher* in the sermon-construction process and in fashioning the "word of God." This implication, however, is not reflected in several uses of the term in Scripture.

For instance, in Jeremiah 1:9-10, *Jeremiah* is a "herald," but is appointed to *uproot* and *build again.* That is, *Jeremiah* is central to the proclamation and the process. In this way, the term *kerysso* indicates the strong *prophetic* ministry of preaching, which seems to carry a much more powerful connotation than that of the "town crier" who is indifferent to the message.

After all, in Second Testament terms, the preacher has been laid hold of by Christ (Philippians 3:12).

Further, when Jesus read his ministry-initiating text from Isaiah 61:1-2 (cited in Luke 4:18-19), he says that his mission is to *proclaim:* to *evangelize* the poor and *proclaim* freedom for prisoners and sight for the blind. But then we see something significant just a few chapters later. In Luke 8:22, Jesus sends a report back to John (in prison) that the blind see, the lame walk, the lepers are cured, the deaf hear, the dead are raised, and the poor are being evangelized. He hasn't just been *proclaiming* that message; he's been *acting* on it. For Jesus, proclamation *(kerygma)* didn't just *report* a message (as would a herald announcing a king's edict). *Kerygma* meant putting his words into action. He perceived his proclamatory ministry as an *enacted* one, thus suggesting a much stronger definition of preaching than mere *reporting.* For him, preaching was rhetoric that transformed lives in dramatic ways; his practice of ministry reflected what he said.

But there's one more implication that comes from the structure of this text in Luke 4. Jesus identifies these three "categories" of listeners as "the oppressed" (the economically oppressed, the politically and spiritually oppressed, and the physically oppressed). They, in turn, are released to proclaim "the year of the Lord's favor." Thus, Jesus defines his ministry as one of *proclamation (kerysso)* at the same time that he *empowers* the released ones to carry on that same ministry, one of "proclamatory empowerment." The *preacher,* in this sense, is granted power over the oppressed.

3. *Αγγελλω (angello)*

Closely related is the Greek word *αγγελλω*. Its root means *to announce.* It is the verb form of *αγγελος (angelos), messenger* (or, as it is usually translated, *angel).* This word also has many derivations that provide slight nuances to oral communication. Among them are:

- *ευαγγελλω (euangello)* (Acts 5:42 is its passive form): *to evangelize*
- *αναγγελλω (anangello): to declare* (Acts 20:27)
- *απαγγελλω (apangello): to announce,* as in Acts 17:30
- *διαγγελλω (diangello): to proclaim* (Luke 9:60)
- *εξαγγελλω (edzangello): to make known* (see 1 Peter 2:9)
- *καταγγελλω (katangello): to proclaim* (as in Acts 17:23)

Of course, any *announcement* (the *αγγελλω* derivatives) has to do with a *messenger service.* A person communicates a message to someone. The individual messenger is sending a communiqué of some kind, often on behalf of another person, such as a herald for a king, or a prophet or evangelist on behalf of God.

4. *Μαρτυρεω (martyreo)*

This verb (from which we get our English *martyr)* is the word *to witness.* Of course, witnesses were martyred, but the word in itself simply means *to bear testimony*, to talk about what the eyewitness has seen. The *μαρτυρων* (martyron) is an eyewitness messenger who is simply telling what he or she has seen.

5. Όμιλεω (homileo)

Όμιλεω (from which we get the word *homiletics)* actually means *to be together* or *communicate.* It is found in Luke 24:14, 24:15, and Acts 24:26. It implies open discussion or sharing. Όμιλειν *(homilein)* is a word for communicating *together,* or, even, dialog. In that sense, it is a good word for the *transactional* approach to human communication (as we will see in Chapter 5). *Homilies* in the early church became commentaries on Scripture, and today the word implies *short sermons.*

Each of these terms refers to a form of monological presentation within a group. While many homileticians suggest that these words are synonyms that refer to the same "ministry of the Word," my understanding, instead, is that they define slightly *different* ministries of oral proclamation that are used in different situations. They should not be construed to imply all preaching as we know it and as we are discussing it here: they are similar *proclamatory ministries* with nuances of meaning.

But however else we may understand these Second Testament words for "preaching," it is clear that *teaching (διδαχη)* is a different ministry altogether. I would even go so far as to say that teaching from the pulpit is not preaching at all: the cluster of "preaching" words are distinct from the word for "teaching." But in order to more fully appreciate this difference, we will continue to discuss the teaching ministry so that we can more adequately understand the ministry of preaching.

THE TEACHING MINISTRY

Teaching, at its heart, is an action by which information is passed from one person to another. It implies that one person, or source of information, has more knowledge than the other, and thus, has something worthwhile to pass on. But teaching is a broader ministry than that. Yes, the teacher *informs* the student, but according to three pre-eminent purposes.

THE THREE PURPOSES OF TEACHING

In his Great Commission (Matthew 28:19-20), Jesus commands his Church to *make disciples.* This is the only command in the Great Commission; all other verbs are participle forms. That is, our call as followers of Jesus is not to *evangelize* ("baptizing" probably indicates this evangelistic ministry). Winning people to Jesus is only the *beginning* of our responsibility to make disciples. Every act of ministry in the Church, then, every meeting, every goal that is set, every activity that is carried on, should be oriented to making Christian disciples of others and better disciples of ourselves.

One strategy of doing that, as Jesus states in this Great Commission at the end of Matthew's Gospel, is by *teaching.* And the ultimate goal of teaching is to bring students to more mature discipleship.

How does that happen? As we consider the *purposes* of teaching, we eventually discover three general classifications that indicate foundational approaches to the teaching ministry. They pertain to *all* teaching, whether for disciple-making or for general, secular education. But they do help us understand three different foci when it comes to teaching as a disciple-making process. They also build on each other, from the lowest (first level) to the highest (third level), progressively and developmentally. Figure 2.1 is an attempt to show what I mean; that diagram will guide the subsequent discussion.

Figure 2.1

Purposes of teaching:

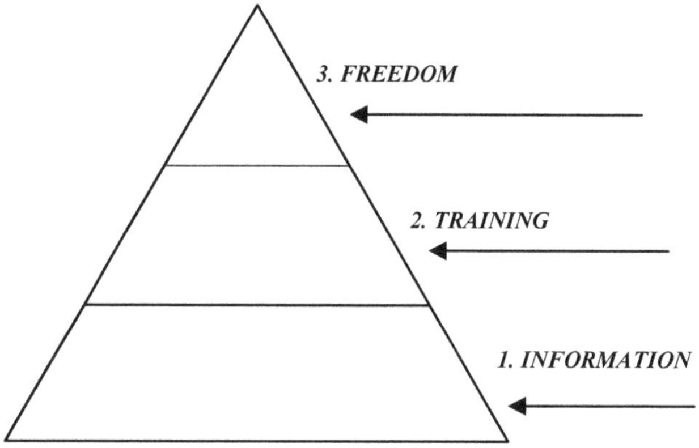

1. **TO SHARE INFORMATION**
    The first ("lowest") and most basic purpose of teaching is to *pass on information.*
    In a Christian context, teaching has several functions. Certainly, it *conveys doctrine or truth,* that which we *believe.* This is the ministry of 1 Timothy 4:6-11; Titus 1:10-11, 2:1; and Hebrews 5:12. Of course, one purpose of this ministry in the Second Testament is guarding against *false* doctrine (as in 1 Timothy 1:3).
    Teaching also *applies the Christian faith.* It helps disciples develop and understand their faith, recognize their responsibility for social concerns, and grow in knowledge of the Bible and every other aspect of discipleship (see 2 Timothy 2:25, for example).
    Finally, teaching *trains* the Christian to follow *a Christian lifestyle.* These are behavioral guidelines for the Christian disciple (especially as seen in 1 Corinthians 4:17; 1 Timothy 6:2; and Titus 2:2-3, and 2:9).

2. **TO PREPARE FOR A JOB OR PROFESSION**
    The second purpose of Christian teaching is to prepare the disciple for a profession, job, or ministry.

This second level of teaching moves one step beyond conveying information. It *does something* with the information: it shares information *in a particular way.* Now the teacher passes on information *for a purpose* (as we see in 2 Timothy 2:2), to *equip* the disciple for a particular role or ministry in the church (as in Ephesians 4:11-12), to be a deacon or youth leader or to help in the soup kitchen. This purpose becomes *formalized* when the disciple is prepared for *professional* ministry through formal theological education, as reflected in 1 Timothy 4-5 (though theological education implies the next purpose of education as well).

3.   TO FREE THE INDIVIDUAL

The third purpose of teaching is for the *growing freedom of the individual.*

This highest educational calling is to help the disciple *keep on learning* for the rest of his or her life, with no dependency on the teacher. It means helping the disciple learn *how to process new information.* Learning, after all, isn't something that should only happen when there is a teacher present.

This approach to teaching builds on the relationship between the disciple and *Jesus* rather than the disciple and the *teacher.* It is the kind of education that leads the disciple *"out of his or her own shadow,"* to introduce him or her to new horizons, worlds, and experiences, and *stretches* the disciple to grow toward a deeper and richer maturity.

With this end in mind, teaching *raises questions* for the disciple's consideration, challenge, and growth. Rather than merely providing information and answers for that disciple, it also identifies *issues* that the student must take into account for his or her own decision-making.

Thus, the third purpose of teaching asks the right questions, points to the right resources, and seeks underlying issues that influence the question under study. It is, above all, a *learning*-oriented discipline rather than *teaching*-oriented. Here, the teacher recognizes the needs of the individual disciple, realizes that individuals learn information in different ways, remembers that adults learn through tension, and recognizes that information must be adapted to the student if it is to be life-changing.

So the teacher's ultimate task is not simply to pass on information, but to pass on information that helps the student tackle a question from a different perspective, solve a theological or biblical problem in a more satisfactory and fulfilling way, and think for him or herself through the lens of an emerging Christian worldview. The best teachers do not *discover* and then *pass on* insights; they help *the student* discover insights for him or herself. The emphasis is on how the student *learns* more than what the teacher wants to *teach.* Learning implies *processing, adapting,* and *"owning" information.* A *scholar* is one who studies and discovers new insights, but a *teacher* is one who helps the *student* become that scholar. No wonder James writes that teachers are to be judged more severely than those with other gifts (James 3:1)!

This is all to say that when the preacher identifies great textual insights and passes them along from the pulpit (like pouring information into the open-topped heads of listeners), teaching is *not* at its best. That kind of teaching fulfills only the lowest educational purpose, and, if we had time to look at educational methodology, it does it poorly. Yet this is the kind of teaching that most often happens from the pulpit. The lecture format disseminates information, but that information is never fully appropriated or *learned* by the disciple. To assume that a notebook full of good biblical insights, collected from Sunday morning sermons, means that the disciple has *learned* anything is to misunderstand how learning takes place.

Finally, this discussion brings us to one further issue in the educational ministry.

DOMAINS OF TEACHING

Essentially, there are three basic ways in which learning occurs. The first is in *formal teaching sessions,* through lecture, discussion, or any classroom situation that is understood to be a "teaching" environment (this is the forum when teaching is done from the pulpit).

But we must not discount the importance of learning *informally,* that which comes through on-going experiences of life and living. Students who are taught according to the third purpose of teaching most adequately grasp this second mode of learning, as they are set free to pursue their own learning.

There is also a third way in which learning happens. It comes from those informal teachers who *set an example* (as in 1 Corinthians 4:16, 11:1; and Hebrews 6:12 and 13:7). Here, the *way* you teach is as important as *what* you teach. Students generally remember the teacher, not for what the teacher *knows,* but for who the teacher *is.* They respond to the teacher's *love,* hardly ever to the teacher's *doctrine.*

Each of these practices in which teaching takes place is important, but the third purpose of teaching (setting the student free) happens most effectively when all three domains are engaged. Teaching from the pulpit uses only the *formal* classroom situation, which is the least effective domain of teaching for *learning.*

PREACHING-TEACHING DISTINCTIVES

What does this have to do with the preaching ministry? There *are,* of course, elements of *information* in every sermon, but what do we do with this "teaching" (informational) aspect of preaching?

First, we need to understand the purpose of preaching. If the purpose of *teaching* is to pass on information, train for a job, or encourage the freedom of the student, then *preaching* is to *persuade, motivate* or *inspire* listeners to believe or act on biblical truth. The focus of preaching is on what the listener must *do*—it is *a call to action* or *a change in attitude.* It is *directive.* In preaching, the listener is *confronted with a decision,* and by the design of the preacher, the *choices are limited.* This is not always the case with teaching.

In Figure 2.2, I have tried to spell out some of the distinctions between these ministries. In certain of the following categories, I have used the most basic (information-sharing) purpose of teaching to better identify the distinctions under discussion.

Figure 2.2

The preaching-teaching distinctive:

	TEACHING	PREACHING
Guiding verse:	Proverbs 9:9	Romans 10:14
Purpose:	1. Pass on information 2. Train for a profession 3. Set the student free	Persuade, motivate, inspire, or convict
Orientation:	*Learning*	*Responding*
Environment:	Formal or informal "classroom"	Worship
Usual Method:	*Lecture* and/or *discussion*	*Proclamation:* a call to action or change
Goal:	Love God with the *mind*	Love God with *heart, body,* and strength
Use of the Bible:	We *talk about* the text	We are *confronted by* the text
Approach to the Bible:	*"Academic"* study, where information is to be *learned* or *memorized*	*Devotional* material is to be *applied*
Openness:	*Many* possibilities, views, and options are identified	*One* perspective is given: that of the preacher
Choices:	The listener is free to make his or her own decisions	The listener must decide about the *preacher's* biblical call to action
Anticipated response:	*Thought* and *incorporation*	*Action* or *inspiration*
Use of information:	*Explanation:* to *convey* facts, data, or insights	*Proclamation:* to *apply* facts, data, or insights
Arena:	Private or public	Always and only public
Recipients:	"Pupils"	Mutual participation
Response:	*Verbal:* for the *student's* clarity or the emergence of new or growing ideas	*Nonverbal:* for the *preacher's* guidance or support

WHAT IT MEANS FOR OUR PREACHING

These observations lead us to several important concerns regarding the preaching ministry. Among them are the following:

First, *both* preaching and teaching are *vital* ministries of the church. We must not minimize the importance of either one.

Second, many current preaching texts are actually about the *teaching* ministry of the pulpit (expository, verse-by-verse explanation or sharing brilliant insights about the text). We need to read those books critically.

Third, the basic difference between teaching and preaching is between *explanation* and *proclamation.* Teaching seeks to *explain;* preaching seeks to bring the listener to a point of *conviction.* Preaching is a word from God for these listeners in this situation. Occasionally, an informative preacher hits upon preaching; and sometimes a preacher becomes informative. But if you want to preach, your guiding purpose when you step into the pulpit should ultimately be *proclamation for conviction, inspiration, or decision.*

Fourth, when the preacher *reflects* on the Scripture, tries to tell listeners what it *means,* or offers *insights* that *explain* the text, the pulpit is being used as a lectern. When your sermon is *topical* or *informational*, it is teaching. When your desire is to share information, doctrine, or propositional convictions, or if you have thought up several interesting things to say about the text, you are preparing to teach. Sadly, most sermons end up being *informative* like this. When good Christian thoughts come pouring over the top of the pulpit, it becomes a lectern, and little happens other than that biblical or doctrinal information is passed along (unfortunately, with very little *learning).*

Fifth, when preaching is *explanatory,* informative, or the reading of a good "biblical essay," it tends to be difficult for listeners to pay attention or follow. What kind of teaching happens when the pulpit is replaced with the lectern? The only option, because of the monological nature of preaching, is that a *lecture method* must be adopted, which, of course, is the worst and most ineffective pedagogical methodology you can use. The teacher passes on brilliant insights that he or she *has already discovered.* Consequently this is of little *learning value* to the listener. (This is why an emphasis on *learning* rather than teaching is so important in the teaching ministry.) Using the pulpit for a lectern means that the teaching ministry is done poorly, *neither* ministry gets done very well, and preaching *never* gets done in the life of the congregation. The Church loses on both counts!

Sixth, when you teach, your "pupils" have the option of "playing with" both what the text says and how it might apply to their lives. That's part of training them to be free to think for themselves. With preaching, though, you don't want to give them that option. Your intent, as the preacher, is to bring them to a point of decision on a particular biblical truth.

Seventh, when the biblical (or thematic) *message* is the most important aspect of your sermon, you are probably resorting to teaching. This approach is based on an inaccurate understanding of "message" or "word" in the Bible.

"Word" was oral language—a dynamic, relevant thing, not static like written language (we'll talk more about this in Chapter 6).

Finally, if there are already teaching opportunities in your church, don't sacrifice your preaching to do more teaching! If teaching is *not* being done, start as many opportunities as possible. Then begin to use the pulpit for preaching rather than as a lectern for teaching.

Again, I want to be clear in stating that teaching is a critical ministry in the life of the Church. More than ever, the Church needs biblical and theological teaching. Christians, for the most part, are biblically illiterate. Pastors and local church leaders have not done a very good job, on the whole, of strategizing for disciple-making and its various stages of development.

But just as both cooking and baking are important in the kitchen, so teaching should in no way *replace* the preaching ministry! I am arguing that teaching should be done in *other places than the pulpit.* The Church needs strong teaching, but it also needs strong preaching. People will *not* be convicted or motivated or challenged to change unless we rededicate our pulpits to the preaching ministry. When teaching moves out of the worship environment, it makes room for an even stronger preaching ministry, and only when that happens can transformational preaching regain its rightful place in the life of the kingdom.

In summation, while both teaching and preaching involve information-sharing, the significant question you must ask is what is your purpose for sharing this information or insight? If it is only to disseminate information, to share your brilliant textual insights with your listeners, you will be teaching. But if your heart is focused on *persuading* or *motivating* your listeners for a change in their attitude or behavior, then you will more likely be preaching.

Section I:
The Transaction of Preaching

We now begin to examine the first of the three components of the preaching ministry, that of the "transaction." This is typically called the "delivery" of the sermon, but for reasons I'll discuss in Chapter 5, I've rejected that terminology as inaccurate and misleading.

There are two sub-sections here. The first (Part A) argues for an adequate understanding of human communication, since preaching must be recognized as an oral, *one-to-many* form of communication. There are five chapters in Part A. Progressively they help us understand what happens in pulpit discourse.

The second segment of this Section (Part B) argues for the essential role of the *preacher* in the preaching event. Preaching is an *incarnational* act, and rather than trying to be "invisible" (under the mistaken guise of wanting *Jesus* alone to be evident in the pulpit), the preacher is an *essential and integral* component of the preaching event. There are two chapters in Part B in which we will discuss this important role.

Section I:
Part A:
Preaching as Human Communication

In this first Part of Section I, we will be examining significant human communication theory and how it helps inform the preaching task. In Chapter 3, we will study the standard theory of human communication. It is important because it is the theoretical construct upon which almost every preaching textbook bases its approach to preaching. As we will see in Chapter 4, though, this is a seriously flawed foundation upon which to understand what happens in the preaching event. These two chapters will be followed by a more legitimate (though complex) formulation of human communication theory (Chapter 5), but one that more adequately describes what actually happens in human communication, and in a way that enhances the art form of preaching.

The final chapters in this sub-section discuss the important distinction between oral and written language forms and why oral proclamation (using formalized conversational language) is the very best style of preaching to adopt. The final chapter of Part A examines *methods* of preaching, where I will argue why I believe that *preaching without notes* is the most freeing and powerful form of preaching, and the one that is most engaging and "hearable" for those who listen to preaching.

CHAPTER 3
The Standard Theory of Communication

COMMUNICATIONS 101

Early in my first pastorate (in the mid-70s), my wife, Ellen, and I team-taught a couples' class on the subject of marriage. One session dealt with communication; the book we used included a chapter on human communication theory. It was my first introduction to the subject, and it was helpful to know how "messages" get distorted in marriage. (I still remember that one of the less active class members remarked afterward that he found it very helpful and would like more of that kind of study.) This lesson, I found, was very interesting for me, too, and was probably one reason why I later went on to study communications in my doctoral program—I wanted to learn more about that theory of human communication.

Almost fifteen years later, in my doctoral work, I discovered that human communication is a far more complex system than I understood at that time. I discovered that many different approaches and theories had been conceived over the years (I had recognized only one in that first plunge). Sociologists, anthropologists, psychologists, and behavioral scientists had been attempting to understand human communication for centuries. I discovered then that my first introduction to human communication theory was inadequate and misinformed. But it started me on a journey of discovery.

Because preaching is ultimately a *communicative* experience, it is important to understand it *as* communication. To do so, I want to begin by discussing that theory of communication that so excited me early in my pastorate. It is a commonly-held understanding of human communication that

47

informs almost every preaching text I've seen, such that it is accepted almost without question.

MATHEMATICAL COMMUNICATION

The theory about which I'm speaking was originally presented in a paper in 1948 by Claude Shannon, and subsequently published the next year in a book called, *The mathematical theory of communication.* The book also included an important introductory essay by Warren Weaver, and, thus, the theory came to be known as the *Shannon-Weaver theory of communication.*

Shannon was an engineer at Bell Telephone Labs and a professor of science at the Massachusetts Institute of Technology. At that time, it was necessary for a theory to be developed that would enable information to be transmitted over telephone lines. Basing his study on the work of other theorists, Shannon's premise was that communication could be understood *mathematically* (almost every page of his little book is filled with complex mathematical formulas). Its approach is a highly complicated accounting of theorems, trigonometric function sets, probability equations, and logarithms suitable to an advanced mathematical textbook.

Shannon's colleague, Warren Weaver, was an executive with the Rockefeller Foundation. Weaver's contribution simplified the mathematical formulas but also broadened Shannon's ideas to include *human* communication. Indeed, Weaver applied this theory to *"all* the procedures by which one mind may affect another . . . (including) written and oral speech . . . music, the pictorial arts, the theatre, the ballet, and in fact all human behavior." Thus was born the mathematical theory of human communication, also known as the *linear* model of communication. (It is called "linear" because human communication is depicted as a left-to-right *directional* movement in a single line.)

The theory is based on what Shannon called *entropy,* by which he meant the potential breakdown in communication. Entropy is the degree of *randomness* in any system, which leads to a statistical probability of distortion in any message that is being communicated. The more that entropy is *reduced,* the clearer is the communication. And entropy is reduced when *interference* in the system is minimized.

THE MATHEMATICAL MODEL

As you can see in Figure 3.1 on the next page, the Shannon-Weaver "schematic diagram of a general communication system" is fairly straightforward:

Figure 3.1

The Shannon-Weaver Model of Communication:

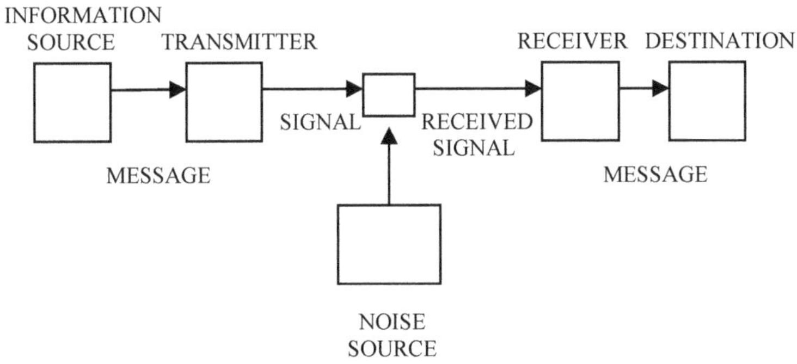

Very simply

When Shannon first developed his theory, the diagram and its explanation provided a very simply-designed conceptual model. (Perhaps its simplicity is the reason why it became so well accepted.) Basically, this "linear" model says that when a message needs to be sent, it must be encoded by an information source (a "Sender"), sent by a transmitter using a particular signal, move through a "channel," and be accepted and decoded by a "Receiver" in such a way that it will be understood at its destination. When there is no "noise" (or interference) in the system, the message is received in its entirety and with complete clarity: its meaning will have been perfectly encoded, sent, and decoded. We can easily understand the genius of the system, and how important such a theory was for telephone communications.

When this theory is applied to human communication, it helps us understand how information is transmitted between people. So just for fun, let's see how this actually works by taking an example from Wednesday night's choir practice.

Preparing the anthem

Here we are in the choir room on Wednesday night and, after an hour of warming up and rehearsing, Mr. Pomeroy, our church's Music Director, wants the choir to prepare a particular anthem for Sunday's worship. (In this case, it is one of my favorites: Virgil Thomson's arrangement of "The Lord's My Shepherd.") To do so, Pomeroy must communicate this information to all the members of the choir. While this seems like a pretty straightforward process, it actually includes several complicated processes.

Entropy

Pomeroy's first decision has to do with limiting all *possible* information to only that which he wants to convey: the title of the anthem. That is, in this particular announcement he won't include information about buying a new car, what he ate for dinner, or his upcoming vacation (though he might talk about these experiences just because he's a member of this community). This is what Shannon means when he says that communication "is associated with the amount of freedom of choice we have in constructing messages." But, for now, Pomeroy only wants to announce the next anthem the choir will rehearse. So he *limits* all *possible* information (including his choice of words and phrases) from all *potential* things he *could* say. This is a first attempt to *reduce entropy,* which, in turn, will minimize the possible confusion of his listeners.

Pomeroy must also further limit his information to particular *details* he wants to convey. Along with the name of the anthem, he might decide to talk about its composer, the color of the sheet music, and any introductory information he may want to share about it. He might choose to read Psalm 23 before the choir first tries to sing the anthem. He has many choices of what to talk about, but his guiding purpose is to try to *reduce possible confusion,* since his goal is to communicate his intention as clearly as possible. Thus, the most effective communication will be a *complete negation of all confusion.*

Redundancy

There's another important element in the linear theory that makes it a bit more sophisticated. Weaver introduces the term *redundancy,* by which he means that the freedom of choice of which words or phrases to use *next* in an utterance becomes more and more restricted as the utterance continues.

Let's turn back to Pomeroy's anthem announcement. To let the choir know what anthem they'll be rehearsing next, he must choose particular words and phrases, and decides to start with, "The next . . ." That is, out of an almost infinite number of ways he could have begun this sentence, he chose these two words. But now his choices for the third word, while still also almost unlimited, are more restrictive than when he started. He could, for instance, say "day," "project," or "person" now, but if he doesn't want to sound psychotic, he couldn't very well add, "yesterday, "ocean," or "later." The further he gets into the announcement, the more restrictive are his choices. So he adds one word or phrase at a time in order to complete his message.

Eventually, Pomeroy produces this string of words: "The next song we're going to sing together is . . ." There are still many options for what he *could* choose next, such as "on page 29," "one of my favorites," or "from the 23rd Psalm," (but, again, he couldn't very well say "grapefruit" or "exonerate" or "quickly"). At this point, the *potential* choices of filling in the blank are far fewer than are the choices he had before he started. This is redundancy, and Weaver says that English is about 50% redundant, that about half of our word choices are "under our free choice, and about half . . . are controlled by the statistical structure of the language."

If we understand the basic ideas of entropy and redundancy, we've got a pretty good handle on the theory that was formulated by Shannon and Weaver. But there's one more piece of the model that came from a different source.

THE CONTRIBUTION OF NORBERT WIENER

The year before Shannon and Weaver published their little book, another scientist at the Massachusetts Institute of Technology, Norbert Wiener, published a book called *Cybernetics*. (It means "steersman," a term he borrowed from Greek.) Building on Shannon's paper from 1948, Wiener was particularly interested in applying mathematical formulation to computing machines, nervous systems, visual imagery, pathological disorders, and brain functions. (Shannon and Wiener both claimed mutual participation in the development of the mathematical theory.) Wiener argued that human communication and language are socially-driven biological phenomena, and ended his book by stating that with his theoretical model it would be possible to construct a machine that could play chess. However, in this initial work, he made little application to *human* communication.

Two years later, though, Wiener published another book called, *The human use of human beings* (subsequently edited and republished in 1954). It was a social scientific view of communication, stating that "society can only be understood through a study of the messages and the communication facilities which belong to it." He was particularly concerned about the control of human over machine and the communication between human and machine and machine and machine. Wiener was most interested in "the transmission of *messages*" and in the *meaning* of those messages.

Again, following Shannon and Weaver, Wiener identified *entropy* as the rascal to be tamed in communication. He claimed that the more a message is *probable* or *predictable,* the less "information" it contains. So when receivers *know* what to expect in an utterance, the information can't very well be "new." Confusion, then, comes with unexpected or new information. It is a result of a lack of clarity and order. Thus, for Wiener, entropy is ultimately a measure of *disorganization.*

Feedback

But Wiener also proposed another idea that had a significant impact on the Shannon-Weaver model. It was that of *feedback,* which he defined as "the property of being able to adjust future conduct by past performance." It was *feedback,* for Wiener, that led to *learning;* indeed, feedback was responsible for the advancement of the human race over other life forms and other kinds of systems. Adequate feedback, he argued, enabled confusion to decrease and order to increase, and only humans are capable of learning in this way. So, Wiener understood the human as a biologically evolved animal whose intelligence is a result of complexity, not the result of a "soul." He further reasoned that eventually "we could have a machine whose intellectual capacities would duplicate those of human beings." (In fact, he used this theory to develop an anti-aircraft firing system during WWII that adjusted itself according to its past performance.) Weiner, of course, was a prophet: building on Shannon and Weaver, he prepared the way the explosion of computer technology we see today. Machines, indeed, are duplicating human intelligence.

THE FULL LINER MODEL

With the addition of Weiner's feedback loop, the linear model has been re-designed in various ways. Here is one way to depict it:

Figure 3.2

The Shannon-Weaver Model with the Feedback Loop:

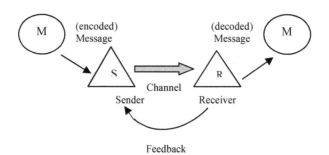

Feedback

The diagram helps us readily see where "breakdowns" ("noise" or "interference") can occur in any part of the system. If the message (M) is not clear to the Sender (S), for instance, or the encoding is not exact, or if the channel has a lot of extraneous noise in it, or the Receiver (R) doesn't understand the vocabulary and cannot accurately decode the message, or the Receiver decodes a particular word or idea in a way the Sender didn't intend (a different connotation), the wrong message will be communicated. One little "noise" problem anywhere in the system can create miscommunication. It seems to be a very complex process.

The case of Selma and Reese

Let's consider another little exercise by applying this model to two people, Selma (Sender) and Reese (Receiver), who actually met each other at Pomeroy's choir practice last Wednesday. It's now Friday, and Selma wants to let Reese know that she wouldn't mind seeing him socially, so she thinks about *what* she might say to him. She also has to decide *how* she wants to say it, because she doesn't want to drive him away, nor does she want to encourage him too much. Her brain finally conceives of just the right message, which she must now make as clear as possible so as to minimize entropy. This is all part of the *conceptualization* process.

Now she must decide on the channel through which she will send the message. She could telephone Reese or write him a note, but, in this case, she decides to send him an email message. Thus, the internet will be the channel. (If she decided to telephone him, the telephone wires would be the channel; if she were an artist and wanted to express her feelings in watercolor, her canvas would be the channel.)

Now she must *encode* the message in understandable language. So she turns on her computer and brings up her email program, and then starts to type the message. After some amount of typing and thinking, back spacing and retyping, Selma finally has written everything she wants, and then she types in Reese's e-mail address that he gave her last week, and hits the send button. Now her message is being *transmitted.*

Almost immediately (if there are no system or internet problems), Selma's note arrives in Reese's Inbox. When he opens up the message, he receives the encoded signals. That is, he sees particular ordered marks on his computer screen that he must now *decode* into meaning. Since he and Selma both speak English, and he has had a lot of practice translating these marks into words, this isn't difficult. So he reads the message, and gets the idea that Selma is interested in him and wouldn't mind spending some time with him. He's correctly *decoded* everything Selma wanted to communicate, as far as he knows. Her message has been adequately "received."

But Reese has a problem. There, on his computer screen, he reads that Selma is inviting him to meet her at the zoo on *"Thuesday."* Yikes! He can't tell if she means "Tuesday" or "Thursday" (a problem of encoding or transmission). Here is "noise" in the system: entropy is rampant! However, because of this breakdown, Reese now *feeds* information *back* to Selma, and, not wanting to seem too eager, he sends a return message later in the day: "I'd like to see you at the zoo, but did you mean Tuesday or Thursday?" With this clarifying question, Selma, red-faced, realizes there is entropy in her message, and, with a little more care this time, sends him the correct spelling: "Tuesday."

Actually, we go through this process every time we talk or write. The simplest message can include a continual process of encoding, decoding, and feedback, all repeated many times, and we aren't even aware of it. Feedback helps the Sender send a more accurate message and the Receiver receive in a more precise way the intended meaning.

Without question, Shannon and Weaver's work, with the contribution of Norbert Wiener, became absolutely foundational to the development of technology in the latter half of the 20th century. The mathematical model, with its understanding of entropy, redundancy, and feedback, enables us to hear and recognize our children when they phone home (though I understand that our *voices* are not actually transmitted through the system; instead, electrically-encoded information gets transmitted and those impulses are then decoded into new electrical information at the other end). This model has been of inestimable help in developing "computer languages" by which our desktops and laptops "speak" to one another. The model helps us identify and minimize potential noise or interference in any communication system. If the system "works" properly and interference is virtually eliminated, messages are transmitted correctly and clearly (as most of them are today).

LINEAR PROCLAMATION

The Shannon-Weaver model is complex enough when we're talking about a simple typed message, a one-on-one conversation, or a short hand-written memo. Preaching, however, is much more complicated. It is a one-to-*many* form of communication; there is not just *one* Receiver in the system, but, potentially, hundreds or thousands. Further, when preaching occurs, a single individual stands before a congregation and talks for 20 or 30 minutes. That's a much more complicated piece of communication than a one-sentence "love note."

Still, we can learn much about preaching from this model. When we preach, we undergo the same process that we saw with Pomeroy and the choir and Selma and Reese, but in a more complex and sophisticated manner. We aren't even aware of all that is involved, and, in fact, we've become so good at public communication by now that it happens naturally; we don't even think about all the processes we're going through when we preach—we just do it!

But let's run through the system quickly. Let's say that you decide on a sermon idea ("inspired" by the Holy Spirit and Scripture), and you want to get this message from your head into the heads of your listeners. (That's how James W. Cox [1985] understands preaching: "The purpose of preaching," he writes, "is to get what is in the mind and heart of the preacher into the mind and heart of the hearer.")

Your preaching idea, then, is fashioned into a sermon, which is carefully written in your study, and honed and perfected so every word is exactly right. You then step into the pulpit with this nicely-fashioned message, and you "deliver" it by way of a channel (a clear amplification system, high-quality speakers, and a minimum number of crying babies). When every word of the message gets safely to the congregation (the Receivers), they then "decode" the language they have heard. It is *your* responsibility as the preacher to use words that are understandable and *their* responsibility as listeners to pay attention. And we expect the Holy Spirit to do his part, too. When everything works right, the listeners "hear" and understand the same message you conceived and encoded in your study.

ENTROPY

Of course, preaching is never perfect. You are not a perfect preacher nor are your congregational members perfect listeners. And because no environment or system of public communication is perfect, there are plenty of opportunities for interference. The Shannon-Weaver model helps us understand potential "noise," which, in turn, leads to entropy. One of your responsibilities as a preacher is to minimize entropy as much as possible. You do so by eliminating everything you can that might create confusion in the transmission of your message. Where might some of these "breakdowns" occur?

Well, you may have a general idea of what you want to preach, for instance, but the message may not be *clear* in your mind. Thus, you will not *conceptualize* it properly. Maybe you want to preach about love, but you are not sure if you are talking about God's love for us or our love for each other. That leads to a confused message. Or maybe you aren't sure whether you are preaching about private or public forgiveness. So you just throw it all in there and pray for the best. If you don't know *what* you want to say (a common problem with many sermons), your listeners won't be able to figure it out, either. So if you want to impact them with biblical truth, you need to *reduce entropy* by clarifying what you will preach.

But suppose you clearly *understand* your message (it is the nature of God that you are preaching about), but you don't *encode* it accurately. You may not have time to choose exactly the right words to express the idea. Or you might use vocabulary that your listeners don't understand (like "Hypostatic Union"). When you "preach over the heads" of your listeners, you are creating "noise" in the system.

The *channel,* too, can have distractions in it, such as a screeching fire engine honking its way through the neighborhood, or the temperature of the room, or young people whispering in the balcony. Or the public address system might have a crackle in it that distorts your words. Often there is an open door or a distracting sign in plain view of everyone. You can reduce entropy in the channel by picking up stray papers that are lying around or checking to make sure that the "cry room" is available to young mothers. Do what you can to minimize possible distractions.

In most cases, your listeners will accurately *hear* all the words you send them. However, they still might *understand* but *misinterpret* your words because of ambiguous language. They may have a very different idea of "fatherhood" than you do, for instance. This "connotative noise" between decoding and meaning suggests that listeners actually "receive" a *different* message than what you intend. If there are no opportunities for verbal feedback while you're preaching, you may not know if your message is getting through or not—your listeners have no chance to seek clarification.

Entropy is a useful concept when it helps you take responsibility for clarity in your preaching. There are, of course, many "systemic noises" over which you have *no* control, but your preaching will improve simply by reducing entropy in those parts of the system over which you *do* have control.

REDUNDANCY

Redundancy also comes into play when you preach. From the very beginning, from the time you first get an idea for a sermon, you begin the process of redundancy, of limiting your choices. You naturally restrict all the *possible* texts and topics. Then you restrict what you *could* say from any text. You restrict your arrangement pattern and stories you want to include. From one step to the next in the sermon construction process, you narrow your choices.

Redundancy continues when you step into the pulpit. From the outset, you choose and then utter your first word, which, in turn, restricts your options for what you'll say next. When you say, "Jesus . . .," for instance, there are many options for the next words, but they are limited (you can't say "modern art" here, for instance, if you want to make sense). And when you extend your utterance with the words, "Jesus died for the sins of the . . .," there are still many options (such as "world," "unjust," or "Jones' family"), but the *potential* choices are far fewer than when you started. Your choice of vocabulary in any utterance gets more restrictive as you go along.

Now, put yourself in the pew, where, as a listener, you are forced to "play along" with the redundancy principle. At the beginning of each utterance, your preacher starts talking about an idea in a certain way and her word choices become more and more restrictive as she continues. You hear one word after another, and, because there are still choices all along the way (even though they get more restrictive), you have to keep listening to her to see how she is going to be complete her thoughts. It's one reason why oral communication *keeps* people listening, and why the use of startling or unusual words in unexpected places can be so engaging—or confusing.

But not only is every expressed thought based on redundancy, but so is the whole sermon. It gets more and more narrowly-focused as it goes along, moving from one *phase* to another. We *naturally* "hear" a sermon in this way. A single-focused message that progresses easily from thought to thought builds toward a natural and understandable conclusion. It's easy to follow. But when a different structural component is suddenly introduced (or a new idea or ill-fitting information), the interruption causes confusion for the listener, because it is an *unnatural* progression.

FEEDBACK

Finally, we turn to the concept of *feedback*, which, of course, becomes important to the preaching event. As the preacher, you stand at the door afterward to shake hands, and some of your members speak to you: "That was a good message this morning, Pastor!" or "I'd like to talk further with you about what you said," or, dread the thought, "You weren't up to your usual standard this morning!" This type of feedback is what is called *substantive verbal* feedback. It helps you know how to adapt your preaching style, content, structure, or "delivery" the next time. Of course, in traditional African-American preaching and that of some holiness traditions, there is a *verbal dialog* between preacher and congregation during the preaching event itself. With that kind of *instantaneous substantive verbal* feedback, you learn to adjust your content and style immediately.

But there are other kinds of feedback that are important to know about, too. *Nonsubstantive verbal* feedback occurs when listeners talk with their neighbors during the sermon (or mutter under their breath). And teenagers sometimes talk distractingly in the back row. You can never tell if these voices have anything to do with your preaching—that's why they are called *nonsubstantive.*

You may also notice *nonsubstantive nonverbal* feedback, such as when Mrs. Thorngate looks up at the ceiling. You don't know what, if anything, it means: she could be disagreeing with what you just said, thinking about lunch, or just stretching her neck.

Finally, *substantive nonverbal* feedback is the most noteworthy kind for preaching. When you detect riveting eye contact from your listeners, or you see them nodding in agreement or shaking their heads in disagreement, or they are sitting on the edge of their seats and leaning forward to get every word, or leaning back with arms folded, that's substantive nonverbal feedback. Nothing is actually *said,* but these are important signals. In a "quiet" preaching environment, this is the most productive kind of feedback you can experience, because it is immediate. Of course, your ability to recognize it requires that you be fully engaged with your listeners throughout the preaching experience, and that you actually *want* them to "hear" what you're saying.

Thus, feedback comes not just after you leave the pulpit, but also *while you are preaching* (even in non-vocal preaching traditions). If you are alert, you will learn to "read" these paralinguistic (nonverbal) clues as an *immediate response.* If you are flexible and comfortable enough in the pulpit, you can adjust your preaching style accordingly.

THE VALUE OF THE STANDARD THEORY

This, then, is the standard theory of communication, and these are some of the reasons why it is so well-accepted and promoted. As we have seen, it is helpful for understanding the whole preaching process. It challenges the way we formulate sermons. It encourages us to think about the "system" of communication and where breakdowns can occur in it. It helps us consider the kind of vocabulary that will best be "received" by our listeners and how to put our sermons together in a way that will be understandable.

The linear model also stimulates us to think of messages that "relate" to our listeners. It forces us to reflect on *how we think* about our sermons. It revitalizes our use of stories and examples that "speak" to our listeners so they can understand what we want to say. It helps us clarify *why* we are preaching a particular message, and to work out messages that are *simple* (without being simplistic) and "graspable."

However, while the Shannon-Weaver model provides these useful insights that help us better strategize our preaching, the basic problem with it is that it really isn't how we humans communicate at all! In the next chapter, we'll look at some of the defects of this model, and then, in Chapter 5, examine what I find to be a more profitable approach to human communication and preaching.

CHAPTER 4
The Substandard Theory of Communication

TYPES OF COMMUNICATORS

Bryden and Scott (1994) suggest that there are four types of communicators. There are the *unconsciously incompetent.* They are unsuccessful communicators and never know why.

The *consciously incompetent,* too, are unsuccessful but are aware of it, and generally want to change. (Perhaps a lot of preachers fall into this category.)

Then there are the *unconsciously competent.* They are successful but don't know why. Indeed, there are many servants of God who are exceptional preachers, but they don't have any idea what they are doing right.

Finally, there are the *consciously competent.* They are good communicators who understand why. They understand the theory of good communication and its practical application, and know what has to happen in order to "connect" with their listeners.

Good preaching means being a good communicator. It doesn't necessarily mean that you must know *why,* of course, but the purpose of responsible theological education (in this case, training for preaching) is to help you not only become a good preacher, but to know why. These chapters on human communication theory are an attempt to help you become *consciously competent.* But keep in mind that it isn't enough if you simply *understand* how to be a good communicator. You must also put into *practice* good communication skills—otherwise you're wasting *your* time and the time of your listeners. That's why it is important that we learn to think critically about preaching, and, in this case, to get a sense of what the standard model of human communication actually teaches us.

THE UNDERCURRENT OF THE LINEAR MODEL

The communication theory of Shannon and Weaver (known as the *mathematical* or *linear* model) has become a standard description for understanding human communication. We've seen the "surface currents" of this model, but now our thinking must move to the undercurrent which is far more powerful and often runs in the opposite direction of the surface waters. It is this undercurrent that now demands our attention; now we start thinking about *people* rather than machines.

When we use the linear model as our guide, it describes what we think communication *should* be like. Unfortunately, it is not a very accurate or helpful approach. Indeed, if you quickly thumb through Shannon and Weaver's book, it doesn't take long to realize that it has little relationship to the act of speaking. Yet the model is found or alluded to so frequently that it is hardly given a second thought.

So let's try a different way of looking at things. That is, if we're serious about human communication, shouldn't we be observing actual *people* who are communicating with each other? Shouldn't we be paying attention to those who think and write about communication from the standpoint of *human beings?* The theory that emerges from *this* observation and reflection should then help us build a more accurate theoretical foundation for preaching—one that is based on actual human interaction. That's the subject of this chapter and the next.

If that's where we're headed, why would I spend such a significant amount of time discussing the linear model if I am now going to discredit it? Well, as we saw, there is some value in it for preaching. But, further, as I've said, it is so *standard* that it is accepted without reflection or analysis even when it is being criticized. Thus, it is important to understand the linear model as *standard theory* so that we can reflect more intelligently about what human communication is *really* like.

This chapter, then, will look at this mathematical model as a *substandard theory* of human communication. As we will see, there are a host of problems with it. This exercise, in turn, will prepare us to do some fresh thinking about human communication in general and preaching in particular, subjects that we will tackle in the next chapter.

THE LINEAR MODEL AS SUBSTANDARD

When we compare the linear model in relationship to actual human communication, it falls far short. The following critique falls into two broad categories. The first is a discussion of several characteristics of the linear model that are *inaccurate* in its depiction of human communication. The second section identifies several elements of human communication that are *not represented* by the linear model.

INACCURACIES IN THE LINEAR MODEL

There are several ways in which the mathematical model of Shannon and Weaver does not adequately reflect what happens when human beings talk with each other. Let me mention ten of them.

1. It suggests that human communication is mechanical.

First of all, the linear model was designed in 1949 for *telephone communication*. Indeed, Shannon did not design the theory so the world would better understand *human* communication. Weaver and Wiener made this application. But humans are *not* telephones, computers, or machines. This seems an obvious observation, but it is hardly noted by the communication specialists who adopt this model for human conversation or monological public communication. *Linear* implies a *mechanical process* rather than a *human experience.*

In actuality, human communication is *temporal*, not linear. The linear model perceives communication as a directional, pre-completed, *incisive* process rather than a strung-out series of incomplete language-chunks, offered piecemeal, bit by bit, as one utterance and then another, each one adjusted by its reception. (Yes, that's the way we produce oral language, as we'll see in Chapter 6.) Talking *doesn't* happen in sentences; we humans communicate *in time*, not in a structured form or diagram. Talking is a phenomenon that is fluid and *relational,* not mechanical.

2. It approaches communication negatively.

As we have seen, the linear model is driven by a *negative view* of communication. That is, it is more interested in *entropy,* in how communication *breaks down* in the transmission of a message than it is in stating positively what communication actually *is*. It forces us to look for *interference* in transmission as an explanation for communication failure, when other causes might be the actual problem (such as one's attitude, a broken relationship, or status issues). At heart, the linear model recognizes reasons why good communication *doesn't* happen rather than helping us see what actually *does* happen.

3. It promotes a "delivery" metaphor.

The linear model presupposes that a message is pre-formed and encoded by a sender, and then "delivered" to a receiver. This idea of "delivery" is a common (and popular) phrase used in most preaching circles, that the preacher *"delivers a sermon."* (In fact, it's very difficult to talk about the preaching event without mentioning "delivery.") This metaphor is clearly derived from the linear model, and it helps us identify some of the problems that come with a linear understanding of human communication.

There are at least two referents for this metaphor. One is that of *delivering a baby* (a rather ironic interpretation for those traditions where only men preach!). But the idea is clear. The preacher "gives birth" to a sermon that has been incubating over a period of time (usually a week, but often much longer than that). When the preacher steps into the pulpit, the baby is "delivered," full blown and mature for the listening congregation.

The other referent is that of *delivering a package* (from the post office or local pizza parlor) or a *newspaper* (the term "good news" supports this metaphor). The preacher has formulated a wonderful "message" which is now "delivered" to the congregation, much like the paper carrier who tosses my morning newspaper in the driveway.

Whatever our mental image, it implies that the preacher conceives and writes the "message" during the week, and then "delivers" it from the pulpit on Sunday; it is now "sent off" through the public address system to its recipients. In both of these forms of the metaphor, we unfortunately find inappropriate (though uncritically accepted) images of preaching that lead to impotence in the pulpit.

It begins with the idea of a carefully-crafted and ready-made *message.* Because the linear model emphasizes *information* transmission as the most important element of human communication, it stands to reason that the more carefully defined is that message, the better chance it will have of being accurately received. This leads to the homiletical practice of *careful honing of the manuscript* before it can be "sent out." The real "work" of preaching, then, happens *in the study,* in the development of an exacting and carefully-worded manuscript that is then *read* in the context of worship. The model naturally favors *written* language over *spoken,* arises from our concern for *literacy* rather than *orality,* and replaces the pulpit with the lectern (as we saw in Chapter 2). Preaching becomes a message-event rather than a *relational* one, and the *manner* of "delivery" doesn't matter as much as the content of the message (congregations, rightly, are more forgiving of pastors who don't preach very well than they are of those whose sermon *content* is suspect).

Further, preachers tend to be uncaring "senders" in this model. When *information* is the only important component of pulpit discourse, the message is put together in the study and read from the pulpit. The more time the preacher spends in careful, exacting preparation of the manuscript, the more "sanctified" the message. And the transmission of that message is not very important, either, as long as interference is minimized: crying babies are kept away and the amplifier is cranked up to such an extent that the listeners can get every nuance.

How different this is from the way we talk with each other! What really happens in conversation is that messages are formulated *as they are communicated*—in *dialog*—not *prior* to the interaction as the linear model suggests. Of course, good preaching is well prepared, but most informal conversation is not pre-scripted before it happens. And informal conversation is a much better place to begin our understanding of human communication than mathematics.

Further, the linear model implies that if the manuscripted "message" is what is most important, *anybody* can step into the pulpit and read it. A Russian friend tells me of a pastor who had been traveling all week, but arrived back home just in time for worship. When it was his turn to preach, he began to read his manuscript, stopped, looked puzzled, and leaned over to his wife who was sitting in the front row. "What did you mean by this, dear?" he asked. She told him, and he then went on with the rest of the sermon. In the Russian context, it would have been inappropriate for the pastor's wife to preach the sermon she wrote, but this story characterizes the linear model's emphasis on *message* as the most important element of communication. It really doesn't matter who transmits (or "reads") the sermon, because the most significant part of the process (its writing) has already been finished.

But preaching, as *human* communication, involves a preacher who must be an integral component of the event. Preaching is a far richer experience than just the communication of a message. If that's all that's involved, why not have the congregation read the manuscript silently or watch the preacher on videotape? *Preaching,* to be preaching, implies that the human agent is present in face-to-face proclamation.

When the *manuscript* or *message* is more important than the *people,* the relational element of preaching is neglected. Even when the sermon is *read* from the pulpit by the one who wrote it, the preacher is indicating a relationship *with the manuscript,* not the listeners. The best way to avoid this problem is to preach extemporaneously, which I'll talk about more fully in Chapter 7.

4. It rejects human uniqueness.

When *message* is so strongly emphasized (as it is with the linear model), the uniqueness of each *preacher* and *listener* is not accounted for, because *any* "sender" will transmit the same information in the same way. This, of course, is possible with computers that have the same basic components and use the same programming language, but with human communication it is not possible. The individual and his or her style and personality *always* have a bearing on what the message is and how the message is conveyed. Different people will "transmit" the same message in different ways.

Further, the linear model supposes that communication (sending a message) is something that is done *to* the listeners who are not really very important to the process of communication at all. When the *message* is the most important component of preaching, both preacher and listener are diminished; the *exact wording* of the sermon is of far greater importance than the *human* communication of the preaching experience.

5. It supports the listener as a passive participant.

Next, the linear model doesn't account for the importance of *listening.* In spite of arguments to the contrary, linear communication implies that the listener is a passive "receiver" (until "feedback" time). The process of encoding is the responsibility of the sender, who must encode that message in a way that the receiver will best understand. It is hard work to convince anyone to engage in "active listening." "Active listening" theory, while very helpful in interpersonal communication, actually supports the deficiency of this linear model: it's far easier to be a lazy participant when you are on the "receiving end" of information.

But in real human conversation (whether it be one-on-one or one-to-many), *all* participants become *active and integral* in the process. *All* participants contribute to the *development* and *content* of the message that emerges from this interaction. (Our next chapter will discuss this subject more fully.)

6. It creates an *entertainment model* of preaching.

Communication *doesn't happen* without participants, but the linear model, with its strong emphasis on the *message*, suggests that the "receivers" are there simply to "accept" whatever "message" the sender "delivers" to them. This, in turn, leads to a congregation that expects the preacher to *entertain* them. If the preacher is boring or nothing happens in the interaction, it's the *speaker's* fault. (We even say that preachers with good public speaking skills are those who can hold an audience's attention during an entire sermon.) It's a natural result of this model.

Of course, the preacher is responsible to attract and maintain the congregation's attention throughout the preaching event, but the truth is that *no* communication happens unless all participants in the communication event are fully engaged in the process, and no communication really happens unless the communicants *are* involved. That is, only those who are actively engaged in the process of preaching really get much out of it.

7. It promotes a feedback myth.

When a computer communicates with another computer, one machine accepts the sent information only if both are speaking the same computer language, and only if all the signals are clear and without distortion. If the receiving machine doesn't understand, it is programmed to send back an "error" response. Just this morning, for instance, I sent an e-mail message to Bulgaria, but got an almost-instantaneous response that said my message had an incorrect address and, thus, wasn't "delivered." When that "feedback" happens, the first machine, its operator, or the server has the chance to clear up the problem.

This "feedback" element of the linear theory was essential to the development of telecommunications and computer interaction, but it isn't an accurate description of human communication. Actually, "feedback" means that the "receiver" is now *transmitting* information, and, thus, becomes a "sender."

Further, in human communication, the process of sending and receiving signals happens continuously. When people talk informally, there are very few instances in which "feedback" actually comes only *after* the sender has finished transmitting a "message." When humans communicate, there's *continuous* interaction between all parties all the time.

Unfortunately, the feedback myth gets applied to preaching. It suggests that the only "feedback" the preacher gets comes at the door after worship. By then, it's too late, except for what the preacher can learn for next time. This is not very helpful for that particular sermon, of course, but it also isn't very descriptive of what happens in human communication.

8. It relies on the myth of language equivalency.

The linear model also implies a one-to-one correspondence in language, that the exact word used by the "sender" is understood in the same way by the "receiver." But a "logically perfect" language (where a single word stands for a single referent) simply doesn't exist. There is no single word, for instance, that describes *you* and applies *only* to you and to no one else. Likewise, if each of us described the same chair, we'd do it in a different way—there isn't just one word that applies.

Linguists also talk about the *denotative* and *connotative* aspects of language. Denotation is a word's dictionary definition; connotation is the emotional *meaning* of that word that varies from person to person. Thus, ideas, objects, and words can have different *meanings,* depending on how they are talked about and the contexts in which they are used. There's no such thing as one word carrying the same meaning from "sender" to "receiver."

9. It promotes the myth of the perfect sermon.

Further, the linear model teaches us the *lie* of the *perfect sermon.* When you adopt this particular frame of reference, you are forced to spend all week laboring toward the *perfect* biblical insight that is included in the *perfect* manuscript with the *perfect* story that sums it all up. In short, you strive to design a *perfect* sermon. Anything less is *imperfect.*

Of course, there's no such thing. Frustration sets in if your best exegesis, the most perfect truth-bearing stories, and the right sermonic structure don't come together by the time your manuscript is completed. The implication is that you didn't have enough time to prepare and that an ideal sermon *could* somehow be produced if only you had a few more hours (or weeks or years). When you keep hoping the ideal sermon will blossom, your preaching will always be *uncertain,* because an "imperfect sermon" can't be preached as authoritatively as if it were *perfect.*

More realistically, a sermon is a product of the *best* gathered materials, the *best* possible exegesis, and the *best* structure you can put together in the time you have. But it's never "ideal" or "perfect," nor should you expect it to be. Given our limited time and resources as preachers, we must seek *excellence,* not perfection, in our preaching. We can't expect to do more. When my wife and I were preparing for missionary service, our trainer reminded us of something one of his mentors said: "All I can do is all I can do, and all I can do is enough." That's good advice for the preaching ministry.

10. It supports the myth of recall.

Finally, the linear model, with its emphasis on the importance of the message, implies that sermon *recall* is the most significant indication of "successful" preaching. That is, congregational members, after the preaching event is past, are supposed to *remember* the message of the "ideal" sermon. (There were "three points" in the former paradigm because it was supposed that a listener could only *remember* three points.)

But preaching shouldn't be *memorable* as much as it should be transformational *at the time it is happening.* Transformational preaching leads to a Holy Spirit-led, life-changing experience *during the preaching event* itself, rather than afterward.

LINEAR EXCLUSIONS

Along with these *inaccuracies* in the linear model, there are also several elements of human communication that are *not* represented or taken into account by this approach. The linear model is silent on at least the following nine issues.

1. It does not account for the **relational dimension** *of human interaction.*

We simply cannot escape the *relational* element of human communication: every time we communicate with other human beings, a *relationship* is either being *worked on* or *established.* The linear model indicates that the only important purpose of communication is *the transmission of information,* and it can happen between two impersonal parties. It is focused on the right *message* rather than the *people* who are involved.

But the relational aspect of human communication can never be dismissed, because both message and relationship *work together.* Sometimes, the strength of the *relationship* will "carry" the information or message. (For instance, the trusting *relationship* I have with my congregation will help me convey a difficult message on sin.) On the other hand, the *message* I preach may develop a good *relationship* with my listeners. (If I am a guest preacher, for instance, with a comforting message about death and dying, and there is a listener in the congregation who is facing death, my *topic* will establish a strong trust between that listener and me, particularly if she perceives me as a supportive person with a helpful message.) Similarly, poor preaching (where the preacher is impoverished in communication skills, not a bank account) is forgivable if the *message* is relevant and meaningful.

Further, the relationship *between* those who are communicating influences the orientation or outcome of the *message.* Describe an experience to a friend who knows you intimately. You'll do it very differently than when you describe the same experience to someone who doesn't know you. (In ethnomethodological circles, this is known as "recipient design.") It's a very natural part of communication: your *knowledge* of the listener influences how you talk and what you say.

We also *negotiate ourselves* every time we meet and greet other people and talk to them. (We'll talk more about this in the next chapter.) Relationships, both individual and corporate, are *always* being maintained or altered in some way in human communication. This is especially so in the preaching event.

This entire discussion is simply to point out that *personalities* and *relevant messages* always interact in human communication. *Relationship* and *content* work together, and the linear model does not depict this phenomenon.

2. It rejects simultaneity.

When we observe people who are actually talking with other people, we discover that one person does not speak and then the other politely respond with "clean" feedback (as the linear model implies).

In actuality, there's no such thing as "feedback" when humans talk (as I said earlier). We might initially think that "feedback" is just a *reversed process,* where the "receiver" becomes the "sender." But when we observe humans talking with each other, we discover that *all participants* in the interaction are *always simultaneous "senders" and "receivers."* In fact, the idea of feedback should be eliminated altogether when we're talking about humans in conversation. We are always giving out vocal and/or paralinguistic signals at the same time that we are "reading" these same clues from others. Sometimes everybody in a small group talks at the same time, which makes no sense to the linear model (and most of these people have no problem understanding what everybody else is saying!). Because humans send and receive information simultaneously, we practice a more complex process than the linear model leads us to believe.

Myron Chartier (1981), in his wonderful little book on communication and preaching, offers a valuable critique to the linear approach. Recognizing current scholarship in the field of human communication theory, he reconstructs a diagram that adds a great deal of complexity to the linear model. For him, communication is a *two-way* system of human interaction, with simultaneous sending and receiving of information. And even though his new model *maintains* the linear approach with its emphasis on *message,* he points us in the right direction to rethink what really happens when people talk.

This phenomenon of simultaneous sending and receiving of information happens both in one-on-one conversation and one-to-many communication experiences. In preaching, for instance, the congregation is always *sending* information to the preacher, at the same time that they are *receiving* information from the preacher. Congregation and preacher don't "take turns": both "send" and "receive" information at the same time, and without ever stopping. This mutual communication process comes through sounds (language) and paralinguistic signals (like eye contact, body posture, and yawning). It means that the messages being sent by the listeners are critical to the preaching event, and an alert preacher will "read" this information and respond to it *as it is happening,* just as he or she would in conversation. Even when verbal forms of feedback are not encouraged, as in "quiet" preaching environments, all members of the transaction are still engaged in the process, *if communication is happening at all.*

3. *It ignores the* **complexity of information transmission.**

The linear model basically says that human communication is only concerned with *words*. But the interaction that takes place in human communication is a far more complex experience than what is seen in the "channel" of the linear model. Communication involves a living, developing, and highly complex *interaction* of personalities, dreams, skills, strengths and weaknesses, likes and dislikes, impressions and intuitions, and different learning styles. Information is shared through any number of signals, data that simply have no way of being represented by the linear model. It cannot, for instance, account for *kinesics* (body language, gestures, facial expression) or *proxemics* (body position, distance). *Attitudes* and *impressions* are also important elements in how "meaning" is transmitted and understood by those involved in the communicative "event," but these influences on human interaction are simply not represented in the linear model.

4. *It cannot account for* **narrative *and* metaphor.**

We will see in Chapters 16 and 17 that, for the most part, we learn about reality and truth through *stories, events,* and *experiences.* Our lives are organized around narratives, not factual data, and the linear model cannot express the transmission of truth in this way. A computer, for instance, does not yet have the capability of *understanding* a story: it only understands *language* in one-to-one correspondence (or as close as it can get).

Neither does the linear model account for *metaphor*, which conveys a great deal of information without being *exacting*. Conceptual metaphors, in particular, carry information that far exceeds the words that are used. "Messages" that come through narrative or metaphor sometimes carry an emotional or convicting "punch" in a way that rational talk cannot do. These linguistic "enhancements" are essential to understanding the message that is communicated, but cannot be explained by the linear model.

5. *It does not account for* **reality construction.**

The rhetorical construction of *reality* cannot be configured in the linear model. Yet it *always* occurs in human communication. The speaker is always "framing reality" for the listener. How a doctrine, story, or argument is talked about is the way that the "receiver" is forced to *perceive* it. Thus, the speaker's description *becomes* reality for the listener.

This has tremendous implications for preaching, because reality construction is a powerful communicator of "truth." But this kind of information cannot be identified by the linear model, which simply isn't equipped to define information transmission in this way.

6. *It cannot account for* **community communication.**

Communication happens on several levels at the same time. Verbal and paralinguistic signals are exchanged, for instance, in one-on-one and one-to-many forms of communication. But there is also a *social* level at which information is communicated. "Social knowledge," for instance, communicates a great deal of information without *specifying* or *teaching* that information.

By "social knowledge," I mean that every culture has generally-shared information that doesn't have to be "proven" all the time—it is just understood. The culture in which I am raised follows certain practices that I automatically adopt, but I may never have been *taught* these customs. For instance, Russian Baptists stand before and after every meal and one of them prays aloud, and they do it without a "leader." When I ask how they know when to stand and who is going to pray, no one seems to know—they just do it. These kinds of social customs are evident in every culture. How do we know, for instance, when it is and is not appropriate to cross the street against the light? We somehow learn this kind of "cultural awareness" (often through observation), but the linear model cannot account for how that information is *transmitted.*

It's the same with "insider" language in the Church, which is often oriented around local culture. The phrase, "the blood of Jesus," for instance, means more than the *blood* of Jesus to most Christians: it carries information about salvation and sanctification in a way that "outsiders" do not understand. This is what Rod Hart (1971) means when he says that language *unites* a "doctrinal group" as well as conveys information.

7. It cannot account for ambiguity.

The mathematical model assumes that language must always be clear and concise for good communication to happen. However, we also know that there is an important role for *ambiguity* in our social order. Eric Eisenberg (1984) argues that *ambiguous language* unites communities in which it is used, where exacting definitions would destroy that unity. Organizational mottoes (a church slogan like "loving God, loving others") or "insider language" (such as "born again") provide unity and cohesiveness in every organization, even though these phrases may mean something different to different individuals in that community.

I had breakfast this morning in Prague with a friend whose name is "Ramblin' Rex." Rex is an itinerant blues singer in the Czech Republic (though you might see him from time to time in California, Oregon, or New Orleans). He talks openly about his faith and his remarkable conversion story (he came from a hippie culture, smoked dope, did sex, and drank regularly). When he shares his testimony in public schools, prisons, and jazz clubs throughout the Czech Republic, he talks about when he "got saved" or "found the Lord." In fact, Rex joyously characterizes *everybody's* conversion as having "got saved," "found the Lord," or both. Those phrases are characteristic of the kind of Christian "community" from which Rex comes. It means something to those from within that tradition.

Much Christian language, like that, unites us, but it is ambiguous enough to mean different things to those who use it. Eisenberg says that this kind of language helps establish and maintain *social organizations*. People unite around this ambiguity because they think that others interpret the language in the same way they do.

Inexact language, like that, carries a variety of messages. The same is true for symbols. Think, for instance, of how differently the American flag was viewed during the Viet Nam war and after the terrorist attacks on September 11, 2001. The same symbol can mean different things to different people at different times: it carries social information. This is the case, too, with Christian symbols, such as the cross, baptism, and communion. Each has a different connotation to different people in different communities, and people get passionate about them! The "information" is almost inexpressible and certainly not communicated by exacting linear language.

Ambiguity in language and symbol, then, communicates and unites, but it can't be characterized by the linear model.

8. *It cannot account for* oral language structure.

The linear model does not understand how humans communicate *orally*. As I already said (and we will see more fully in Chapter 6), when we talk, we don't *speak* in logical sentences or complete thoughts. Oral language is fluid. It depends on *sounds*, not dictionary definitions, and conversation comes in small "chunks" of information that are emitted one at a time. The whole message isn't completed and then transmitted, as the linear model suggests. It comes bit by bit, often with "repair" and other adjustments along the way, clumping along first with clear direction but then adding backfill, and always with nonfluencies (like "er," "um," or "you know.") This pattern of talking is not as clearly "directive" as the linear model shows.

But, more significantly, when we're talking about preaching, listeners learn to "hear" language in this way, too, not in the more compressed structure of written language, or in the exacting style that comes when a "message" is already *completed.* With oral language, the listener learns to hold small "thought chunks" in abeyance until the next few "chunks" are produced, and, with back-and-fill interpretation, the message gets understood. Human conversation is not as "clean" as the linear model suggests.

9. *It cannot account for* inference.

Finally, when "chunks" of discourse are produced orally (and heard aurally), one at a time, the listener must make *inferences* about information that isn't specifically stated in what the speaker says. These inferences are a natural element of human communication, but are not accounted for in the linear model.

Let's look at an example. Suppose I am telling you about a friend who preached last week, and I say to you, "After her sermon, four people came forward," you might assume that four people were responding to the gospel proclamation that day. In making that assumption, you are supplying information that I didn't give you. Now, I really meant that four deacons came forward to serve communion. In the next chunks of discourse, you'd quickly learn that I wasn't talking about salvation responses, but about the next part of the worship experience. You'd adjust your previous inference.

This is the way we engage in conversation all the time. That is, we make assumptions based on social knowledge, the context of the conversation or communication, our relationship with each other, and plausibility structures. We make and then correct those inferences, if necessary, as we get more information. This keeps us engaged in the conversation.

This kind of inference in language also happens through the *enthymeme,* a tool of deductive reasoning. It's a word used by Aristotle, and it has to do with filling in the missing step in a statement of logic. Here's what he meant:

Formal logic comes through what are called *syllogisms.* A "normal" syllogism looks like this:

> If A is B *(the major premise),*
> and C is A *(the minor premise),*
> then C is B *(the conclusion).*

The syllogism is a way of making sure we're communicating accurately with each other.

Let's look at a couple of examples. Ephesians 2:5 says that all Christians (A) are saved by grace (B). I can draw a conclusion from that: if Florence (C) is a Christian (A), it follows that she (C) is also saved by grace (B).

Let me try another: all Swedes (A) are hungry (B). John (C) is a Swede (A), therefore John (C) is hungry (B). This syllogism follows the pattern, of course, but there's something wrong with it. This example actually points out the two conditions that are necessary in order for a conclusion to be correct: the major premise must be true *for all cases,* and the particular instance in the minor premise must fall within the class with which it is associated. In this case, I happen to know that John is a Swede (the minor premise is correct, then), but I also know some Swedes who are *not* hungry. The major premise (that all Swedes are hungry) is, thus, faulty, and, for this reason, the syllogism is not true.

This brings us to the *enthymeme.* The enthymeme, for Aristotle, is an *incomplete syllogism.* An enthymeme is a construction that leads us to accept a *conclusion* without one of the premises. It is based on assumption and inference.

So, for instance, I just found out that Phil has been baptized by immersion. Nobody actually *told* me this, and I didn't *see* his baptism, either. I know it from a short lunchtime conversation I had with you. You said something in passing from which I was able to *infer* that Phil has been immersed: you told me that he is a member of the "Solid Believers Mountaintop Chapel" down the street. I already knew that all members of "Solid Believers" (A) are baptized by immersion (B). (The chapel is led by a fundamentalist pastor who only allows those he baptizes to become members.) So here, then, is the major premise. When you told me that Phil (C) is a member of "Solid Believers" (A), I heard the minor premise (which I hadn't known), that he is actually a "member." Therefore, I was able to infer a conclusion: that Phil has been baptized by immersion. The syllogism was incomplete, but I filled in the missing information by *inference.*

Again, making inferences and filling in missing information are something we do all the time in human communication, but the linear model has no way to explain these phenomena.

SO WE MOVE AHEAD

Shannon and Weaver's mathematical theory of communication has been an extremely important model for technological advancement, particularly for telecommunications and computers. But it has also been adopted (without critical evaluation) as the *standard reigning* model for human communication. It is sometimes useful, but, as we have seen, there are serious weaknesses in this model when we use it to describe the way humans communicate. Unfortunately, it has influenced the way we have been taught to proclaim biblical truth from our pulpits.

In this chapter, I have tried to present the linear model as an *inaccurate* depiction of what really happens in human communication, and also that it does not adequately represent many elements that are present in human language when people talk.

If you have adopted the Shannon-Weaver model for your preaching, but want to be a *competent communicator,* you will have to begin with reconceptualizing your theory of human communication. Of course, your ability to preach doesn't really depend on which theory of communication you hold. What really matters is whether you are able to "connect" with your listeners. If you can't do that, all the theory in the world won't make a bit of difference.

But if you do need to *change* your approach to preaching, begin with your *theory,* because *conceptual knowledge* leads to responsibility. *Theory informs* and then *drives practice.* You have a vital message to proclaim, and you should become the *very best* you can in communicating it!

The stage is now set for yet another look at human communication, one that I call *transaction,* and it is to this subject that we turn in the next chapter.

CHAPTER 5
Transactional Human Communication

COMMUNICATION ISSUES

When one person attempts to pass a simple idea to another (a single-purposed one-to-one communication event), the linear model has some usefulness. A message is conceived, encoded, and transmitted to a listening "receiver." Of course, if it were possible for a person to communicate in this way without anything else "human" or "systemic" intruding on the event, a mechanical, mathematical, technological approach is suitable. But as we have seen, the linear model is *unlike* anything that happens when real people are actually engaged with other *real* people.

But now we start to think about *one-to-many* human communication, of which preaching is one form. For this kind of communication event, the linear model may seem to be more relevant than for that of one-to-one communication. After all, a *monological* presentation from a "sender" to a group of "receivers" seems a perfect fit for the linear model.

But let's not forget that preaching is still a *human* activity. As such, it embodies an *even-more complicated* process than one-on-one conversation. *Any* human interaction, after all, is far more complex than one person encoding a message and transmitting it to another and getting feedback if it's misunderstood. But where there are many human beings involved (as in preaching), communication doesn't get simpler—it gets much more complicated—and the simplistic linear model becomes even more profoundly irrelevant.

So where do we turn for a more adequate theoretical model? Well, if we agree that preaching is actually *human* and not *mechanical* communication, we should look for a theoretical orientation that conforms to this basic understanding. I suggest that we look at the only sensible place to start—with *informal human conversation.*

Why begin here when we know that preaching is a *formal, one-to-many* rhetorical presentation? Well, shouldn't *public* speaking be only an extension and "formalization" of informal, over-the-back-fence conversation? When we think about preaching and listening this way, it makes sense. After all, our earliest language acquisition comes by speaking *informally* and *conversationally;* only later do we learn *public address.* Perhaps one reason why public speaking is the most feared experience any human must face is that we have removed it from the "conversational" category. Talking with other humans should come *naturally* to us—we cut our teeth on it!

Yes, public speaking (and preaching) *is* a more formal way of communicating (we have to be careful about being too informal in the pulpit). But if we begin with the assumption that preaching is *conversation,* our pulpit language will communicate far better than if we assume it to be a *mechanical* process. We can always adjust the informal to be more formal, but we really can't make a linear, mathematical model resemble anything that looks like humans talking with each other. So it's better to base our theory on how *humans* talk rather than an informational model that describes how *machines* talk. When we recognize preaching as an *extension of conversation,* the experience is much more natural: we will speak more freely and our listeners will hear more clearly.

If we take this approach, there are two important questions we must ask.

WHY?

In these past two chapters, we have examined and evaluated the linear model of communication, an approach that assumes that the *only* purpose of human communication is to *transmit information.* But is this a legitimate assumption? *Why* do humans communicate? I find at least three basic reasons.

The first, of course, is that we *do* communicate because we have information to share. There are times when we have something important to say or there is a particular "message" we want to convey (as in preaching). The linear model is useful for helping us sort through some of the issues related to the transmission of information. But we must be careful not to leave it here. There are at least two additional reasons why we talk with other people, neither of which can be accounted for by the linear model.

The second is that we communicate just to *socialize* with others, as, for instance, when we need companionship. When a young couple is building a relationship, the *topic* of conversation isn't nearly as important as the time they spend together. Or look at me. I'm an introvert at heart. But there are times when I *need* companionship, when I *want* to talk with my wife or one of my best friends, and it doesn't really matter *what* the subject of our conversation is. (In fact, sometimes I have to figure out *what* to talk about!) I'm really only aware of my need to *talk* with somebody else, face-to-face. It's a function of being human. For socializing purposes, *what* is talked about isn't as important as the *human interaction* that accompanies the talking.

Thirdly, sometimes people talk for *psychological* purposes. We talk because we are expressing a need for power or love or protection, or to ease our fears (like whistling while walking through a cemetery). Sometimes we talk just to vent our anger or pain, by cursing or screaming. The *content* or *information* isn't as important as the cathartic *action.* When people communicate for psychological purposes, the "message" that is communicated isn't the informational *content* of the discourse. It's a "message" that comes through volume and passion and torn robes—through the *act* of communicating itself.

I'm raising this question simply to point out that humans sometimes "talk" because we are working on a relationship or taking care of personal business, and it doesn't matter what the subject matter is. This is the domain of *feelings* and *attitudes,* not data transmission. That's quite different from thinking that we always have *information* to convey whenever we open our mouths.

HOW?

Similar to the "why?" question is the "how?" *How* do we communicate with each other when we're in conversation? The linear model assumes that we use only carefully-encoded words and exacting language. But it doesn't take much observation to discover that we speak with far more than "vocal noise." We use gestures and facial expression and tone of voice and volume and body language and spatial distance. All are important to the communication process. These "paralinguistic" signals work *alongside* the "linguistics" of communication.

This is what Gregory Bateson (1951) claimed. He said that there are always two ways that information is passed between human beings, what he called *report* and *command.* By report, he meant the *content, information,* or *message* that is "sent." *Command,* on the other hand, refers to the way the message is communicated, which is dependent on the *relationship* between communicators. *Report,* for instance, is the story line of the Prodigal Son; *command* helps you know if that story is meant to be freeing or confrontative. "Aren't you fun?" can be either a sarcastic put-down or a wonderful word of encouragement, depending on how it is said. The content *(report)* is the message; the way it is said (the *command)* determines how the speaker understands its meaning.

These two levels of human communication (the *what* and the *how)* are always present. The combination of verbal (language) and nonverbal (paralinguistic cues like gesture, proximity, and inflection) is natural to how we talk. Of course, the clearest communication happens when words and paralinguistic cues are consistent. Sometimes, as we know, *report* will send a very different message than *command,* as when, for instance, you say to your spouse (with great disgust), "Yeah, I'm really happy that you made *those* arrangements!" And perhaps you've experienced the preacher who shouts angrily, with a grimace and eye-fire, *"God loves you"* with the unvoiced but implied meaning, "You dirty rotten skunks!"

I'm simply pointing out that *how* we pass messages or talk with each other is a much more complicated process than what the linear model implies. The Shannon-Weaver model is concerned with only one component of communication—the transmission of information. It was designed for that, and for that it is valuable. But human communication is much more complex than that, and we need to lay aside the linear model in favor of theory that more accurately defines how *humans* talk.

In its place, I am suggesting that we turn our attention to a different way of understanding human communication. This is what I call a *transactional approach.* As you will see, "transaction" takes into account more of what happens when humans talk, and is particularly helpful when we reflect on the preaching event.

John Dewey, the great philosopher, first introduced the term "transaction." Dewey, along with Arthur Bentley, co-authored a book in 1949 called, *Knowing and the known,* the same year that Shannon and Weaver's book was published. (Unfortunately, it was Shannon and Weaver's book that captured the attention of communication theorists, even though Dewey and Bentley were far more insightful in depicting human communication.)

In their book, Dewey and Bentley are concerned with semantics (the study of meaning). Dewey argued that *knowing* something emerges from human *interaction:* "knowing is cooperative and . . . integral with communication." What he meant was that communication is a transaction between individuals, and out of that communicative relationship, a message (or meaning) emerges. That is (and these are my words), humans must be locked into a "relational dance" if there is to be meaningful conversation. Messages and meaning don't exist apart from this relational element of interaction. Dewey argued that meaning emerges when any information, description, or a particular "point" or perspective is heard through a relational channel, when a "receiver" is able to think through, examine, and then relate that information to his or her own worldview.

TRANSACTIONAL COMMUNICATION

John Stewart (1990) picked up where Dewey and Bentley stopped. Stewart argues that there are three levels at which we can understand human communication. First, it may be perceived as an *action* experience, where the communicator transmits information to a receiver (this is depicted in the linear model of communication). It is *directional* and *purposeful.*

The second level takes us one step further. Here, communication is *interaction.* Interaction includes the action experience, but it also implies a continual involvement and interplay of all participants in the communicative process. It thus takes into consideration the *relational* dimension of human communication. It understands communication as a living, complex engagement of personalities and dreams, skills and attitudes, strengths and weaknesses, likes and dislikes, impressions and intuitions, with different learning styles and interests.

But there's one more level at which to understand human communication. Stewart identifies this as the *transaction,* an approach that, again, *includes* action and interaction, but then he moves us one step further. As Stewart understands transaction, it is the engagement of *displayed personality.* He means that all parties are continually "interpreting themselves for others" and "reading" signals from others at the same time (what I call "simultaneous feedback"). This moves the idea of "transaction" one step beyond what Dewey and Bentley had in mind, but it is a significant component of the transactional nature of public discourse.

In the rest of this chapter, then, we will consider the interesting subject of the *transaction.* We will look at transaction's *relational, message,* and *meaning* components, and throughout this discussion, I'll be relating the transactional experience to preaching.

1. RELATIONAL

Whether we are talking about conversation between two people or mass communication (such as preaching), *people* are communicating with each other. And whenever that happens, there is the mutual interplay of all participants in the engagement. This is the *relational* element of the experience. Indeed, whenever humans are involved in the communication process, we simply cannot ever dismiss the relational component. Even when I stop to ask directions from a stranger, I am carrying on a *relational interaction* at the same time that information passes between us. We can't ever escape it. This component is so strong, in fact, that Watzlawick, Beavin, and Jackson (1967) claim that the relationship is "mediated by communication."

Let's look, then, at several implications of this relational dimension of human communication.

First, the relationship is between people

In preaching, of course, the preacher is the "central player" in the process of communicating biblical truth (as Philips Brooks once said, preaching is "truth through personality"). But the preacher is also *relationally* engaged with each of the listeners and the group as a whole. Sermons are never preached to a blank sea of faces or a wall of humanity, but with living, breathing, rational human beings. They are real *people,* actual *persons,* not objects or automatons, as the linear model would have us believe. Each person is a unique *individual*—a living, breathing, *thinking* human agent, with a unique personality and perspective on life, a sense of humor and/or fiery disposition, with distinct experiences, a particular worldview, and a unique personal taste in food and clothing. Bring a batch of us into a room and automatically the relational component begins to work its magic. So when we engage in human communication (no matter whether it's one or many), we are communicating with individuals, not objects or ideas of persons, but actual *people.*

Without this relational dimension in preaching, very little happens! Preaching requires that preacher and listener (or preacher and congregation) be fully *engaged* with each other. Preaching activates a relational component of life, one between *people.* Unfortunately (as I've already said), reading a manuscript from the pulpit indicates a relationship between the *preacher and the text* rather than between *preacher and listener.* This results in a broken relationship with the listeners. Thus, either there is a transaction between preacher and *people* or between preacher and *message:* the first will transform lives, the other is irrelevant, or, at best, distant, to its listeners.

Second, the relationship is both individual and corporate

In public (or mass) communication, there are two processes of relationships engaged at the same time. The first is the one-to-one communication between the preacher and the individual, which is, of course, compounded by the number of people present. Each of these private *relationships* is unique, and the resulting *message* between each pairing of preacher and person is therefore always unique.

But there's also a *corporate* relationship on which public communication operates. The preacher preaches to the *assembled body,* a one-to-many type of relationship with the congregation as a *whole.* (Except on rare occasions, the preacher doesn't tend to target a single individual: most messages are directed to an "assembled body.") Further, the corporate relationship is just as active and engaged as that between individuals. For instance, if a preacher feels (through verbal or nonverbal cues) unappreciated by the congregation, she might assert her personal authority in the sermon without even knowing about it. Or a pastor might preach much more tentatively or gently if he feels the congregation is disagreeable that morning. A "public face" is always present in one-to-many communication.

This is one reason why the same message can be preached a second or third time in different settings. Because of the corporate relationship, the same message is never the same. It is not so much that the individual listeners are different but because the corporate relationship is different.

Third, the relationship begins with the preacher

Because preaching is a monological, one-to-many event, the preacher is the one who manages and monitors the relational exchange. Stewart (1990) says that when we meet other people, we continually *present* and *monitor* our own self-definition *as we interact* with them and as we respond to their self-definitions. *We define ourselves* in relationship to other people. Thus, whenever we interact with others, we continually *negotiate* the presentation of ourselves. We are always presenting, interpreting, and altering our self-perception and self-presentation every time we encounter others. Human communication, then, is *fundamentally* relational; it is an experience by which we display ourselves to each other.

Transaction for preaching implies, then, that whenever a preacher preaches, a public "face" is being presented. My *self-awareness* is always introduced and clarified in every preaching event, depending on how I "read" other participants in the process. Look at what Berger and Luckmann (1966) write:

> *I* hear myself *as I speak; my own subjective meanings are made objectively and continuously available to me and ipso facto become 'more real' to me . . . (L)anguage makes 'more real' my subjectivity not only to my conversation partner but also to myself.*

This means that when I, as a preacher, reveal myself through public communication, I am, at the same time, also "solidifying" my own self-understanding. I am never merely voicing a "word from God" when I preach, because every sermon is accompanied by some changing information about me.

Third, in many ways, the preaching *transaction* begins before the preaching event, because it is based on prior assumptions, experiences, knowledge, and the preacher's relationship with these listeners or others like them. In this sense, preaching includes the "whole" of an experience, not just the static "delivery" of a completed, fixed message. The transaction engages the "whole" of the preacher, but it is the *message* that is still the focal point of the preacher's exchange. That "message" is filtered and voiced through the person of the preacher who, in turn, gives shape to the meaning that bursts within the listener. Indeed, *without the interaction, there can be no message!*

Finally, and most interestingly, in public proclamation the preacher is not only engaged in *self-presentation,* but also rhetorically constructs the *listeners.* Preaching, thus, has power to *create* listeners who reflect on their own self-awareness and presentation through the preacher's discourse, but who are also positioned by the preacher to respond in a particular way.

Fourth, the relationship engages listeners

The preacher initiates and guides the stream and pace of information, as well as the "course of the discourse," but the listener must be fully engaged if any *transaction* is to occur. The listener is not simply a *receiver* of information, but actively *contributes* to the relationship *and* to the formulation of the message. Something *transformational* happens through the relationship and the message.

A friend once told me that he was in a college class that redirected a professor's style of teaching. Through collaboration on the part of class members, every time this boring professor would start walking toward the door, the whole class would yawn, pass notes, get restless, and talk to each other. But when the teacher moved toward the window, they would sit on the edge of their seats and get very involved in his lecture. Within a couple of weeks, the teacher was lecturing by continually staring out the window!

This suggests that the listener has great power over the preacher and, thus, the discourse. Congregational members are not just passive listeners. Their hopes and dreams, their own thought patterns and attitudes, their sorrows and strengths, their weaknesses and interests—all contribute to the communicative process. Most of the "listener-sent" information perceived by the preacher comes from paralinguistic sources. It is not "feedback," but is, rather, *active communication,* both *relationally* and in the formulation of the message.

Indeed, these traits help fashion the meaning of the message for that listener, quite apart from what the preacher may intend.

Further, the preacher displays and changes his or her self-perception through public exposure, and the same happens to the listeners. The relationship *between preacher and listener* is developed or altered as all engaged participants construct, reveal, and monitor their self-definitions. Any preacher can learn a great deal about any listener just through observation during the preaching event.

Thus, preaching is a complex process of selves engaged in self-perception and self-presentation and, through it, biblical information is shared and understood. Thus, *both* the preacher and listener work together in the transaction and both contribute to the *relationship* and the *message*. Everyone in the preaching transaction is *actively engaged* in the communication process at the same time—it is *never a one-way event.* This is what Plato meant by *dialog:* it is out of discussion and interaction that "truth" emerges.

When we define the *preaching transaction* in this way, the whole concept of preaching takes on a different reality. It's a radical departure from the linear model. No longer is preaching merely an *action,* where one person "delivers" a message to a group of silent and distant receivers. Preaching requires an engagement that makes it an *interaction;* the experience is one more event in the on-going, *relational* dialogue between preacher and people. Of course, relational factors are already at work before the sermon begins, especially when both preacher and listeners know each other well. For this reason, Clyde Fant (1987) recommends that the preacher, in imagination, stand about a third of the way into the congregation. The exercise reminds us that preacher and congregation are inextricably connected in the preaching experience, and it is out of this engagement that a message emerges and transformation happens.

2. AN EMERGENT MESSAGE

The word "communication" comes from the Latin, "to have in common." Communicating, then, implies *commonality* among participants, in both relationship and *information.* In preaching, for instance, preacher and congregation are *commonly* engaged together in a unique relationship, but they must also use *common* language if they are to understand a *common* message based on *common* ideas and values. Preaching breaks down when there is no "common ground" between pulpit and pew.

When the sermon begins, an *informational* dialog joins the *relational* dialog. The *message* is important, but in a different way than the linear model suggests. Because preaching is a *transaction* between engaged participants, a unique "message" emerges that *could only be developed* when this unique biblical truth is proclaimed by this unique preacher among this unique mix of people in this unique setting. We assume (through the linear model) that this *proclaimed message* is actually the message, but when we understand preaching as transaction, it is more accurate to say that the preacher's discourse, while the primary contributor to the message, is not actually the message itself. Rather, the message is the *product of the preaching event.*

Another way of saying this is that a *transaction* is necessary for a *message* to emerge. Or, in other words, *a message develops in the interaction that could not have occurred apart from that interaction.*

Let's unpack what I mean by this.

First, the **preacher** *is the primary contributor to the message*

The preacher conceives of, fashions, and then presents a fully-formulated biblical discourse in the preaching event. This introduces the subject matter of the transaction. The sermon also provides the foundation by which biblical truth impacts its listeners, and sets into motion the process of the *transaction.* Ultimately, the origin of the *message* and *meaning* are dependent on, and emerge from, what is stated by the preacher.

Biblical truth is never without a context. It needs an application or "location" for it to be meaningful. It was given birth in the biblical world. Now it must be nested in ours. And by identifying that truth and then proclaiming it, the preacher brings it to birth *within the listener.* There is never a "pure" message that can be separated from a context or a transaction. Ultimately, this means that the prepared sermon undergoes a transformation *as it is being preached.* And it is out of the *relationship* and the *prepared information* of the sermon that the message develops.

Second, the **transaction** *contributes to the message*

Humans who communicate for social or psychological reasons interact without having to pass *information.* The transaction, on the other hand, expands the interaction with the *informational* component, because in a transaction, a *purposeful message* emerges. Here is where Stewart's *action* and *interaction* join forces. In linear terms, the speaker has particular information to encode and transmit to a listener. For preaching, the "sermon" provides the *content* of the exchange, but it is the relational interaction with and between participants and information that create the transaction.

Both preacher and listener, then, must be engaged in *proactive* communication ("proactive preaching" and "proactive listening"). If the sermon is irrelevant or distant, and the preacher is disengaged from the transaction (as often happens with reading a manuscript), little will happen. And if there are no engaged listeners, there can be no *message.*

Third, **self-presentation** *contributes to the message*

As I mentioned earlier, Stewart (1990) extended Dewey's definition by suggesting that a "transaction" is not just directional and relational, but is also an engagement in which participants *define themselves* in relationship to other people. This continual *negotiation* with others influences how others respond to us as they perceive how we present ourselves. Thus, when humans talk, this display and alteration of self in the transaction influences not only how the message is communicated, but its content as well.

Fourth, content *and* relationship *contribute to the message*

We have already seen that two "channels of discourse" *(content* and *relationship)* interact all the time that there is human interaction. Like the two levels of the George Washington Bridge where traffic flows in both directions on two levels at the same time, the *content* of a message and the *relationship* between all the conversational participants are always interacting, both at the same time and between all those who are engaged in the transaction. So Niedenthal and Rice (1980) identify preaching as a "shared story." In African-American preaching, for instance, the interaction of message and relationship is carried out vocally through a dialog between preacher and listener (a "creative partnership," according to Henry Mitchell [1990]). That kind of verbal interaction doesn't usually happen in European-American preaching, but the African-American context provides a visible (and vocal) model of what should also be happening "silently" when only one of the participants is speaking: *the message is formulated while the relationship is developed.*

It is also evident that, when these two interactive channels of content and relationship are busy and productive simultaneously, one of them tends to "carry" the other. This dominance depends on the situation, the relationship between the people involved, and the message being communicated. That is, as I said earlier, sometimes the *relationship* encourages the development and acceptance of the *message,* and, at other times, the *information* or *content* helps develop the *relationship.* Sometimes the *real* subject of the discourse is the proclaimed message, and sometimes it is the *relationship* between the participants. But the most powerful sermons are those that engage listeners with a relevant and convicting *message* that is also carried by a strong, caring relationship.

What I'm saying is that the *message* can never be separated from the *relationship* between the preacher and individual congregational members. And because they influence each other, the *relational interaction* determines the quality and, to a certain extent, the substance of the *message.*

Fifth, an open system of influences *contributes to the message*

Every transaction between human beings operates within a *system.* Communication includes many, many influences other than just the transmission of information: environmental factors (like heat or light, pollen count, sounds, and room appearance), thoughts, speech patterns, prejudices, disposition toward the subject, individual perceptions, word denotations and connotations, volume, emphasis, the relationship and spatial distance between participants in the interaction, personal history and personalities, the amount of value given to different linguistic and paralinguistic cues—the list is practically limitless. And these influences operate in an *open system* of communication.

An open system exchanges information, materials, and energies with its environment. As with any living system, all these components interact with and influence each other. Because the communication event takes place in a system of influences, any one of the components can influence the whole, and every one of these influences impact the resultant message and its meaning. A change in one part of the "system" changes the other parts.

The linear model depicts human communication as a "closed" system. The factors directly involved in the communicative process ("sender," "channel," "receiver," "message") are "protected" or isolated from their environment, as, for instance, when signals are sent between computers. "Noise," for the linear model, is an *invasive* component in the communicative process—it comes from outside the system, and harms the system.

But human communication (and preaching) actually happens in an open system. There are any number of environmental, personal, and group influences that can change the course of informal conversation (a minor story detail can determine the next story, the honk of a horn reminds a speaker of something else, or a high temperature leads to exhaustion that, in turn, means a trite response rather than a sharp retort). A *transaction* includes too many uncontrollable factors (such as attitudes, body posture, values, grimaces, colors, and worldviews). Some people or cultures are *suspicious of* or *offended by* certain paralinguistic cues (such as spatial distance, body language or odor, eye contact, certain gestures, dress, or accent), while other individuals from other cultures *trust* people through the same paralinguistic cues. A change in one small element of the system, when there are human beings also present, has the potential of changing everything else. A transactional model suggests that all these components are natural elements of the communicative process, not deviants or detractors from it.

It also means that all systemic components in any transaction contribute to the development of the message. As each influence or element changes the system, the resultant relationship and message are changed. This, again, is a reason why every transaction is unique, even when the same sermon is communicated with a different group of listeners. Every transaction is unique because the people engaged in it are unique. Each person has a different personality, each responds to the sensory environment differently, and each sends out unique "self-presentation" signals. And the group identity that is formed by these individuals combines with the environmental factors and individual relationships to contribute to the communication event. When these blended signals are "read" by the preacher, the relationship changes, as does the resultant message, particularly when the preacher is engaged head-on with listeners in a transaction that includes biblical truth and noteless interaction.

It follows, then, that the *message* that emerges from preaching arises from a series of *influences*. It can hardly be a linear, directive message whose primary purpose is that the listener be able to duplicate it exactly. Rather, a "message" emerges *because* of the event, the system, and the participants, all engaged *together.*

Ultimately, the relational element of human communication, and the systemic environment in which it occurs, and the information or message that is formulated out of the transaction, all contribute to *meaning* for the listener. Indeed, it is *meaning* that matters most.

3. THE CONCEPT OF MEANING

In the preaching transaction, the preacher and listeners are continually negotiating both the relationship *and* the information, which leads to a final message. And this negotiated message becomes *meaningful.*

Meaning, then, is what happens in the heart and mind of the listener. Thus, the goal of transformational preaching is not simply to present a message, but for that message to be transformed into *meaning,* that the listener's heart be changed. George Swank's (1981) *dialogic* approach to preaching says just this, that preacher and listener are both involved in bringing about the sermon's "meaning." But the preacher is not the only contributor to the message or to its emergent meaning.

There are two implications of *meaning* for the preaching event.

First, meaning "resides" in the individual

The *message* arises from the *information* that is transmitted, the way in which it is shared, and the *relationship* between the preacher and listener. Meaning *emerges* when biblical truth, relationship between preacher and listener, and Holy Spirit come together, but meaning always "settles" within the listener. Truth resides within the biblical text, but the interpreted *meaning* of that truth comes in its application and relevance to each listener.

Charles Kraft (1996) argues that meaning resides in individuals. It does not exist in the external world and is not inherent in the message, even though the words and symbols restrict possible options. Meaning, in this way, is constructed by the receiver; it belongs to the domain of the *listener.* This "locates" meaning not in the text or the preacher's intention, but within the listener.

In Mark 7:20-21, Jesus says, "What comes out of you is what defiles you. For from within, out of your hearts, come evil thoughts . . . " Thus, for Jesus, *incoming* information is not the problem. Jesus says that it is the person's heart that does the clarifying and interpreting. The real problem is what people do with what they hear. This puts the responsibility for the *meaning* of a message directly on the listener. When the preacher preaches, a *message* emerges from the transaction, but the *meaning* of the message comes from within each listener. Meaning is the *uniting* of the developed message with the "set" of the listener's heart. This happens when listeners are transformed by what William S. Howell (1982) calls an "internal monologue," which inhibits, constrains, and focuses the message and the relationship between the communicating parties.

This is simply to say that, in preaching, the spoken word of the preacher is only one element (though of primary importance) of the *meaning* that emerges for the listener. The preacher is responsible for the sermon's content, and is the one who initiates the confrontation and guides the listener to it and through it. The preacher *constructs* and *fashions* the discourse. But the initial discourse that is generated by the preacher can be adapted, changed, directed, even rejected by the listeners in the process.

Thus, all the work I do on sermon preparation in my study is only part of the process whereby the biblical truth will transform my listeners. To state it even more radically and strongly: the emergence of proclaimed truth, the word of God, is *dependent* on the preaching event. A sermon's meaning arises in the mind and heart of the listener *only* because of the transaction; the confrontative power of the proclaimed biblical truth will be transformative only through the preaching event.

Ultimately, *meaning* is out of the control of the preacher. There may be a disparity between what the preacher says and what the listener actually *hears.* And the relationship between listener and preacher may undergo many changes through the course of the preaching event, from strong to weak or distrust to respect. The sermon's content may also be accepted without reservation as the "word of God," discarded completely, held in abeyance, or tentatively identified as the preacher's "opinion." And, of course, it is possible for listeners to move existentially between attention and inattention, comprehension and confusion, and/or toward or away from a strengthened or broken relationship all within the same preaching event. But the listener must be *engaged* (both relationship and information) if "meaning" is to emerge for that individual.

Any of these responses may come within any individual listener, and may be broadly seen in different members of the same listening congregation, but there will be little transformation without personal engagement. The message is so heavily influenced by the listener's personal issues that these private responses "translate" the preacher's message into that person's own worldview or theological system. The resultant *meaning,* then, may be completely different from what the preacher intends.

In the final analysis, *meaning* arises from the *truth* of the proclamation, the *person* of the preacher, the biblical text, the preacher's whole *discourse,* the *relationship* between preacher and people, the listener's *receptive* influences, a host of *environmental* factors, and what the *Holy Spirit* is able to do in and through the preaching event.

Second, the Holy Spirit is active throughout the process

The proclaimed "word of God" is something more profoundly and uniquely personal for the listener than the prepared sermon that the preacher brings to the preaching event. Biblical truth becomes meaningful because of the activity of the Holy Spirit. The Holy Spirit is present within the text as the inspired and authoritative written word of God. The Holy Spirit is active within the preacher when a message is conceived and formulated. The Holy Spirit transforms the ordinary auditorium into holy space, sanctifying every corner and crevice. The Holy Spirit is alive in the preacher's proclamation, relational dynamic, and self-presentation from the pulpit. The Holy Spirit, active within each listener, interprets the biblical truth and its message for that listener, in his or her own terms. The Holy Spirit integrates and massages all the bits of the "open system" of the communication event, together with the orienting message of the preacher's discourse. The Holy Spirit brings those personally-relevant elements together and creates within each listener a particular "meaning." It is Holy Spirit-action on the emergent message within each listener's mind and heart that brings about *meaning* for that engaged listener. Meaning is, above all, a *cooperative* effort that is brought into being by the Holy Spirit who translates all the present factors into what he ultimately wants the listener to comprehend. Indeed, the emergence of *meaning* is a *spiritual phenomenon.* As such, it is the very domain in which the Holy Spirit works.

This is why every listener, seated in the same room, hearing the same sermon, can be impacted by a different message from the same proclaimed biblical truth. Transformation comes from the interactively-developed, Spirit-interpreted *meaning* of the message.

Of course, just because "meaning" is taken out of your hands as a preacher isn't license for you to say *anything* you want in any *manner* from the pulpit. Nor does it imply that it makes no difference *what* you preach. It is precisely because of your Spirit-infused motivation, *because* you identify and proclaim clear biblical truth, and *because* you use all the persuasive ability you can muster that your listeners are *confronted* with biblical truth in such a way that they must respond to it. Without your purposeful *intention,* as the one who initiates and commands the discourse, there can be no confrontation between listener and text, and little release of the Spirit.

This implies, of course, that you be prepared spiritually, and that you be absolutely clear about the biblical truth you are proclaiming. Only when your listener is held captive by your discourse, only when he or she is locked with you in the "relational dance" of preaching, only when your message is as *direct* as you can make it, will the Holy Spirit be free to confront and challenge that listener with holy *meaning.*

SUMMARY AND DEFINTION

I want now to put all of this together in a definition of *transaction* for the preaching ministry. Of course, in light of our discussion, we can expect this definition to be deeply complex, but such a definition will bring together what I mean by transaction. I offer, then, the following:

> *The preaching transaction is a Spirit-permeated, one-to-many human interaction, resulting in a "message" that is initiated and given focus by proclaimed biblical truth. The message is shaped by all persons engaged in the interaction, and is characterized and governed by each participant's monitoring of his or her self-perception and self-presentation. It is a message that emerges through an almost infinite number of interactive interpersonal and environmental influences, and results in a unique Spirit-interpreted meaning for each listener.*

This rather awkward definition is oriented toward the *systemic production* of meaning that emerges from a message that is initiated by the preacher through *proclaimed biblical truth.*

By this time, it should be clear that there isn't going to be a diagram of the transactional model. Human communication is far too complex for it to be represented by a simple picture. After all, when preachers preach, the experience includes the *decision* to say something and then the making of sounds with vocal cords, mouth cavity, tongue, and lips. It makes use of facial muscles and body parts, gestures and postures. It involves proxemics and spatial arrangement, the structure of language, and the preacher's relationship with each listener and with the whole congregation. It concerns the passion (or lack thereof) with which the preacher engages the topic. It entails semantics and linguistics, structuralism and philology, phonemics and phonetics, and morphology and ethnomethodology. It is concerned with how the ear takes in sound through tender membranes and little bones and transforms those sounds into meaning. It involves all kinds of informational and environmental factors. It engages all participants as continual contributors to and receivers of the experience, all interactive exchanges, and all verbal and non-verbal cues. It includes languages and language groups and the development of languages. It includes linguistics and its influence on the ways different classes of people communicate with each other. It includes cultures and local customs and all the past and present experiences of each person. It includes inflection and volume, non-fluencies, visual acuity, tones of voice throughout, attitudes, dispositions, worldview, intonation, and dialects. It includes the environment in which communication happens, nuances of speech, personalities, and what makes each person laugh or be irritated. It includes the pace of utterances, denotations and connotations, and all the personal histories and social contacts and group memberships and hopes and dreams and attitudes of all the participants. It includes smells and vision and perceptual acuity.

How can all of that, and more, be put in a simple diagram? Human communication is so complex, with so many overt and covert methods by which each individual *constructs* messages (through language, gestures, and/or art forms) and ways that each individual processes *incoming* information, that it is impossible to diagram something that would make sense.

Taken altogether, I'm arguing for an *approach* to human communication rather than a *model*. It is too awkward to represent all the influences that impact a single coherent experience. It makes the preaching event a highly complex and incomprehensible process, and causes us to wonder why God has chosen *this* method to proclaim His good news to all creation, particularly by imperfect human beings!

Ultimately, I pray that this discussion helps us recognize and value the complexity of human communication. In the end, our preaching depends on it!

CHAPTER 6
Orality and Preaching

WHEN PREACHING IS PROCLAMATION

When preaching is understood as a *transaction,* it implies an interpersonal engagement between preacher and listener. That relational connection only happens when the *sounds and structure* of the preacher's language are naturally "listenable." And that *relational* language works like *glue* that keeps preacher and listener engaged together in the event. It makes the preaching experience *immediate.*

When biblical proclamation comes by way of *oral language,* God's word more dramatically captivates, confronts, and challenges the listener, and more powerfully calls that listener to respond.

LEARNING TO TALK

Each one of us learned to communicate *orally* before we learned to read and write. When you were just a baby, you learned language through *sounds.* You heard these sounds from your parents and others who gathered about your crib, and then you started to mimic those sounds. And eventually, after a great deal of trial and error and experimentation, you appropriated language.

It is easy to see why *orality* is the most *natural* way we communicate—it is how we initially *learned* to express ourselves. Writing and literacy came later, long after we knew how to *talk.*

Of course, being raised in a literate society, we were also taught to read and write at an early age. Our parents picked up books that they read to us when we were infants, and, by so doing, were socializing us as "little humans" into a literate social order. Reading provided comfort and connectedness with our parents, but it also trained us to *listen to* written language (we *hear* a lot of it during the rest of our lives, even though it is unnatural). Unfortunately, this passion for literacy tends to devalue orality as a *natural* form of human communication, which, in turn, drains language of its real power.

It used to be that a person's *spoken* word was a bond. God's covenant with Abram was oral (Genesis 12:1-4), and Abram believed the *word* of the Lord (Genesis 15:6). Today, in our literate society, we trust only signed documents that are exactingly worded, with lots of suspicious fine print.

I'm not suggesting that we shouldn't be literate. Not at all. What I am arguing is that oral and written languages are two different *styles* of communication. They have emerged in human history for different reasons, have different grammatical structures, and require different types of "receivers." Most importantly for our purposes, preaching becomes awkward when we replace the free-flowing *speech* of oral language with the exactness and compression of *written* language.

I'd like now to take us on a little excursion back in time to reflect on the appropriation of language. This exercise should, in turn, prepare us to better understand orality's importance for preaching.

THE DEVELOPMENT OF HUMAN LANGUAGE

As a child, I acquired language through *listening* and then *speaking.* So did you. In a way, that *individual* experience is an example of how language developed in human history. Anthropologists tell us that orality is the most *natural* form of human communication, and that, from earliest human history, language was *oral.*

But how did the human race start to learn language? Several theories have emerged that speculate on how language originated. One is that onomatopoeic outbursts (like "ouch!") or imitations of nature (such as the "groan" from a swaying tree, or a "cuckoo") were the beginnings of language. Others have suggested that language began as a *description* of a particular person (many First Testament names have their origins in descriptions of people, as in Genesis 16:13-14 and 17:19). Plato added a different twist, that a name reflects the *nature* (rather than *description)* of a person or object. Thus, when Jesus gave Simon his new name *Peter,* or *Rocky* (Matthew 16:13-19), he was calling him to a new *nature.* These approaches indicate that early scholars logically assumed that intelligence developed *before* language, and that language, coming later, *reflected* the process of thinking. It was believed that language is the way by which thought is known.

That idea was finally rejected in the 4th century before Jesus. In Socrates' dialog with Cratylus, Plato offered the most compelling argument up to that time, and it is still a commonly-held position by anthropologists today. Plato maintained that thinking without language would not have been possible, because thinking *uses* language. Instead, he reasoned, thinking and language probably developed *together,* and *language* evolved as *humans* evolved. Today, we also know that the ability to walk upright created the possibility of *vocality,* so it is most probable that language was not *invented* as much as it was appropriated by *necessity,* when developing, bi-pedal humans needed to interact for food, safety, shelter, or companionship.

Language, then, arose from a confluence of ability, usage of vocal cords, the evolution of intelligence and thought, the need to name things, the development of culture, and the emergence of human personality.

WRITING

Anthropologists believe that we humans have likely been speaking with each other for 500,000 years. Writing, on the other hand, came on the scene only about 5,000 years ago. But as literacy became the norm (as it is today), more and more attention was paid to *written* communication, in such forms as clay tablets, papyrus, parchment scrolls, then books, libraries, and, today, computer disks. Writing has become so much a part of our culture that, in our literate society, we automatically think of "words" as something *written* rather than *spoken.*

But at the time that writing was first emerging as a popular form of communication, written language was recognized as problematic and was greeted with a great deal of suspicion. In another of Plato's dialogs (called the *Phaedrus),* Socrates relates the myth of an Egyptian god named Theuth who brought writing to earth. Thamus, the King of Egypt, doesn't like this new development. He argues that writing is bad because it leads to *forgetfulness,* and that through writing, *ignorant* people (without the benefit of instruction) will be able to teach others. Socrates adds that writing is a *danger* to social life and relationships because it *isolates* people from each other. Further, words put on paper will be clear and certain (and, thus, *believed)* just because they are written down. People who are not necessarily interested will then have the ability to read material that they don't comprehend. Plato, too, joins the discussion, saying that writing eliminates any relationship between writer and the argument being espoused, which, in turn, calls into question the writer's integrity. True discourse, on the other hand, is inscribed in the *soul,* and only comes through face-to-face dialog.

There is some truth in all of these early objections to written language, but because we appropriate written language as easily as speech, we don't give much thought to these arguments. And because we are a literate people, it is difficult for us to separate these two forms of human communication.

THE WRITTEN-ORAL DISTINCTION

One of the predominant differences between written and oral language is their *structural* characteristics, that is, in how they are both formed and received. Written language is structured by compact *sentences* that express a complete thought. Words are usually carefully chosen to express exactly what the writer intends. And written information is "received" by *reading,* which gives the recipient time to process such *condensed* information. That is, the *reader* controls the pace of information intake with written language, and can do it as quickly or slowly as is necessary.

Oral language, on the other hand, is characterized by the *chunking* of small bits of information in rapid-fire progression. That pattern of speech is either a *reflection* of how we think or it *taught* us how to think. Oral language, of course, is "received" by *listening,* which means that it is *heard* by bits and pieces, as it is given. Those chunks, which come at the *speaker's* pace, must be grasped by the listener and put together in a way that makes sense.

Most of us have studied written *grammar* as the "stuff" of proper communication, but few of us have been trained to speak *conversationally.* That's because speaking informally comes *naturally* to us, and, thus, we don't have to be trained to do it. Writing and reading, on the other hand, are *unnatural* and so must be learned.

But let's take a closer look at oral language and conversation. If we're going to begin here for communication from the pulpit, it is important that we get a good idea of how oral language is constructed and heard.

ORAL PRODUCTION

I'd like to challenge you to listen in on a conversation between a couple of your friends. Listen critically if you can, to see how language is produced. If you are able to observe and listen in *super slow motion,* you'll start to understand how speech is produced in ordinary conversation. You might even try to figure out a way to write down exactly what you hear.

What follows is a very small bit of an imaginary conversation, but it provides a good example of what *speaking* and *listening* are like.

CHUNKING IN *SUPER SLO MO*

Let's suppose we are talking informally after class one day, just for socialization purposes. In the course of our conversation, it happens that I want to tell you about a basketball game I attended over the weekend. This then becomes a *goal* for me in a very small part of our interaction. It, in turn, sets things in motion for what I will say. That is, I have an *idea* that I want to express, and, without very much thought, I now call upon particular *linguistic* (words) and *nonlinguistic* resources (such as gestures, head nods, and voice inflection) to meet this goal.

I do this by starting to produce particular sounds (what we call "words"), one after the other, in a short phrase. This is the first "chunk" of information that I verbalize. If it is of average length, it is what I can express in approximately 6 words, or about one "talking breath" that lasts about 1.6 seconds:

Oh, yeah, I uh went to the, ah

This "chunk," of course, is too short to give the whole idea I'm trying to express, but it's a start. So, to this "partial information" I take a quick (usually unnoticed) breath and add another "chunk" of approximately the same length:

First Union Center on hhh (a quick breath)

I then produce another chunk, and another, and another, all of which are strung together in a series of statements that are linked in some way. Each of these units of speech is separated by a slight pause or breath, and frequently includes an *and* with a lot of *ers* and *ums.*

Using this pattern, then, I keep building toward the idea or thought I'm trying to express. Each additional chunk is determined by how much I was able to articulate in the previous chunk, or how clearly it came out (I might have to *repair* something I said), or, sometimes, by how the whole string is being *received* (if, for instance, I see a look of bewilderment on your face: *the First Union Center,* for instance, is where Philadelphia's professional basketball team, the *76ers,* plays). This chunking effect is consistent with what Weaver meant by *redundancy:* each expressed thought unit narrows or limits the possibilities for the next one.

This, basically, is how oral language is produced. We humans don't actually speak in *sentences* (those are the "stuff" of *written* language). Rather, we speak in a series of *mini-phrases* that are strung together to make complete *thoughts.*

After a very few short seconds and all this work of trying to say something, I have produced the following:

> *Oh, yeah, I uh went to the, ah*
> *First Union Center on hhh (a quick breath)*
> *Saturday,*
> *uh with Ellen you know,*
> *and ah ah we were up in the nosebleed section and uh*
> *we had one of those*
> *basket of nachos*
> *(pause)*
> *bas-kets*
> *(pause)*
> *and uh I slopped that cheese stuff*
> *uh over uh*
> *all down my shirt!*

As you can see, this discourse doesn't *read* very well, but it would sound quite natural if you *heard* me say it. This whole *linguistic strategy* for speaking also includes three particular characteristics that are important for us to understand.

1. Transitions

In order to produce coherent thoughts this way, these "chunky" utterances have to be somehow connected together. It happens by conjunctions (usually *"and"),* brief silent spaces, longer breaths, or these bits of *"er"* and *"um"* utterances that we call *nonfluencies* (sometimes they are an indication that I am trying to think about what to say next). I just keep adding chunk to chunk until I've produced as many of these short phrases as I feel are necessary to complete my idea, or until I am interrupted (as often happens in conversation). Either at the beginning of each new chunk, or between these chunks, I try to link them in some way. Thus, the words *within* each chunk demonstrate internal coherence, but each chunk is also connected by linguistic or paralinguistic devices to the chunks that come before and after it, and all the chunks are related to the main idea or goal I have in mind.

2. Adjustments

While this is happening, I often find myself having to *repair* something I said incorrectly. That is, sometimes I *restate* what I just said, or *correct* it, or *back and fill.* (In the example, you notice that I misspoke "baskets," thought about it briefly, and then inserted the correction in the next chunk.) Sometimes I *abandon* the beginning of an utterance that I realize isn't going to accomplish what I thought it would (as in the *uh over uh* in the second to the last utterance). That is, sometimes I decide to *revise* what I said in an earlier chunk, so that the idea I am conveying makes better sense to my listener (or me).

Of course, I never really move "backward" in conversation by making these repairs. Each chunk is produced, and once it is released it cannot be taken back. But later chunks help modify errors in earlier ones. This is a natural part of speaking and listening, and we don't even *hear* it when it happens.

This is why I say that human conversation is *temporal,* not linear. Exactingly-encoded, completed thoughts don't just come pouring out of our mouths in a straight line, as the linear model suggests. Verbal presentations of human ideas come in twists and turns, are uttered bit by bit, stated and then repaired, until the speaker is happy that his or her purpose has been finally achieved, or until he or she is interrupted.

Further, *listening* to this kind of language is very *natural* for us, too. It is also easy to see that *written* language is quite differently structured, and in a way that is *not naturally* hearable.

3. Threading

If I am not interrupted, I eventually come out at the end of the process with a completed thought. When I speak, I keep that main purpose ever before me. It leads me along, bit by bit, chunk to chunk, assertion to repair, one phrase after another, until I feel the idea is completed and my goal is achieved.

But when we listen analytically to orally-produced language, it seems as if the speaker has passed through a confusing, tangled maze to get to the end, much like Theseus following Ariadne's scarlet thread to escape the Labyrinth. But that thread is critical. It's the *main idea* I want to express. For every oral contribution I make to a conversation, I first have a goal or idea I want to express, and then that goal guides the construction of each chunk and how I link the chunks to each other.

Of course, it all happens very, very quickly, and without conscious thought by any of us. That's because we've been speaking (and listening) a whole lifetime, and most of us are well-practiced at it.

HOW WE LISTEN

Producing oral language is only half of the communication event. We have also learned how to *listen.* So, in my imaginary conversation with you, we laugh because I messed up my shirt at that game. But now you, too, want to take a turn in the conversation. My snack story reminds you about a hockey game you attended when a woman spilled a Coke on your head. So you're now going to tell that story, and it's my turn to listen to you. And when I listen, it happens something like this:

HEARING

Basically, I *hear* information in reverse order. I appropriate chunk after chunk of information that you utter and *then* have to figure out what your goal is. Again, if we slow the process way down, we'll see how it happens:

When I listen to you speak, I listen with a *task* in mind, and that is to discover the *meaning* of what you are trying to say. (Usually, you won't tell me the purpose of a thought, idea, or story, so I have to *discover* it.)

So I hear a chunk of language, and then another, and another, as you produce these little units of speech. These chunks, of course, are heard through sounds, but they are also accompanied by *nonverbal* (or paralinguistic) cues, so I actually *see* language being produced, too (listening typically involves both aural and visual signals). I see your eyes light up, and your gestures, and your body language, and I process that incoming information along with the sounds you produce. (You, in turn, see my frown or smile as I respond to what I hear and see, and you alter your chunks of speech accordingly.)

As I listen to this string of thought-units, I have that ultimate task in mind: to discover the thread you are following. All the time I am listening, I want to learn *what* you're talking about. If you have expressed yourself clearly, I will nod and laugh along with you, and we'll discover that we have done a pretty good job of communicating orally!

This, then, sets the pattern for listening. As a listener, I am engaged and attentive, because I desire to sift through all the chunks, repairs, fill-ins, and nonfluencies to get to your idea. This *pattern of listening* is what keeps my attention. (Of course, when I am forced to listen to *written* language, this natural listening ability is completely offended. Written language forces me to think in an *unnatural* way.)

We now come to five additional characteristics of listening that must be addressed. They, also, are important for our preaching.

1. Filling categories

As I listen, I not only try to follow your *thread of thinking,* but I also conceptualize the bits of incoming information you are uttering. That is, we tend to *categorize* what we hear. Words and chunks are related to large categories and then subcategories, and each subsequent chunk of information helps redefine those categories.

For instance, I hear you use the word "slap," a word that could be assigned to any number of possible big categories. But because your main subject is "hockey," I immediately consider which of these might be relevant (without *thinking* about it). That is, you could be talking about a confrontation with a woman who *slapped* you, a negative personal assessment (a "slap in the face"), or a swift movement of a hockey stick against the puck (a "slap shot"), all of which could conceivably be used in a "hockey" story. That is, the general context in which the word is used is important, but with the chunking pattern of language production, I usually don't have enough immediate information to make a category assignment, so I must wait for more information before I can define what you're talking about.

Further, a word or chunk must not only be related to a large category, but once the large category is identified, I must also assign it to a subcategory. I am still trying to figure out what exactly you mean. That is, I still have to work out the right *kind* of slap.

As it is, in your next chunk, you mention "slap shot," so I immediately eliminate the "slap on the cheek" and the "slap in the face." I know that you're talking about a particular kind of hockey play. So I have now identified the broad category. But now I have to learn the "point" of your sharing this information: was it a significant shot that scored the winning point? Or did you mention it because you could *hear* the slap sound? If it's important to the story, I, as the listener, have to *wait* for further information to get a complete picture.

Well, in the next chunk and the one after that, I finally discover that you are referring to a *slap shot* that came whizzing over the Plexiglas and almost hit you in the head—and that's when the woman behind you fumbled her Coke and dumped it on your head.

All the while I am trying to make sense of what you are saying, you just keep moving on, backing and filling, repairing misstatements, and inserting nonfluencies—all in an attempt to get me to understand what you've got in mind when you started out. Of course, if I *miss* one of your defining words or my attention is distracted or I *misunderstand* something you say, the whole meaning of your string of chunks can be misunderstood.

All in all, it's a complicated process, but it happens *instantaneously* and without thought. And we are *very* good at it.

2. Making inferences
This discussion about categories, then, leads us to a second important characteristic of listening. It has to do with *inferences*. I, as the listener, must sometimes decide for myself how the chunks fit together, since the information you give me is not always complete. You *assume* that I know what you are talking about or that I understand particular references you make or the specific vocabulary you use. So a lot of the time, I must decide *how* these chunks relate to each other. Thus, in order to make quick sense of incoming language, I must make little "jumps" of logic to connect the pieces.

For instance, you say to me, *"I got to the stadium er ice rink and um entered through the G Gate the one on the left there um you know which one."* I *infer* that you parked your car first (because the stadium is only accessible if you drive there). I also *infer* that you had a ticket already, and that you knew approximately where your seat was located (because you went through "G Gate"). You didn't actually *tell* me those pieces of information, but I had to *add* them to your story so I could make sense of your discourse.

Come to find out, in the next string of utterances, you tell me that you did *not* go in the right gate after all and had to walk a long way around to find your seat. But that, too, is part of the *inferential* process: I discover later that my assumptions *weren't* accurate. Typically, speakers tend to be very good at inferring what listeners assume, and listeners are very adept at making inferences that correctly "fill in the blanks." In fact, our whole language system is built on these inferences. Speakers simply don't have the time to fill in every exacting detail of everything they say.

3. Holding information in abeyance

The third characteristic of listening is that most of the time we listeners must *retain* chunks of information in our minds until we get additional information. That is, I must hold an idea *in abeyance,* hoping it will make sense with later utterances. I hear one little bit of a thought and have to keep it in my mind until you fill in additional, clarifying details later. Essentially, it means that I understand chunks of language *retroactively.* My brain holds these little thought-units for a short time until I can relate them to later chunks, but all so that I can grasp your main idea.

Sometimes, too, the speaker *assumes* that listeners know something that they really don't. In those cases, too, I must hold that information in abeyance until later. Often, inference helps, because additional information is *not* given and I have to assume some other details to make sense of what is said.

When we preach, we can use the principles of *inference-making* and *holding information in abeyance* to our advantage. For example, I don't have to explain every little detail of a story—my listeners can draw inferences. And since my listeners are *used* to holding information in abeyance until it is clarified later, I can introduce ideas in the sermon that will be tied together later. For instance, phases of a sermon's argument may not have to be fully explained until the end of the sermon. Or when I tell a story that helps fulfill an immediately-prior point, I usually don't have to say, "Here's an example of what I mean." My listeners are able to make the connection *automatically,* even if it is only after I finish the story. I just tell it without an interruptive transition. This practice helps keep the interest of my listeners, since they must stay engaged in the encounter if they want to follow what I am saying.

4. Comprehension rate

Scholars recognize that oral language is generally produced at a rate of between 100 to 150 words per minute, but human beings can comprehend about 250 words per minute. This means that even if you speak very quickly, my mind has a lot of extra time during the listening process. When you speak at a "normal rate," I can comprehend what you're saying at double the rate you are able to speak. This gives me a lot of opportunity to think my own thoughts while I am listening to you speak.

This difference, of course, creates problems for congregational members who are listening to your preaching. Your pace (speaking at an ordinary "conversational rate") moves along at about half that which your listener can hear and comprehend. So if your sermon isn't very captivating or interesting, your listener will be easily distracted by his or her own thoughts and will miss a lot of important "incoming information."

5. Selective inattention

Finally, the immediate attention span of most of us is about 20 seconds. After that short time, our focus has to shift. When we are *reading* and this happens, we just take a short break (usually only a micro-pause). If we "miss" what we were reading because of this little break, we simply *reread* the passage. (This is possible, of course, because the reader has control over the *pace* of incoming information.)

But this need for a rest in the middle of intensive *listening* presents a problem for preaching, because the *preacher* controls the pace of incoming information. This is true whether the preacher is speaking or reading, but the process is complicated when the preacher *reads*. Oral language is based on *sounds* and *repetition; written language* is made up of *dictionary words* that are packed together and *non-repetitive*. Further, the *structure* of written language is highly compact and carefully-honed, and trying to *listen* to it is an *unnatural* aural process. When that happens, listeners very naturally *disengage* from the listening process because listening takes so much concentration. Unfortunately, if the subject matter isn't captivating enough or the discourse isn't structured for aural reception, those listeners may not ever "catch" back up with the discourse, and they get lost altogether.

This is why *exacting* word studies and *long explanations* are the worst form of pulpit discourse. People simply cannot "hear" (or appreciate) all that fine-tuned language. It's one reason, also, why the consistent use of *stories* helps keep the listener's attention. Stories, when well told, attract and keep attention, and they serve to pull an "escaped thinker" back into the sermon.

All in all, hearing oral language, like producing it, is a complicated process. But, again, we have learned how to listen so that we don't even think about it. Through years of practice, we are *very good* at it.

And finally, because speaking and hearing are *natural* processes for human beings, we should seriously consider the benefits of preaching extemporaneously (as we'll see in the next chapter). This "formal conversational" style of public proclamation not only calls upon our *natural* ability to speak, but also the *natural* ability of our listeners to hear. Ignoring this process severely *diminishes* the potential power of the spoken word.

STRUCTURAL DIFFERENCES

When we put all this information together (along with other scholarly information) and think about how differently oral language is structured from written language, we can draw some important conclusions that are helpful for the preaching ministry.

These differences are outlined in Figure 6.1 (on the following two pages). In that chart, I have compared these two distinct forms of human communication, and what each means for *producing* and *receiving* language.

IMPLICATIONS FOR PREACHING

While I've been referring to preaching throughout this chapter, I now want to expand on what I've said by returning to what I believe are the two most critical issues that this study raises for us. After all, transformational preaching happens only if you "connect" with your listeners: if there is no *listening,* there is no communicating, and, subsequently, no transaction, and, therefore, no *preaching.*

The first of the two concerns is that if we want our listeners to be impacted with biblical truth, we must reject the use of *written language* in the pulpit. Transformation comes with *engagement,* and engagement happens only with the "glue" of oral language.

The second issue is that when we *speak* publicly, we almost invariably use words that are familiar to us, and, thus, words that tend to be familiar to our listeners. But this practice can lead to sometimes-distractive "slangy" language or discourse that is "too ordinary" for the pulpit. This, in turn, can lessen the impact of our preaching. *Public* discourse demands a more formal, respectable use of language, so we'll look briefly at this concern as well.

1. LISTENERS, NOT READERS

When you sit in a comfortable chair in front of your fireplace and read a good theological book, *you* are in charge of the pace of incoming information. You read at your own leisure. If you encounter a challenging idea or discover that you have missed something, you return to reread the same page or paragraph (over and over again if you need to). This is the nature of reading, because written language is *compact* and *condensed* (like some of the information in this book).

Now think about how it sounds when that same book is *read* to you (that is, in an *oral setting).* You, as a listener, immediately have a problem *hearing* it because written language is not structured like oral language. (Written language, of course, *looks* good to the *eye,* but it certainly doesn't *sound* natural to the *ear.)* That's because it's too "compressed." There are no pauses between chunks, no repair, no "backing and filling." There is little need for *inference,* as with oral language. Everything is neat and tidy, and it is simply not *natural* for us to listen to that kind of input. *Listening* to written language is uncomfortable and, ultimately, exhausting. Because of that, you are likely to miss a great deal of what the author has to say when a book is *read* to you.

Figure 6.1

Written-Oral distinctions:

Written	Oral
1. **slow pace** (writing is very slow; reading is at the pace of the reader)	**fast pace** (created at 100-150 wpm; comprehended at 250 wpm)
2. **encoding information (writing) is visual and tactile; decoding (reading) is also visual and tactile**	**coding is oral; decoding is aural and visual** (through paralinguistics; the structure is listener-dependent)
3. received **at the *reader*'s pace** (the *reader* is in command)	received **at speaker's pace** (the *speaker* is in command)
4. the **reader can** always **review** written material	the **listener must keep up** with the speaker
5. **linear**—in English, for instance, it moves left to right on a page (Hebrew is opposite)	**temporal**—it takes place in *time*, not space
6. generally it is **planned and organized**, not spontaneous	generally it is **"unplanned"** (especially conversation)
7. **permanent**—language is for preservation, for reading later	**fleeting**—usually for the immediate situation
8. writer *assumes* **an audience**	**speaker** is in an immediate relationship with an **audience**

9. **monological; one-way**	**dialogical** (usually)—it is for *interaction*
10. **compact, condensed, rule-bound**	**repetitious, strung out** (in chunk form)
11. **word** boundaries are indicated by spaces	**word boundaries are usually not given,** except between chunks. The listener must "design" space between words.
12. **written punctuation** comes in marks on a page (comma, semi-colon, etc.)	**oral punctuation** comes in **pauses, inflection, volume, intonation, nonfluencies**
13. **reader is self-prepared** for input	**listeners are captives of the situation;** interest must often be *developed*
14. **sentences** tend to be **simpler but longer**	more **complex structure** but **shorter phrases**
15. vocabulary tends to be **conservative**	greater **vocabulary** *innovation*
16. tendency to use more **complex words**	generally **simple, concrete words** are used (with fewer syllables)
17. **fewer qualifiers used**	**more qualifiers** tend to be used
18. **active and passive voice are used**	the tendency is to speak in the **active voice**
19. tends to be **formal and impersonal**	**personal references** are frequent
20. **antecedents are clearly defined**	**vague antecedents are** used ("it," "this," "that")

In the same way, when the preacher reads a *written manuscript,* listeners are subjected to a very *unnatural* communicative experience. They have to "translate" written language into oral language, an exercise that takes a lot of energy and concentration, and it's much easier for them to "escape" the event. It doesn't matter how masterfully a memorized sermon is recited or how expertly a printed sermon is *read*—it still uses *written* language. (Even "writing like you speak" uses the structure of written language.) A manuscript of *any kind* calls upon language that is compact and logical, and when it is read from the pulpit, the listener *hears* it *awkwardly,* and it doesn't take long before that brain-exhausted listener has to escape for a little mental vacation (usually, it takes only a few minutes for most listeners to "tune out" the manuscript-reading preacher). The preacher, of course, keeps his or her own rate of "delivery," and the listener, who is hopelessly lost, never gets re-engaged because of the incoming barrage of such heavily-compressed language.

Further, *sight* is important in both written and oral forms of communication. With written language, the reader sees the page. But in conversation, the participants see *each other.* It's part of the *relational* dimension of the transaction. So, while the oral preacher keeps eye contact with the *listeners,* the manuscript preacher must watch the *script.* The *oral* preacher is *relationally* engaged with *people;* the *manuscript* preacher's relationship is with *words* on a page. That means that when preaching is an *oral/listening* experience, the listeners are drawn into the discourse, and, thus, there is a much better chance that they will be transformed by biblical truth. But when the manuscript is *read,* the preacher's attention and relationship is with the *printed word,* and the listeners are relegated to bystander status.

Ultimately, when we confuse the *writing/reading* and *speaking/hearing* pairings, little communication actually happens.

As a preacher, you are proclaiming the most important message in the world. But if you want your listeners to actually *hear* and be confronted by the message you're communicating, you will only effectively reach them through natural, *orally-structured, conversational* language. When you use language that is meant for *listening,* you will be *talking with* your listeners, not *at* them.

Transactions are developed through *oral language.* For the most part, *orality* develops relationships. It creates or builds the people-connection while *uniting* the preacher and listener in the common preaching experience. And that relational dimension to language use *reinforces* the content power of the sermon.

2. USING "FORMAL CONVERSATION" IN THE PULPIT

Aristotle argued that the bigger the audience, the more "distant" is the point of view of the speaker. "Group" implies the use of loftier language and more expansive horizons than you might use in one-on-one conversation. Audience size, then, impacts the speaker's choice of vocabulary and perspective. This seems to be a natural phenomenon for public speakers, so it isn't something that you have to spend a lot of time thinking about.

This means that whenever you stand before a group of people, your discourse will be more naturally *formal*. The problem, however, is how to balance the more *hearable-structure* of oral language with a more publicly-acceptable *formal* tone and grammar. There are several ways to resolve this tension.

First, "conversational" language implies the use of a limited number of *words*. Deane Kemper (1985) tells us that an unabridged dictionary of English has about 500,000 listings. Most adults recognize about 90,000 words *when they are written*. But studies have shown that when we are involved in everyday conversation, we use only about 600 different words. When specialized language is taken into consideration (such as "church language" or insider "professional terminology"), most people have a working vocabulary of less than 1,000 words. Of those, effective preaching, in appealing to the common denominator of a diversity of listeners, will generally use only about 600 words—the capacity of the typical listener's ability to comprehend. This means that we shouldn't try to develop an expansive pulpit vocabulary, because it will only confuse or distract the ordinary listener.

Second, pay attention to the words that you use. *Shorter, good-sounding, sensuous nouns and verbs* captivate the listener and will make an impact. *Figures of speech* add spice. *Inclusive language* (for women and minority groups) is essential, not only so you don't offend any of your listeners, but so that you create an environment where everyone is welcomed in the kingdom. *Statements* rather than commands are more acceptable to listeners, and the use of "we" rather than "you" keeps the *relational* dynamic alive that is so important. However, Deane Kemper (1985), again, reminds us that we don't need to use as many words in preaching as in writing, since gestures, tone, facial expression, and body language help to convey meaning.

Third, vocabulary plays only a partial role in a "formal conversational" style of preaching. "Oral grammar" is also important. By this I mean adapting written grammatical rules to oral language production. That is, in a literate society, we learn to speak "correctly," using grammar from written language. For instance, in writing it is improper to split infinitives (not *"to* persistently *pray"* but *"to pray* persistently"). It is improper to use hanging prepositions (not "the store which I went *into"* but "the store *into which* I went"). It is improper to use nominative forms with prepositions (not "for Ellen and *I"* but "for Ellen and *me").* It is improper to identify yourself before others (not "me and the choir" but "the choir and me").

These "writing rules" (and others like them) are helpful in creating a *formal speaking grammar*. If you use this kind of "formal conversational" language in the pulpit, your preaching will sound more "listenable" (or "lofty") to both the highly literate and the uneducated. And if you are concerned about offending very informal listeners, remember that they won't have any trouble understanding your more formalized conversation, particularly because they immediately recognize the "larger context" of public speaking about which Aristotle writes. It is generally the case that a *slangy* public speaker will offend both those who use "formal" language and those who do not.

Thus, because it is a *one-to-many* type of human interaction, preaching requires a more "ceremonial" type of oratory, or what I call a "formal conversational" style. When you speak to a group, speak *naturally,* but, at the same time, demonstrate a greater formality than you would in informal conversation. I would thus recommend that you *train* your speech to include these kinds of strategies, since much of your pulpit talk will reflect your customary "patterns" of speech and not always those that you thoughtfully prepare ahead of time. This is why I would suggest that you develop a *natural speaking style* for in and out of the pulpit.

This brings me to my final, and perhaps most important, consideration. It is that you *be yourself* in and out of the pulpit. If you naturally use a more formalized language in private speech, keep it in the pulpit. If you are used to speaking in slang, minimize it in the pulpit, but without compromising your identity and uniqueness as a preacher. This will serve you well.

CHAPTER 7
Working toward Transaction:
A Question of Style

START AT THE END

In my understanding, the "word of God" is something that is *fashioned* for proclamation, but then comes to fulfillment *through* the proclamation. This "event" (the "presentational experience" of preaching) is what concerns us right now. It is usually called the "delivery" of the sermon, which, in most textbooks, comes at the end of the process, only after some instruction about the construction of a sermon. So shouldn't this topic of "delivery" wait until we talk about the content and structure of preaching? That makes sense, of course, but there are two reasons why I want to discuss the *end* of the process right now.

First, *how* we preach directly follows from our discussion about oral language and the transaction of preaching. It is important for us to see what the pulpit experience looks like *in actual practice* if we're serious about transactional proclamation.

But second, and more importantly, I find it helpful to talk about presentational styles *before* we think about content and structure, because your personal conviction about how you will present the sermon in the pulpit will *inform* the rest of the sermon construction process. This chapter comes at a transitional point between our discussion about human communication and the sermon construction process so you can make a decision *now* about your presentation style. That decision, in turn, will help you know how to "read" the rest of this book, and how to spend your valuable sermon preparation time later.

STYLES OF PRESENTATION

There are five basic styles of presentation. I have had personal experience in each of these methods, but within five years of starting to preach consistently (after five years of experimentation), I settled on the last (extemporaneous preaching without notes) as my only mode of transaction.

I want to briefly describe and analyze these styles by looking at the use of preparation time, how anxiety plays a role, and the advantages and disadvantages of each.

I. IMPROMPTU PREACHING

The first style of presentation is *impromptu* preaching. It is used by those who believe that the Holy Spirit inspires the preacher, but only in the moment of preaching. It is often the preferred method of those preachers who have little or no preparation time, and is heavily relied upon in Eastern Europe.

Basically, impromptu means *preaching without preparation*. The preacher flips open his or her Bible, points blindly to a verse or passage, and starts commenting on it. Sometimes there is a little bit of forethought, but not enough to work out legitimately what will be said. In some of the contemporary holiness traditions, this is the only *Spirit-led* approach to preaching that is acknowledged. Early African-American slave preachers effectively proclaimed their messages in an impromptu manner, but that was because of a brilliant but simple formula that was followed. However, without this kind of orienting framework, impromptu preaching generally doesn't work very well.

I was interested to discover that one of the earliest Baptist splits came over this issue. John Smyth, in 1607, insisted that true worship must come "from the hart." He believed that spiritual worship would be compromised by use of any written helps, including prayer or hymn books. Smyth even denied the public reading of Scripture during worship, claiming that Jesus closed the scroll before he started preaching (in Luke 4:16-21). Preaching, too, had to be completely spontaneous, otherwise the Holy Spirit was not in control, and, because his pastor used a manuscript for preaching, Smyth left that congregation.

Preparation time

Impromptu preaching, in its most extreme form, requires no *preparation*, so I will assign it 0 hours. Little or no time is spent on writing, and little or no time on preparation. Sometimes, an impromptu preacher might spend an hour or so in preparation, looking for and praying over a text prior to preaching from it. But without serious preparation time, preaching under these conditions isn't much different from a complete lack of preparation. (Of course, with a little training, a simple design, and an hour of preparation time, a very good sermon can be preached, but I don't recommend this strategy on a permanent basis.)

Anxiety

Since the unprepared preacher doesn't know what he or she will say beforehand, *anxiety* tends to be very high, from the beginning of the preaching experience right through to the end of the sermon. Sometimes this high stress will lead to boredom with the process, and, subsequently, to boredom for the listeners.

Advantages

There are a few *advantages* to this style of presentation. First, preparation time can be used for other ministries, like visitation or administration. It also *demonstrates,* in a very practical way, a reliance on the Holy Spirit. And, because the preacher is free from a manuscript, it is likely that there will be good eye contact with the congregation.

Disadvantages

The *disadvantages* to impromptu preaching far outweigh its advantages. For instance, the preacher who preaches spontaneously tends to repeat him- or herself from week to week and within each sermon. Unfortunately, this often leads to dreadful, dreary sermons, and, because of the theology behind the style, poor preaching ends up to be the fault of the Holy Spirit.

There is also a tendency to preach on known texts or a few restricted favorite themes. Further, it gives way to the human tendency to *give advice* and often leads to too much exposition. Sometimes it is accompanied by a "preachy" tone that puts the preacher in a super-spiritual position, through which he or she becomes separated from the "sins" of the congregation. And without preparation time, there are few stories, examples, or other support materials that keep the sermon interesting and the congregation engaged. Often, it sinks to the level of mere explanation and teaching.

Most often, an impromptu style leads to *theological preaching.* The preacher calls upon texts with which he or she is already familiar, and seldom is able to deal legitimately with the uniqueness of a specific text. When a "pet" theology or topic is preached, the preacher ends up wandering from theme to theme or verse to verse ("Bible hopping") and without distinct structural "phases" that are easy for the listener to follow. Sometimes, of course, an impromptu preacher will stick to one text (certainly a preferred approach), but then tends to rely on the structure of the *biblical text,* which is fine for reading but often awkward for hearing.

Evaluation

For the above reasons, I do *not* recommend preaching without preparation. The only (infrequent) exception may come when your sermon preparation time is used up with two funerals, an overload of unexpected counseling, additional administrative preparation, and a wedding or two.

Recently I was invited to preach in a region of churches in Romania on a week-long visit. In order to keep my preaching fresh, I "played with" the impromptu style by taking a "standard sermon" and putting it together in a new way or including a different story, sometimes just before preaching it. Thus, I would formulate a "new" message out of an old one, or use a different story with a different emphasis. This attempt at impromptu preaching, of course, came only after I had developed my own consistent style, had already decided on a "standard form" for this particular sermon, and after preaching for 25 years. I do not otherwise recommend it.

However, even if you have only one or two hours of preparation time, you can preach effectively. Though this procedure is not what I would consider *impromptu* (it does involve some preparation), you should be able to preach adequately on those rare occasions when you have little preparation time. Choose a text and single truth from within that text. Then jot down a quick outline that will help you keep "on track" with your sermon. Or, better yet, use a simple formula into which you can "insert" the sermon's content. You might try, for example, an *opening story, text development, and one more convicting story* to conclude. With this simple formula, you can develop the middle phase of the sermon in several ways: present a *problem* the biblical truth raises for our lives, a *solution* for that problem that comes from the text, and then an *evaluation.* Or, with a single idea in mind, you can *chronologically* work your way through the biblical story in a way that highlights that single idea. Writing a quick outline or using a simple formula works better if you are consistently in the habit of careful preparation and you use the impromptu method only when you are pressed for time.

However, *if you have the opportunity to prepare* (and the Lord gives all of us the same amount of time every week), there is *no reason* to preach impromptu sermons! Doing so denies your call to preach and the development and maturing of your gift. Spiritual gifts don't always come fully developed. They need to be practiced, learned, and brought to maturity.

If you are used to preaching without preparation, I encourage you to take the time that God allots you for your ministry to try another presentational style. You might be surprised at how much more dynamic your preaching can be!

II. MANUSCRIPT PREACHING

This brings us to the second method of pulpit presentation, which is almost the opposite of impromptu preaching. It is the careful preparation of a manuscript that you carry into the pulpit and *read.* You might read it poorly or you might read it with such excellence that the congregation doesn't even know that you are reading it. Either way, you follow a fully written document when you step into the pulpit. Your preparation time is spent getting the right wording to "deliver" to your listeners.

Preparation

Preparation for manuscript preaching is, of course, longer than for impromptu preaching. A typical manuscript preacher might allow about 20 hours for this method. About 15 hours will be spent carefully writing the manuscript, and about five in preparing the manuscript for reading. This often includes writing in the margins, color-coding words or phrases, or blocking paragraphs for emphasis—almost anything that helps you follow the manuscript and present it in an easy manner.

Anxiety

Anxiety is barely evident, but when it is, it exhibits a far lesser degree than with any other style of presentation. Of course, anxiety can be somewhat high when you begin the process of sermon-construction, but as you fashion your manuscript, your anxiety will decrease. At the time you step into the pulpit, there is hardly any anxiety, as long as you have a firm hold on your manuscript and the lights are on!

Advantages

There are *advantages* to manuscript preaching. It allows you to bring accurate language to your preaching. It also frees you from anxiety prior to worship so you can mingle freely with arriving worshipers, teach a Bible study, and, even, worship freely during the early part of the service. Further, you don't have to *remember* the details or structure of your sermon. And it is a valuable method for "restrictive" settings, such as when you must preach with a time limitation (if, for instance, your morning worship is broadcast on radio or television, or you are invited to preach in an extremely sensitive circumstance, as with a high-profile funeral or political situation).

Disadvantages

As with impromptu preaching, there are many more *disadvantages* to this style of presentation than there are advantages. We have already discussed the difference between oral and written language structure, and this is one of the strongest arguments against reading from a manuscript. It uses *written* language that is structured for *reading,* not for listening. As we saw in the previous chapter, trying to *hear* written language is unnatural. It saps the power of the spoken word. The compact, exacting nature of written language is difficult for listeners to follow, since they must first "translate" the written structure into oral meaning. Most listeners find it too exhausting an experience, and it doesn't take long before they lose interest.

But there's also a problem for you as a preacher. When you read a manuscript, your attention is on *what you are reading,* because you don't want to lose your place. This orientation detracts your attention from your *listeners* and away from the heart of your message, and eliminates the possibility of a genuine *transaction* taking place.

Further, the sermon tends to use *polished language.* Manuscript preachers generally hunt for vocabulary that is *exact,* because careful choice of vocabulary helps fashion what they want to say. Unfortunately, this is often not the kind of language that is immediately recognizable by *listeners.*

There is also a decided lack of spontaneity and freedom in the pulpit. In a closely timed service, there is little flexibility. If the music leader takes too much time, or a lay leader prays too long so that the service is running long, you have no way of adjusting your preaching time.

Finally, manuscript preaching is informed by the Shannon-Weaver model of communication, which, as we have seen, promotes an inadequate understanding of human communication. It says that a static message is transmitted to static receivers. As such, the manuscript invades the preacher-listener relationship by keeping the preacher from engaging his or her listeners in a *transactional process.* The preacher's attention and eye contact tend to be more manuscript-centered than listener-oriented. Indeed, the *preacher and manuscript* are in relationship with each other, and the congregation only *overhears* the message, which, in turn, minimizes the direct impact of the message on the lives of the listeners. We simply cannot separate *person* from *content* or *messenger* from *message* in oral communication, even though reading a manuscript attempts to do this. It also dismisses the *relational* element of oral discourse, where one preacher is in relationship with one audience during one preaching experience. When a manuscript is read, it disembodies the preacher from the message. No transaction takes place because there is no human relationship being worked on. A *read* sermon is a *disassociated* message and will not be transactional.

Evaluation

I tried manuscript preaching when I first started preaching, but soon found it too awkward and restrictive, and so moved away from it very quickly.

Manuscript preaching tends to be very popular in the West, perhaps for two reasons. First, as we've just seen, the standard understanding of human communication (the linear model) supports it. But secondly, it drastically reduces the preacher's anxiety just before and during the preaching event. The preacher has far greater control over the language used in the pulpit, because the sermon is carefully honed in the privacy of a quiet study.

Generally, this approach leads to "reading a sermon" rather than "preaching." For this reason (among others mentioned above), I do not encourage this style of preaching. Those who use a manuscript are simply not able to experience the real exhilaration, power, and freedom of the *preaching event*.

III. MEMORIZED PREACHING

This brings us to the third style of presentation, which is a *formalization* of manuscript preaching. Memorizing a sermon means taking a well-honed manuscript and memorizing it, word for word. In doing so, you gain the advantage of maintaining eye contact with the congregation, because there is no manuscript in front of you.

Preparation

Preparation time is one of the greatest problems with this method. You may need 30 or more hours for each sermon if your memory is good enough to "capture" the sermon in that amount of time. You still need 15 - 20 hours for writing and rewriting the sermon (the same amount as for manuscript preaching), and the remainder of the time for memorization.

Anxiety

There is a great deal of anxiety with this style, which tends to be high before the construction process begins, lower when you start memorizing, but since you must *recall* the whole thing in the pulpit, it is extremely high when you begin preaching.

Advantages

There are *advantages* to this style. Certainly, you can maintain the accurate language and phrasing that took all that time and energy in your study. You can also maintain better eye contact with your listeners than with reading. And you certainly don't have to worry about misplacing the manuscript or having someone walk off with it!

Disadvantages

Of course, there are major *disadvantages* to this style of presentation. In fact, this method *keeps* all the disadvantages of manuscript preaching but adds additional ones. Because you are essentially *reading back* a written manuscript (though you are reading from memory), your preaching will *sound* like it is being read, even without a manuscript in front of you (it still uses the *structure* of written language, too). And you might feel that you have to preach the sermon as rapidly as possible so you don't forget it.

Further, this style of presentation just takes too much time for memorization, particularly in the context of pastoral ministry.

You will also realize that there is a lack of freedom or flexibility to change anything in your sermon, if that becomes necessary (more so than with manuscript preaching). Usually, memorization means that words and phrases "trigger" the next ones. If you are interrupted for any reason, or forget a portion of the text, it is sometimes difficult to "find your place" again.

Then, as with manuscript preaching, your relationship is with the *manuscript* (even though it remains "behind" your eyes), not with your listeners. Your main focus of attention is on trying to *recover* the sermon rather than the importance of the *message*. Finally, when it's done well, your listeners may be more impressed with your *memory* than your *message*.

Evaluation

My experience with full memorization has been minimal. I have memorized *parts* of sermons, but my memory isn't reliable enough to have attempted the memorization of a full sermon. Besides that, I never really had the time or desire to fully memorize a manuscript.

For the strong negatives to this style of presentation, its "canned" approach in structure and recall, I would also not recommend it.

EXTEMPORANEOUS PREACHING

As we have seen, the first three styles of presentation are problematic and should not be used for your "normal" preaching week after week. There are *some* occasions in which it might be important to borrow one or more of these inadequate methods, but, for the most part, I suggest that you reject them in favor of a style of presentation that suits a better *reception* of your message.

We now come to the preferred method of preaching. It is what I call *extemporaneous,* and there are two approaches to it.

The word "extemporaneous" needs defining, since it is used in different ways by different homileticians. Most often, "extemporaneous" is understood as a synonym for "impromptu." However, I am using it here to mean preaching that is *well-prepared but presented with few or no notes.* It is not spontaneous or "off the cuff" preaching. Nor is it memorization. The flow of the sermon, its main ideas and stories, and its *direction* are all remembered, but not most of its *language.* Manuscript *writing* is important in order to preach extemporaneously, but the manuscript is used only to *prepare* the preacher for the preaching event; it stays in the study.

Thus, extemporaneous preaching doesn't mean a *lack* of preparation. It just requires a *different use* of preparation time. Indeed, *less* preparation time can sometimes lead to *better* extemporaneous preaching.

Manuscript and memorized styles of presentation are what I would call *sermon-centered* preaching. They focus your listeners' attention on the *manuscript* or your *recall* of it. They give you *control* over the vocabulary and sentence structure, but it really doesn't matter what audience is sitting there or the kind of environment in which the sermon is preached.

Extemporaneous presentation, on the other hand, is *listener-centered.* It forces you to meet and confront your *listeners.* You are building and developing a *relationship* with them, refocusing yourself to meet your listeners because *they* become the center of your communicative attention.

And in keeping with oral transaction, your relationship with the congregation is united with your *message.* This unity gives you a more *natural expression* in the pulpit, where your language tends to be *formally conversational,* and, thus, very naturally *hearable.* Ultimately, if you want to *communicate* in an oral setting, you must get away from manuscript and memorization, and preach *extemporaneously.*

With this definition in mind, then, let's look at these two approaches to extemporaneous preaching. The first is preaching *with notes,* but the preferred method is to preach extemporaneously *without notes.* The rest of this book is oriented to help you preach in this preferred style.

IV. EXTEMPORANEOUS PREACHING WITH NOTES

If you want to try preaching extemporaneously with notes, you step into the preaching role with a few comments written on a single sheet of paper (or less). These notes provide a reminder of the direction in which your sermon is headed, as well as some specific information that you might want to remember (such as statistics or dates).

Preparation

For the extemporaneous preacher who uses notes, *preparation* can be done in 10 – 12 hours. It takes about six to eight hours to write the rough and final drafts of the sermon, and between two and four hours to prepare for the preaching event itself (which often means rewriting and rearranging notes).

Anxiety

Anxiety tends to be fairly high before you begin writing, depending on how much pre-work you've done. It lowers as the manuscript is finished, and then gets somewhat higher again just before you step into the pulpit. Of the five presentational styles, extemporaneous preaching *with notes* is the second lowest anxiety producing method at the moment of preaching (next to manuscript preaching), and it certainly has that to commend it.

Advantages

The advantages of extemporaneous preaching with notes are many. You will be "conversational," and, thus, easier to "hear" than if you read a manuscript. Also, you are far more alert to the situation, environment, and influence of the listeners during the preaching event than when you are tied to a manuscript or trying to recall a memorized sermon. Extemporaneous preaching with notes leads more naturally to a *transactional* experience with your listeners, as you are able to make adjustments to your discourse. The notes help guide you through the sermon, but it is fairly easy to depart from them if you have to. It also means that you will more naturally maintain eye contact with your listeners. And your gestures tend to be natural, since they *accompany* what you are saying.

Disadvantages

There are also a few disadvantages to this style. Of course, as with both kinds of extemporaneous presentation, the language you use will not be as accurate as it would be if you were to use a written manuscript. This might make you feel awkward at first because you may find that you cannot recall exactly the right word or phrase you want to use. But remember that listeners *expect* this as a natural part of orality. They are used to it, and there is no reason to be embarrassed by it. It simply makes their listening more natural.

It is also true that you may, from time to time, forget specific wording and phrasing in the sermon. You had rehearsed everything, but now when you are preaching, you draw a blank. Your notes can help you remember, but not if they are too generally written. For this reason, you may have the tendency to rely on your notes too much, and thus be tempted to establish a relationship with your *notes* rather than with your *listeners,* and, in that way, destroy the transactional experience.

A final disadvantage is that using notes can sometimes restrict your freedom of thought in the pulpit, since you are bound to follow the way your notes were composed in your study (in a different environment).

Evaluation

Preaching with notes is perhaps the most popular style of preaching in the West apart from using a manuscript. The amount of notes varies from "almost-manuscript" to the very skimpy. Some preachers who bring notes into the pulpit resort to reading them (not much better than manuscript preaching), and some preachers hardly glance at their notes at all. But this kind of extemporaneous preaching "involves" you as the preacher more fully in the preaching event than if you are trying to transmit words from a manuscript.

However, when you use notes, you are still bound by them. Your freedom is still hindered, and if you happen to misplace your notes or can't read your writing, your ability to communicate with your listeners will be hampered. So, while this style of presentation is much preferred over the previously discussed methods, we turn now to a "more excellent way."

V. THE PREFERRED STYLE:
EXTEMPORANEOUS PREACHING WITHOUT NOTES

A transformational *transaction* in preaching most naturally and easily happens when you preach without notes, and it is for this reason that I recommend it and practice it.

Unfortunately, preaching with "no notes" is sometimes a derogatory designation that means you are preaching without *preparation.* However, preaching without notes is effective only *with* adequate preparation.

Actually, if you go through the process of writing, rewriting, and outlining (as we'll talk about it later), there is really no need for notes. You already know the "flow" of your sermon because you have written it, rewritten it, and practiced it. And often, you discover that notes are *interruptive* to the transaction. So why not experience the real *freedom* that comes when you proclaim biblical truth *without* notes? There is no preaching style more powerful or convicting than stepping into the pulpit and carrying on a biblical, life-changing *transaction* with your congregation, and being completely free of notes to do it.

Preparation

When we take into consideration some advance planning strategies (the subject of Chapter 23), preparation to preach without notes is, perhaps surprisingly, only eight to ten hours. Of this, six to eight hours will be spent on collecting materials and writing and rewriting the manuscript, and about two hours preparing to preach. The total preparation time, as you can see, can be less than with other styles, but it is *how* you spend the time that is important.

Anxiety

Anxiety is the greatest problem in preaching without notes. It is high when you begin the sermon construction process, lowers as the manuscript gets written, but, as with memorization, it again gets very high when you step into pulpit. You have nothing to jog your memory once you've started. You are on your own, guided only by your Spirit-inspired memory. And that can be frightening! However, you also learn that anxiety can be important because, when it is controlled, it will *energize* your preaching (we'll talk about managing anxiety at the end of this chapter).

Advantages

Preaching without notes *keeps* all the advantages of extemporaneous preaching with notes (except for *having* the notes), but also *adds* several advantages.

First, you experience an exciting freedom in the pulpit. It is much easier to engage your listeners in a *transactional* event without the burden of notes. You are also freed from the burden of impressing people with your *memorization* skills, so that the power of the *message* becomes most important to them. You experience a unique *oneness* with your listeners. There is more meaningful eye contact and a *directness* about the proclamation that is difficult for your listeners to escape, so they are more apt to *stay with you*. Ultimately, the act of locking your listeners with you in this transaction of preaching is an absolutely unequalled and joyous spiritual experience!

Another advantage of preaching without notes is that your sermons, by necessity, will be simpler (which does *not* mean *simplistic).* That is, by remembering the *flow* of your sermon, your preaching will not tend to be filled with highly complex ideas or structures, which listeners can't follow anyway. The progression of your sermon will tend to be streamlined and easy for your listeners to grasp, which, in turn, challenges you to use more stories and narrative forms (which are more "hearable," too). Further, this whole approach minimizes *exposition* and *explanation,* which also carry little impact for your listeners. You will be more direct and more easily understood, and, thus, your messages will be more *engaging* and more *convicting* for your listeners.

Preaching without notes also incorporates the "best of both worlds": adequate, Spirit-led *preparation* with reliance on the *spontaneous* work of the Holy Spirit. Thus, even after preparation, you have freedom to adjust your sermon if there are last minute concerns or circumstances that support your message, additional insights into the text as you preach, or if you forget part of your sermon, you have the immediate ability to change its order. This enables you to adapt more naturally to the immediate situation, such as the relevance of a solo to your message, interruptions (a passing fire engine), an early Sunday-morning automobile accident of one of your members, or a shorter time for preaching than you expected.

Finally, you don't have to worry about keeping track of a manuscript or notes on Sunday morning. Wherever you go, you are "free." If the lights go out or if you have to meet in the church parking lot because of a building problem, you can still preach. If you sense the need to step out from behind the pulpit, you are free to do so. You have freedom in the immediate impact of the congregation's contribution and influence in the process of the transaction. Preaching without notes increases your *options.*

Disadvantages

The disadvantages, actually, are few, but they are important. The primary one is that your anxiety is high when you step into the pulpit. Your greatest fear is that you will have a lapse of memory and forget something. It happens. (And it may startle you so much that you'll decide never to try it again!) But it's part of the balancing process of learning how to simplify your sermons so that you will most strongly impact your listeners. It *is* true that interruptions can be distracting, though it is easier to manage them with this style than if you are preaching from a manuscript or by memorization.

Evaluation

I have been consistently preaching without notes since 1977, and I am a strong advocate of this style of presentation. Because preaching is *oral* communication, preaching without notes makes the most sense. It creates an environment in which the preacher most naturally engages a *transactional* communicative experience with listeners. It is most easily *heard* because it uses naturally-spoken (though somewhat formalized) conversational language. And it makes the best use of the preacher's limited preparation time. At the same time, it offers the immediacy of "spontaneous," Spirit-directed movement and language in the preaching event.

Preaching without notes can be an exhilarating experience—for you and your listeners. As you think through the issues we've discussed, I hope you are interested enough in extemporaneous preaching without notes to try it. Once you make the decision, you will be more open to the actual practice of putting a sermon together in a way that makes preaching without notes easy and instinctive. It most naturally takes advantage of the oral environment in which preaching happens, and incarnates the biblical message in you as the preacher.

ENGAGING THE TRANSACTION

Finally, before we leave this section of the text, there are four additional issues we should look at when we're talking about oral communication. We'll briefly examine anxiety control, mnemonic strategies, gestures, and elocution.

MANAGING ANXIETY

How can anxiety be reduced in preaching? Actually, this is a question every preacher faces, particularly those committed to preaching without notes. Let me offer a few ways you can help manage it in your own preaching ministry.

To begin with, as I've said, a little nervousness is natural and can be extremely helpful! When you step into the pulpit, anxiety can actually *energize* your preaching. Of course, when there's too much of it, it can be incapacitating, and that's when it becomes a problem. But when there is "just enough" adrenalin flowing through your body, it can be exhilarating and empowering. So here are some strategies I've learned that might help you manage your anxiety.

First, be as *prepared* as possible. Don't short-cut your preparation time.

Second, *remember your listeners* and their need to hear this "word" from the Lord. Human communication is always *relational*. It is always between *people*. *They* are the reason for your preaching and for this message. So talk to them about this matter that is of great importance to their lives—that's what preaching should be (we'll discuss this subject more fully in Chapter 14).

Third, *focus on your thesis and the development of your sermon*. It will help you remember where you are going and how you plan to get there. If you forget part of your sermon but know your thesis, you can always jump over particular phases of the sermon to emphasize the "point." Remember that your listeners don't know what you were planning to say in the sermon. Your greatest desire is to get them to understand your thesis as it develops the truth of Scripture.

Fourth, find your best weekly preparation schedule so you are *prepared* well *but not bored* with your sermon by the time you step into the pulpit.

Fifth, it is extremely helpful to *know your first line* and opening story. I have found that, once I start talking, I'm on the way!

Sixth, *take a few deep breaths* before you step into the pulpit. And *pray!* You are here now because the Lord has called you here and has a message He wants your listeners to hear.

Seventh, it helps to *walk with confidence* to the pulpit. Behavioral psychologists suggest that your *behavior* is inextricably connected with your *attitude,* and that *changing* your behavior will often change your attitude. So even if you don't *feel* secure, you can still *act* as if you know what you're doing. It will make a world of difference in your self-esteem and your anxiety management: if you *walk* with confidence to the pulpit, you will *feel* more confident.

Finally, when you preach without notes, you might find it helpful to *include more details* in your preparatory manuscript than you will use in the pulpit. This eases the tension of having to remember *everything* when you start preaching. Jot down more biographical details than you will use, or additional statistics. Or glance at an additional story that you don't plan to include in your sermon. This way, you'll have more than enough information if you happen to forget something.

MNEMONIC DEVICES

You may also find *mnemonic strategies* useful in your preaching. These are memory devices that help you remember the flow of your sermon when you are preaching without notes.

There are many such strategies you can use. One that's worked well for me is to take the *first letter* of each major phase of my sermon, and use those letters to make a word or sentence. For example, I once preached a sermon that

I called, "Two foundations are better than one," from Acts 4:32-33. I built the sermon around three "phases" from the text: *new* Christians do evangelism, *mature* Christians provide nurturing support, and *all* work together in one mind and heart. This led me to my use the initials "E" (for evangelism), "N" (for nurture), and "O" (for one). But then, to make the progression even more memorable, I thought of a nonsensical sentence by which to remember those three letters, and came up with "Elephants need oranges." (Even after all these years, I still remember that silly sentence!)

Here's another possibility: try to associate each phase of your sermon with a particular place in the sanctuary where you preach. When you mentally move around the room as you work your way through your sermon, the room actually becomes your "sermon notes."

Sometimes, I *do* take a few notes into the pulpit with me, such as when I need to remember particular details about a person's life (birth date, family members, major accomplishments, or identification with particular places, etc.). I do this because I want to talk about real people and places, but also because there might be a well-read listener who knows something about this particular person or historical character.

GESTURES

As we saw in Chapters 4 and 5, human communication is not only concerned with *what* is said but *how* it is said (the *report* and *command* of Gregory Bateson [1951]). This *command* component of communication has to do with *paralinguistics*. It includes body language, proxemics, tone of voice, emphasis, and other visual and aural elements that accompany the words that are used. These cues help us understand how the *information* and the *relationship* are being developed during this particular interaction.

Because visual cues play such an important role in effective communication, the topic of *gestures* is important for preaching. Typically, gesturing means using your hands and arms, though it can also mean facial expressions, body movement, and use of the head. Most preaching texts include helpful suggestions for natural gesturing, while others seem to put too much emphasis on developing the *right kinds* of "gestures." Actually, gestures help add the "presence" of your personality to the preaching event, but only when they are natural. Indeed, the most important aspect of gesturing is to *be natural. Trying* to gesture is always unnatural. So here are a few guidelines for gesturing.

First, don't *make* gestures—just *gesture!* Your gestures should be a natural expression of who you are, what you are saying, and how you ordinarily talk. You shouldn't have to plan them. Rather, use your body movement and hands and head and facial expressions as you ordinarily do when speaking with your friends.

Second, your gestures should *complement* the *content* of your sermon. They are helpful when you want to emphasize important words or phrases. Just be careful that you don't punctuate *everything* you say, otherwise your gestures become meaningless.

Third, your gestures should be *appropriate* to the cultural situation in which you are speaking. Preaching to a crowd of 3,000 demands different gestures than sitting in a small group. Cultural sensitivity is also important if you are a visiting preacher: wearing a ring or necktie, gesturing wildly, or using particular stories, are inappropriate in some places in Eastern Europe. Try to be natural without being offensive.

Fourth, when trying to be natural, sometimes it is helpful to think about what *motivates* a gesture. There are several possibilities: a word or phrase that needs *emphasis,* a *conviction* or *feeling,* your own *personality*, or to *indicate something or someone more easily described with movement than words* (as pointing out a listener who is really engaged with you).

Fifth, it is important to use a *variety* of gestures. While you want to be natural, you can also expand your repertoire of gestures. Haddon Robinson (1980) says that we can produce 700,000 distinct elementary signs with arms, wrists, hands, and fingers, so you might want to experiment with some additional options than those you ordinarily use.

Sixth, your listeners will follow you more easily if you use *spatial* arrangement. What I mean is that you should keep persons, objects, scenes, and future and past tenses in particular spatial locations in the room. Then, refer to those places consistently. It makes your sermon and progression of ideas much easier for your listeners to follow. And your own movement in telling a story should be natural to the listeners so it will be easier for them to follow: you can "live out" a story by moving around the platform, for instance.

Seventh, learn to *reverse your gestures.* This makes it easier for your listeners to follow what you're saying, because you will confuse them if you use your own point of reference. Ordinarily, for instance, we envision the past to the left and the future to the right. But when you are preaching, you should gesture in *an opposite way* so your listeners will not be confused: they will *see* you point to *their left* when talking about the past (which is where the past is for them), even though you point to your right. They will *see* you turn pages in an imaginary Bible from right to left, which is natural for them, even though you are turning those pages from left to right. Gesturing like this is opposite your natural perception, so you'll have to think about it and practice this reversal of gestures. You certainly don't want to interrupt the flow of your sermon if you have to keep saying, "My right, but your left."

Finally, let me also encourage you to be on the lookout for your own *annoying* gestures. We have all heard speakers who jingle coins or keys in their pocket while they are in front of a group, but they are completely oblivious to the distraction it causes. As a young preacher, I unknowingly kept sweeping my hand across my forehead to get my hair back into place. I didn't realize I did it until a friend pointed it out (for which I am still deeply grateful). I had to work consciously to change that nervous habit because I knew it was distracting. These, of course, are *nervous gestures,* and we should be on the alert for them in our own preaching situations.

ELOCUTION

Projection and *enunciation* (called *elocution)* are also important elements of oral transaction. You could study these skills at length, but there are really only two significant principles to keep in mind:

1. *Make sure that your listeners can hear you.* There are enough potential difficulties with communication without introducing *hearing* problems. Whenever possible, use a public address system. Minimize noise distractions. If your listeners can't *hear* you or the words you use, it will be difficult for them to understand your *message.*

2. *Make sure that your listeners correctly understand the words you are saying.* This is not to suggest that you must become a great orator. If you want to do that, this book is really not for you. That might require the intricate study of speech communication principles and vocalization, and a great deal of public speaking in a large auditorium, practicing expansive gestures with vast audiences. It might include formalized language and diction, weighty vocabulary, and how to correctly emphasize words. But I suggest that most of these disciplines will come *naturally* to you, if you really want to *talk to* the people who are listening to you.

If you can follow these two guidelines, you'll be fine. If your listeners can't hear you or understand you, there isn't much sense in your wasting their time—or yours. Just try to be a *natural* (but formal) conversationalist in the pulpit. *Talk with* your people, though from a prophetic posture. Be aware of *them.* Be concerned about *them.* Know what you want to say to *them.* It is important that you speak loudly enough to be heard by all of them and to speak as clearly as you can. But, generally, if your focus is on *them,* you will communicate more clearly than if you try to figure out everything you're doing wrong. Be as focused as possible, love your people, and engage them in this transaction of preaching. If you do that, you *will* communicate effectively. That's what counts.

Taken altogether, if you want to be a convicting, transformational preacher, *don't sweat the small stuff!* Don't worry about the issues that many preaching texts focus on: gestures, elocution, tone, inflection, and the "crisis" of too many nonfluencies ("er"s and "um"s). These are all *minor concerns.* Just be yourself.

Of course, if you are secure enough in your preaching, you might ask a friend to critique your presentational style, diction, gestures, and/or distracting movements. Change those actions or gestures that they see as annoyances, but do so with the specific intent of being able to more passionately and directly communicate the word of God. It will be of great benefit to the power of your preaching in the future.

Section I:
Part B:
The Preacher in Transaction

We move from thinking about the communicative *event* that I call the "transaction" between preacher and congregation to the actual and necessary presence of the *preacher* in the preaching event. It is what I identify as *incarnational preaching*. Preaching is not for the faint of heart, nor for the proud. It emerges from the preacher's encounter with the living Spirit of God that leads to a new awareness of self and a relevant encounter with God's people.

This Part of Section I includes two chapters about the centrality of the preacher in the preaching event. The first calls our attention to the uniqueness of each preacher (as God intended); the second is an examination of the importance of the preacher's theology to the transactional preaching event.

CHAPTER 8
The Each in Preach

JEWETT

One day in the 19th century, a young man sat in the gallery of the British House of Commons and listened to the majestic eloquence of John Bright. That young man went home resolved to be a lawyer. The day before he was to sign his name to a law career, he was walking through his village and met his Sunday School teacher. He said to his teacher, "Tomorrow, I am signing articles in a law office." The Sunday School teacher said: "That is a great profession!" But then his face clouded over, and he whispered, "Henry, I had always hoped you would be a preacher." That young man went home in deep thought and, in the solitude of his room, heard the call of God "as clearly as the morning bell rings in the valleys of Switzerland."

So it was that John Henry Jewett entered the Christian ministry. In Great Britain and then in the pulpit of Fifth Avenue Presbyterian Church in New York City, he became an extraordinary preacher. He knew his calling and gave himself to it.

Here was a young man traveling his own road in life. He dreamed of an exciting future, but was nonetheless open to God's call. He said, "Lord, I am here. In spite of what I know about myself, in spite of my failures and imperfections and weaknesses, I give myself to You to use in any way You want." This kind of willingness doesn't require a man or woman who is perfectly fashioned to be a preacher. It only takes someone who is *willing,* willing to respond to God's *best use.* So it is that God calls *ordinary* men and women to preach.

YOU-NIQUE

What makes *you* unique? In asking that question, I'm not advocating that you be content with your imperfection and sin, but that you accept yourself in your own humanity as you strive to grow as a disciple of Jesus Christ.

You don't need to study psychology to recognize how extraordinarily distinctive you are. You were raised in a one-of-a-kind environment (even our two sons were *not* raised in the same home environment—they have different brothers!). You developed a particular personality, experienced life in ways peculiar *only* to you, and were trained and educated as an incomparable human being. Your cultural heritage and language contributed to your character. Your genetic code and every one of your relationships contributed to your uniqueness. Your personal history, the values you've been taught, and all the existential pain you've experienced contributed to your individuality. There's almost no limit to the influences that have made you who you are (and the same is true of every other person who has ever lived). You are unique and special, like no other. No two of us *are* ever, or *have* ever been, alike.

It's the same pattern we see in the created order. What a wonderfully complex creation it is—we should rejoice in the way God made it. Look at the majestic towering Sequoia tree and the heart-breaking beauty of the Weeping Willow. See the timidity of the deer, the treachery of the termite, the temerity of the bulldog. Reflect on the patience of the robin, the perseverance of the ant, the persistence of the housefly. God is the Genius Creator of *diversity,* not uniformity.

It's just one more evidence of the way God made *people*—each one a reflection of His great complexity. Of all the vast millions of faces in the thousands of racial and ethnic groups in all the history of the world, no one has ever looked just like anybody else (identical twins come close, but even they have their own special look—just ask their parents).

This discussion, of course, implicates *you* as a preacher. Jesus created you and calls you as a *unique* individual. But he doesn't invite you to become somebody *different*—otherwise, why waste all that creative power? From a special and unique beginning, and a life filled with unique experiences, he calls you to *continuing* uniqueness. You are not expected to be like anybody else.

Yes, he works on our sin and imperfection, our immorality and self-centeredness—that's why he died and why he comes to us as a risen Lord. He continues to improve us, sanctify us, and reorient us. But that doesn't mean we are expected to *conform* to be like somebody else. If Jesus wanted you to *be* somebody else or be *like* somebody else, he would have created you that way. He wouldn't have wanted somebody just like *you* if he had created you to be somebody else.

A BIBLICAL RATIONALE

The Bible provides good support for this view of the unique created individual. Let's look at some major biblical images.

THE POTTER AND CLAY

Here is the potter as she sits at her wheel, spinning that slick gray mud between her slippery palms. She can do with that clay whatever she wants. From the same lump, she can make a cooking pot, a coffee mug, a flower vase, or a statuette. The shape is of *her* choosing. And she can put whatever color glaze she wants on it or paint any design she desires.

When Isaiah prays, "we are the clay, You are the Potter" (64:8), he accepts his own "moldableness." God is like the Potter, fashioning us in whatever way He wants. The Apostle Paul says it, too, that God, the Potter, has the right to make *anything* from the same lump (Romans 9:20-21). We are in God's Hands. He fashions us as *He* chooses.

But there's something else here. The potter also creates the pot *as it is being fashioned.* There is a general design to it in the potter's mind from the outset, but the small idiosyncrasies and character of the pot emerge as it comes into being. Every artist experiences this creative process. An emerging piece of art begins with an idea or design, but takes on its own unique beauty *as it comes into being.*

That is exactly what happened when I was writing this chapter. It began with an idea I had of the preacher's importance, and then became a series of disconnected thoughts about the subject. Then I wrote and rewrote the material, edited and refocused and rewrote it again, and organized and reorganized it. I massaged and manipulated it in my office in Prague, on my computer in East Norriton, Pennsylvania, in Brjansk, Russia, even in the Pittsburgh airport, all over the course of five years. I pushed it and prodded it and kneaded it until it ended up the way you're now reading it. Sermons happen like that, too (though with narrower time restrictions). And I, as a preacher, have been fashioned like that, over the course of a lifetime. You have been, too, because *God continues to fashion each of us as He works with us.*

I like that image of our lives, and of us as preachers. As we grow, as we develop, as we practice our craft, we are being fashioned by the hand of God. The making of a preacher takes a lifetime. But it begins with an ordinary man or woman who is submitted to the will of God.

Dr. Wiard Popkes, when he was the distinguished New Testament scholar at the Baptist Seminary in Hamburg, Germany (now located in Elstal), was once invited to preach in the northwestern part of Germany. Before the service began, an elderly woman greeted him and asked him where he was from. "Hamburg," he stated proudly. "I teach at the Theological Seminary." "Oh," said the woman, "is that where they make preachers out of ordinary people?"

That's the business in which God plays a major role: making a preacher out of an ordinary man or woman who is submitted to His will.

How about you?

A PHILIPPIAN CALL

This rather astounding biblical truth is also found in Philippians 3:8-17. Here, Paul is presenting a case for our uniqueness. The heart of the passage comes in verse 12, where he writes, "I press on to take hold of that for which Christ Jesus took hold of me."

I used to believe that this meant that Jesus had in mind a perfect, ideal "self" of each individual when he called that person to faith. The world had encrusted that "perfectness" with imperfection and sin-scars, so the lifetime the individual spends following Jesus is a way for that person to *get free* from those sinful habits and find new life at every turn. The more closely the disciple follows Jesus, the more Jesus "takes off" these encumbrances of imperfection. We are continually moved ahead to the ideal for which Jesus "grasps" us. That's a very important interpretation of this verse.

But now I am coming to understand the passage differently. Now I see that all the experiences of life *give shape* to the ideal that Jesus has in mind. Life in the world does not "pile on" imperfect elements that have to be shed before we can get back to our perfect image. Rather, everything that has happened and will happen *contributes* to my unique, ideally-developing self. My trials, experiences, relationships, physical looks, giftedness, and interests have all contributed to who I am. So I can celebrate them (even the painful ones!), because each one contributes in some way to *who I am becoming* under the Lordship of Jesus Christ. I do not mean to imply that he *brings about* catastrophes in my life to fashion me in a certain way, but that he uses *whatever happens* to bring renewal and adjustment to my developing life and character. My greatest obligation as a Christian is only to trust him and seek his perfection *through* every trial and treasure of life. Then he is able to use those experiences for my, and his, *good* (see Romans 8:28).

I think that's the idea Paul develops throughout this passage. In verses 8 and 9, he writes that the *past* is trash because of Jesus' doing. All of the past has been used up, like the sweet juicy segments of a ripe orange. They were *so* good, but there are leftover seeds and orange peels that have to be discarded now. In the same way, the good has been sucked out of all my experiences of life. They have had their impact, their influence, but all that is left is the refuse, the rubbish of what *was* valuable. It had its developmental use in me, but now I put it behind me through the ongoing experience of the death of Jesus. That's what Paul says in verses 10 and 11, that what is important in life is defined in the light of Jesus' death and resurrection. That is, I am able to put *behind* me the garbage of my experiences because I share in the death of Jesus.

And then comes the heart of the passage in verse 12, when Paul focuses attention on the perfectly-emerging *me*. Here he writes that I *strive* for, *press* on, *grasp* that which I am "attaining" (note the use of this verb in verse 11). It is an *active, positive* word, not a *taking off* but a *putting on*. It is not a *letting go* of what is imperfect, but of *obtaining* that which is so much better. *Every new experience contributes to my perfection!* So I ask, *"Who* am I *becoming?* For what *purpose* is Christ calling me, grasping me?" As a preacher, how am I *being* fashioned—even here and now, today?

This posture then sets me up for the next step in the process (verses 13 to 16). Now Paul presents the whole Christian life as "a great race," a running "pilgrimage." There is improvement all along the way. I strain forward, pressing on for the high calling of God in Christ Jesus. This is an intentional effort to become somebody I am not yet. It is this *ideal* (verse 16) which I am called to "live up to." It is not a reference to separate pieces or experiences of life that I must "cast off." Rather, these are elements I continue to *appropriate. I live up to what I am attaining!* That is, falling back into my old habits doesn't suit the new being that I am becoming. Jesus says that I am not to put new wine in old wineskins (Matthew 9:17), and I am not to look *back* when I put my hand to the plow (Luke 9:62).

Finally, in verse 17, Paul talks about the importance of *role models.* Again, he encourages me, his reader, to become like him. But why? In its context, it is so I as the individual Christian can keep growing and emerging as the particular, distinct, special person Jesus is calling me to be. The whole passage is a call to a future, to a new *me!*

How about you?

IMPERFECT PREACHERS IN THE BIBLE

Let's look at Scripture in another way now by trying to describe *common* traits of preachers we find in the Bible. That "ideal" image, in turn, should help me become more of the kind of preacher Jesus expects me to be, to more adequately know what I should be like in the pulpit and what I should say. So what is that "ideal" biblical preacher like?

If we were going to do this right, of course, we would have to engage in a comprehensive study of all the preachers in the Bible, line them up next to each other, identify their character traits, examine their messages and contexts, and try to understand the responses of their listeners. What do you think we would find? Could we confine all their common traits to one side of a page? In actuality, we'd find that there aren't any two of them who are alike.

We also would discover that none of them were *perfect.* Were we to examine the lives or attitudes or personalities of just a few of the preachers in the pages of Scripture, we would discover that they were all blemished sheep, all spotted and imperfect. Jonah was angry and rebellious. Isaiah strode around naked (20:1-4). Jeremiah buried his unholy underpants in a hole by the river just to make a point (13:1-11). Elijah got terribly depressed and asked to die (1 Kings 19:4). Ecclesiastes (the one called "the Preacher") lived in despair, the eternal determinist. John the Baptist was a hermit with a bad diet. Peter was impatient and had a shaky faith (Acts 8:20). When Stephen preached, he got off to a good start, but then he started *accusing* his listeners and lost his life for it (Acts 7:51-53).

And Paul, the one who asks us to imitate him, was fearful (2 Corinthians 7:5). He was accused of being bold when writing his letters but timid when in person (2 Corinthians 10:1). He told his enemies to castrate themselves (Galatians 5:12). In a difficult meeting, when James managed conflict by gentle reasoning and compromise (Acts 15:13-21), Paul met the situation with anger and separation (Acts 15:36-40). He claimed Roman citizenship to save his neck (Acts 22:25). And he was sometimes a boring preacher (Acts 20:9).

Not any of them conformed to a "standard" that we would apply to the "perfect preacher."

If we think about it, though, these were preachers who were *called by God.* They weren't perfect in any way. They were only open and responsive to God's holy call. They were people *becoming, in process,* and they had a tremendous impact on the kingdom of God. Each was a special and unique person, and, while imperfect, God *used* each one in his or her uniqueness.

How about you?

PERSONALIZED CONTENT

In case we think the *messages* of biblical preachers are presented consistently, let's look at case studies of three of them and see how the *content* of their preaching varied. That is, if these preachers were perfect, we might also assume that there was a standard approach to each subject on which they preached.

Let's briefly examine Jonah, the Samaritan woman, and Paul. Here's the issue: each has been called to preach about *repentance.* Jonah is commanded to preach to a foreign nation. The Samaritan woman preaches at her own initiative to the people who live in her own town. Paul, in response to a general call to preach repentance, goes to Jews and Gentiles wherever he can find them. The theme was repentance for all three of them, but how did each go about conveying that message?

JONAH

In the little book that tells this wonderful short story, Jonah is the reluctant prophet. He first runs away from God's call to preach repentance to Nineveh, but through extraordinary events, he finally agrees to go. When he does, he marches (angry) right into the heart of Nineveh and preaches a very direct, smack-'em-in-the-heart, confrontational message. He doesn't want to be there at all, so he keeps his message short. In fact, the writer of the story records it as a one-liner: "Forty more days and Nineveh will be destroyed" (3:4). There is no indication that Jonah has any other discourse than that (perhaps it's because the story is about *Jonah,* not Nineveh, and not even about repentance). Jonah just announced the end of the world for the great city of Nineveh. He was pretty certain of his preaching ability, too, since he *knew* they'd repent and he'd see no fire (4:1-3)!

Well, of course, all the people believed God's message and, from the wealthiest to the poorest, they humbled themselves before God (3:5). Even the king humbled himself and issued a proclamation of repentance (3:7-9). But Jonah felt like a fool because the destruction that Nineveh deserved *didn't* come! God is merciful when people respond to the proclaimed word. But instead of bringing joy to Jonah, he sulked about it.

SAMARITAN WOMAN

Jesus met a woman at the Sychar well (John 4:4-42). She was a prostitute (or, perhaps, only very promiscuous), and hardly a worthy preacher. But after she met Jesus and was *accepted,* she went to town to preach. With holy boldness, she called the townspeople to meet Jesus for themselves because of her own experience of being forgiven. "Come and see a man who told me everything I ever did!" she cried (John 4:29). That's hardly the message of a woman who hasn't found forgiveness and freedom. She was joyous, and her sermon emerged from that repentant and forgiven heart.

Hers is not a *condemning* sermon about repentance and forgiveness. Instead, her positive, personal experience eventually brought people to Jesus— a very different approach to preaching about repentance than that of Jonah.

PAUL

One of Paul's many sermons is recorded in Acts 13:16-41. He is in the synagogue in Pisidian Antioch, preaching a message of repentance to the Jews. How did he fashion that message? He first provided a historical overview of Israel, 450 years in slavery, then the coming of the judges, Samuel, and the two kings, Saul and David. Then he got right to Jesus (and John, too), and talked very directly about the cross and resurrection and forgiveness of sins (v. 38).

But we don't find any call for repentance! Paul seemed only to want to *inspire* the residents of this little village to *understand* Jesus in a new way. The town's Gentiles came to hear Paul preach on the next Sabbath (v. 44), but that made the Jews so jealous that they expelled Paul and Barnabas from town.

This, of course, was a more elaborate sermon than the previous two we examined. But one thing is clear: each preacher fashioned the message differently—in his or her own way. The *truth* was the same, but the sermons were different because the preachers and the contexts and the people to whom they were preaching were different.

Here, again, we see the uniqueness of each preacher and each preaching situation. Because I am different, I, too, would have preached in each of these situations in a different way.

How about you?

HUMBLE BEGINNINGS

In Romans 15:18, the Apostle Paul writes that he will only preach about "what Christ has accomplished *through* me." He thus indicates that his experience is essential to his preaching, that his *self,* with all his imperfections and sin, cannot be separated from the work of his preaching. Because his life has been impacted by the resurrection power of Jesus, his preaching has become relevant and transformational, particularly for the Gentiles.

I am not arguing that we preach only from personal experience or only about spiritual matters that concern us as preachers. But it does imply that *every message* is filtered through the preacher's own personhood and personality. The preacher cannot escape the power of biblical truth that is proclaimed. When it has transformed the preacher, it is likely to be transformational for the listener. That kind of incarnational preaching, while centered in the preacher, is Spirit-directed and Spirit-driven, and it takes severe humility to be engaged in the preaching ministry in that way. Who, after all, would dare claim to be a worthy prophet of the holy God? It's what David Bartlett reflects in the title of his little book, *The audacity of preaching* (1962).

Paul continues this same thought in 1 Corinthians 1:18. The message of the cross is foolishness to the world, he says, but, at the same time, it is the power of God for us. God uses this foolish message for purposes of salvation (verse 21). The gospel message is foolish, and, as such, it requires my own personal humility to proclaim the word of God that comes in and through me. *Uniqueness* does not imply pride and sole competency. It is only when I am humble enough and foolish enough to preach the cross that the miracle of God emerges in the preaching event. This "foolishness of preaching," according to Paul, is the way God has chosen to make redemption effective and applicable. We can't persuade a person to believe in God. Faith is not an act of the intellect. It is a moral creation produced by the interaction of God's Spirit and my spirit in willing obedience. "Intellect comes in afterwards," writes Oswald Chambers (1950), "to explain what has happened."

Rather than stepping aside from the preaching event, the incarnational preacher gets fully engaged in it: body, heart, mind, and soul. Biblical truth is channeled and enhanced *through* the preacher, in such a way that the same truth from the same text is different when filtered through a different preacher.

I've found that to be the case in my experience. How about you?

PRIVATE REFLECTION

You may be starting to think about your preaching ministry in a different way. It is a holy task, yes, but it is a ministry to which God calls you from out of your *ordinary* experience. Preachers are not greater "saints" than other disciples: we are just given a different role and responsibility in the Body of Christ (see Romans 12:6 and 1 Corinthians 12:10, for instance).

So, with this discussion behind us, let me summarize what I mean by incarnational preaching.

1. PREACHER-STARTED

First, *all preaching begins with you as the preacher.* The text from which you speak, how the sermon is formulated and understood from that text, what you specifically say about the text or subject, the elements that you see in it and exegete from it—all are functions of who you are as the preacher.

2. BE YOURSELF

Because transformational preaching is *incarnational*, be *yourself* in the pulpit. *You* are unique in all the world. *You* have been chosen to use all that you are in your preaching. *You* have been called to offer this sermon to this people at this time. Remind yourself periodically that if God wanted someone else to stand in your pulpit or preach this sermon, He would have appointed somebody else to do it. Don't try to be a different kind of preacher than you are and don't try to "get out of the way" of the preaching event. Those who say, "I only want others to see *Jesus* in me" generally end up calling attention to themselves through their lack of self-esteem (which is very different than *humility*). But *you* are the key to transformational preaching. Those who fully engage the text and present it authoritatively from a position of *personal* strength are the ones who "reach" people with biblical truth. It happens when you "embody" the message. God's "word" needs to come fully alive through *you,* as a living channel through whom it is given.

3. GIFTEDNESS

As a unique preacher, you have *charisma.* The dictionary says that charisma is an inspiring character trait of individuals that "secures the allegiance of large groups of people." Ben Witherington III (1995) defines charisma as the ability to strike "responsive chords" in an audience. That is, you are a *catalyst* who is called to convert the latent feelings of your listeners into action. That's what *charisma* means for preaching, but it's a gift that takes courage and confidence. Only when you are strong enough to be yourself can you step out confidently with the kind of message God wants you to proclaim.

4. SELF-CONFIDENCE

Preaching, while it is *incarnational,* is not an opportunity for you to call attention to yourself. It is an occasion in which you are to call attention to *biblical truth.* But only when you are self-confident can there be enough power for the truth to be evident to your listeners.

The pulpit in St. Stephen's Cathedral in Vienna is a work of art and an interesting sculpture. It is carved from marble. The preacher climbs the circular steps to preach good news, but there, underneath him, is a little man opening a window in the pedestal. It is a self-portrait of the sculptor calling attention to himself, an artist's expression of what the old preacher once prayed, "O Lord, give me a high opinion of myself!"

A desire for *pride* is sinful. That's not what I'm talking about when I speak of the confidence required for incarnational preaching. *Self-esteem,* the opposite of pride, is holy. It means that we understand our full acceptance by Jesus Christ, in spite of our imperfections. The healthy preacher recognizes her own strengths and weaknesses, gifts and inabilities, talents and limitations, and praises God for this unique creation. She steps into the pulpit with assurance that the embodied word of God here and now comes from a rightly prepared *person.*

There is a cautionary note here. If you are "filled with yourself," very self-conscious, or are afflicted with low self-esteem, transformational preaching is a difficult approach. With little self-confidence, you may be uncomfortable actually *engaging* other people. Yet, that is what is required in the transaction of preaching, that *listeners* be engaged with biblical truth. But the focus of attention is not on *you* as the preacher. You are just the mediator, the go-between. You want your *listeners* to understand what you are saying. And when your attention is on your message and *communicating* that message, you may find, as I have, that your own self-esteem is also strengthened.

5. NO PERFECT SERMON

If you believe that preachers must be perfect, you probably also think that sermons, too, must be perfect. In our imperfect world, that, of course, can never happen. The search for the *perfect* text or perfect sermon will end in frustration. Given the time constraints of ministry, and the imperfections in your *not-yet-arrived* status, you will very rarely find exactly the right story or text for your proclamation. You will need to be content with what you have in hand in your given circumstances, and use the evidence of who you are *at the moment* to the best advantage. That's important when you preach incarnationally.

6. KEEP BECOMING

Your participation as a unique individual in the preaching event implies that you keep becoming who God is creating you to be. Your own Spirit-led approach to the text is as important as the text itself. Your theological maturity determines what the "message" will be about. But you aren't yet perfect. By following Jesus even more closely day by day, you will keep developing as a Christian and as a preacher.

Through your experience, relationships, study and reflection, the Spirit of God is bringing something to life in you. And under the Lordship of Jesus Christ, you are being made into a unique and special preacher. "What is Jesus now doing in me?" is the orienting question we should all ask ourselves. What Jesus is accomplishing in you is what you ultimately preach. Warren Wiersbe (1995) writes, "God prepares the person who prepares the message." And Bishop William A. Quayle once wrote, "Preaching is not the art of making a sermon and delivering it. Rather, preaching is preparing a preacher and delivering that."

Preaching is a lifetime of work as you continue to *become* a unique individual and a unique preacher.

CHAPTER 9
Incarnational Theology

THEOLOGY OF THE INCARNATIONAL PREACHER

Incarnational preaching says that every sermon begins with you as the preacher: your perception of God, the selection of a passage of Scripture (even if you follow a lectionary), how you handle the text, what specific exegetical elements you "discover," the purpose of the sermon, how you approach the whole process, and how you ultimately design the sermon. And let's not forget your *relationship* with the congregation, whether implied or specified. Almost everything about the preaching ministry is *preacher-oriented.* From *conceptualization* to *event,* the entire preaching process is a demonstration of the *preacher's* responsibility for the preaching task.

In light of this understanding, the preacher's *theology* must be examined, because it is the preacher's worldview, personality, training, and theological understanding, more than anything else, that determines the kind of sermons that will be fashioned and preached.

A PREACHER'S "THEOLOGY"

What, then, is *theology?* Funk and Wagnalls (1975) defines it as "the study of religion," which takes in a lot of territory. The term itself, of course, comes from two Greek words *(θεος* and *λογος)* which mean "God" and "word," which together do not mean "the word of God," but, rather, the "study of God." It has come to imply the *discipline* of Systematic Theology, which we might say is the study of how mature Christian thinkers have understood the revelation of God.

We begin here, because the theology of others down through the centuries has forged the *Church's* theology. We don't come as "outsiders." We wrestle with theology from within a tradition of Christian thought. We hear stories of God's intervention or inaction. We read about a God Who reveals Himself, from the Bible, books we borrow or purchase, and periodicals to which we subscribe. We hear sermons that expound the nature of God. We know God from our own observations of life. Our minds continue to reflect on how the world and universe *make sense.* As thinking Christians, we are always attempting to better comprehend the reality of God and His interaction with our lives and our world. This, then, is what I mean by personal "theology." Even though it comes from many influences, it is an intensely personal business. In the final analysis, it is the way that we as individuals *make sense of God's interaction in our world.* It suggests that your (and my) *personal theology* arises from several sources and that it has *everything* to do with our preaching.

Oswald Chambers (1950) writes, "We begin our Christian life by believing what we are told to believe, then we have to go on to so assimilate our beliefs that they work out in a way that redounds to the glory of God." For Chambers, our understanding of God's interaction in the world begins with what others tell us, but then we must work it out for ourselves. And by "assimilating" it, we make it consistent. Ultimately, theology comes to rest within us as individuals.

Your "theology," then, is your own *personalized* attempt to observe and understand God's interaction in the world. That is what I call *reality.* What is "real" for Christians emerges from an integration of observations, science, relationships, life events, studied information, and our understanding of God's role in all of it. It is based on *perceptions* that are restricted by a person's background and culture, traditions and reading materials, education and conceptual ability. Most significantly, your ability to coordinate and conceptualize *anything* is entirely dependent on who you are and where you have come from.

Of course, since you *continue* to experience life, new experiences and information *change* your perception of reality. Thus, your *theology* develops and matures as you continue to live through and observe more and more experiences of life, and as you take them into consideration. Theology, then, becomes a *life-long* pursuit for every one of us. It is a necessary discipline of discipleship, and something that should never get encrusted, as it did with the Teachers of the Law in Jesus' day.

As a preacher, you are entrusted with the word of God. As such, you must be intentional about developing your own *consistent* and *rational* theology. In making sense of God's interaction with our world, as you gain new information to understand or adapt those perceptions, you *integrate* these new experiences and this new information, and it is *processed* almost daily. Sometimes you interpret new experiences in light of what you already understand. Sometimes you find that a new experience cannot be understood in your current theology and you have to change something (either you ignore the new experience or you change your theology). The more you study Scripture, the more you gain new biblical insights about the character of God. The more you encounter Christians with different experiences and worldviews, the more you read insightful works by professional theologians, the more relationships you develop that force you to broaden your understanding of God and an increasingly complex universe, well, the more your theology grows and emerges. If you close yourself off to new information, you could find yourself one day confronted with such great contradictions that you would be in danger of abandoning your faith altogether. It happens. But the important concern here is that, as you grow and develop, you want to gain a more and more *consistent* view of reality, one that most completely manages as much as possible of what you have understood and experienced up to that point in time.

This brings us to an examination of the components that interact and cooperate in the development of your personal theology.

COMPONENTS OF REALITY

As your theology is enriched through fresh intellectual information and new experiences with a living God, there are three primary influences that contribute to your comprehension of Who God is and how God interacts in your life and world. Not only do these three components *contribute* to your theology, but as time goes on and you become more observant, learned, and experienced in your discipleship, they also cooperate to develop *consistency* in your theology. As you grow, your ideas and lifestyle become more conformed to how you understand Who God is and what He expects of you.

These three components are what I identify as *Existentia* (all that makes you unique, and the most critical piece of the puzzle), *Doctrine* (the "truth influence" of the community in which you live), and *the Bible* (the final written authority for your faith). All three work together to create your *personal theology.*

Figure 9.1 offers a conceptual diagram of what I mean. In brief, *Theology* (our understanding of what is *real)* develops through the interrelationship of *Existentia, Doctrine,* and the *Bible.*

Figure 9.1
The preacher's theology

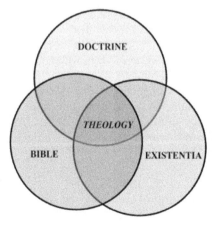

Let's look, then, at what I mean by each of these components.

"EXISTENTIA"

Existentia is a term I use to refer to all that makes you unique as an individual—all of what we talked about in Chapter 8. Your initial comprehension of God depends on what you were taught about God, how you understand your conversion experience, and your own observations concerning spiritual matters (how people behaved in your church community, for instance). But it also includes the social norms that you were taught, the customs you practiced when you were growing up, and your experiences in school. You were born into a particular culture with a national identity. You learned certain prejudices from your parents and interpreted their good and bad actions in a particular way when you were young. That is, your view of reality *begins* with who you are—your training, background, all the jobs you did, and everything else about you.

However, your personal experiences don't only implicate how you *first* understood God. They *continue* to do so throughout your life. You find particular elements of Scripture important in your tenth reading of it because of the attitudes that you have developed. You are now attracted to a particular theology not just because of your upbringing, but because of new social experiences you've had. You participate in the life of the church in a different way now because your relationships and personality have changed. All of your background contributes to how you understand the ways that God continues to influence the world.

So how you understand God, the Church, your Bible, and the Christian life is entirely dependent on who you are. Your ability to think broadly, to resist temptation (or not), and to develop a love for biblical exposition—or narrative—is all a function of who you are.

You are *unique.* You are a *product* of God's creative ability and your environment. Your understanding and worldview are *fashioned* by who you are, but who you are also *limits* your comprehension. Your *experience* tells you how to interpret life and the nature of our world and how God interacts with His created order. This is all to say that your *personal perception* is the key to understanding God and the world and is critical to your understanding of theology. *All theology begins here*—with who you are and what experiences you have had and all your training.

But that isn't the only component of your theology. If it were, there would be no consistency or authority in the Christian faith. So we add two other components of theology to our personal experience. They help us develop a more consistent and accurate understanding of Who God is and His influence on the world.

"DOCTRINE"

The second component of personal theology is what I identify as *Doctrine*, as those principles or foundations of faith that we understand as *truth.*

Doctrine is that which faithfully represents Who God is. It is, as Paul writes, that which *"conforms* to the glorious gospel" (1 Timothy 1:10-11). He is suggesting that if anything is *contrary* to the gospel as we know it in Jesus Christ, of God's love for all individuals, it is not "sound." The gospel, for him, is the standard against which we are to judge whether doctrine is true or not. That is its purpose. It is what Jesus meant when he said, "I am the Truth" (John 14:6). That statement is the centerpiece of John's discussion of Jesus as the fullest revelation of God (John 14:7-11).

But how do we know what is *true?* Jesus is, yes, but how does that truth relate to our broader belief systems? And what *is* doctrine?

There is a certain theological perspective that argues that doctrine (or "Truth") is *propositional,* that it exists "out there" somewhere. It is *reified,* something that *is:* there *is* something identifiable as Truth in the universe.

There's another approach, however, that suggests that doctrine is *community-determined.* It is decided by a particular faith posture or denomination. It is what is true *for a particular culture* or *tradition* or *group* of people. For those who hold to this position, there isn't really any *universal* Truth, because truth is only a function of the community that defines it.

This argument, of course, is one of the major questions raised by Systematic Theologians and philosophers, and I'm not going to solve all of its complexities here. On one hand, if nothing is *universally* True, we can't very well talk about the Christian gospel as right for every person, which, in turn, challenges the whole of Scripture. On the other hand, who *decides* what is true and what isn't true? If truth is community-related, then isn't it defined by majority opinion (which seems to be the project of the Jesus Seminar)?

How do we solve this dilemma? I suggest that *both* positions are correct, that doctrine is both *propositional* and *community-recognized.* There *is* universal Truth, yes, but it is the *community* that determines what it is, because the *community* to which we belong always focuses our faith. Indeed, early Christians sought consistency in Church doctrine by submitting themselves to one another. Heresy was understood as teaching that was contrary to what the *community* believed, and heresies were minimized when those "stray teachings" were brought under authority of the community (Priscilla and Aquila's handling of Apollos in Acts 18:24-26 is a good example).

Since the understanding of "true doctrine" in the early Christian community emerged directly from Scripture—from the First Testament writers and their contemporaries—so we, too, turn to the Bible in our quest to understand the nature of doctrine. When we do so, we find a consistent presentation through both Testaments.

THE BIBLICAL VIEW OF DOCTRINE

In the development of the biblical canon, particular *communities of faith* emerged. Rather than a single coherent "biblical" view, each of these communities comprehended, in their own way, how God dealt with His Chosen People. For instance, in the First Testament there were different theological and historic perspectives within the deuteronimistic and Chronicler communities. And it is likely that most Second Testament books, such as the Gospels, emerged from *communities* associated with that particular writer. These communities held to their own doctrinal perspectives, and each kept its own slightly different theological orientation, guided by its own "plausibility structures."

But, at the same time, these different "doctrinal communities" also maintained a consistent view on what "doctrine" is, so let's now look at what they say.

הקל

In First Testament Hebrew, the word "doctrine" is *"lequach."* It is variously translated as "instruction," "teaching," "learning," or "beliefs" (see its usage, for instance, in Deuteronomy 32:2, Job 11:4, Proverbs 4:2, and Isaiah 29:24). In all cases of its use, it does not refer to a *fixed body* of Truth. Rather, the term indicates *information* that is fluid and adaptable to a changing world. Doctrine, according to the Hebrew language and First Testament usage, is truth that is understood *through a changing community.*

Διδασκαλια

In the Greek language of the Second Testament, the word usually translated "doctrine" is *"didaskalia,"* which means "teaching" or "substance." It is used 19 times, 17 of them by the Apostle Paul. The two non-Pauline references come in Matthew 15:9 and Mark 7:7, where, in both cases, Jesus is citing Isaiah 29:13—as references to the First Testament understanding of doctrine.

Thus, the Second Testament word for "doctrine" is a Pauline one, and when we track his references, we find that he takes two approaches. First, διδασκαλια indicates beliefs that are *contrary* to his understanding of the gospel. True doctrine is something from which people *turn* in order to "hear what they want" (as in 2 Timothy 4:3). In this text, Paul is expressing concern about doctrinal problems in the local church that Timothy is serving. Those who believe or are teaching truths that are contrary to the Christian gospel are motivated by evil, which is generated by deceiving spirits, hypocrites, and liars whose "consciences are seared." The metaphor is a powerful one. *Searing* stops the flow of blood. In this case, that which stops the *continuing flow of ideas* is perceived as evil. These good Christian believers are abandoning the faith by following authoritarian leaders who do all their thinking for them. Thus, it is a *negative* view of teaching to which Paul is responding; it is what doctrine *is opposed to.*

But Paul also uses the term to identify teaching that *conforms* to the gospel (as in 1 Timothy 1:10). It refers to that which is *held in common by a local community.* In Titus 1:9, for instance, it is something that is "taught." In 1 Timothy 4:16, it is something that *belongs* to Timothy ("your" doctrine). And in Titus 2:1, he writes that the Christian should adhere to that which is in accord with *sound* doctrine, which, in this context, is *community* belief. Thus, for Paul, doctrine is foundational to the Christian's experience. But the individual is not free to determine other truth than that which is held by his or her *local community*. It is, in this sense, a *positive* perspective on doctrine.

So, in both Testaments, doctrine is the *community's* understanding and definition of truth.

This is much in keeping with contemporary thought, as well. George Lindbeck (1984), writing from a cultural-linguistic perspective, argues that doctrine is a community-generated guide to the beliefs of individuals. It brings us back to Peter Berger's (1967) "plausibility structures," as elements of truth that are identified within every community. Their purpose is to help members of that community know what is doctrinally or behaviorally *correct* (or *true*).

So we talk about different "doctrinal communities." Because of particular understandings of Scripture, doctrinal communities have emerged that center around their own "sacred" truths. Pentecostals, for instance, focus on different "truth" than Baptists do. Orthodoxy is oriented around still other "truth." Fundamentalists understand the faith differently from those in the evangelical tradition. Calvinists are different from Armenians. Southern Baptists, United Methodists, and Roman Catholics are all different, but all adhere to particular truth that is a "portion" of, and reflective of, that which is universally and biblically True.

There is one more element of doctrine that is important. Eric Eisenberg (1984) has demonstrated that the most significant doctrine, or "community-teaching," comes in *generally-worded, ambiguous* postulates rather than carefully-defined, exacting ones. It is critical to a community's *unity*. Eisenberg discovered that ambiguity in a corporate mission statement is essential to keep a "doctrinal community" together. It's the same in a church community: doctrine that is too narrowly defined often becomes divisive, because there is no room for individual interpretation.

For instance, when the phrase "born again" describes a disciple of Jesus in a local church community, it helps define membership, but only as long as the term remains somewhat ambiguous. So, for some members of that community, it means a "sinner saved by grace." For others, it refers to "regeneration." For still others it is a sign of ongoing repentance and forgiveness. And for a few (as Jesus uses the term in John 3), it identifies *religious* people who are dissatisfied with their religious practices. But when "born again" is consistently defined in the same community to refer *only* to one of these categories ("religious people who have gone astray," for instance), it can alienate other members of that community. So when a local community defines exactly what "born again" means, many members of that community who would otherwise be comfortable with the designation soon discover that the definition doesn't really reflect their own experience. So either they become spiritually isolated and remain in that community as "outsiders" or they look for a different community that defines their faith more accurately.

This is one of the great challenges for communities of faith. If there is to be cohesion and unity, doctrinal statements must be narrow enough to define the boundaries of faith but ambiguous enough to allow personal interpretation.

This is all to say that "doctrine" is a concept that reflects universal Truth (as found in the Bible), but it is narrowed in a way that specifies truth for a particular community of faith. These communities cohere around doctrine. And that community doctrine (or truth) also contributes to the individual member's private theology, which, in turn, contributes to that individual's understanding of reality. Oswald Chambers (1950), again, writes, "The business of faith is to convert truth into reality."

"BIBLE"

The third element of one's personal theology is *the Bible*, the written Scripture as the revelation of God. The Bible is a unique Book that comes both from the hand of God and the particular writers who were confined within their own contexts and cultures.

The Bible, as its words challenge and change us, must be our very Source Book for faith and practice. It guides our lives and our thinking. It gives shape to our theological perspective. It helps us interpret our experiences of life and the adopted truths of our doctrinal communities. We use it in our preaching, because we want our listeners to understand and respond to what it says. It is God's Book for us.

This is why personal devotions, Bible study groups, and legitimate continuing education in biblical studies are so important. They help our understanding of God and the world to be focused not just by our own limited experience and community, but by revealed Scripture. We also use the Bible for our preaching, and a commitment to never-ending study and growth encourages us to develop a holistic understanding of Scripture, which, in turn, yields a richer and more fully-developed text when we preach.

This commitment to a more significant understanding of and appreciation for Scripture also leads us to one more characteristic of the biblical record that is important for our developing theology and, subsequently, our preaching.

BIBLICAL TRUTH VS. BIBLICAL THEOLOGIES

The Bible demonstrates that God's truth was "made real" within the local circumstances of those to whom it was initially spoken or written. This "relevancy of truth" to a particular time and place means that biblical truth was *localized* or *contextualized.* But the truth was also related through the *theologies* of the writers, and those *personal* understandings of God's interaction in the world are also evident in the biblical record.

For example, in Philippians 3:12 (as we saw in the last chapter), Paul suggests that life experiences are "added" to our growth. As we take them on, each experience helps to "perfect" us as we grow more toward fullness in Jesus Christ. But that's not the only biblical perspective on how we grow. There are other passages, such as Isaiah 48:10 and 1 Peter 1:6-7, that indicate that our lives undergo a process of *refining*, like gold or silver which is purified by fire. This theology "subtracts" imperfections in our lives. These are two different theological approaches to the salvation process. Both are "true," but they present quite different *"theologies"* expressed by different biblical writers.

Or notice what Peter preaches to Cornelius. He says that Jesus is a person who was obedient to God, so God *appointed* him to be Messiah (Acts 10:42), similar to his sermon in Acts 2:36. But for John, Jesus is *pre-existently divine* and comes to earth to fulfill his purpose (John 1:1f, 13:3, etc.). These are opposing theologies of Jesus even though they are both biblically "true."

I am suggesting, then, that the Bible has many "theologies," all of which are *truthful,* but very clearly different. So, then, what is *truth* in the Bible and what is *theology*? And how can we know?

I perceive the difference in this way. There is a *broad category* of truth that could be considered "universal Truth." Theology, though, is only a *personal understanding* of that universal Truth. In the Bible, God has revealed Truth to and through finite writers who had to make sense of it in their own way (thus, through their own *theologies).* It means that when we are reading the biblical writers, sometimes we must "move up a level" in our understanding of Scripture, to get *behind* or *above* what the writer is saying so that we can arrive at the more general Truth.

In the first example above, for instance, the Truth is that *Christians are called to be perfect* (Matthew 5:48). That perfection, while never realized on this earth, implies life-long growth. That *truth,* in turn, is reflected through the *theologies* of these two biblical writers: either our life experiences *add to* that perfection, or our negative experiences are *subtracted from* that perfection. The *truth* is that we grow in our discipleship; the two *theologies* offer options for how we understand it.

In the second example, the Truth is that *Jesus' purpose was the salvation of the world.* Peter and John have different understandings of how that happened: Peter's *theology* suggests that Jesus was appointed *after* he got here, John's that he was appointed *before* he got here. Neither is right or wrong—both are merely *reflecting* what they know to be true, that Jesus is Savior.

Let's look at one more example. What would you say is our basic nature: are we *good* or *bad?* And, subsequently, what is our natural destiny when we leave the earth? These are questions with at least three "theological" solutions in Scripture.

The first is that our basic nature is *neutral:* we are either good or bad. But it really doesn't matter, because it is our *sin* that ultimately condemns us. In Romans 2:1-16, for instance, Paul implies that God is a Judge Who deals justly with our sin. Because He is a holy God, He is forced to condemn us when we leave this life. Jesus, though, through his death and resurrection, *rescues* us from the wrath of God (Romans 3:21-26). He died with our sin. He "paid the price" for us. He took our place. And he provides an escape from judgment for us: when we believe in Jesus as Savior and Lord, we are saved (Romans 10:9-10).

But there's another "theology" of salvation in the Second Testament, one that suggests that human nature is basically *good.* It comes in the idea of "ransom" (as in Mark 10:45 and 1 Timothy 2:6). A "ransom" is offered for a person who has been kidnapped. The image is of a person who was "at home" at one time, but then was led (or stolen) away (by the devil or the world). When Jesus *ransoms* us through his death, he pays off the kidnapper and we are brought *back home.* Given this metaphor, we were "at home" to begin with (thus, part of God's family), and through no fault of our own, we were stolen away. But Jesus, through the cross, died to *redeem* us. We were not bad people—it was not *our* sin that got us kidnapped—it was somebody else's fault. But when we trust Jesus to ransom us, we are brought back home.

But there's yet another "theology" of the human predicament in Scripture. It suggests that, by nature, we are *bad.* We are automatically *destined* to end up in hell, because we are naturally self-centered rather than God-centered. When Jesus saves us, he comes to snatch us out of that involuntary spiraling plunge into hell (as seen in Luke 8:12, John 3:16, Romans 5:9-10, 1 Corinthians 1:18, 2 Corinthians 2:15, Ephesians 2:5, and 2 Thessalonians 2:10). Here, we are not brought *back* home, but, rather, we are brought to a *new position* in life, where we now live *toward God.* This theology, too, is evident in Scripture. Salvation is a glorious experience of rescue from our evil nature.

Which is right? They *all* are, of course. They are simply different ways of understanding the inexplicable truth that a loving Creator God wants to "save" His people. Each of these theologies helps relate salvation to different people in different circumstances under different conditions at different times.

And this leads me to one more observation about the theologies of biblical writers. It is that of *relevance.* There is value in recognizing different theologies, because different truths may be applicable to different situations to which you are preaching. That's why it is important that you *continue* to study the Bible's text, social environment, and history, and learn more and more about what its words would have meant to its original readers or hearers. These theologies of the writers, lying within a divinely-inspired text, continually temper and shape our own doctrinal positions. This enables you to preach a message of the *lostness* of humanity to one audience, and *ransom* to another; why you can preach *predestination* to one difficult problem faced by your listeners and *free will* to another group in different circumstances.

However, the ability to *recognize* the difference between truth and theology in the Bible is a function of your own maturing discipleship and emerging theology. Consistency in biblical interpretation comes only through serious study and reflection and a long acquaintance with Scripture and with Jesus. Your *understanding* of the Bible will grow as your *knowledge of* and *experience with* Scripture grows. The more biblical information you discover, the more your view of Scripture will be expanded and broadened. And that growing perspective will account for a greater number of observations about God's interaction in your life and world, and, thus, will contribute significantly to your growing, emerging personal theology.

If nothing else, we should remain open in our perceptions of how God interacts with our world and in what the Bible teaches. Problems arise when we declare that a *theological* position in Scripture is the *only* truth there is.

THE EMERGENCE OF THE PREACHER'S THEOLOGY

These three components influence your perception of God and His interaction in the world (what I am defining as your view of *reality*). But these three dynamics aren't isolated from each other. Far from it. In fact, as I've shown in the diagram in Figure 9.1, it is their *interaction* and mutual *influence* that shape and develop your personal theology. What I mean is that the more integrated your Existentia, Doctrine, and Bible become, the more consistent will be your understanding of reality (your Theology).

Further, when these components interact with each other, friction may begin to emerge between them. That can be good, because the friction brings about change, and this change leads to greater consistency in your personal theology. Let's then look at a few examples of how these components interact.

DOCTRINE AND BIBLE

The community's *doctrine* and the *Bible* frequently lead to tension. That is, there may be conflict between what the Bible says and what the community teaches. Serious Bible study can challenge sacred beliefs.

For instance, let's observe how suffering is understood in two different areas of the world (an issue with profound consequences today). In Latin America, evangelical Christians have faced suffering and injustice for many years. "Principalities and powers" have included political oppression, persecution from other religious groups, and economic upheaval. How have these believers responded? That is, what is "truth" for them? Through their own study of Scripture, they have recognized that these injustices arise *from the world,* from *Satan,* and from *human sin.* Suffering, as a tool of the Devil, must be overcome, because political, economic, social, and personal liberation comes only in Jesus, who leads them to fight against these injustices. Because of this approach, they have developed a "theology of liberation" which encourages them to seek out and conquer those abuses of human rights.

In Eastern Europe, on the other hand, evangelical Christians have had the same experience of suffering and injustice. "Principalities and powers" have included political oppression, persecution from other religious groups, and economic upheaval. How have these believers responded? That is, what is "truth" for them? From their own study of Scripture, they have recognized that these injustices come from the *hand of God.* Suffering is important in that it helps Christians grow and mature in their faith, and these believers who live in nations under former communist regimes have learned to *welcome* suffering as a sign of faithfulness. After all, personal liberation comes in Jesus, who frees them existentially from the restrictions and bondage of this world. Because of this approach, they have developed a "theology of acceptance" or "theology of survival." In Eastern Europe, a new "Suffering God" theology is just now emerging. Suffering is *welcomed* as a tool of God for the perfecting of the saints, because liberation comes only in one's personal relationship with Jesus Christ.

Now, when we bring the Bible to bear on these different doctrinal positions in Latin American and Eastern Europe, what do we find? Well, we see in Luke 4:18-21 that Jesus, reading from the Isaiah scroll, clearly states that his mission is to proclaim *release* from suffering and injustice. And in Acts 12:5-11, Peter is *released* from prison because believers were praying for it. These references lead us toward a *Liberation Theology,* like the Christians in Latin America.

But we also note in the "beatitudes of Luke" (Luke 6:20-26) that Jesus calls the poor "blessed," an indication that poverty is to be welcomed. And Peter writes that Jesus suffered *to set an example* for his followers (1 Peter 2:20-21). These references lead us toward a *Suffering God Theology* like that of Eastern European Christians.

When we take into account the "whole counsel of God in the whole of Scripture," the Eastern European view is broadened by Jesus' citation of Isaiah that suffering should *not* be perceived as "normative," but is to be rejected. And they can learn from Peter's *release* from prison that such liberation is important. On the other hand, Christians in Latin America will take into account Jesus' suffering (1 Peter 2:20-21) and the value of poverty (Luke 6:20) as biblical contributions to their doctrinal position. Each of these communities of faith can grow in their "existential" perspective by bringing it into contact with Scripture.

Deeper biblical studies will lead to a broader understanding of the doctrinal views of any community, views that must be balanced with those of other communities. The more we learn about the Bible and from the Bible, the more it challenges our "too-neat" doctrinal positions and well-considered faith systems.

DOCTRINE AND EXISTENTIA

The same kind of interrelated experience emerges between Doctrine and Existentia, where community standards (Doctrine) help the individual Christian interpret different experiences of life, how to *respond* to life, and how to understand God's relationship with His people (Existentia).

For instance, suppose you were raised in a home and church that teaches predestination. You lost a child to an accident. The doctrinal base of the community helps you understand that experience, that God is somehow responsible for the death of your child. Everything that happens in your life is a result of God's loving hand. So you must try to reason out why He would do such a thing. With help from the community, you would arrive at satisfactory answers.

But if you were raised in a free-will community, you learn that these kinds of problems arise from a complex but well-ordered universe that is filled with human nature and self-centeredness, and that God doesn't bring calamity upon His people, nor does He control everything. But He loves every single person in the world. Jesus showed us that, and he suffers with us. The "doctrine" of this community would cause you to understand things differently.

Of course, because every community is made up of people, when a member of a community *rejects* the community's doctrinal position, it can also lead to change in that community's understanding of the faith. Thus, the influence can be mutual.

So Existentia is interpreted by Doctrine and Doctrine by Existentia. By living in community, the individual learns how to understand and respond to personal experiences through these community standards.

EXISTENTIA AND THE BIBLE

The Bible also helps individuals understand their experiences in life.

Unfortunately, it is most natural that our personal theology begins with Existentia, and then we go to Scripture to prove it. We have all had experiences where we've sought out Scripture to back up what we believe.

It is important, however, that we not simply turn to the Bible to *support* an already-arrived at position, but that we come to the Bible and let it speak freshly to us in all its confrontational, life-changing power. Only when that happens will the Scripture adequately "conform us" to the will of God. This influence of the Bible on our Existentia is the purpose of biblical preaching: it applies Scripture to everyday life, helping people understand and *interpret* their lives in the light of biblical truth. But this same impact happens through personal study of the Bible, and we should always be encouraging this process.

Here is a young woman, for instance, who was raised by a cruel father. She learns from the Bible that God is *not* like that after all. Indeed, the God of Scripture is a loving and kind Father. That image of God Who is like a Father helps her understand her own *human* father's imperfection and sin. It challenges her easy notion that God is like her earthly father by suggesting that her earthly father is only a poor imitation of the God Who is revealed in Scripture. Were her father perfect, he would have been reflecting the love of God in his relationships with family members. So the Bible challenges and informs an uncomfortable existential experience, which, in turn, can even lead to forgiveness and healing.

The Bible is one of the most potent spiritual influences we Christians have to challenge and change our understanding of experience. But you, and I, must learn to read it with open hearts if it is to adequately "read us."

THE RESULTANT THEOLOGY

These three components of Existentia, Doctrine, and the Bible, then, interact to fashion your *personal Theology*. The heart of theological maturity comes as these three circles move closer together. As that happens, your personal *Theology* becomes more and more coherent. That's why continual growth is so critical. Only when your *Theology* is constantly being renewed and adjusted will you discover fresh insights for your life and captivating preaching for your listeners.

We come, finally then, to look at some implications of your personal theology for your preaching ministry.

IMPLICATIONS FOR PREACHING

Incarnational preaching suggests that *what* you preach is always more than what the Scripture says. After all, *you* are fashioning the "word of God" in this preaching event. So a consistent and thoughtful theology is important, one that naturally incorporates your current knowledge, biblical awareness, and personal experience. The foregoing examination of *Existentia, Doctrine,* and the *Bible,* and the subsequent *Theology* that emerges from their interaction, are extremely important for your preaching ministry. It will influence your preaching in at least the following three major ways.

1. AS A PREACHER, YOU ARE UNIQUE

Incarnational preaching is predicated upon your uniqueness as a preacher. There is no one else in all the world's history who has been, or is, just like you. No one has emerged from the same environment as you. Because of your own very privatized experiences and community relationships and understanding of Scripture, no one else, past or present, has the same theological perspective that you have.

Along with your "anointed" call, you bring your own theological perspective into the pulpit, like it or not. It has been fashioned both from what you could not control (your parents, upbringing, and many of your own experiences) and also from your experiences, training, and relationships over which you have had some amount of control. Your theology has to do with your creativity and understanding of Scripture; it is completely dependent on who you are, what you have experienced and continue to experience, and where you came from. Your on-going study of Scripture, your observations of life and understanding of your relationships, and your increasing awareness and evaluation of your community's Doctrine continue to *perfect* your understanding of how God relates to you and your world.

But your perspective is also *limited* by your experiences, the doctrinal communities that have influenced you, your acquaintance with Scripture, and your own finite mind. You may seek doctrinal purity, but you'll be frustrated—it is, in many ways, an exercise in futility. After all, your knowledge, perception of reality, and worldview (all that makes up your theology) have been *rhetorically constructed* from the environment in which you were raised, and *continuing* experiences and reading and discussions and observations are also rhetorical constructions that *continue* to contribute to your growing understanding of life and God's ways.

2. YOUR THEOLOGY HELPS LOCATE BIBLICAL TRUTH

Your privatized theological perspective also determines how you approach and preach every sermon. Preaching, after all, is the proclamation of biblical truth through a particular preacher. It is a *personal* business from which you cannot escape: who you are and what you believe and the Holy

Spirit's influence in your life *process* the truth of Scripture that is embedded in the theology of the biblical writers. Seek balance, but, above all, celebrate your uniqueness! If God has called *you* to preach, don't minimize what *you* bring to the preaching event. After all, *how* you preach a particular passage of Scripture is dependent on everything you are.

When you come to a particular passage of Scripture, it is your emerging theology that helps you recognize, understand, and frame biblical truth for preaching. So when you come to a text, it is *your theology* that enables you to recognize what is "preachable" from that text. That's why a different preacher (of greater or lesser theological maturity) will identify a different preaching truth from the same text you're using. It's important to understand the important role that your own theology has on your preaching, even though truth and theology are not easily separable.

How do you keep from preaching your own theology rather than biblical truth? Well, you can't easily know, but remember that false and true prophets are known by their fruit. Oswald Chambers (1950) provides a helpful insight:

> *If a man is talking the truth of God, those who listen will meet it again whether they like it or not; if he is not talking God's truth they won't come across it any more. Whenever the grand simple sanity of the Holy Spirit's interpretation is wanting, hold the matter in abeyance. The one stamp of the right interpretation is its "warm" natural sanity; it is not fantastic or peculiar, it doesn't twist your brain, it makes you feel, How marvelously simple and beautiful that is!*

This is helpful. The truth you preach should be rational, understandable, and natural—not strange. It is a truth that should be understandable by a "baptized" reason, and it should be demonstrated in other texts. It will thus be proclaimed elsewhere in Scripture and heard again by your listeners. But if it is a "strange" doctrine, you won't come across it again and your people won't hear it again.

3. YOUR THEOLOGY CONTINUES TO DEVELOP

In order to maintain a consistent theological perspective, you will want to keep developing an integrated biblical perspective on God and His interaction with life in this world. It calls for an ongoing study of the Bible, reflecting on your personal history and experiences and personality in light of the gospel of Jesus Christ, and comprehending the ways your doctrinal community understands and practices its faith. It is a continually developing process. And whether you have no training or have completed significant formal theological education, you still have much to learn and a great deal of growing to do. Your spiritual formation has emerged from the tools and experiences of life and your ministry and all of your past, but it continues to emerge as it becomes perfected. But will it continue to grow and be stretched through resiliency and freshness, or will you encase yourself in a protective theology that will become encrusted over time? Your education is never "completed" nor your spiritual life "perfected."

So preach your *convictions* and *affirmations,* not your doubts. You are a growing Christian, and what you know and understand next year will be more broadly-based than your understanding right now. The next time you preach *this* text, you come with a different theology to a different situation, because you continue to grow in a balanced understanding of how God interacts with the world. It doesn't mean that you'll just stop preaching because you aren't yet perfect. Rather, keep on preaching by *affirming* what you *do* believe right now, in the best understanding you have of your faith and the Bible.

And because your theology changes with new experiences, continuing theological education is critical. Take advantage of *taught* courses, seminars, and discussion groups, because through *formal* experiences, your theological bias is challenged from an external source—something you can't experience in the same way when you rely only on your own insights. Increasing biblical and doctrinal information, and different experiences in life, will mature your understanding of God's interaction with the world. After all, a continually-developing theological perspective will more satisfactorily respond to the questions of increasingly-sophisticated church members. That's why it's important that you keep studying and growing in your theological awareness.

If you are growing as you should, your theology becomes more consistent and better able to account for more experiences of life. Existentia, Doctrine, and your biblical understanding will come more into balance. For the rest of your life, continue to develop a consistent and thoughtful theology. It needs to be biblical and doctrinally correct for this community, and "comfortable" for your own growth as a Christian. Your theology of tomorrow emerges from your theology of today.

Ultimately, you must preach what *makes sense* to you. Your theology is a way to understand God's Self-revelation and His interaction in the world. Your preaching task is to present a biblical vision of God's revelation and to call your listeners to conform to this *truth-ful* word from God. To do that, you want to present a consistent and coherent theology, one that is continuing to develop, that takes into account more and more of the things you are learning and experiencing, and your growing understanding of Scripture.

Section II:
The Content of the Sermon

We turn our attention now to the *content* of the sermon. As with Section I on *Transaction,* there are also two parts to Section II. The first (Part A) is a presentation of what I mean by *biblical* preaching. This portion contains six chapters (10 to 15) that provide the main biblical material in the sermon. Part B has two chapters (16 and 17) that discuss the importance of narrative and story forms in preaching.

Section II:
Part A:
Biblical Content of the Sermon

As we turn our attention to the sermon itself and its biblical content, there are several issues we face. *Biblical preaching,* as I understand it and will explain it, is proclamation focused on a single biblical truth drawn from a single biblical text. In this Part, we will look at four simple steps in getting to a specific preaching thesis (including a chapter that encourages us to preach to the needs of our listeners). But before we look at those five chapters, we will study the concept of biblical authority, which is foundational to the preaching task.

CHAPTER 10
Biblical Authority
for Biblical Preaching

FOUNDATIONS OF BIBLICAL AUTHORITY

When I visited a pastor's conference in the Philippines in the winter of 2001, one of the keynote preachers read a biblical text and then preached for 45 minutes without reference to it. It wasn't until his last sentence that he finally made mention of the text he had chosen.

Early in my pastoral ministry, I was invited to attend a *Basic Youth Conflicts* seminar. Day after day, Bill Gothard "proved" his approach to youth issues by citing Bible verse after Bible verse, using an overwhelming amount of proof-texting to support his views. His compilation was not biblical, though it certainly sounded like it.

We have all heard sermons like these—those that hardly refer to the Bible at all and those that include biblical references in every breath. Unfortunately, both extremes badly abuse the Bible, and both present problems for preaching. When the Bible becomes whatever its user wants it to be, it loses its power. Indeed, the Bible is the Book of the kingdom and is foundational for us as preachers, but only when we let its own truth speak to us and through us.

More to the point, we should not be as interested in reading the Bible as in allowing the Bible to read us. Only then does its truth penetrate the depths of our souls. Only then is the Holy Spirit able to change us from the inside out.

This happens when Scripture is read privately, of course. It also happens in preaching, but not when we bombard our listeners with a barrage of Scripture—that only serves to bore and confuse them. But a single biblical truth drawn from a single text has the ability to penetrate the mind and heart of the listener. When the Bible is treated so that a single living truth is proclaimed with authority, that truth becomes invasive and confrontative and inspiring and the Holy Spirit goes to work.

Thus, along with the authority of the preacher (which we've only briefly mentioned earlier), we come now to talk more fully about the authority of the *Bible* in the preaching task. Transformational preaching brings these two powerful structures together, and when they are united, they lead to a potent pulpit ministry.

HOW WE ACCEPT THE BIBLE

As we begin to talk about the authority of the Bible, there are a few important questions that will help you sort out your view of Scripture. Your response to these issues will not only reveal how you accept and understand the Bible for your own life, but also how you use it for your preaching.

1.   What *is* the Bible? Are the *individual* books as important as the *collection?* Do you see value in what a *particular* author and book has to say, or does the individual writer only have significance in light of the *whole?* That is, do you accept both biblical *and* systematic theology, or only systematic theology?

2.   Similarly, to what extent are the writers "present" in the text of Scripture? That is, do you accept the influence and evidence of both human and divine authorship? And is the human presence visible in *all* of the Bible or only parts of it?

3.   Is the Bible to be *revered,* honored, and put on display as a *Holy Book?* Or does its value come only when we *use* it in a very practical way, as a *handbook* for living?

4.   What is the *main intent* of the biblical message? Is it for salvation? Or love? Or judgment?

5.   Has the Bible been inspired, written and transmitted primarily for the use of those in the *kingdom,* or are its principles of life meant for *everybody* in the world, even those who don't accept it? That is, should biblical truth be imposed on secular society and governments?

6.   Must the "word of God" have a context, or does it exist quite apart from any relevancy to life in our world? That is, must we deal with the contexts in which biblical truth was first revealed, or were the original circumstances unimportant?

7.   Similarly, does *genre* make a difference in what truth is and how it is communicated? Does the "literature nest" in which we discover biblical truth really matter?

8.   Is the Bible a Book in which we *find* the "word of God," or *is* it the written "word of God"? Are we more inclined to accept a "ghostly" Scripture that we don't really have *(Scripture* is really "above" the text), or do we accept and trust what we actually have?

9.   In the same way, when we come across periodic "contradictions" in Scripture, would they be completely clarified if we had a *perfect* or *ideal* version of the Bible? If so, are these contradictions in the original *manuscripts,* or are they only present because of inadequate *transmission* or *translation?*

10. Is the Bible inspired for *factual data and historical accuracy,* only for *truth,* or *both?*

How you answer these questions, and others like them, will influence how you approach and work with Scripture in your preaching. They relate to issues of biblical *inspiration* but also to biblical *authority,* which are two distinct areas of study. I have not included a chapter specifically on inspiration in this work (and am assuming that the reader has already settled that issue in some way), it is the subject of biblical authority that has more relevancy to our preaching, and it is that subject that now occupies our attention.

When we talk about the authority of Scripture, we are brought face to face with two very important theories, those of *inerrancy* and *infallibility.* As we consider these human-generated theoretical positions, they, in turn, force us to wrestle with some of the questions we've just examined.

THE INERRANCY PROBLEM

Inerrancy is a term that has been used widely in recent years, generally as a code word that helps identify "true believers." However, because it has been applied in so many ways and is loaded with so many different meanings, it should be carefully defined.

In *popular* usage, "inerrancy" is an attempt to understand the holiness of the Bible. Those who hold to this position usually mean that the Bible is *factually and literally true* and *without error.* Inerrancy, however, at its core, is the belief that the Bible is free from error *in the autograph copies* of Scripture. By *autograph copies,* we mean the "first draft copies," or the "originals," of the biblical writers. These are the books or letters that the authors first wrote in their own handwriting, none of which has ever been found (of any book or letter of the Bible).

Martin E. Marty (1981), perhaps tongue in cheek, explains the roots of the inerrancy theory. It began in the 19th century when a British theologian came to America with a new idea. He claimed that God is a God Who takes risks and Whose divine nature and character are "inherently" present in the Bible. An orthodox theologian from Princeton Seminary (the guardian of conservative Christianity of the day) heard the Englishman speak of this "inherent" word of God, but he heard it as the *"inerrant"* word of God (the English drop their "h" sound from time to time). As a result, the term *inerrant* became a new way for conservative Christians to define Scripture.

The initial meaning of inerrancy given by this British theologian, then, was that the Bible was *inherently immersed* with the divine character of God. But because of inaccurate hearing, the term took on a life of its own, referring to the absolute, *literal* acceptance of Scripture. Today, "inerrancy" is a sword wielded by Christian fundamentalists. It has become a watchword by which they root out heresy (and, often, legitimate Christian discipleship), and a standard by which they decide whether *somebody else's* faith is pure or acceptable. They are well-meaning, but they use inerrancy to coerce doctrinal statements from their brothers and sisters, and, thus, committed disciples of Jesus are forced to believe what someone else *wants* them to believe. In its wake, inerrancy has become a divisive rather than helpful term.

But *inerrancy* is a concept that is not generally understood by those who profess it. It is a not a *biblical* word (it is not found in the Bible), but, more importantly, it argues a theoretical position that doesn't accurately represent the character or reality of the Bible. It puts theological constraints on a living Scripture. There are those who use this term broadly to mean that the Bible is inspired and authoritative (a posture that is clearly in keeping with evangelical Christian faith), but the correct meaning of inerrancy, that only the *original manuscripts* were without error, is where the term (and the concept) has difficulty.

If we take its root meaning, there are at least six fallacies of the *inerrancy theory.*

1. An unprovable argument

First, *inerrancy* is an argument from silence. There are no original manuscripts, so we can say anything we want about them. I *could,* for instance, argue convincingly that *no* original manuscript was written in human handwriting, or that all "autograph copies," without exception, are filled with misspellings, crossed-out words, insertions, and incorrect grammar. I *could* argue that each manuscript was written in a mysterious, unknown *language* that was completely unique to that single book or letter, but then was translated into Hebrew, Aramaic, or Greek. The problem with these positions is that we have no way to prove or disprove them. We have no basis upon which to accept these arguments because we have no autograph copies to examine.

In the same way, just because the theory of inerrancy *sounds* good, that doesn't make it different from the arguments I've just offered. There are no manuscripts to back up the theory.

2. Which Bible?

Second, in the early years of the Christian Church, there were different Christian traditions that emerged (primarily at Rome and Constantinople). Each held its own books as sacred and canonical. Many Christian denominations in the world, even today, accept the *Apocryphal* books as part of their tradition (these *Intertestamental* books are tucked away between the First and Second Testaments).

There were also other letters and books in the early Church. Along with the 27 books we currently have in our Second Testament, the earliest Christians had other manuscripts for their use, such as the "Shepherd of Hermas," "First Clement," and Paul's "Epistle to Laodicea" (mentioned in Colossians 4:16). When the Second Testament canon was finally adopted (late in the 4th century), one of the principles of accepting a book was that churches were actually using it.

The question then is, "Which books should be included in the *true* biblical canon?" Does "without error" refer only to those books that are in *our* current Bible? What about the books that are accepted as canonical by Roman Catholicism and Eastern Orthodoxy? What about early Christian letters that dropped out of use? If we only count those books that the *inerrantist* identifies as canonical, which inerrantist do we trust? And who decides who is right?

I am not arguing that we should include or exclude any book. What I am suggesting is that there is no agreement about which books *should* be included in the biblical canon. Even Martin Luther questioned the validity of James, Jude, Hebrews, and Revelation. The question we must ask of the inerrantists, then, is what books are without error?

3. Earliest manuscript

Third, if we promote the *autograph copies* as the only significant edition of the Bible (as the *inerrantist* does), then we must suppose that what was written in those earliest manuscripts is *all* that should be included in our authoritative Scripture. But it is clear that the story of Jesus and the adulteress (John 7:51-8:11) is *not* in the earliest manuscripts. And the saying of Jesus reported by Paul in Acts 20:35 is nowhere in the original Gospel accounts. The woman taken in adultery is a story that was probably circulated and included by a later editor; Paul includes the non-Gospel quote of Jesus, which came to him from somewhere outside the Gospel tradition. Should we then omit these references just because they were not in the "autograph copies" of the original writers or speakers? We would lose an important story and saying of Jesus were we to settle only on the *autograph copies* as authoritative.

4. Translation

Fourth, the translation of Hebrew, Aramaic, and Greek into English and other contemporary languages raises problems. Is it erroneous, for example, for a translator to choose one wording over another? *Translation* can never be done on a one-to-one basis, so which translation is *inerrant?*

In a few cases, different *translations* provide contradictory messages. For instance, the Hebrew word אף *(aph)* can be translated as *but* or *and,* which, in turn, can lead to very different understandings. The NRSV, for instance, translates the words of the Bride in the *Song of Solomon* 1:5, "I am black *and* beautiful," while the NASB translates it, "I am black, *but* beautiful." The first rendering suggests that black and beautiful are naturally-paired terms, that *black is beautiful.* The other suggests a more racist view that blacks are ordinarily *not* beautiful, but in this case, she definitely is! Who is to decide which one is the *inerrant* translation?

On the other hand, if inerrancy only deals with the original (autograph) manuscripts, it also must be concerned with original *languages* and not a translation. This is problematic for the inerrancy theory, because many arguments arise from *translations* rather than the original languages.

5. Not our Bible

Fifth, and perhaps most significantly, inerrancy teaches that the autograph copies are the only legitimate Scripture we have because they are the only documents without error. That means that the Bible *as we have it* is not authoritative. It can be dismissed as "inaccurate" or "corrupted," leaving the *individual* interpreter as the authority who determines which parts of the Bible are to be accepted and which rejected. And this posture ultimately leaves us without any written authority.

6. The meaning of "error"

Finally, we must define the meaning of "without error." Does it, in fact, mean that there are *no mistakes?* How do we accept Second Testament references like Mark 1:2-3 where the author clearly states that he is quoting "Isaiah" (the term "prophets" is a later addition), but he then includes *Malachi 3:1.* Do we consider that an "error"?

Or does, perhaps, the idea refer to *mistakes* in the actual *handwriting* or *grammar* of the autograph copies? If the Apostle Paul (or one of his scribes, like Tertius, for instance [Romans 16:22]) chose an inaccurate word at one point and scratched it out to fix his mistake, or if he blackened out a certain letter because he realized he had misspelled a word, would that constitute an error?

Or does "error" mean that *no editing* could have taken place? For instance, the writing of the Pentateuch is attributed to Moses. But Moses may not have been able to write *anything* in Hebrew, just because that language was still in its infancy (in its written form, at least). The earliest Hebrew writing that scholars know about comes in the *Song of Deborah* (Judges 5), dated at about 1250, just about the time of Moses. Certainly no one would have been able to *read* the language. In the oral culture of early biblical times, what would have been the point of writing it all down? The question is whether or not Moses had to have actually *written every word* of the Pentateuch for it to be "without error." Or, if the "original document" was, indeed, written down later (by oral tradition and editing), would the inerrantist accept that *edited* version of the orally-produced text? It would have been the "autograph" copy, and, thus, appropriate for the definition.

Or perhaps "without error" means that there are *no contradictions* in the text. But what does "contradiction" mean? For instance, did Jesus contradict himself when he said, "Whoever is not against you is for you" (Luke 9:50), and, in the same Gospel, "He who is not with me is against me?" (Luke 11:23)? These are two distinct sayings that are quite different (and contradictory). Of course, we can understand them as having been spoken in different contexts and meant for different circumstances, but the inerrantist cannot allow for contextualization of Scripture, because that implies different truth for different occasions.

Or what about the inclusion of the book of *Ruth* in the First Testament canon? It is clear from Deuteronomy 23:3 that no Moabite may enter the assembly of the Lord "through the tenth generation." And Nehemiah says that no Moabite should ever be admitted to the assembly of God (Nehemiah 13:1). Is it a contradiction, then, that *Ruth's* book, herself a Moabitess, is included in the First Testament canon? (Even more significant is the listing of her name in Matthew's account of the lineage of Jesus [Matthew 1:5].)

And there are accounts of the same story that clearly present contradictory information, as in 2 Samuel 24:1, where it is *God* Who directs David to take the census, while in 1 Chronicles 21:1, it is *Satan*. And the Synoptic cleansing of the Temple comes at *end* of Jesus' ministry (Matthew 21:12-13; Mark 11:15-18; Luke 19:45-48), while John puts it at the *beginning* (John 2:13-16). And in 1 Kings 15:1-8, we find a very different characterization of Abijah than we do in 2 Chronicles 13:1 – 14:1. The accounts cannot be harmonized, unless we recognize that they are two different historical or theological perspectives given by two different traditions (the deuteronomistic and the Chronicler's), each of which has its own unique historical perspective. When we try to *harmonize* the accounts, we destroy the integrity of the texts.

And, of course, John's account of Jesus' death takes place on the Day of Passover *Preparation* (John 18:28, 19:14, and 19:42), a day *earlier* than the Synoptic view (see, for instance, Mark 14:12 and 15:42). An inerrantist cannot manage this tension with any satisfaction.

It is clear that the best manuscripts we have *do* contain "contradictions" (by inerrantist standards), and there is nothing to suggest that an "autograph" copy wouldn't contain the same problems.

Perhaps, though, inerrancy doesn't mean *factual* or *textual* "contradiction" after all. Perhaps it means that there is no *doctrinal* error. And when we come to this realization, we return to the understanding that doctrine is about *truth.* Now we have come to a very different position from that of inerrancy. Now we are talking about *infallibility* (which we'll look at shortly).

When we talk about doctrinal truth, we also remember that the *community* identifies what is doctrinally "true" for its own members (as we saw in our discussion of "plausibility structures" on page 139). Is speaking in tongues, for instance, a legitimate spiritual gift in the contemporary church (1 Corinthians 12:10 and 14:27)? Some communities of faith agree that it is, without question. But other communities believe equally strongly that its manifestation has ended (1 Corinthians 13:8). The "right" *(truthful)* answer depends on the particular community from which you come. This implies that different communities have different "truths," a position which is untenable for the inerrantists. (We might, of course, claim that "right" doctrine is only that which conforms to either the Apostles' or Nicene creeds, but one of those creeds makes no mention of the Holy Spirit, the other no mention of the Bible.)

I do not raise these questions because I am trying to disprove the Bible. Nor I am arguing against the sanctity, inspiration, or authority of our Scripture. Far from it! I honor the Bible as the *only* inspired and authoritative Scripture that comes from the very breath of God. What I *am* suggesting is that a rigid *inerrantist* theology leads to difficulties with *the text as we have it,* and we should look elsewhere for a theory that more adequately *reflects* what we actually have in the Bible that we read and from which we preach. Indeed, the problem is not with *doctrine* or the *text,* but with the *theory.* Can we not find a theory that accounts for all these differences without destroying the sanctity and integrity of the Bible that has been so painstakingly preserved for us?

My position is that the *whole written Scripture,* as generated and transmitted by the Holy Spirit, working through fallible human beings, *is* the inspired and authoritative written word of God. We have no other. If we are to be serious and intentional about our discipleship, we must use the text we have. *The Bible as we have received it* has been preserved and transmitted by the Holy Spirit. *The Bible as we have received it* is the Book through which God speaks to us. *The Bible as we have received it* is the only authoritative document for our preaching. If we are not committed to the authority of the text *as we have it,* we can never be certain that the truth we proclaim is, in reality, the word of God.

Thus, by rejecting the inerrancy theory, I am not rejecting the authority of Scripture. I am simply arguing that the *theory* is faulty. Actually, most of those who use this term may, in fact, mean something else by it. It is probable that they mean that the Bible is *infallible,* and we turn to that more-adequate theoretical posture now.

INFALLIBILITY AND AUTHORITY

This second term, *infallibility,* is often thought to be synonymous with "inerrancy," but there are at least two differences between them. First, infallibility is properly used of the *transmitted* rather than autographed text. Second, infallibility deals with *truth* rather than facts.

Infallibility, then, is the belief that the Bible *as we have it is incapable of error in its communication of truth.* It upholds the integrity of the Bible we hold in our hands, with all of its different theologies, "humanness," and marvelous breadth of literature.

Further, while *inerrancy* is mistakenly based on errorless *facts* and *text,* infallibility rightly rests on errorless *truth.* It affirms that there is *nothing* in our Bible that relates a contradictory or mistaken *truth,* in any possible way. We can utterly trust the dependability and trustworthiness of the Bible in its communication of spiritual truth.

That's why an infallible Scripture is essential to transformational, biblical preaching. The received Bible, as the written word of God, is the very foundation upon which our preaching is based. Scripture is trustworthy and stable as a communicator of God's truth. Truth, ultimately, has its origin with God, and the Bible, in its entirety, is our only inspired and authoritative resource for that truth.

This posture also means that we don't accept certain parts of the canon as *more* authoritative than other parts. *Red letter* editions of the Bible (where the words of Jesus are printed in red) or the custom of standing to read the Gospel lesson in worship, are rhetorical actions that indicate a preference for the words of Jesus and the Gospels as somehow "more authoritative" than other portions of Scripture. Paul writes, for instance, in 1 Corinthians 7:10 that the advice he gives is really not his, but the *Lord's.* Does that claim make this verse *more authoritative* than what he says two verses later, where he writes that his advice is only *his* and *not* the Lord's? Of course not! To say so suggests that certain portions of the Bible are "more inspired" and/or "more authoritative" for our preaching than other portions. Yes, some Scripture may be more *useful* or *usable* for preaching, but that does not deny the *authority* of those less-helpful *preaching* texts.

Either the whole Bible is inspired or none of it is—we can't play guessing games about it. When we start to do that, we disempower the authority of Scripture for preaching, because we are then never really *sure* if we are speaking an authoritative word from the Lord.

AUTHORITY IN A CLOSED CANON

Frank McConnell (1986) argues that the Bible is a self-contained witness about itself, and its *self-reference* gives the Bible its own authoritative stance. Northrop Frye (1982) adds that the two Testaments act as twin mirrors that reflect each other (the First looking ahead to the Second, and the Second finding fulfillment in the First), making the entire biblical canon a self-interpreting "closed space." For instance, rather than attempting to *prove* God's existence, the First Testament *assumes* His existence. Likewise, the Second Testament *assumes* the centrality of Jesus. The only actual proof that Jesus lived comes only from the biblical record itself, as a *sacred* account of Jesus' life and ministry. Actually, one of the "proofs" of biblical authority comes from the way Jesus, as Son of God, Savior, and Lord of life, recognizes the authority of Scripture.

Because of the Bible's "closed," self-reflective posture, then, we understand that 2 Timothy 3:16-17 speaks for *all* of the biblical canon. We could, of course, infer that this text only refers to the "Law and Prophets" of the First Testament, since that was the only officially-recognized "Scripture" at the time of Paul. But there is another Second Testament citation that broadens this perspective. 2 Peter 3:16 infers that *Paul's* writings were considered "Scripture" (early in the second century A.D.). Thus, there is a Second Testament witness to its own "Scripture-ness." If Paul's letters are "Scripture," then, does not his reference to inspiration also refer to his own writings and others of the Second Testament? This, then, is *self-proclaimed* authority, *from* the Bible *about* the Bible. The authority, however, ultimately comes from within the province of God. Accordingly, biblical authority is *intrinsic*. It is an *internal* authority that resides in the text itself. That is, the Bible does not point to or draw from anything outside itself to "prove" itself.

ARENAS OF AUTHORITY

As we think about the issue of biblical authority, we must ask about the *purpose* for which the Bible is "God-breathed," or authoritative. Our answer is readily supplied in the same text where the word for *inspiration* is used (2 Timothy 3:15-17). Here, it is clear that Paul has four purposes for the Bible's "God-breathedness."

First, it *leads us to salvation* (verse 15). The ultimate function of Scripture is that we may understand the salvation of God in Jesus Christ.

Second, it *helps us understand Christian doctrine* (verse 16). This purpose has both a positive and a negative focus: it is for "teaching truth" (verse 16—a positive) but also for "correcting" or refuting error (verse 16—a negative). Thus, it helps us not only know *what* we must believe, but also what we should *not* believe.

Third, it *instructs us in a Christian lifestyle* (verse 16). Again, there is both a positive and negative focus for how the Bible applies to practical living. It is to "correct faults" (a negative) and for "training in righteousness" (a positive). Again, it is useful to help us know both *how* we should live and how we *should not* live.

Fourth, its purpose is to *equip us for good works* (verse 17). As we study and apply the Bible's truths to our lives, we become better equipped to serve our Lord and his kingdom.

Taken altogether, then, the Bible's purpose is for the benefit of the *Christian.* It is our handbook for salvation. And it helps us demonstrate our salvation in good works because it instructs us on *what* to believe and *how* to live. It helps us understand *what* to believe and what *not* to believe. It helps us know *how* to live our lives as Christians, what *is* appropriate interpersonal and social behavior and what is *not* appropriate. Because Scripture is God-breathed, we accept it as our written authority for faith and practice.

At its heart, all of these stated purposes fall within the domain of *truth,* not *fact.* That is, while these four functions help us understand what the Bible is *for,* they are also *limitations* to its authority. We must be careful not to extend the authority of Scripture beyond these biblical bounds (for geography, science, or history, for instance, though contemporary archaeological studies continue to demonstrate remarkable consistency between the Bible's record and their own disciplines). But when we assume biblical authority for other than faith and lifestyle matters, we impose issues and principles on the Bible for which it was never intended. In the process, we exchange the authority of Scripture for the authority of our own ideas.

Ultimately, though, the authority of Scripture must be *attributed* if the Bible is to be infallibly understood. Indeed, biblical authority has no authority for those who do not perceive its divine origin, or those who do not *choose* to accept its authority. While the Scripture is inherently authoritative through its inspiration, it *only* becomes authoritative for the reader who *acknowledges* that authority, or the listener who hears an authoritative Scripture proclaimed from the pulpit. Once a person becomes a member of the "community of faith" through personal faith in Jesus Christ, the Holy Spirit interacts with that sacred Book and its reader, and *meaning* arises. But for those who choose not to engage the transaction, no transformation will happen.

Infallibility means that the Bible will not *fail* us when it comes to truth about what to believe and how to live. In many respects, it demands a lifestyle that is counter-intuitive and even contrary to that of the world. When we accept and apply Scripture to ourselves, we discover that the Bible challenges our attitudes, beliefs, and lifestyle, and forces us to conform to and adopt the standards of the kingdom rather than the world.

THE VALUE OF SCRIPTURE

Finally, I want to identify my own personal conclusions from what I've said in this chapter. That is, there are three primary reasons why I believe the Bible to be the infallible, authoritative written word of God.

First, the Bible is *authentic.* There seems to be no attempt to *propagandize* its readers by using unethical strategies that could easily happen if someone were to try to "sell" us on its principles and practices. Our Bible comes by human hands. If it were "made up" (as a *Holy Book* might be), it wouldn't contain different styles or divergent accounts. This diversity or divergence proves its *authenticity,* in the same way that no two signatures of a person are identical. A counterfeiter will copy an original signature exactly— that's how authorities can detect a counterfeit signature. *Difference,* when looked at this way, proves authenticity.

Second, the Bible is *trustworthy.* Its message "works" when I take it as my own. The Holy Spirit speaks to my life today, just as he has in past centuries. He changes me through it. It is a *living* book that ultimately makes sense. *Uncanny* truth is revealed in it. When I accept it in faith, it becomes an essential element of my Christian worldview and lifestyle. The written word of God then becomes the *residential* word of God in me.

Third, the transmission and preservation of the text lead me to believe that it is the *reliable* written word of God, that God has had His hand in its transmission and canonization. Again, when I seek to understand God and His truth for my faith and lifestyle, and I make an effort to apply that truth, it makes sense, even when that application may be contrary to what the world tells me. The Scripture is always reliable.

What does this mean for our preaching? Simply this: we understand the Bible to be inspired and authoritative for what to believe and how to live. We accept the Bible as having been written to a particular culture and context, that every utterance had meaning for those to whom it was first spoken or written. Truth is eternal, but only when we understand clearly how its truth related to those first hearers or readers can we then apply that same truth to our lives. But apply it we must, because this collection of inspired books by inspired writers comes from the very heart of God. It is, beyond all comprehension, God's authoritative Book that reveals His truth for our world today.

So, once we recognize these characteristics of the Bible for faith and practice, it also becomes our authoritative, trustworthy, and reliable authority for preaching. Those of us who speak *from* the Scripture also speak *for* the Scripture as we continually *reconstruct* its authority whenever we use it. When the Scripture is foundational to the preacher's proclamation, the act of speaking from it establishes his or her authority to speak and, at the same time, establishes the authority of the text.

CHAPTER 11
Principle One: Single Text,
Single Truth

THE TEMPTATION WITH TOO MUCH INFORMATION

There are two temptations you might face when you preach, especially the first or second times you try it. Both temptations emerge because we see the Bible as a great, gigantic collection of biblical themes and important truths that relate to the spiritual needs of people. There's so much information in there that you aren't sure what to do with it all.

The first temptation, then, is to include as much of the Bible as you can. Your listeners, after all, are biblically illiterate, and the more information you incorporate, the more they are going to learn. Besides, citing a lot of Scripture will demonstrate that you are no stranger to the Bible and its themes. So you approach the Bible thematically and systematically, with the decision to include *everything you know* about spiritual matters. After all, 20 minutes is a long time to preach. (The problem, of course, is that if you have to preach again next week, you won't have anything to talk about!)

There's a second temptation you might face as you think about all the biblical material there is to preach. The amount of important information is so overwhelming that you are frozen in your chair just thinking about it! You don't know *where* to begin (because you might start in the wrong place), so you just sit there and let your mind wander off into deep space, praying that the Holy Spirit will "lightening-bolt" you with just the right message.

Actually, these temptations aren't bad. They indicate, at least, that you want to preach from the Bible. That's good. But, while the task is daunting, it is also much easier than you think. You shouldn't preach everything you can think of (that would be preaching your own theology, anyway), and you don't have to sit, overwhelmed and passive, waiting for an interesting idea to come out of the blue. (You can start with a congregational need, for instance, or a single text that stimulates you.) Rather, if you decide to preach from a single text (and do it professionally and with passion), you'll find that your listeners will respond to your preaching because of your clarity of thought, and you will also have years and years of material to work with the next times you preach. (If you have doubts about this, look at Figure 21.1 on page 313.)

The way to combat these two temptations is to focus on a single topic or theme about which you want to preach, and then find a single text that informs that theme. (By "text," I mean either a verse or a series of verses. It is usually a sequential passage of Scripture, though this isn't always the case.) Of course, you might also be drawn to a particular text first, in which case you then focus on a single preaching theme within it. This is the subject that occupies our attention in the rest of this chapter.

A RATIONALE FOR "SINGLE TEXT, SINGLE TRUTH"

The first principle of biblical preaching is to *focus your sermon on a single text,* choose a *single theme* within that text, and identify a single biblical truth related to that theme. As we talk about this principle, I first want to discuss *why* it is important to focus on a single text and use a single biblical truth, and then we'll look at some practical ways of starting the process of sermon development. Beginning here, with this chapter, we're also going to build *one sermon,* step by step, chapter by chapter, as we work through four principles of biblical preaching. That way, you can see how they work in actual practice.

But first, there are several good reasons why biblical preaching focuses on a single text and single biblical truth.

1. UNQUESTIONABLE TRUTH IS PROCLAIMED

When I discover truth embedded in a single text, I can say without hesitation that here is a word from the Lord. I can stand on it because I see it clearly right here, *in a particular text.* Indeed, I *know* I am preaching biblical truth because I can identify it here and I have already accepted the *Bible* as authoritative. Thus, a single truth, revealed in and through a single text of Scripture, can be counted on to embody the authority of the whole Bible.

Further, drawing a truth and developing it from a specific portion of Scripture *authenticates* the authority of the entire Bible every time I do it. The authority of Scripture is *made real* through the authority of what *this* particular biblical text says.

2. IT MINIMIZES QUESTIONS OF PERSONAL AUTHORITY

When I discover a single biblical truth in a single text in the Bible, I don't have to wonder if I've legitimately put together different bits of Scripture to arrive at a legitimate preaching truth (as I do when I preach theologically). That's because theological and expositional preaching tends to advance a doctrinal system, and usually quotes a lot of Bible to do it. But citing biblical reference after biblical reference is only an attempt to "manufacture" the *preacher's* authority; it doesn't reflect the authority of Scripture. That is, I never know if my systematic theology is accurate or representative enough of the whole, so I can never really preach it with authority. But if I uncover a *single,* relevant, contextualized biblical truth from a *single* passage of Scripture, I can say without hesitation that this is a word from God. I can preach it with authority.

I once worked with a youth director whose peers told him to preach with "more authority." He didn't really know what that meant, so he just added more Scripture references (a *theological* approach) and shouted louder. His preaching never did get very authoritative, because he was only preaching his own doctrine. But if he had relied on discovering a single biblical truth within a particular text, he could effectively have said (in a calm manner), "This is what the *Lord* says. I know it because we see it in *this* authoritative text. And, as a result, I have no doubt but that the Holy Spirit confronts us through it today!"

Theological preaching promotes the *preacher's* theology and, thus, is never authoritative, in spite of all the Scriptural references it might include. *Expositional* preaching, as well, tends to focus on a single text, but it tries to explain *many* biblical truths in that text. Thus, *expositional preaching,* too, is derived from the *preacher's* authority, because there's no consistent rationale for why those particular points are chosen.

Both theological and expositional preaching are derived from the preacher's systematic theology, but *systematic theology* is simply not authoritative; its role is to frame the great doctrines of the Church. It is a human attempt to make sense of complex theological data. But there's nothing very engaging about these systems when people are forced to hear them from the pulpit. I am not suggesting that you *refrain* from proclaiming great doctrines of the Church. But when you do that, they should emerge from a single text of Scripture rather than a compilation of texts. And they should always be relevant to the needs of your listeners. As A. W. Tozer (1960) once said, "There is scarcely anything so dull and meaningless as Bible doctrine taught for its own sake."

People are hungry to hear an *authoritative word* that is relevant to their lives, not a theological treatise. Proclaiming a single truth from within a single text *is* authoritative, because that truth is clearly identifiable in a particular place in an authoritative Scripture. When you do that, you don't have to be timid about it. Instead, you can assert that truth with clarity and conviction.

3. SPECIFIC APPLICATION

Third, Scripture is authoritative not because of its theological *explanation,* but because of its *application.* Your authority as a biblical preacher comes when a single truth of an authoritative Scripture is *applied* to the human condition. This is what gives the proclamation and the Scripture its authenticity. Your listeners understand the authority of Scripture when they see this single truth applied relevantly to their lives.

4. A LIVING PORTION

Fourth, the Bible comes alive because a *single passage* of Scripture comes alive. When a single text is explored in its own context, and the truth from that text is made relevant to the contemporary context, the Bible is brought to life. It becomes "real," a legitimate particular situation in which and to which the word of God was made known. On the other hand, there is no "life" in a cut and paste job of many, many texts, because there tends to be no "story" in *systematic theology.* When listeners hear a single text expounded in a living, relevant way, they have the impression of a powerful, living Bible.

5. COMPILATIONAL CONFUSION

Fifth, there is a difference between a *compiled* truth and an *evident* one. When I preach from a compilation of texts or biblical citations to "prove" a truth I want to convey, there are at least three consequences.

First, it creates confusion for my listeners. There is just too much quoting going on, and sometimes the verses I choose only make sense to me. My listeners, in the flurry of my presentation, don't "hear" them all or understand how they conform to what I'm saying.

Second, putting a lot of texts together generally means that I am *supporting my* theology by Scripture rather than *developing* a single *biblical truth.* Proof-texting is an attempt to be "biblical," but it only means that I am calling on Scripture to support my own theological position.

Third, when a group of texts is used to support my theology, it tends to lead to *dogmatic* presentations. When that happens, my proclamation relies on *my own* authority, not that of the biblical text. This, of course, makes me *sound* biblical, but I am, in actuality, again, only preaching my own theology. So I have to be dogmatic, because that's the only authority I have.

What's the alternative? When I choose and stay with a *specific text,* the single text fuses my *incarnational* authority with *biblical* authority. The single text helps me *focus* my preaching, too, because my sermon is "connected" to a specific context. I can preach with authority, because there is no question that this truth is drawn directly from Scripture rather than my own mind.

6. FREEDOM

Sixth, it is *easier* to preach from a limited text. I have lots more freedom. When the *whole Bible* becomes my resource for putting a sermon together, where do I start and stop? Which portions do I select for my sermon? How do I know *what* to include and *how* to include it? I skim over the surface of biblical texts and am never forced to wrestle with any of it. That's hard work!

It's actually much easier to force myself to stay with a single text. Now my mind is not as confused as when I try to contemplate the *whole* Bible. Now I actually experience the freedom that comes from *within* a single passage. After all, true freedom always has boundaries.

7. DEPTH

Biblical preaching from a single text also enables me to dig more deeply into the Scripture. When I flit from text to text, or use several texts to support my "point," I only really scratch the surface of biblical truth. Jesus told a parable about a treasure in a field (Matthew 13:44). The guy who finds the treasure buries it again and buys the field. That is, that kernel of truth is *contextualized* in the field in which it is found; it is useful only within the confines of that field.

Finding preaching nuggets is like that. When you concentrate on a single text, you are more apt to discover important biblical insights that can be applied to the need or situation of your listeners. When you skim the surface of a lot of biblical material, you only demonstrate that you are a *theologian*. But that is never the same as the *authoritative* biblical truth that emerges from the study of one particular passage of Scripture.

Having seen the rationale for focusing on a single text, then, we now move on to the practicalities of what this means for our preaching.

THE MILKING STOOL OF TEXT USE

In those places in the world where milking cows is still done by hand, the wise dairy farmer still uses a milk stool. That little stool is important because it easily tips over. If the farmer is irritating Old Betsy, she takes a swipe at him with her foot, and he easily rolls with the falling stool. He doesn't want to get trapped sitting there on a four-legged stool, unable to escape those hard shin-kicks.

The same is true of biblical preaching, because single text preaching resembles a milking stool. Like the picture in Figure 11.1, single text preaching rests on three legs.

Figure 11.1

The three-legged stool of biblical preaching

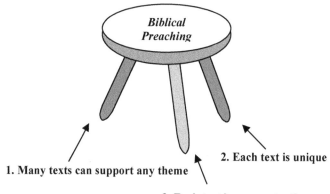

The first leg indicates that there are *many texts* that address the same biblical theme. The second is that each text contextualizes the theme *differently,* and each potentially has something different to say about that theme. Third, every text has *many preachable truths* within it, but the biblical preacher focuses on only one of them.

Let's look at each of these legs of biblical preaching now.

1. LEG ONE: MANY TEXTS CAN SUPPORT ANY THEME

You have decided to preach about a particular theme, and you need to find a text. The first leg of biblical preaching says that there are *many texts* that contain truth for any theme or need. That is, every general preaching theme has many "potential" passages of Scripture that can focus that theme.

For instance, let's say I want to preach on the "love of God." There are many possible texts from which to choose: 1 John 4:7-12, Hosea 11:8-11, John 3:16-17, Psalm 86:15, Romans 8:31-39, or Deuteronomy 7:12-14 (to mention only a few). In the free church tradition, I can preach on whatever text I want; I must simply decide which one to use.

Knowing there are many texts, then, frees me up to know that I won't have to preach everything there is to know about the love of God, nor that I have to find a whole batch of texts to support whatever I want to say about God's love. I will tackle the theme from only *one* of several possibilities.

2. LEG TWO: EACH TEXT IS UNIQUE

Next, I recognize that every text is *unique.* It is different from all other texts. So, texts that deal with the same theme have different approaches to that theme. Even when two or more texts are telling the same story (like the deuteronimistic history of 1 and 2 Kings and the Chronicler's perspective in 1 and 2 Chronicles, or the "Feeding of the 5,000" in all four Gospels), there are *distinct* elements within each telling that lead to distinct presentations of biblical truth. Or we could use any of the three "lost" stories from Luke 15, all of which are about the love of God. But each one has a different "slant" on God's love, or a different way of demonstrating God's love. The particular writer, context, and need make each text unique.

So, because each text is unique, the text I choose should lead me to a different sermon than if I were to choose a different text. I have great freedom to know that, whatever text I choose, there will be *relevant truth* within it, and I can let the text reveal its own truth in its own context for my particular theme.

3. LEG THREE: EACH TEXT HAS MANY TRUTHS

When I examine my text, I now come to realize that it has many preaching themes and many biblical truths within it. If I try to preach about all of them (or even some of them), I would have to make a decision about which ones to use and which to omit. Thus, I would be using my own theological understanding to make the choice, and, thus, will begin to develop a theological sermon rather than proclaiming a biblical truth I might discover.

As a biblical preacher, I know that I only have to choose *one* theme on which to build my sermon, and when I identify a single biblical truth from that theme (which we'll talk more about in the next chapter), I know *without question* that I am proclaiming biblical truth rather than my own theology. I don't try to include them all, otherwise I will confuse my listeners, plus I will be *teaching* the text rather than proclaiming a single living truth from God.

Expositional preaching encourages me to lift out as many preaching themes as I can find and all the "points" I see in the text. But *preaching* for transformation implies orienting my sermon around only *one* of these themes, and only *one* biblical truth.

If I want, then, to focus on a single suitable text, how do I go about *finding* it? How do I narrow my choices? And how long should a text be?

HOW TO PICK A TEXT AND THEME

There are essentially three ways to go about choosing a text and a preaching theme.

1. WHEN YOU BEGIN WITH A TEXT

One beginning point is to work with a text that is already chosen. For example, if you use a lectionary, as do the Baptists in Hungary, you will be provided with a text. In many liturgical traditions, there are three possible texts from which to choose. However, trying to bring the three selections together often leads to doctrinal preaching, because your *theology* is what makes sense of them. Thus, you will generally want to choose only *one* of these texts. While you may have to make a choice, still your choices are limited.

Similarly, if you are preaching a series of sermons from the same biblical book, your decision of a text is already made for you. You might, for instance, be preaching through the book of 1 Corinthians, and the next text is Chapter 12:1-6.

But now you must identify and select a single preaching theme from within that text. How do you do that?

Sometimes themes will emerge almost at random. Sometimes they will come to you because of a particular story you want to use in the sermon. Sometimes a need in your congregation or a world event will raise an insight from the text. Sometimes you already know what you want to preach from the text and that's why you came to it in the first place. Most of the time, a single overriding theme will emerge as you study and wrestle with the text.

You start, then, by making a mental (or paper) list of the different *themes* you see within the text. What *could* you say about this text? What is it all about? Is salvation talked about at all? Or is it about God's providence and care? Does it deal with relationships or work in the church?

With any text, you are likely to see three, four, or many more preaching themes. But now you must make a choice.

One *only, please!*

Reuel Howe (1967), after discussing hundreds of taped sermons with those who have to *listen* to them week after week, concluded that people in the pew "complain almost unanimously that sermons often contain too many ideas." Because every text has a lot of ideas in it, many preachers think they have to capture and preach as many of these ideas as possible if they are going to be faithful to the text. But this, again, is *theological* or *expositional* preaching, because the preacher can never plumb the depths of any text.

So if you want to preach biblically, you will need to isolate *only one* of the preaching themes from within your text.

This process depends on several factors: the sophistication of your personal theology, your frame of mind at the time, why you chose this text to begin with, the congregation to which you are preaching (and their needs), and the environment in which you will be preaching. Taking these and innumerable other issues into account, you come to your text and spend time with it again. You read it and ponder it and reread it and wrestle with it until one main theme comes to light, for this particular sermon at this particular time with this particular congregation. Sometimes you will see several competing themes in the text, and you will have to resolve the tension by deciding what the main, overriding theme seems to be. This, then, will be your preaching theme. And this preaching theme will enable you to focus your attention on the biblical truth you want to proclaim (we'll examine this process in the next chapter).

Unfortunately, the process whereby you seek out a single preachable theme is not exact. Of course, your theology has the primary role in identifying and selecting this preaching theme. As we saw in Chapter 9, it is from an awareness of your personal experience, your community's doctrine, and the Bible that your theology emerges. And it is that theology that enlightens the text for you and which enables you to identify a preachable theme from within it. Preaching is a personal business; that's why you can preach a particular text in one way, while another preacher will engage the text very differently.

2. WHEN YOU BEGIN WITH A THEME

Biblical preaching does not imply that you *start* with a text. Sometimes that will happen, but not always. More often than not, you will begin with an idea or theme, and then you have to locate a suitable text for your subject. In those cases, how do you find a text? Here are some suggestions:

First, use your *memory*. When you call upon your own memory for texts, you might settle on one that is useful for this particular topic or need.

Second, *marginal notes* in a study Bible can be helpful. Often, you start from memory by identifying a text that is "close" to something that might work, but you then use the marginal notes to track down a more suitable text.

Third, use your *concordance*. Seek words that relate to your subject. You might have to spend some time checking different possible words and potential texts, but such a search often brings about interesting possibilities that you wouldn't otherwise have considered.

Fourth, use other *reference works.* A Bible dictionary or topical Bible can be useful for locating particular texts for preaching. And look in your sermon resource file, or computer software. Finding a *story* about the topic may remind you of or lead you to a particular text. And if your hymnal includes biblical citations, that can be very useful.

Fifth, develop a *filing system* where you file away sermon topics, themes, or texts under particular headings, such as the church, evangelism, leadership development, or crisis situations. (We'll talk more about this in Chapter 24.) You may have to sort through these files for subjects, stories, and the texts to which they direct you, but it can be time well spent.

These suggestions will help you find a text when you begin with an idea.

3. NARROWING YOUR CHOICE

Now let's suppose that you've located *several* possible texts. How do you decide which one to use for this particular sermon? There are three guidelines to help narrow your choice.

Relevancy

First, remember that each text is unique, so it will have different truths that will inform or illuminate your theme. Choose the text, then, that includes information that will be most useful to the particular situation or need to which you are preaching. It is sometimes helpful to read quickly through all potential texts until you discover the one that seems to be most relevant.

Recency

Another strategy when you have many possible texts is to pick one that you have *not* used before, or one from which you have not preached for a long time. You will consider this option, of course, when the "relevancy principle" does not lead you to a particular text. In the long run, this procedure adds variety to your choice of preaching texts.

Reinforcement

There is one more option you might want to keep in mind. When you construct your sermon, you can use one text as your main, governing text for the sermon, but other texts as additional activating resources in the sermon (we'll talk more about this in Chapter 16). In this way, you can include several different relevant texts or stories in your sermon. But remember that you only want to use *one* text and the biblical truth *from that passage* to guide your sermon's development. The other texts only serve as reinforcement.

Two case studies

Let's take two examples to follow this process from theme to text. Let's suppose you decide you want to talk about *gifts.* From your memory, you realize you could preach from 1 Corinthians 14 or Romans 12 or Ephesians

4:11-12 or Hebrews 2:4. But you read these texts and do some thinking, and, finally, you decide that you will try 1 Corinthians 12:7-12. You know that *every* Christian sitting in your congregation has a God-given gift to be used in kingdom service.

This text will focus your sermon and offer insights to your listeners' situation. But because of the principle of textual uniqueness, this text will provide a *different* sermon than would a choice of any of these other texts. Your decision to use this text means that you will not include a lot of information from 1 Corinthians 14 or Romans 12 or any of the other texts (except as you use them to *support* your thesis—which we will discuss later). Nor will you include a lot of information from 1 Corinthians 12:7-12 that is *irrelevant* to the use of gifts. The specific text from which you draw your truth will be limiting, but, in that limitation, you will discover great freedom.

Let's look at another example. Suppose you've decided on a general theme of how God uses *ordinary people* to carry out His work in the world. So you let your mind wander for a while and see what texts or stories come to you. After some thought, you decide you can see this theme developed in the stories of Abraham, Moses, and David. But you check other resources, and decide you could also discuss the call of Matthew or Paul, too, or you could give your listeners a list of the great number of biblical characters who were chosen for particular ministries (perhaps from Hebrews 11). That's a good idea, too, but you reject it as not very convicting or relevant to your listeners right now.

As your mind sifts through the possibilities, you start to think about Isaiah's call in Isaiah 6. You've always liked this text, but realize that you've never preached on it before. With it, you could easily focus your sermon on how Isaiah heard God's call and how he responded, and you decide that if you approach your subject this way, your listeners might potentially be convicted of God's claim on their lives. Your decision means that you won't include other texts to develop your ideas about God using ordinary people. Nor will you talk about other interesting details in Isaiah 6 that have nothing to do with God calling ordinary people. You've found a text, and you will use that text alone to focus your theme. Now you are able to move on to the next three principles in developing a biblical sermon.

4. LENGTH OF TEXT

Finally, many beginning students wonder how long a text should be. The general principle is that it should be long enough for a *context,* but short enough to contain *one idea* or a single preachable theme. Typically, the text will tell *one story* or present *one completed thought.*

More specifically, I generally choose a text that is between one and 12 verses in length. However, the choice of a text depends on the local situation, expectations of the listeners, the amount of time allowed for the sermon, and the culture. There should be enough text to include all that I want to say, but limited enough that there aren't too many themes or issues that will lead me away from one focus.

There are, however, four special cases that require explanation.

1. A larger context for a short text

Sometimes, I want to preach on a single verse of Scripture, but the verse isn't developed enough to provide an adequate context. So I will *focus* my attention on that one verse, but *contextualize* that verse within a longer text. For instance, if I preach on Psalm 23:4, I will frame that verse within the context of the whole 23rd Psalm.

2. A summation section from within a longer text

Sometimes, I may want to develop a theme that includes a very long text or period of time. In those cases, I may want to use a shorter text for the Scripture reading. The story of Ezekiel and the prophets of Baal, for instance (1 Kings 18:1-40), is much too long a passage to read from the pulpit, but is a great preaching text. In this instance, I may use the full story in the sermon, but select a smaller portion of it for my Scripture reading, one that encapsulates the biblical truth I want to emphasize (we'll look at this principle in the next chapter).

Or sometimes, I might want to summarize a book of the Bible or a specific chapter. For example, I want to make the point in the Ephesian letter that those who have responded to Jesus are members of the "elect." Since this idea doesn't "reside" in only one portion of the Ephesian letter, there are many parts of the book that I can use to support this truth. In that case, I choose a *theme verse* that encapsulates that truth (such as Ephesians 1:13-14). These verses, then, provide the guiding focus of my sermon, even though I will look at the whole book.

3. A theme text for a story

Sometimes, when focusing on a larger story or character's life, I will use a *portion* of the whole text or person's life and apply this portion to my listener's need. For instance, if I am using Joshua's life to encourage my listeners to be strong and courageous when facing life's obstacles, I *could* draw references from Exodus 17-33, Numbers 11-34, Deuteronomy 1-34, and the whole book of Joshua (all of which would be too much). Instead of doing that, I will preach from a single text, so I decide that my main source will be Deuteronomy 31:7-8. I will then keep coming back to this text as I share incidents from other stories in Joshua's life that reflect his strength and courage.

Or I might want to use the experiences of the Apostle Paul to demonstrate what it means to live by faith, and will draw from many examples in his life. In this case, I will find a "theme verse" from the book of Acts or one of Paul's letters that emphasizes that particular biblical truth, and then build the sermon around that theme.

This same strategy could be followed in summarizing a whole book. Philippians 4:4, for instance, could become a guiding verse for the entire book.

4. An "outside" summation text

There's one more option, and that is to use *another biblical text* that clearly expresses the truth I want to proclaim. This other text will orient my sermon, but I will be *summarizing* a larger block of material or story to develop that truth. In this case, the *content* of most of my sermon will come from outside the specific text that I am using, but it will be that single text from which I will draw my biblical truth.

For instance, 2 Corinthians 7:1 could be used as a wonderful "theme verse" that frames the stories of all the saints listed in Hebrews 11. In this case, the 2 Corinthians verse interprets how I tell each of the stories in Hebrews 11.

Or suppose I want to use the whole story of Jesus' life, but focus my listeners' attention by viewing Jesus as a *servant.* So I choose Philippians 2:6-7 as my main text. These two verses don't provide any narrative account of Jesus, but they *encapsulate* his life story with the truth I want to proclaim. So I draw my theme from the Philippian text, but build my sermon around different incidents in Jesus' life that support that basic truth.

THE PRACTICE OF SERMON CONSTRUCTION

We're now going to start a process that we'll carry out for the four principles of biblical preaching. That is, we're going to work on the *same sermon* in each of these chapters, under this heading. My hope is that it will help you see, in a progressive way, how a single sermon might start to come together.

STEP 1: SINGLE TEXT, SINGLE TRUTH

To begin the process, I choose a single text and preaching theme. I can do it in either order.

For our purposes here, let's begin with a theme. I think about my congregation and decide, for several reasons, that I will preach about the *love of God.* I start to think about possible texts: Romans 8:31-39, Psalm 23, 1 John 4:7-12, and John 3:16-17. After reading through these, and following some of the marginal notes in my old Bible, I decide to preach from John 10:11-16. I haven't preached from this text in a long time and I'd like to give it a try again. This choice of a text now forces me to refocus my theme from the love of God to the special case of the love of Jesus (or God). This is entirely acceptable.

I also now realize that my choice of text will restrict what I can say about Jesus' love of people. That's because it is a unique text. If I were to choose a different text (and there are many, many of them), I would have something else to say about the love of Jesus. But I've made my choice and I'll see where it leads.

This, then, is all there is to the first principle of biblical preaching. It's time to move on to the second principle, and we'll look at that in the next chapter.

CHAPTER 12
Principle Two: Single Thesis

LAST THINGS FIRST

Transformational preaching begins where the sermon ends, with questions that identify the preacher's intention: *"How* do I want my listeners to respond to this sermon? *Why* do I want to preach this text? *What* is the biblical truth saying to this particular group of listeners at this particular time?"

These questions lead us to a *desired outcome.* That is, when I preach biblically, I am not content simply to *transfer* biblical information from mind to mind; I expect some kind of *response* from my listeners. If listeners are to be transformed through my preaching, I must first know *why* I am preaching this sermon. Defining this purpose is the most critically important step in sermon construction. It is what I call the *thesis.* It is this purpose, in turn, that will determine the focus, content, and structure of my sermon. It helps me know what to include and exclude, how to fashion the sermon's argument, and where the sermon is headed.

THE CORNERSTONE

Actually, the thesis functions very much like the cornerstone of an ancient building. In biblical times, the cornerstone was the most important stone in the whole structure.

Today, of course, the cornerstone is the *last* stone to be put in place. It tends to serve a *ceremonial* function. When I was a youth, I was a member of the Burton Baptist Church in Grand Rapids, Michigan. When our new building was completed out on Plymouth Road, we held a dedication service. At that time, a special document (signed by all the current members of the congregation) was placed in the cornerstone and sealed up, right next to the front door. It was the last piece of the building, and, as far as I know, my name is still in there.

But in the world of the Second Testament, the cornerstone was the *first* stone to be laid. The ground was cleared and the building mapped out, and then the cornerstone was cut. It had to be absolutely, perfectly square, because the set of the walls was determined by the orientation of that single stone. When other stones were set in place for the walls of the building, every one of them was oriented to that single cornerstone. (This process is a key to understanding Ephesians 2:20 and 1 Peter 2:6.)

In the same way, the thesis acts like the cornerstone of the sermon. It helps you decide what fits and what doesn't fit in your sermon. It also helps you know how to *design* the sermon once you've collected all the building stones. Without a thesis, you're likely to get an awkward, poorly-constructed, confusing sermon, because if you don't know *why* you're preaching this sermon, your listeners certainly won't be able to figure it out, either.

The remedy for this kind of thematic and structural confusion is what I call the *thesis*. It is the thesis that gives you a *singular* orienting focus to your preaching.

So, how do you get to a *one-point, intentional, purpose-driven* sermon? It begins with your theology as a preacher (Chapter 9), the text from which you are preaching (Chapter 11), and the situation in which or to which you are preaching (Chapter 14). But the most significant piece of the whole business is the *thesis statement* that you'll develop. Once you've selected your text (as we did in the last chapter), it is time to determine what you are going to do with it. That's the function of the thesis.

As would be expected, the "discovery" of the thesis is where preaching becomes indistinct as an art form. Just as the artist has to follow certain principles (rather than "rules"), so the preacher works from *principles* that help define the direction of the sermon.

What follows, then, are five simple steps that will help you determine a thesis statement. This thesis will guide the content and construction of your sermon, and getting it right will save a great deal of time and indecision when you start to put your sermon together.

FIVE STEPS TO A THESIS

Developing a thesis statement requires a lot of practice, so as we move through this exercise, we'll look at one primary example, and follow it through for each step. I'll also provide three other "practice" examples without much discussion. And, then, at the end, we'll come back to the example we're following through each of these chapters.

Of course, the decisions I make in each of these steps are not the only possible approaches. I am only offering *examples* of one way I might develop a thesis. I recommend that you try it on your own. If you do so, I would expect that you will arrive at a different decision, simply because you and I are different preachers and the people and situations to which we'd be preaching are different. That's just as it should be!

When these steps are completed, your thesis, hopefully, will be simple and straightforward: it should give you a "nutshell sentence" that answers the question: *why am I preaching this sermon?*

With that in mind, here, then, are the texts we'll be following through this chapter:

Primary text

I have decided to preach several sermons from 2 Thessalonians, and my first message will come from Chapter 1:3-5:

> *³We ought always to thank God for you, brothers and sisters, and rightly so, because your faith is growing more and more, and the love all of you have for one another is increasing. ⁴Therefore, among God's churches we boast about your perseverance and faith in all the persecutions and trials you are enduring*
> *⁵All this is evidence that God's judgment is right, and as a result you will be counted worthy of the kingdom of God, for which you are suffering.*

"Practice" texts

Along with this primary text, let's also use three different types of Gospel texts as our "practice examples" (I won't write them out here):

John 3:16 (a well-known doctrinal verse)

Mark 6:30-44 (the feeding of the 5,000, a miracle story), and

Luke 15:11-24 (the story of the Wayward Son).

We will use these four texts to illustrate how a thesis statement might develop as we practice the following five steps.

The thesis process, basically, begins after I know my text. But, as we saw in the last chapter, there is often a close relationship between finding a text and discovering the preaching theme (the first step in writing my thesis). However, for this exercise, let's assume that I have identified my text without reference to a theme, so I now begin the process of working through the five steps to my thesis.

STEP 1: IDENTIFY A PREACHING THEME

The first step is to identify a general *preaching theme* within my text. The preaching theme is the basic idea of what I want to preach about in this sermon. Let's remember that every text has many of them and I have to choose just one.

Let's now apply this first step to my "case studies."

Primary text

First, let's list all the themes we find in 2 Thessalonians 1:3-5.

1. In verse 3, Paul *thanks God* for people in the church. He even boasts about them in the next verse (not a bad idea for any pastor to do from time to time!).
2. In verse 3, Paul honors faith that is *demonstrated.*

3.   Paul praises an *increasing love* among the church members (verse 3).

4.   In verse 5, Paul mentions God's *judgment,* which could be understood as an "End Times" reference.

5.   We see the importance of being counted *worthy* of God's kingdom through personal faith (verse 5).

6.   The idea of *suffering* is also present in verses 4 and 5. It is suffering that builds Christian *character.*

7.   Verses 4 and 5 also imply that *church relationships* are important when Christians persevere through difficult times.

So, from this short text and with very little thought, I have detected at least seven preaching themes (there could be several more), without spending much effort on it. This is not the time to carefully define these themes; I just want to list them.

The important first step, though, is that I want to isolate *just one* of these main preaching themes from the text. I do that by asking which of these ideas, when taken with my contemporary situation and my own inclination, best represents *Paul's* thought. So, as I read the text over again and again, I ask if Paul is really talking about the kingdom (theme 4). I don't see it this time through. Does it have to do with God's judgment (theme 4)? Yes, but perhaps only incidentally—it doesn't seem to be the way this passage is focused. One by one, I contemplate the possibilities.

But I am sitting in Brjansk, Russia, working on this chapter. Given the immediate context of Christians in 21st century Russia, I am currently very sensitive to the idea of suffering Christians (theme 6). This, then, is the way I *read* the text this time through. For me, it becomes clear that this is where Paul's real heart lies in writing these words. Suddenly, the text takes shape, and the theme of suffering becomes my obvious "preaching theme." Were I in another setting or aware of other needs, I might notice that the text is about the development of Christian character, and that suffering is just one way in which character is developed. But, for now, it is clearly the suffering theme that encapsulates my understanding of this text. My theme, then, is *suffering for Jesus.*

"Practice" texts

Without much explanation, let's look at some of the potential preaching themes in my other three examples.

John 3:16: If I understand the salvation message of this "gospel in a nutshell," it is through personal belief in Jesus that God demonstrates His love for the people of the world. But that isn't the only way to preach this verse. There are other truths here, as well. For instance, salvation is depicted as being rescued from a natural descent into hell. And the verse speaks of the nature of humanity, our ultimate destiny, and Jesus' identity as the Son of God. While all of these preaching ideas revolve around a common theme, each of them is unique and distinct from the others. But I pick the following: *God's love is a demonstrated love.*

Mark 6:30-44. In the story of the "Feeding of the 5,000," we see many different preaching themes, too. Jesus is clearly presented as a miracle-worker (vv. 42-44), but he is also a shepherd who cares for lonely people of the world (v. 34). We also notice that people are attracted to Jesus (vv. 31, 34). But then there's the miracle of sharing food, that we should share what we have with others (v. 37). All of these preaching themes, along with a score of others, are there. But I pick the following: *Jesus loves people.*

Luke 15:11-24. It is possible that the story of the Wayward Son is an allegory rather than a parable, because it lends itself to an interpretation of many details rather than having a single point, as do most parables of Jesus. In this story, we see the power of sin over our lives, and the depth of sin in the pigpen. We see a good definition of repentance, as a change of heart and then action. Here is the theme of the rescue of an individual rather than love for a large group. But perhaps most powerfully, we see the loving embrace of a father who runs out to meet his son. But it's not only the story about God the Father Who loves the lost individual; it is also the kind of love that Jesus demonstrates—in some ways, it is a story about him. So I pick the following: *God reaches out to lost individuals through Jesus.*

A first examination of these texts, then, reveals many different preaching themes. Of course, different preachers can preach different messages from these same texts. The important point, though, is to work through these evident themes and select only one for this sermon.

STEP 2: WRITE A STATEMENT OF BIBLICAL TRUTH

Out of all the possible biblical themes I see in the text, I have selected one of them. But now, drawing from that theme, I want to isolate a simple declaration of biblical truth from that theme. The truth, then, emerges from this particular text, and *it is this truth that will determine the content of my sermon.*

So, starting from my theme, I now want to fashion a statement that describes the truth I see in it. That is, what does this text say about this theme? I also ask what my "theological reason" tells me about this passage, in light of my own *existentia* and *doctrinal community?* What seems to be the "plain meaning"? Personal observation plays an important role in identifying biblical truth.

I might have to spend more time reflecting on the text, but now from the perspective of my preaching theme. I look at the characters, physical movement, "hot words" (particular vocabulary or phrases that jump out at me or don't seem to fit the story line), the development of thought or the argument in the passage, or its tension. What is being "opposed" or to what issue is the writer responding? Is there anything *unusual* here, any elements of the story, such as behavior or attitudes, that stand out? How does this passage compare to other texts I know about? I also might ask the standard "reporter"-type questions: who, what, when, where, why, and how. And I ask myself what it is I don't understand about the text. Or I bring the theme to bear on the contemporary context of my listeners. Texts are living, breathing, relevant things, and when I set a text beside a situation (or bring a situation to a text), otherwise unimagined truth may emerge.

Any of these questions might lead me on a journey of discovery that takes me down many fruitful paths. It sometimes takes time to do this investigative work, but it can yield wonderfully insightful fruit for the discipline of preaching.

But, ultimately, when I frame the biblical truth, I want to answer the main "action" question: "How does God *act* here?" Or "How does the story's character *respond* to Jesus?" Or "How are we directed to *behave* from this text?" That is, what does this text declare *in action form* about the theme?

So, I want to *"actionalize"* my biblical truth. I write my statement of biblical truth *as an action,* in a way that God or a biblical character acts, or we are compelled to act as a result of God's word. Truth statements that are written as statements of doctrine are extremely difficult to work with; they lead to doctrinal or theological preaching, and do not help me formulate my sermon. If I can word my identified biblical truth as an action, it makes my job much easier later.

For instance, to say "Jesus is Lord" is too broad a statement as biblical truth. This is an important *doctrinal* truth, but it gives me no direction for my sermon. "God is love" is another important doctrinal truth, but it is not helpful for developing a persuasive sermon. Statements of this kind lead to *explanatory* sermons (How did Jesus become Lord? What was the role of his death and/or resurrection in the salvation process? What does his kingdom look like? Etc.). When I identify biblical truth as a statement of doctrine (using an "is" type verb), it keeps my preaching on a theoretical level, and, thus, tends to become informational rather than transformational.

Thus, I want to write my statement of biblical truth as an *action sentence.* So I say, "When you follow Jesus as Lord, you enter a new kingdom," or "Because Jesus is Lord, he calls me to follow him," or "As my Lord, Jesus gives me purpose in my life." I then have a much clearer directive for my preaching. Instead of "God is love," I write, "God loves sinners." When biblical truth is expressed as *action,* something happens as a result of that biblical truth. It then has a greater chance of being relevant and meaningful to the lives of my listeners.

Again, as with deciding on my theme, there is no rule for this discovery. But when I take time here, the statement of biblical truth I develop is critical to helping me understand and focus my thesis.

Primary text

Let's return, then, to 2 Thessalonians 1:3-5 to write a statement of biblical truth. It should be a natural development from the preaching theme I've already identified. My theme has something to do with *"suffering for Jesus."* There isn't any action in that, so I re-read the text and write the biblical truth in this way: *"When I suffer for Jesus, God counts me worthy of His kingdom."* Now I have a pretty good idea of what I'm going to emphasize in my sermon.

"Practice" texts

When I do the same for my other examples, I come up with the following:
John 3:16-17: God acts on *His love for the world.*
Mark 6:32-44: Jesus, the Shepherd, feeds spiritually hungry people.
Luke 15:11-24: Like the Father, Jesus goes out to minister to outcasts.

A cautionary note

There's a concern that needs mentioning at this point. It has to do with what is *preachable truth* and what is not. That is, texts are filled with little ideas and side issues and interesting details that can easily be developed into "truth" statements, but that do not accurately reflect substantive Christian doctrine. Or they may be so trivial that it is silly to preach about them.

But how can you know what is "trivial" and what is not? How can you know that the truth you have isolated is really "preachable"?

Let's look at a few examples to exaggerate the point. In 1 Chronicles 11:22, for instance, Benaiah went into a pit in a snowstorm and killed a lion. Does that text suggest that we should hunt lions only in winter? Probably not—that point is irrelevant to biblical truth. This kind of detail helps us *understand the story,* but that doesn't make it *preachable truth.* It leads us to recognize the courage and, perhaps, perseverance of Benaiah, which are good character traits for God's faithful people. But it doesn't necessarily mean that we should hunt lions in the snow.

Or you might notice that Mark mentions *green grass* in his version of the "Feeding of the 5,000" (Mark 6:39). Might that mean that God expects us to keep beautiful lawns? Probably not. When we read Mark's account carefully, we realize that this detail is probably an intentional reference to Psalm 23, and, thus, provides a clue to the reason why Mark tells this story. The detail of "green grass," in itself, is certainly biblically true, but it isn't *preachable* truth.

And the image of a young man running *naked* in the garden (Mark 14:51-52) doesn't support public nudity, but it may mean that Mark is giving us an eyewitness account. It also points us ahead to the presence of the *young man* in Mark's startling conclusion (see 16:5), who is now clothed in radiant clothing (the same word used of Jesus' robe in the Transfiguration account). The story's detail, then, may not *be* a preaching truth, but it often *leads* to a preaching truth.

My advice here is four-fold. First, *look for details* in the text, because they are very important. However, most of the time, their purpose is not to call attention to themselves, but to point to a more significant truth. Figure out what deeper truth the detail is telling you.

Second, *avoid the trivial.* Preach only what is solidly biblical and central to the biblical record. Try not to preach about bits of information that have little relevance to living in the kingdom of God. Look for biblical details that have *eternal* rather than *extraneous* significance. Examine truth in light of history and/or eternity. Ask yourself if this interpretation would have made sense to a first century Christian, or if it will make sense in the 25th century.

Don't waste your listeners' time with the trivial—they can find plenty of it in their own lives.

Third, remember your *personal theology.* It is the "central processing agent" for helping you determine biblical truth. But remember, also, that your personal theology grows and develops. It isn't yet complete or perfect. Thus, you can only preach the text according to your own theological sophistication at the time. If you reflect back on a sermon you preached last year and realize now that it was trivial or irrelevant, then you have grown and learned something, which, in turn, should help you avoid that more limited perspective next time. As your personal theology matures, you'll get a growing sense of what is preachable biblical truth and what is not. Above all, preach what you can *affirm,* not what you doubt.

Finally, your theology helps you identify biblical truth, but the biblical truth, once it has been identified, must live "on its own." Your *theology* must take a back seat to your statement of biblical truth. Indeed, your theology should be constrained, informed, and re-fashioned through the truth that is revealed from within the text you have before you. Let the truth speak from its own context.

STEP 3: IDENTIFY A NEED OR DESIRE

This third step has to do with the particular situation to which I will be speaking. We'll deal more fully with this issue in Chapters 14 and 15, but for now, I want to identify a particular need or desire to which I will direct this biblical truth. I may already have considered this issue when choosing my text or theme, but now is the time for me to focus my thinking. Will I speak to a *need* (minimizing anxiety, or lack of fulfillment) or a *desire* (finding the narrow way as a Christian, or wanting to use one's gift in church ministry)? Will I preach to the *personal* need or desire of *individuals,* or will my sermon be oriented toward a *corporate* need or desire (of the church or community)? Often, needs or desires come to my attention only after I identify a particular biblical truth from the text. And sometimes no specific need or desire will come to mind, but I *am* able to focus on the general *human condition* that is addressed by this biblical truth.

I find that if I can clearly pinpoint answers to these questions and identify a circumstance in my immediate environment that needs addressing, or tackle a situation to which I have had an urge to preach for a long time, my sermon will be more direct, relevant, and powerful.

Primary text

As I contemplate 2 Thessalonians 1:3-5 here in Brjansk, I become aware of a congregation that faces almost constant suffering or persecution. In America, I am mindful of those who are passed over for a job because of their Christian faith. I am also aware of those who feel isolated or oppressed because of their faith who need encouragement. So I decide I will preach this sermon to *those who are taking a public stand for their faith and are facing embarrassment or ridicule because of it.* By preaching to his need, I also realize that I will be encouraging my listeners to be *public Christians* among those with whom they live, study, and work.

"Practice" texts

Here are statements of need or desire for our three other texts:

John 3:16-17: I've become aware that most members of my congregation are *insecure in their faith.*

Mark 6:32-44: *There are a number of regular worship attenders who have not yet become disciples.*

Luke 15:11-24: *I have just learned about homeless people living in the neighborhood park.*

STEP 4: DETERMINE YOUR RHETORICAL INTENT

A *rhetorical intent* is an expression of my own desire for how I want my listeners to respond to this biblical truth. Do I want them *to feel* a certain way? Do I want to change an *attitude* or a *behavior?* In what way would I like my listeners to *act on, respond to, change their minds about,* or *be inspired by* this biblical truth?

It is important to keep in mind that preachers are naturally and inescapably engaged in *rhetorically constructing* the faith of their listeners. There is an indirect and almost unintentional *framing of reality* that comes with any oral presentation. But the word "rhetorical" can also imply intention. It becomes *direct* when you, as the preacher, practice *persuasive discourse.* It happens when you desire to *move* your listeners, or get them to *change* as a result of the biblical truth you are proclaiming. *Rhetorical intent* implies that, because God has revealed a particular biblical truth through His written word, your listener's attitude or behavior *must* change. *Rhetorical intent* has to do with the kind of *response* you'd like to see: a change in an *attitude or feeling, behavior,* or *understanding.* This purpose, in turn, will help you decide what tools of persuasion you will use: stories, examples, argument, logic, or all.

But for now, I am asking the question, "So what?" In what way do I want my listeners to *respond* to this biblical truth? It isn't enough to proclaim truth or raise interesting insights about biblical truth. If I am going to be a biblical *preacher,* I want my listeners to *do* something, *believe* something, or *act* in a different way as a result of this text. Biblical truth demands it.

I would like, then, to suggest two specific ways in which to preach for results. There are variations on each of them, but these two simple categories will help focus your preaching to be more *transformational.*

Inspire

The first is by *inspiration.* Information becomes inspirational when it "strikes home," when it hits a responsive chord in the listener. It is a *helpful, uplifting,* or *encouraging* word. Inspirational preaching helps my listeners see and understand their lives, or doctrine, in a new light. It motivates them to become something better or to see their faith from a more positive perspective. It deals with attitudes, not behavior.

Inspiration encourages people with hopes or dreams, to become something that they are not. It draws them ahead, gives them something to reach for, and lifts their sights. Its opposite is bullying, pursuing, provoking, and condemning.

There are two ways to move a donkey. You take a big piece of lumber and smack him as hard as you can across his back end and he will jump forward a wee bit. Or you dangle a carrot in front of his eyes, and he lurches forward trying to retrieve it. Inspiration is dangling the carrot.

People are *inspired* like that—not by criticism or condemnation, but by offering them stories that encourage them to become something better, that lift their sights, that help them dream what the Christian life *could* be. Inspiration offers them models of those who are *succeeding.*

Inspiration is a valuable preaching tool. When I want to change a person's belief system, it is far better to *inspire* new ideas than to *argue* or *explain* a new way. When I want to offer people a better vision for the church, it is far more persuasive to *inspire* that image of what *could* be than just to discuss the details of the vision. When I want nonbelievers to comprehend the fullness of the gospel, they will understand it more quickly through inspiration than explanation.

Notice that *inspire* does not mean *inform!* Most *informational* preaching that addresses a personal, corporate, or community need, hardly ever does. That's because it is *explanatory* rather than *persuasive.* But inspiring or encouraging preaching is *persuasive.* It has the intention of *lifting the sights and perspective of* your listeners, not just providing them with important information. So when you inspire your listeners, you want to give them new hope; you want them to gain a different *impression* of the Christian faith or this biblical truth.

Persuade

A second general rhetorical intent is *persuasion.* That is, my preaching sometimes will *challenge* or *convince* my listeners. Sometimes it will *convict.* Generally, my listeners will follow a naturally-flowing *argument* that, when done, will have *persuaded* them to believe or behave in a different way. Persuasion means that I am convincing my listener that a particular *behavioral* or *lifestyle* choice, or a given *action,* is biblical. *Inspiration* doesn't necessarily lead to a particular action, but *persuasion* does: when I persuade, I want my listeners to *act* in a particular way as a result of this biblical truth. I want them to give money, treat each other more lovingly, pray more consistently, or take the first step in becoming a disciple of Jesus. When I persuade, motivate, or convict my listeners of biblical truth, I also try to give them some *practical* ways in which they can act on that biblical truth.

Again, I must make a *decision* about what I will do in the sermon. This step in the process involves a very simple conviction: either I want to *inspire* my listeners or *persuade* them (never just *inform* them). *How* I want them to respond will come next. For now, I only want to settle on whether to *inspire* or *persuade.*

Primary text

For the text in 2 Thessalonians 1:3-5, I decide I will preach an *inspirational* sermon. That is, I don't want to ask them to *do* anything because of this biblical truth. I just want to inspire them.

"Practice" texts

I've also decided to *inspire* my listeners in the first two practice texts, and *change congregational behavior* in the third (that is, *persuade* them):

John 3:16: Because I am orienting this message toward the *insecurity* of my church members, I won't ask them to *respond* in any way. I simply want to help them *appropriate* a different kind of security for their lives. Thus, this sermon will be *inspirational.*

Mark 6:32-44: In this case, I decide that I will not ask my listeners to take a stand for Jesus. Instead, I will present them with a comforting and challenging image of Jesus to whom they will be drawn. I am hoping that, when I am through preaching, they may *want* to follow Jesus as their shepherd, but I decide I won't *compel* them to make a public decision. This sermon, then, will be *inspirational.*

Luke 15:11-24: When I come to my third example, I want to preach the biblical truth in such a way that my members will be *motivated* to work in a soup kitchen for the homeless. This *persuasive* thrust will give them something to *do,* a new way to put their faith into *action.* So, I decide that this sermon will be *persuasive.*

STEP 5: WRITE YOUR THESIS STATEMENT

Now comes the final step of bringing these previous decisions together. After this step, I should know what I really intend to do with this sermon. Sometimes this is the most difficult step in the process because my decisions up to this point often lack clarity or definition. But now I will attempt to compile the prior information into one cohesive whole. It is what I call the "thesis statement."

The thesis is actually *a very simple statement* that indicates what I want the outcome of this sermon to be. The biblical truth will serve as its foundation, it will be directed toward a particular need, and it will indicate an expected outcome of how I want my listeners to respond to this biblical truth, either by attitude or behavior. The thesis puts into a single phrase exactly what I want to happen when I'm done preaching.

I suggest that this statement follow a particular formula. This enables me to be consistent, but it also makes it much easier to put my sermon together. The statement, then, should complete the sentence,

"I want to (inspire or persuade) my listeners to . . ."

Narrowing my intent into this kind of thesis statement isn't always easy, but it forces me to consider the issues we've discussed in these five steps, and it makes the rest of my sermon construction fall into place quite easily. I also try to avoid writing my thesis statement as "I want to (inspire or persuade) my listeners that . . ." This kind of statement leads me to write a doctrinal or theological thesis, which, in turn, leads to *informational* preaching. So I always try to make my thesis *action-oriented.*

Primary text

When I come to 2 Thessalonians 1:3-5, I work at a thesis statement that conforms to this formula. After some manipulation, I end up with the following: *I want to* inspire *the suffering members of my congregation to remain faithful to Jesus Christ when they are persecuted for their faith.*

Notice that I do not include in my thesis statement any of the textual points I want to make. I don't include anything about character development when Christians are persecuted. I don't include how proud I am when my listeners persevere in their faith. I don't include the kind of persecution I'm talking about. I don't provide examples of how their faithfulness can be *practiced.* I will probably include those elements in the content of my *sermon,* but the thesis statement only reflects my ultimate *intention* in preaching this sermon: it is to encourage my listeners to remain faithful. If they get no other message from this sermon, this is the single, simple idea by which I want them to be transformed. Any other insights or materials I include later will add to this purpose, but the thesis statement is not intended to present the sermon's content or outline; it only states, as simply as possible, my reason for preaching this message.

"Practice" texts

Let's now complete the process with our other three examples:

John 3:16-17: I want to inspire *my insecure listeners to trust a God Who* demonstrates *His overwhelming and undeserved love for them.*

Mark 6:32-44: I want to inspire *my listeners who have no leader in their lives to trust Jesus as their Shepherd.*

Luke 15:11-24: I want to persuade *my listeners to serve in the soup kitchen.*

These, then, are very simple thesis statements that tell me just what I want to accomplish in each of these sermons. I encourage you to follow the formula at first, but once you get used to the pattern, don't be too restrictive with your thesis statement. Your ultimate goal is to present as simple and singular a statement as possible that defines what you want to do by the time you're finished preaching this sermon.

None of these statements are perfect, but they will guide my thinking, how I will exegete each text, the way I structure each sermon, the choice of support materials I will include in these sermons, and, in general, how I approach each subject. That is, I could preach these texts in any number of ways, but I have decided that this is how I will approach each one with this particular group of listeners on this particular occasion.

At this time, I also bring my thesis back to the text from which I have drawn it. While this is the subject of the next chapter, it is important to set the stage for it here. After the process of developing my thesis statement, it is important that I now re-examine it in light of the biblical text to see if it still "holds up." This step subjects my thesis to the text. If it adequately reflects the context and content of what the Bible says, it keeps my preaching *biblical* by constraining my own theology. Sometimes I check a few commentaries to see if my thesis is supported—or, at least, not contradicted—by scholars. And, finally, if my thesis doesn't adequately reflect the text from which I have drawn it, I have three options: change my thesis, change my text, or start over again.

This, then, is the second principle of biblical preaching: the single thesis.

MERGING FOR THE EMERGENCE

Ascertaining the thesis statement is not always easy, and the steps I've identified are guidelines more than "rules." But in the same way that preaching is an art form, so is developing a thesis statement. You arrive at the thesis by bringing together all the pieces you have in hand—the text, your own ideas, the support materials you've already got in mind, the immediate circumstances, needs, and/or desires of your listeners, and whatever insights you've gained from thinking about the text. Like concrete, the thesis emerges from the "mix" of sand, gravel, small rocks, and cement.

That is, a thesis is developed as you bring *together* the text, a need, frame of mind, support materials, and a host of other elements. The sermon emerges as you *manipulate* the materials you have in mind and hand. As the rest of the sermon construction process unfolds (which we will be discovering in the next few chapters), you gather your thoughts, ideas, exegesis, and support resources with your "working thesis," think about them for a while, and watch a sermon emerge.

In the process, all of these elements undergo a "transformation" into the "word of God" for this congregation at this time. At the beginning of the process, don't expect your thinking or your thesis to be clean and perfect—it hardly ever is at this stage. Even after processing the five steps, you still only have a "working thesis." Most likely, it will change through the rest of the sermon's development, but it is important that by the time you preach, you have a clear and consistent idea in your mind what you want to say.

A LAST RUN THROUGH

We're almost finished with this chapter, but, before we leave it, let's look at one more example. This time, we'll take it from beginning to end without much discussion.

I'm supposing now that I am preaching a series on Romans, and have decided to begin with the text from Romans 1:1-6.

1. ONE PREACHING THEME

My first step is to look for possible preaching themes in the text. These ideas don't have to be written in complete sentences, or even written down, but it is important that I consider some of the possibilities: *Christians are called and set apart* (v. 1), *God has a long-range plan* (v. 2), *the centrality of Jesus* (v. 3), *what salvation means* (v. 5), and *belonging to Jesus* (v. 6). I'm going to settle on *one* of them, and, because of several factors, I decide to work with the second of these possible themes: *the long-range plan of God.*

2. STATEMENT OF BIBLICAL TRUTH

I now take this general theme and define an exact biblical truth that I want to work with, one that conforms to what the text says. After several attempts and manipulating sentences, I put this truth in the form of a simple action statement: *God has a long-range plan for you.*

3. NEED OR DESIRE

After thinking about the various themes and the text, I now consider the situation in which I'll be preaching this sermon. Because I know my congregation pretty well, I know there will be many nonbelievers present, so I decide that I want to make this *an evangelistic message.* I will focus on their *desire for purpose in life.* I want to point out from this text that even non-believers are included in the long-range plan of God, that God has *their* salvation in His heart from the beginning of time.

4. RHETORICAL INTENT

Rhetorical intent asks if I want to *inspire* or *persuade* my listeners. Do I want them to be transformed in *attitude* (inspire) or *action* (persuade)?

When I ask myself how I want my listeners to respond to this particular sermon, I decide I'd like them to *act* on this message by making a public profession of faith. This means that my rhetorical intent is *persuasive:* for an individual to participate in God's long-range plan, he or she must become a disciple of Jesus. So my focus throughout this sermon will be to invite nonbelievers to become Christians. I don't simply want to present information about salvation, nor do I want to inspire my listeners with wonderful, hopeful images or thoughts about what it means to be saved. When I preach this sermon, I want to bring my listeners to a place where they will be invited to follow Jesus.

5. THESIS STATEMENT

Taking everything together, then, I ask the question: what do I want to say about the long-range plan of God that will help me bring non-believing listeners to a point of decision? This "first thesis" is hard work, because I want to define what I'm trying to say as clearly as possible, but without having much material in hand to work with. But, again, after some frustrated attempts and manipulation, I arrive at the following thesis statement: *I want to persuade my non-believing listeners to become part of God's long-range plan for the world by becoming disciples of Jesus.*

It isn't very pretty at this point, but at least I have a direction for the next steps in the sermon-creating process.

As you will see when you try doing this on your own, *writing* the thesis is not an easy process. But don't give up on it! Its purpose is to benefit *you* as the preacher. You won't use this statement in your sermon. Nobody else will know about it. You spend this time because it helps you get a clear idea of *why* you want to preach this sermon. The more narrowly and simply you define your thesis, the easier it will be to decide what to include and what to exclude from your sermon later on. I cannot say this strongly enough: spending valuable energy here is the most advantageous use of your preparation time!

FIRST THINGS LAST

Finally, there is one more thing to keep in mind *before* you start developing thesis statements. I remind you of it now so you'll approach this bothersome task with greater ease. It is this: your "working thesis" will probably change later. In fact, there may be too many "sermons" already in any of the thesis statements above (in the primary text, for instance, am I talking about God's plan for individuals or the world? How does Jesus fit? Why must people come to Jesus to become part of this plan? Etc.?) But the "working thesis" at least gives me a focus for how I will examine the text, the kind of actualizing materials I will look for, and a starting point from which to structure my sermon.

This means that, most of the time, my "working thesis" won't accurately reflect what my final sermon will look like. The purpose of the "working thesis" is to help me *develop* my sermon. It gives me a first orientation. I won't be quoting it in the sermon, but making this attempt to focus my thinking at this early stage gives me a direction in which to start to work.

If your experience is similar to mine, you may find that your thesis may radically change over the course of the sermon construction process. Thus, I'm not all that concerned right now about developing an exact thesis. I only want a "working thesis" so I'll know what to include in my sermon and how I'll put it together.

Sometimes I will "get" a thesis statement on Monday morning, at the first phase of sermon construction. But sometimes I am *not* able to identify a specific or clear thesis statement this early in the process, no matter how hard I try. As I work with the biblical text and materials I've collected for this sermon, I sometimes find my sermon taking on a very different orientation. Sometimes, I only clearly understand my thesis late on Saturday night at the very *end* of the sermon construction process and final preparation. Even at that late point, I sometimes need to abandon my original intent.

However, by the time I step into the pulpit, I want as clear a thesis statement as possible, at least in my mind. All the components of the thesis should be clear at that point. A sermon isn't a sermon until it is preached, so it is only the *final preaching thesis* that I want to be as clear as possible.

If I don't do that, more often than not my sermon is restless and wavering, like a building without a foundation—or a cornerstone.

THE PRACTICE OF SERMON CONSTRUCTION

We now return to our practical example that we're building from chapter to chapter. In the last chapter, we identified Step 1: the text and singular theme: Jesus loves people from John 10:11-16. Now we begin to work on Step 2: the thesis statement. We'll move quickly through these five steps.

STEP 2: SINGLE THESIS

1. Preaching theme

I've already determined that I want to focus my general preaching theme on *Jesus' love for people.* Not always will I have settled this matter when I identify the text, but now is the time to clearly identify the single biblical truth I want to proclaim.

2. Statement of biblical truth

Now I must narrow that single biblical truth into an *action statement.* Of course, I notice several such biblical truths in this text that relate to my theme. Here are just three possibilities:

    a.   *Jesus is a Good Shepherd who loves his sheep.*

    b.   *Jesus laid down his life for sinners.*

    c.   *Jesus knows all his sheep.*

After thinking a bit about this text and these truths, and considering my target audience for this sermon, I decide to choose the first truth and write it in an action statement:

    Jesus, the Good Shepherd, loves his sheep.

3. Need

The next step, then, is to identify a particular need or desire or target audience. I've been thinking about those who attend Sunday morning worship, and am aware of a group of young people who are not believers, but whom I also know are restless in their search for meaning. This is the group I will target, and, because of them, I am able to identify the need I want to address:

    a restless search for meaning.

4. Rhetorical intent

The fourth step is to decide on my rhetorical intent: do I want to ask for a behavioral change, or will I inspire them? Will I seek action, or attitude? Given this target group, and knowing that they would be embarrassed by being asked to make a public statement of faith, I will not call for action in this sermon. Rather, I want to *inspire* them to think positively about Jesus and his challenging call:

My rhetorical intent, then, is *"to inspire."*

5.   *Thesis statement*

Finally, it's time to write a thesis statement for this sermon. This is the most difficult and time-consuming part of the process, but I finally arrive at the following:

I want to inspire my restless, non-believing listeners to follow Jesus as their Good Shepherd.

This, then, completes the second principle of biblical preaching. Our next step is to bring this thesis back to the text, and it is to that task that we turn in the next chapter.

CHAPTER 13
Principle Three: Thesis Exegesis

THE MUSIC OF THE TEXT

Every text of Scripture is like a great symphony, with different instruments playing different "themes" through different "movements," all of which interact and converge to create wonderful music. Sometimes the brass contend with the strings for control of the melody. Sometimes the tympani demands notice. Sometimes there is tension in the score when one mood tries to replace another. But it all comes together in a full "symphonic experience."

Biblical texts are just like that. They are filled with themes and issues and truths that clamor to be noticed and preached. Often you only notice these things when you bring a particular *need* to them, or when you start comparing this text against that one. But the biggest problem with much preaching today is that it seeks to expose, identify, and explain as many of these themes or truths as possible in order for it to be a "biblical" sermon.

Unfortunately, that's what "exegesis" has come to imply: you must discover everything you can about a particular passage of Scripture before you can preach on it. That kind of exegesis requires an in-depth study of the original language, comparing translations, learning the socio-historical context, fully examining the higher critical disciplines of biblical studies, reading as many commentaries as possible, and isolating, exploring, and contemplating all the themes and issues you can find in the text. This approach may be important for a teaching ministry, but it is too exhaustive if you have to preach week after week. This chapter, then, reexamines the discipline of exegesis specifically for the preaching ministry.

THE EXEGETICAL TASK

This third principle of biblical preaching (what I call "thesis exegesis") has to do with discovering *what the text says* to the listeners to whom you are preaching. It means seeking out a particular biblical truth from within the text and then *using the text to define and orient that truth.* Exegesis enables you to do that. Its counterpart, *eisegesis,* means forcing your own theological perspective upon a particular text.

Exegesis "draws out" what is in the text;
   eisegesis "adds to" the text.

Exegesis submits what *you* want to say to what the *text* says;
   eisegesis submits the *text* to what *you* want
     to say about your subject.

Exegesis is what makes preaching *biblical;*
   eisegesis makes preaching *theological.*

Transformational preaching, at its heart, is *biblical.* That means that we insist on proclaiming biblical truth while, at the same time, minimizing our own theology. Thus, we need to think about many of the issues related to the exegetical task.

For preaching purposes, William Thompson (1981) helpfully separates *exegesis* from *hermeneutics.* For him, exegesis is what we do when we extract biblical truth from its "contextual nest," while hermeneutics applies that truth to a new (contemporary) context. Of course, these two disciplines work hand in hand, and often one informs the other, so they cannot be simply divided as separate and distinct disciplines. However, because of the important issues involved in each, I have adopted Thompson's pattern; this chapter will examine the exegetical task, and Chapter 15 will look at the hermeneutical application.

Some approaches to exegesis suggest that there is only *one* preachable truth and only one "perfect sermon" in every text, and if you want to be a legitimate biblical preacher, you have to fully *process* the text before you can preach on it. The more studying you do, the more apt you are to discover this single "purpose" of the text. Unfortunately, when you cannot spend that kind of time in the study, you are never certain that you are preaching the text "correctly." In your feelings of guilt, then, you are unable to preach *with authority.* You will either be tentative and uncertain in what you are able to claim, or your preaching will become dogmatic, narrow-minded, and/or arrogant. Neither of these approaches is healthy. For this reason, it is important that we take another look at both the nature of the Bible and the exegetical task as it specifically relates to the preaching ministry. That is, how do we, with integrity, understand each biblical text while knowing that we don't have the time to fully study it? How can we preach biblical truth from a text if we don't plumb its depths?

I suggest that we think through three phases of the exegetical process in order to develop a consistent approach to each text we face. Each is relevant to preaching within the time constraints of pastoral ministry. These three phases are 1.) developing and maintaining a particular orientation to the biblical record, 2.) developing consistent exegetical tools that help you interpret what you read, and 3.) bringing your thesis to the text to seek *only those elements of the text that relate to that thesis.* In the rest of this chapter, then, we will examine each of these principles of exegesis. We begin with an overall approach to the text.

I. AN ORIENTATION TO THE TEXT

When you approach any text, it is important that you treat it consistently with all other texts. This *orientation* to the text is dependent on your basic view of biblical inspiration. However, it is possible to understand all the issues related to inspiration and still not have a basic orientation to the text as a whole. So the question that faces every preacher is: "How does inspiration *apply* to my understanding of the text and how I preach it?"

In order to understand what I mean, I want to take you through the three-stage process that brought me to this point of how I *understand* and *accept* the text. My hope is that this discussion will give you a better idea of my approach to the text and why I preach from it as I do. But I also hope these next few pages will encourage you to think through your *own* orientation to the text for your preaching.

The following three steps indicate how my own view has developed over the years.

1. A *LITERAL* ORIENTATION TO THE BIBLE

When I started to read the Bible seriously as a young Christian, I *understood it as I read it.* I believed what it said. I accepted the biblical story as *the story of what happened.* I made no distinction between *the event* and its *telling.* Angels, demons, and miracles were all part of what happened in biblical days, because the event was reported *as it happened.* Some of these events made the biblical world seem different from mine, but that didn't matter. (I realized later that I believed that the biblical world in which these things happened was a very different place from the world we live in today, much like Tolkien's *Middle Earth* or Lewis' *Narnia.)*

This approach to Scripture worked well for me—up to a point. But then something happened to my reading. For me, this change of awareness came quite early, when I thought about Jesus' instruction to pluck out my sinful eye and cut off my wandering hand (Matthew 5:29-30). It didn't make sense that Jesus would promote bodily mutilation as a requirement of discipleship. At that point, I became a more serious Bible *student.* The more I read the Bible, the more frustrating this "first" approach became, and I began to think of biblical texts differently. By the time I got to seminary, I was ready for a significant transition to a new understanding of Scripture.

2. A *HISTORICAL-CRITICAL* ORIENTATION TO THE BIBLE

My seminary education introduced me to a serious *academic* study of Scripture, which, for me, was a deeply satisfying approach to the Bible. Now I was exposed to key historical-critical disciplines of biblical studies. As I have since thought about this approach, I have come to realize that it essentially separates *text* from *event.* These scholarly tools lead to *textual* discovery, to the distinction between *what happened* and the *written record* of what happened. I could now study the biblical writings as literature, as a record of events, quite apart from addressing the issue of what "really" *happened.* This I found to be extremely helpful.

This *textual* emphasis, then, suggests that the Bible is a wholly-inspired *record* of events. I learned where the text came from *(form, source,* and *redaction* investigation), how the text was passed from generation to generation down through the centuries *(textual* investigation) and what the written text or spoken words would have meant to those to whom they were initially directed *(context* analysis). This meant that I could make an application of the biblical record to my own circumstances, because the Bible had become a *living word.* In a way, the *recorded history* could now be separated from the *actual experience of history.* This, in turn, allowed me freedom to apply the truth of *what happened* between God and the world without necessarily accepting all the *explanations* of the written account. These details could be contextualized because of the historical-critical methodology. (It was these *details* of the written record in my first orientation that indicated a different world than the one I live in and that sometimes separated the biblical world from my life.) This second approach was revelatory, though; it suddenly became clear to me that the biblical world was exactly the same world in which we live, and the biblical characters were exactly the same kinds of people we are, except that they lived in very different contexts. Thus, the extraordinary details of the biblical world that don't adequately reflect the world I live in are explainable through the critical tools as *contextualizing discourse.*

I have found these investigative *tools* extremely useful and important inroads into the text. They help me discover the meaning of the text or initial event for the original hearers or readers, which I can then apply to the circumstances or needs of my listeners. (We'll come back to this subject when we discuss exegetical tools for preaching.)

But then I entered graduate school and studied rhetorical criticism.

3.   A *RHETORICAL ASSENT* ORIENTATION TO THE BIBLE

My doctoral studies brought me to a third level of appreciation, one that emerged naturally from the first two. I realized that the second posture's separation of the story from its written form led to the movement to discover the "real" Jesus, a quest that was largely defined by Albert Schweitzer in 1906, and continues through the contemporary "Jesus Seminar," where participants, by casting ballots, attempt to find out what the historical Jesus *really* said. This project, of course, is futile; it attempts to force *textual* issues back onto the event, which cannot be done. It is silly to suggest, for instance, that voting can settle the issue of whether Jesus said that "the meek shall inherit the earth."

This third posture, on the other hand, brings text and event back together. It argues that we know about Jesus (and any of the biblical story) only *because of* the written text. There are no external sources, so we must accept the textual narrative for what it *intends* to say. When we try to bypass the *text* to get to the event (as the "Jesus Seminar" tries to do), we make the biblical story *whatever we want it to be.* Further, separating the event from its telling destroys the integrity of the written record, because, ultimately, we only know the story *from the text.*

This third orientation, then, brought me full circle back to my initial (literalist) posture, but with a more sophisticated understanding. It is what I call "rhetorical assent." It suggests that I must work through what the *text* has to say (the second posture), but by recognizing that, ultimately, I only know the story *through the text.*

This approach implies that a text has *intention.* By this I do not mean that we can attribute *authorial* intention, which most of the time we cannot do. Nor can we assume what *God's* intention was in enabling the text to be created. Nor can we know whether the text was written down by a single individual or by *communities* associated with particular traditions (the deuteronimistic tradition of the First Testament, for instance, or the Johanine community of the Second). Still, from whosever hand, there were *choices made* in compiling and editing the materials. When I speak of the *intention of a text,* I mean that each text is unique, no matter how it is put together or by whom. Each book of the Bible has a particular framework, worldview, theology, and orientation—all of which come together in the text we have. The written record that we have, and *only* this written record, offers a disciplined and intentional approach to God's interaction with the world. As such, we cannot simply dismiss any part of the biblical record by suggesting that something different actually happened than we know about *through the text itself.*

For example, the Gospels (along with Acts 20:31 and, perhaps, a few select passages from Paul's writings, such as 1 Corinthians 7:10-11 and 11:23-26) are the *only* material we have about Jesus. We understand (in written form) who Jesus is *only* because of the text and *only* because of the particular writers' perspectives. The "Jesus of history" is known *only* through the "Christ of faith" who is represented in Scripture. Thus, the Jesus of history *is* the Christ of faith.

We have now come full circle. What has been written arises from an *intention* of the text, as its author(s) included details and commentary that were important to their own telling of the story. In so saying, we have thus *reunited* event and explanation. We take the biblical story *as we have it;* in freedom, we accept the written account as accurately portraying the story because it is the *only* record by which we know the event.

Biblical preaching, then, demands that what we preach be fashioned from the actual text of Scripture; the "incarnated proclamation" is *constrained* by the written text. But this is a very different posture from the first (literal) approach to the Bible, because it relies on the critical/investigative disciplines to discover how the biblical material would have been understood by its first readers and hearers. Only *after* we understand the textual record, when the textual account is accepted *as the story,* can we interpret it for our listeners today.

This orientation to the biblical record, then, brings us back to the question of exegesis. How do we understand the text? And how can we be consistent in our exegetical task so that we minimize our own subjectivity, our *eisegesis?*

II. AN ORIENTATION TO THE EXEGETICAL TASK

This orientation to Scripture, then, recognizes the importance of the *text* of Scripture, and brings us back to the task of exegeting what is evident within the authoritative text. We want to know what the text says and what it would have meant to its original hearers or readers.

Very practically, you won't have time to exegete every text as fully as you'd like to, so it is important to develop *consistent* principles of exegesis. *Consistency* is an important word here. A consistent exegesis helps you discover those valuable nuggets of truth in a text. And consistency helps you avoid the easy tendency to "proof-text" or skim the surface of the text without grappling with what truth may be embedded there. Consistency, however, develops only over a period of years, as you reflect on and study and work with various texts. My own exegetical principles, for instance, have emerged and developed over long years of practice and reflection. There is value in sharing them, as an exercise to help you see how I have settled some of the difficult issues that arise when we talk about various biblical texts. I also challenge you to start now to develop your own principles of exegesis that suit your theological framework. The point is that you want to be *consistent* every time you approach the Bible. If you start now to develop these guidelines, and add to them as you work more and more with biblical texts, it will make your exegetical task easier. As with any discipline, your grasp of what "works" and what doesn't "work" will grow with time and usage.

What follows, then, are some of the principles I use in interpreting specific biblical texts. I try to apply them consistently, though most of the time it is an *informal* application, by which I mean that I don't always think them through every time I come to a text (this procedure would be much too time-consuming). Rather, I recognize that these are principles I follow when I come across a difficult text. I also take these exegetical principles as *guidelines* that help me "discover" the text. They are fluid *principles,* not rigid *rules;* I try to keep my mind alert to each text and what it might say.

EXEGETICAL PRINCIPLES

Exegesis asks me to understand all I can about the text. That is, I want to arrive at clear biblical truth from within whatever text I'm using, truth that would have had *meaning* to the original hearers or readers, which, in turn, provides a clear directive for my listeners today.

To do it adequately and consistently, I use several analytical *inroads* to discovery. While I am prone to think "outside the box," I also trust trained scholars and their insights into Scripture so that I will not wander too far afield from the "normal" boundaries of our historic Christian faith. *Commentaries, Bible Dictionaries* and *Handbooks, Atlases, Study Bibles,* and *other useful resources* help me know if my understanding is *upheld* (or *not contradicted)* by other scholars. And, because I am not an expert in biblical languages, the use of *many translations* of the English Bible helps me understand the original intent of the passage. This kind of scholarship gives me useful information by which to approach each text.

But what am I looking for? And what are the important principles that help me understand the information I find?

Three textual inroads

I begin by suggesting three general principles by which I gain access to the written text. I want to know what it would have meant to its first listeners or readers.

1. The literary inroad. A *literary* examination focuses on the written record of the text. That is, the *type* of literature is important, because different genres will be interpreted in different ways. *Song* and *poetry* (as in the *Psalms)* are different literary forms than *parable* (Matthew 13) and *epistle* (Paul's letter to Titus). Knowing the type of literature helps me know better how to interpret it. *Apocalyptic* imagery, for instance, cannot be interpreted literally and historical accounts should not be interpreted figuratively. The *structure* of the text and its language will also lead us to insights into biblical truth.

Form and *textual investigative* methods are literary in nature. *Form investigation* examines the oral transmission and development of a particular text before it was written down; *textual investigation* seeks to locate the best and/or earliest form of the written material (it wants to discover, as near as possible, what the original writer wrote).

I also want to be aware of the *larger written* context in which my particular text is located, so an examination of several verses before and after the passage helps prevent a misguided understanding of the text. This exercise can also lend additional insight to the text.

2. The authorial inroad. A second "inroad" to the text is finding out who wrote it. For most of the First Testament books, we don't know the answer to this question (this is also true of some of the Second Testament books, such as Hebrews and 2 Peter). But knowing the author can help us interpret more accurately what would have been understood by the first readers, especially if we have other examples of that person's writing and/or theology.

Source investigation is an attempt to get at authorship or, at least, the *sources* of the story. For instance, the J.E.P.D. theory in Pentateuchal and Former Prophet studies is an attempt to understand repetition in the written account. The Synoptic problem is answered by assuming different *sources* of Gospel information. These issues belong to source critical methodology.

Redaction investigation is another way to define authorship. It deals with the editing of the text and the communities of faith from which those texts came. How was the text put together? What choices were made? What is the theology of the writer and/or community?

3. The "first receiver" inroad. God used *imperfect* human beings to produce these books, people who were subject to their own times and limitations. That is to say, the Bible was produced in and through particular historical and cultural contexts, not created "outside" our world and then "handed down" to us. Thus, I want to know the circumstances out of which and to which the discourse was addressed. I want to know what the text said to its original hearers or readers. Only when I can make a determination of what the truth meant in its initial situation can I apply that truth to my context today.

Contextual (or *socio-political) investigation* is extremely helpful in understanding Scripture from the socio-economic circumstances of the day and the particular issues raised by the revelation of the text within its Mediterranean culture. That historical and social milieu was unique. Local culture, particular circumstances, language, thought-forms, topography, and the situation of the local community to which these words were addressed—all are important. Combined, they help us understand the original concerns of the writer or speaker and God's truth in that particular time for those particular people. We can discover some of this information through reference tools, which are potential resources for discovery.

Van Harn (1992) suggests that the preacher must "respect the distance between the text and the pew." That is, the text must be honored *in its own setting* first of all. God spoke then; He speaks now. But I can only know the relevance of the text when I know what it would have meant to its first hearers or readers. This process is critically important to preaching. If I don't understand the text in its own context, if I don't respect the text *historically,* or understand how God spoke to that day and time, I will not be able to make accurate judgments about what God wants to say to our day and time. The biblical record loses its integrity, and so do I as a biblical preacher.

Given these important inroads into the biblical text that guide our exegesis, what then are some of the "principles of discovery" I have adopted?

Principles for discovery

As they have developed over the years, the following guidelines have become "second nature" to my reading of Scripture. They are particularly helpful in uncovering "problem texts." But, in general, these principles guide my reflection on the text and help me discover preachable biblical truth.

Establishing a set of principles is concerned more with *how* I decide to interpret difficult questions than with how I *interpret* each. Many unthinking preachers, in the rush of completing a sermon, interpret each text in a way that *seems* legitimate at the moment, or they take the most literal view, but that approach often results in an inconsistent or contradictory theology.

These following principles, then, provide a way to be consistent in my exegetical task.

1. A questioned understanding. When there are tensions between my *present understanding* of God or Scripture and *new information,* I do not question *God,* my *salvation,* or the *Scripture.* In those cases, I question *my finite and imperfect understanding* of God or Scripture.

2. Progressive revelation. God has revealed Himself in a limited way, through forms and ideas that could be understood by the people to whom that revelation came. But that earlier information was supplanted by later, more advanced information. It means that there is no biblical material included solely for later generations that would have had no meaning for those to whom it was originally spoken or written. (Sometimes, for instance, the Messianic passages of Isaiah are interpreted only as referring to Jesus, and sometimes the Apocalypse is viewed only as a futurist document.) *Progressive revelation,* instead, means that God has chosen to disclose Himself in Scripture little by little so that people in every generation may know Him in a more "full-picture" way than those who knew Him beforehand.

Think of the landscape artist. Working from general to specific, he begins by broadly sketching the framework of his painting, and then he fills in background colors and then foreground colors, and then specific shapes and innumerable details, and, finally, highlights. The former information isn't incorrect or mistaken—it just isn't yet complete.

For instance, the first Commandment says, "You shall have no other gods before Me." God does not say that there *are* no other gods, just that His people are to *honor* no other gods. Actually, it isn't until the time of Isaiah (perhaps 600-700 years later), that God revealed Himself as the *only* God. The people to whom He was speaking in the time of Moses would not have understood Him in any other way. And look at the dietary laws in Leviticus 11. They were important because they revealed a God Who cares about His people and demands obedience. But are the laws eternal? Peter's vision in Acts 10 seems to "fulfill," or reinterpret, those laws. Similarly, Jesus, in Matthew 5:17, says he came not to abandon the Law, but to "fulfill" it.

The principle of progressive revelation can be helpful, particularly when we encounter texts that seem to reflect contradictions.[1] Some of these are "genre" issues, but in many other cases, I understand that earlier texts are

---

[1] For instance, Revelation 7:4 (144,000) doesn't seem to coincide with "all who believe will be saved" (Romans 10:13). And how do we understand the bodily mutilation sayings of Jesus in Matthew 18:8-9 in light of I Corinthians 12:18? How do we understand the "day" of Genesis 1:5 with "a day is like a thousand years" (2 Peter 3:8) with the "Day of the Lord" in Matthew 24:29-31? And in 1 Corinthians 15:51-52, Paul writes that we will all be changed *instantaneously* when the Lord returns, but in 1 Thessalonians 4:16 he writes that the dead in Christ will rise first *when Jesus returns.* So, does the believer who died in Jesus go right to heaven (as in Luke 23:43) or to a "holding place"? And how do we understand God's command that all enemies be slaughtered (Joshua 11:6) in light of Jesus' words in Matthew 5:43-45 (that we are to *love* our enemies)? And 1 Samuel 16:14 tells us that the *Lord* sends an evil spirit on Saul, but in Matthew 12:24-28, when Jesus is accused of *casting out* demons, he says that he can't be in league with Satan, because Satan would not "cast himself out." I raise these queries (all of which have legitimate answers) not to cast doubt on the authority of the biblical text, but to say that these kinds of questions must be faced if we are to preach the text faithfully and consistently.

limited by the "theologies" of those biblical writers, and that those earlier ideas are more completely understood through later revelation.

3. Gospel primacy. This principle is similar. By it, I mean that difficult portions of Scripture may be interpreted in light of the *latest* and *fullest* revelation of God in the gospel of Jesus Christ. The quality of God's love that we know in Jesus, for instance, is a more *complete* image of God than the reports of His warring nature in the First Testament. God loves the world and has revealed a plan of salvation and right way of living for all people who are in His kingdom. Thus, I interpret earlier conflicting accounts of God's activity in light of His love in Jesus Christ. In many cases when I preach from the First Testament, I focus on *other* biblical truth than that of a warring God.

4. Authorial "theology." Each biblical writer has a particular "theological perspective" and worldview, a particular "inspired" understanding of God, and expresses God's Self-revelation in light of that perspective. Thus, the cultural, historical, and theological limitations of each writer influence what a particular text meant for its first hearers or readers. Biblical "truth" is authoritative, but the theological limitations of each writer are *not* authoritative. They are the vehicles, though, through which God chose to reveal Himself. Thus, it is important to unpack the truth from its human limitation. Problems arise when we apply a biblical writer's *theology* rather than the biblical *truth* that was revealed in that particular context.

For example, we see many instances of women who are active in the Second Testament church (Acts 16:13-15, Acts 18:24-26, Romans 16:12, Galatians 3:28, Philippians 4:3, etc.). Paul's instructions for the propriety of Christian women (1 Corinthians 14:34 and 1 Timothy 2:9-10), then, must be understood in the full light of his appreciation of women in ministry. When we take a few obviously contextualized comments of Paul about women in Corinth and apply these directives to all women for all time, it creates problems for the life and ministry of the Church, but also with the responsibility that women disciples have in taking an active role in ministry.

Thus, biblical *truth* is "wrapped up" in the *theologies* (perceptions) of the writers, and exegesis means seeking the *truth* behind the *theology* of the biblical writer. Sometimes, I must try to isolate the kernel of truth that drives the theology. It is *that* biblical truth that reflects a "localization" of the eternal and unchanging Truth that informed the *biblical* writer, and is applicable to our context today.

Further, biblical writers used literary forms. *Truth,* then, is conveyed through many *genres* of literature in the Bible that are essential to its inspiration. There are many different types of literature in the Bible, most of which are *not* to be taken literally or dogmatically. The Bible's poetry and parables, for instance, tend to be personal *reflections* with a lot of emotional response to personal issues more than they are propositional truth (as, for instance, in Psalm 137:8-9). When we limit the Bible only to a formal or literal "science and mathematics" textbook, we restrict God's ability to communicate truth. And we negate most of its power. I'm suggesting that it's more important that we understand *truth* than the writer's *theology*. Sometimes we must crawl behind or underneath the text to discover the more general truth that is at work.

How, then, do we make the distinction between *truth* and *theology?* Unfortunately, there are no easy rules, and the task is a lifelong pursuit, but it may mean that, in some cases, that we accept the Bible's "inspired truth" rather than its "inspired theology." Sometimes, such as when a biblical text contradicts the principles of "Gospel Primacy," I look behind the expression of the particular writer to get at the *truth.* For instance, the "words of God" in much of the First Testament account may, in reality, be the words of the author. In these cases, when what God is *reported* to have said or done contradicts the "Gospel Primacy" principle, the *author's theology* may be in evidence, and I would take those words as the author's *understanding* of the will of God (as perhaps in Joshua 11:6 and Hosea 13:16).

However, I don't *preach* these issues or questions! These are simply principles by which I *investigate* a text. My intent is to discover truth that I can passionately proclaim, with full conviction and without hesitation, as a word from God for us today.

5. A balance of systematic and biblical theologies. It will be wise for you to recognize the on-going tension between systematic and biblical theologies. Systematic theology says that the individual text is understood in light of the whole of Scripture. Biblical theology says that the individual text *constrains* and helps *define* systematic theological principles.

I generally practice *biblical theology* in my preaching. While each text is necessarily understood in light of my own developing "systematic theology," my first inclination is to see what each biblical writer and/or passage of Scripture, taken in its own unique situation, *adds to* systematic theology. I seek biblical truth within each text, and try not to *force* systematic theology on this passage. As intentionally as possible, I avoid *proof-texting* and *eisegesis.*

However, sometimes the limited *theology* of the writer is more evident than *truth* in a particular text. From my growing systematic theology, then, I take the larger biblical message into account, which, in turn, helps my interpretation of a particular (problematic) text (as, above, with Paul's view of women).

6. Event over explanation. Sometimes, when a reported event seems to contradict the "Gospel Primacy" principle, the *event* may be separated from the *explanation* of the event. Because *doctrine* is community-recognized *truth,* and *theology* is a way to understand *reality,* authorial explanation may reflect the writer's view of *reality* rather than propositional *truth* (as in 1 Samuel 16:14, Mark 5:11-13, and Acts 5:1-11).

7. Omniscience and attributed motivation. Akin to the "event over explanation" principle, I also look for motivation that is *attributed* by biblical writers to biblical characters, or, even, to God. This manifests itself in two forms, *omniscience* and *attributed motivation.*

For instance, in Mark 8:2, at the Feeding of the 4,000, Jesus says, "I have compassion for these people." We know, then, that Jesus is compassionate because he *says* so. But in Mark's story of the Feeding of the 5,000 two chapters earlier, *Mark* tells us that Jesus had compassion on the crowd, "because they were like sheep without a shepherd" (Mark 6:34). In that instance, Mark is demonstrating *omniscience.* He is telling us what Jesus is *thinking* and how he is *feeling.* And later, in 12:28, Mark tells his readers what a teacher of the law had "noticed" a dispute. That is, Mark again claims omniscience, that he *knows* the mind of this teacher of the law.

Attributed motivation is another form of omniscience. The author tells us *why* people decide to take certain actions. So, in Mark 8:11, for instance, Mark tells us that the Pharisees came to Jesus "to test him." This *seems* to be their motivation from the question they ask, but it is possible that they first came to see Jesus because they heard he was a great teacher, and then asked him this question only later when they decided to "test him." Yet Mark states unequivocally that this is the reason for their coming. In so saying, he is *attributing motivation* to them. These kinds of examples are sprinkled throughout the Scriptures.

These Markan texts, of course, are not problematic, but there are instances where motivation is attributed to God in a similar way. In Genesis 6:6-7, for instance, God *repents* of His created order, an attribution that doesn't legitimately reflect later revelation, where, for instance, Ephesians 1:3-6 tells us that the *whole plan of God* was known from the beginning (thus, no need for Him to "repent"). In such cases, I recognize these as *theological* understandings of these writers, not *doctrinal* points. When I am seeking biblical truth, I bypass these theological constructs to discover a *preachable truth* behind the way the event is recorded.

8. Exhibitative Gospels. Because the Gospels came out of the Church and not the Church out of the Gospels, these documents are *descriptive* rather than prescriptive. That is, the Gospels tend to *exhibit* life in and issues faced by the early Church. Sometimes we can better understand a Gospel story or parable of Jesus when we consider the situation to which or in which it might have been spoken or written. That is, perhaps some of the Gospel narratives are included because they address a problem the early church was facing. The writers (or tellers) remembered these stories and sayings of Jesus because they found them relevant to the needs of the emerging churches. This principle will often add rich and relevant insight to particular stories of Jesus.

9. Affirmative preaching. I preach only those *truths* that I can *affirm* from the text rather than themes that raise lingering doubts. When I'm dealing with a problematic text, for instance, I always find positive, unquestionable truth tucked away in what might be an otherwise confusing or cumbersome theology of the writer. Since I am proclaiming only one truth in any sermon, I don't have to wrestle with these doubts as I would were I preaching an expository sermon.

As far as possible, then, I try to develop my thesis from a *kernel of truth* in a passage of Scripture rather than its *theology.* Further, I develop my sermon from the *truth* that I have sometimes laboriously unveiled rather than *my path of discovery.* Listeners don't always need to know the details of *how* I exegeted a particular truth (as I might do in a preaching lecture). I discover the biblical truth and then develop my thesis from there. That truth becomes the focal point of the way I deal with the text. So when I *preach* difficult texts, I don't, in most cases, indulge in serious academic argument or discussion from the pulpit about *what the text means,* or *why I have interpreted it in this way.*

These exegetical principles are simply ways that help me understand a passage of Scripture when I encounter difficulty or contradiction. They provide *consistency* to get at truth in the text. In so doing, my intent is to discover truth that I can proclaim with authority.

But let's move past the theoretical framing of the exegetical task and get to its practicalities.

III. THE THIRD PRINCIPLE OF BIBLICAL PREACHING: THESIS EXEGESIS

Having understood the importance of consistent and critical exegesis, I now introduce a simplifying principle to the process of exegesis. To understand it, let me first ask a question.

I hear that you're going to the mountains. What clothing will you take? Of course, your answer depends on your *purpose* in going, *when* you are going, and the kind of *circumstances* you'll be in when you get there. Are you planning to swim, go for a formal dinner at a favorite mountain resort, hike and camp, work in your garden, lounge inside a cabin, or ski? Your *reason* for going will help you decide what to take.

"Thesis exegesis" does just that. It asks what *your purpose* is in preaching this particular sermon, which, in turn, helps you know what particular details you will *draw out* of the text. I am not suggesting a short-cut to the exegetical task, but it does minimize the amount of time you need to spend on exegesis. "Thesis exegesis" asks you to glean only those clues from your text that *support your thesis.*

Let's assume you have isolated the text you want to use. You have also identified the specific biblical truth and written your thesis statement. Now you use your thesis to *control* the information you take from the text. There will be many important and interesting "facts" and theological issues you identify in your study of the passage, but many of them won't help shape your thesis. They will, in fact, make your sermon confusing and complicated, both for you and your listeners. So you not only have to choose elements of the text that *support* your thesis, you also have to *eliminate* much of the textual material that doesn't relate to your thesis.

So you bring your thesis back to the text to identify particular "points" or "phases" that you see in the text that will bring about your thesis. Keep your purpose sharp here. It's why it is so helpful to *know your thesis,* because the elements you draw from the text then help you develop your sermon rather than confuse it. These bits of biblical information become the "hooks" on which you will hang the steps or "moves" of your sermon. They become the *grounds* by which you build your *claim.* Try to discover in the text exactly those details that will help you fashion your thesis, and in a way that brings your listener face to face with the biblical truth.

However, because preaching is an art form, sometimes, of course, you won't have a clear thesis before you return to the text. On those occasions, keep working with the text. Keep thinking it through. Lay a congregational need alongside it. Let various themes speak from within it. The text will soon take on a particular shape for you, and one truth should emerge from within it. And when you identify this truth, design your thesis, and then bring it back to your text to recognize *what* information you will need to support that thesis and what information you can eliminate that *doesn't* support that thesis.

One more point. We've been discussing *textual* exegesis in this chapter, but the principle is also true for other resources you will use (which we'll talk about in Chapter 16). You eventually want to conform *everything* to your thesis by the time you step into the pulpit. To do it you'll have to give up a lot of interesting information from the biblical text and the possible stories you can use. But your preaching will be far more direct and transformational if you preach with a single idea in mind.

WHEN IT JUST ISN'T "RIGHT"

Finally, before we get to some practical examples, suppose you've started working on a theme, recognized a need, identified a thesis and then find, as you start exegeting, that you can't substantiate your thesis with the text. What do you do? Actually, you have three choices.

First, you can *change your thesis* to fit the text. Remember that you can change your thesis up until the time you step into the pulpit. Just make sure you have a clear idea what you want to say in this sermon before you open your mouth, because this *idea* (whatever it is) must, in the end, help you restrict and conform everything that you include and exclude from your sermon, and the way you structure it.

The second option is that you can *change the text.* If nothing emerges from your exegetical study that helps you bring about the thesis on which you have been led to preach, then find another text. (This, of course, is not appropriate if you preach from the lectionary or are working on a sermon series.) But remembering that every text has a unique slant on biblical truth, go back and look again at one of the several texts you eliminated from your initial choice. You might find that a different text *now* (after further development of the idea) suits your thesis more adequately.

Third, *change the need* you are addressing. Because your thesis brings together a congregational need and a particular text, if the text doesn't shed light on the need you've identified, you may want to rethink that situation or need. There are a great number of needs, desires, issues, or circumstances that can be addressed in any sermon, so you might re-orient the direction your sermon has taken.

Ultimately, it is important that you not force an unfitting thesis on a resistant text or an ill-fitting situation. When you do that, it isn't biblical preaching. You then resort to "theological" preaching, which, in turn, often leads you to an *eisegetical* approach to the text.

The next step in the process, of course, is to move from the exegesis to the *application* of the biblical truth, and, for that, we turn to the next chapter. But before we do that, we want to see what I've been talking about in practice.

THE PRACTICALITIES OF EXEGESIS

This principle says that we exegete the text according to the thesis, that we use the thesis to control the information we glean from the text. This third principle of biblical preaching is more a *process* than a single task. Throughout the rest of the construction of the sermon, up until the time I preach it, I will continue to read and contemplate and integrate and submit every element of the sermon to the text. So I will need time to reflect and re-reflect on the text. If I only exegete the text *once* for details, I might miss some valuable textual material. (Sometimes, I have suddenly seen something in the text when I'm reading the Scripture aloud from the pulpit just before preaching!)

When I face the task of exegeting the text, I've already done some of the work, because I had to look over the text to discover my theme, biblical truth, and thesis statement. But now I'm returning to the text with my thesis worked out for more specific elements of the text. Now I want to see how the text supports the thesis I've developed.

When I do that, I notice that something else begins to happen. The textual insights I discover often help *clarify* and *re-orient* my thesis. This is all part of the "emerging sermon" that is the art form of preaching.

Let's look at the example we used in the last chapter. Let's suppose I'm preaching on 2 Thessalonians 1:3-5 (the primary text we used there). You will remember that the thesis was *"I want to inspire the suffering members of my congregation to remain faithful to Jesus Christ when they are persecuted for their faith."*

This text is not problematic, so I don't have to wrestle with most of the principles I've defined earlier. However, there are many, many underlying assumptions about this text that inform how I understand it. For instance, the *Apostle Paul* wrote it (this has implications for other passages within this letter, but not this one). I know that it is a *letter* (which means that I tend to interpret it *plainly*, not figuratively). It is part of the *Second Testament* canon, thus it reflects a knowledge of Jesus. These are the kinds of foundational exegetical principles that I bring, unthinking, to exegete a text like this.

But I now come to the third phase of exegesis where I want to submit my thesis to the text. So I bring my thesis to the text and see what components of Paul's argument support this idea. I see the following five items:

Verse 3:	your faith is growing more and more
Verse 4:	you are demonstrating perseverance and faith
	you have persecutions and trials
Verse 5:	you will be counted worthy of God's kingdom
	you are suffering *for* the kingdom

I may not use all of these, and I may later include others, but I have decided at this point *not* to include their increasing love (v. 3), boasting about their endurance to other churches (v. 4) or God's judgment (v. 5).

Further, these five "points" I've identified do not provide the structure for the sermon, though they will provide *information* for the structure (we'll look at how to put the sermon together later). For now, it is important only to recognize that we bring the thesis back to the text to see how it will be developed and what we can and cannot say about it.

THE PRACTICE OF SERMON CONSTRUCTION

We come now to the example we've been following through these principles of biblical preaching. As a reminder, our text (Step 1) is John 10:11-16, and our thesis (Step 2), from the last chapter, is: *"I want to inspire my restless, non-believing listeners to follow Jesus as their Good Shepherd."* We come now to the task of thesis exegesis.

STEP 3: THESIS EXEGESIS

The principle of thesis exegesis means that I now go back through the passage and identify the themes and issues that seem to relate to my thesis. I want to inspire my listeners to understand Jesus in a way that they will want to follow him, so I will identify elements of this passage that provide that kind of information. These "points," then, inform my thesis. With this in mind, I then make a list of the following "points" about the Shepherd:

1. he lays down his life for the sheep (vv. 11, 15)
2. he "owns" the sheep (v. 12)
3. he knows the sheep (v. 14)
4. the sheep know him (v. 14)
5. there is one flock and one shepherd (v. 16)

I also decide, at this early point, that I will *not* talk about the hired hand (vv. 12 and 13), the story of the wolf (v. 12), and other sheep that are not in the pen (v. 16). This is not to suggest that I would never include these elements, but whether I do so or not depends fully on my thesis. If my thesis changes before I preach this sermon, I might include some of these points. But for now, keeping a lot of detail just because it is in the text will only confuse my thesis, sermon, and, ultimately, my listeners. I want to let my thesis *and* exegesis be as streamlined as possible—it will help the next steps in the development of this particular sermon.

This, then, completes the third principle of biblical preaching.

CHAPTER 14
Preaching to an "Itch"

HERMENEUTICAL LEGITIMACY

Hermeneutics is concerned with the *relevance* of biblical truth to life today. Here is where we talk about *application.* If people don't recognize that biblical truth *applies* to them, it is, essentially, meaningless for them. If biblical truth is not *confronting* or *challenging* or *enlightening* people for where, how, and why they live, the preaching that they hear is, in effect, irrelevant. If the Christian faith is to be a *living* faith, not a *theoretical* one, and the Bible is to be a *living* Bible and not an old dead Book, it will come only when the preacher makes the truth of Scripture *relevant* to the lives of listeners.

WHY A LISTENER-ORIENTATION?

Is theology a "thing," a reality apart from human experience? That is, should *every* sermon be related to a need or desire? Or is it enough just to "talk doctrine"? A lot of preaching is like that, after all. It presents an intricate theological argument based on an assumption that doctrine is "real," that biblical truth has meaning *apart* from life.

It's a theological issue that you will have to settle on your own, and you may want to do some investigation of the great theologians before you settle it. But my personal conviction is that doctrine, biblical truth, and theology are *only* relevant when they are contextual, *only* when they are *related* to real life.

What do I mean when I talk about relevancy to life? Well, first, preaching must be transformational. If so, it must be directed toward *needs* or *desires* that real people face in their real lives. Only when biblical truth is made *relevant* to where and how people live does theology have any significance. That's why I define theology as a personal understanding of how God interacts in our world. If there is no *integration,* there is no "theology." But when truth is applied in a meaningful way, out of that *relevance,* people will be transformed. Transformation never comes about when the lives, concerns, and the issues real people face are not taken into account. So when doctrine is proclaimed for its own sake, when sermons are informational and theological, *transformational hardly ever happens.*

Second, when I talk about relevancy, I am suggesting that biblical truth meets the needs or desires of people (a *need* drives us away from that which is wrong or negative in our lives, while a *desire* pulls us toward something better). Needs and desires produce a *drive for satisfaction,* by which I mean those things that *motivate* real people: a need for certain information, a "mission" in life, a pain, a life-long calling, or fulfillment in a job.

Third, listener-oriented preaching implies that there are many types of needs and desires that people have. There are, of course, immediate *psychological* and *spiritual* needs or desires, but there are also *social* and *existential* needs. There are, indeed, *many* levels of needs and desires that can be identified and addressed in preaching. What I am suggesting is that when *any* need or desire is identified and biblical truth is focused on meeting that need or desire, change is more likely to come about than when the sermon just "talks theology."

Finally, preaching to needs or desires doesn't negate biblical preaching in favor of topical preaching. Instead, *whatever* our starting point, we still bring a need to a specific text and biblical truth (or vice versa). In that way, whether we start the sermon construction process with a topic or a text, with a need or idea or story, in the end, all must converge in the sermon. And when preaching becomes biblical in that way, the Bible has power and relevancy.

But what specifically does it mean for us to be listener-centered in our preaching? And how do we go about discovering the *itches* that our listeners have? If we are serious about preaching that *applies* the truth of God to the situation and circumstances of the listener, then we must consider some of the issues that help us relate to our listeners. It is that topic that concerns us in this chapter.

A QUESTION OF RELEVANCE

If a tree falls in a forest and nobody is there to hear it, does it still make a sound? That old philosophical question has been around for ages. The answer, in a world of sophisticated scientific explanation, is: *of course, it does* (unless we say that sound is only what is *heard* rather than what is *produced).* We know, of course, that sound is a system of waves that moves out from a source. A falling tree *causes* those waves because there is the contact of solid objects with each other. We *know* scientifically, then, that sound waves result from that kind of collision.

Unlike the tree in the forest, though, preaching *requires* listeners for it to be preaching. Preaching *depends* on hearing. Unfortunately, a lot of preachers don't practice this simple truth. They think that as long as a message is formulated and then shot out into the airwaves (even with great gusto and passion), their job is done. It doesn't really matter to them whether or not anybody pays attention to what they say. "Communication," for them, implies the dissemination of information, like putting sound waves into motion. Their words are like trees falling in the forest: sound is still produced even if nobody is there to hear it. And their practice demonstrates that they are perfectly happy with this arrangement. They have listeners, but it doesn't matter whether what they say is relevant to those listeners or not.

But that kind of preaching is a waste of everybody's time. If nobody "hears" the spoken word, it can hardly be called "preaching," because preaching *requires* listeners. And listeners imply *communicating.* Communication, then, requires something *more* than just the *transmission of information.* The audience, congregation, or listeners are *essential* elements of the preaching event.

If we believe that, our preaching must actually *communicate* with those listeners. They become part of the formula of the preaching event; they are taken into account when the preacher speaks. So, a key piece in bringing about a *transaction* is "connecting" with the listeners. They have a *necessary* role in preaching.

That is, preaching is more than telling your congregation what you believe or what you know or all those interesting biblical insights you have discovered. Transformational preaching moves beyond that. It provides a unique and holy opportunity to *persuade* your listeners to respond to the truth of Scripture, to that which you have discovered in your study.

I take a strong position about the eternal value of gospel preaching. But if your message isn't legitimately "heard," if it makes no difference, then of what value is it? You may have the most important sermon in the world, but if your listeners don't "get it," you're wasting your time—and theirs! It's no different than preaching to an English-speaking congregation in Hungarian, without an interpreter. They won't know if your sermon is about Jesus and the Syro-Phoenician woman or the price of potatoes. You may be preaching to a group of interested Muslims, but if you don't speak a "language" they can understand, it doesn't matter how critical or eternal your message of salvation may be. The same is true of your "regular" listeners: if you don't know them or understand them or relate biblical truth to them in a "language" that *they* understand, you're wasting your breath. Ultimately, if you don't *fashion* your message with your listeners in mind, taking *their* thought patterns and interests into consideration, they won't *hear* it.

Your responsibility as the preacher is to capture the attention of your listeners and maintain that interest. It is *your* responsibility to be relevant. The burden rests with *you*, not your listeners, as to whether they actually listen or not, whether they "get the message" or not.

So if you are concerned with "connecting" with your listeners, you must take them into consideration from the very beginning of the sermon-creating process, right through to the completion of the preaching event. This means understanding their own mindset and hesitations, and, sometimes, the disagreements they'll have with the biblical truth you want to proclaim. If you want your preaching to be transformational, it must be fully oriented to these particular listeners in these particular circumstances at this particular time. That's the beginning of transformation.

Toivo Pilli, my friend from Estonia, was visiting America in 1995, and was invited to preach in a small country chapel. On Saturday night, the young pastor of that congregation took my friend into the empty chapel and "introduced" him to members of the congregation. He said, "In this seat tomorrow will be an old woman who just lost her husband. Over here there will be a young family. They just discovered that their 5-year old daughter has a cancer." Seat by seat, pew by pew, my friend was introduced to his congregation for the next morning. Here was a pastor who knew his congregation and their needs, and it was obvious to his Estonian guest that he loved them. That Saturday visit helped prepare my friend to preach the next day.

It's a good exercise to try. Only when you know the needs of your people can you scratch where they itch. Gerald Ray Jordan (1951) writes:

> *The advantage in preparing a sermon with the actual needs of our people in mind is (that) . . . we are dealing with the daily discouragements, the constant frustration and the corroding worries of the people who are before us Sunday after Sunday. We sit where they sit, wear their shoes, and if we are genuinely sympathetic, not merely walk into their hearts and minds, but into their skins! We know what they fear and understand why they are so often defeated.*

The congregation of *itchy* individual listeners, then, is at the very heart of transformational preaching. It is concerned, from its roots, with those to whom this message will become meaningful. And the transformational preacher will want to scratch where they itch.

PREACHING AS GENRE

A need-driven approach to preaching begins with understanding preaching as a particular genre of public discourse. Genre is important because it leads us to consider *audience expectations.* This was how Aristotle understood genre in his *Rhetoric.* The type of *audience* determined the type of *discourse* required. He wrote, "it is . . . the hearer that determines the speech's end and object." For Aristotle, there were only three types of public discourse: forensic, deliberative, and epideictic. These divisions identified different types of *audiences,* and he made the distinction so that public speakers would understand the *expectations* that listeners brought to the event. In turn, that listener-expectation determined the style and content of the speaker's discourse.

Thus, a genre is a type of message or literature that shares common structural and/or content features, and which creates particular *expectations* in its listeners or readers. Within the broad genre of political discourse, for instance, there are different kinds of specialized genres, including political stumping, inaugural addresses, or Prayer Breakfast speeches. Each of these has different structural and content characteristics. But, more importantly, genre helps the *audience* know what to expect. And, subsequently, genre suggests that we should alter our discourse, as Jamieson (1973) says, to meet the "expectations of the audience and the demands of the situation." Thus, genre helps *position* an audience to "hear" a discourse in a particular way.

Preaching, too, is a genre of public discourse. As such, you have certain expectations that frame your sermons. But it also implies that when your listeners come to hear you preach, they also know what to expect. That is, some of the work of preaching is already done for you, simply because of this "expectation factor." For most of our listeners, they are either ready to hear "gospel" or they are expecting to be brought to that point. They probably already expect that the biblical message will be made relevant to them. This is important for how you construct your sermons and how you preach. But you may need first of all to *establish* a need or desire, or help your listeners *recognize* a need they have. Most of the time, your listeners will *not* be aware of their needs or wants, so you have to rhetorically construct those needs for them.

So how, as biblical preachers, do we know the needs, issues, desires, or concerns of our listeners?

KNOWING YOUR AUDIENCE

Being listener-centered in our preaching means that we want to be relevant to our listeners. This brings us to the subject of *context analysis,* one of the important, but infrequently identified, elements of effective preaching.

Context analysis is a process of analyzing the needs of the listeners in the preaching situation. Even if you have been preaching to the same listeners for years, it is helpful from time to time to think about them. When you do this, you will be more inclined to focus your preaching on your listeners from the beginning of your sermon-building process right through to the end. Certainly, you don't have to do this every time you preach. But it is important to be aware of these issues and periodically reflect on them. If you preach to different groups from time to time, then this process becomes even more important.

What follows are six general arenas of context evaluation that can be helpful.

1. DEMOGRAPHICS

First, you should have an idea of your congregation's *demographics.* What are the age groups represented in the congregation? What is its gender split (its ratio of men and women)? Its socio-economic status? Employment percentage and type? Marital status? Racial, cultural, or ethnic backgrounds? Group membership (that is, are there a lot of Veterans, Masons, or Teamsters in the congregation)? What is their theological perspective on worship?

Immediate environmental concerns are important, too, such as the physical setting of the room and its seating arrangement, room temperature, "street" or internal noise, time of day, the length of time your listeners have been sitting prior to your preaching, and particular traditions they would expect.

Or consider the *theological maturity* of the congregation. Is this a group of *new* believers or *well-established* members? Is the congregation *alive* or *unresponsive?* Are there *weak* Christians (those who are so *rule-bound* that they judge everybody else, as in 1 Corinthians 10:27-33), or are they *mature* Christians (who love each other as in John 13:34-35)? Some congregations have a high level of *social* awareness, while others are very focused on *personal* consciousness. Recognizing these characteristics can help you better "connect" with them.

The more of this kind of relevant information you can get, the better you will know your audience, and the greater will be your potential relevance to them.

This is important for preaching because it forces you to be aware of your listeners. Consistent preaching of the simple truths of the Christian faith to a well-educated and theologically-sophisticated congregation may not be meeting their needs for growth as disciples. If 80% of your worshipers are women, but you preach mostly about men's issues, you are probably not meeting their needs. If there have been no non-believing visitors in worship for the past year, you might want to rethink all those evangelistic sermons you are preparing to preach.

2. IMMEDIATE CIRCUMSTANCES

Secondly, it can be helpful to know the *immediate conditions and concerns* of your listeners. What is it that occupies the attention of this congregation on this particular Sunday? Are there particular issues that might be evident on this day? Is there a particular experience that has captured the congregation's attention, such as a community crisis or an event of national or global significance? (I heard about one preacher who, on the Sunday after the September 11, 2001 terrorist attacks on the World Trade Center and Pentagon, completely ignored what had been happening in the world!) So don't forget to look on the front page of the local newspaper, if you want to be relevant, if you want to speak to the issues that concern your listeners. And be aware of *the season* of year (winter, spring, summer, or fall), and the *weather.* Has it been raining for 40 days and nights? Is there nearby flooding, or an imprisoning blizzard?

And don't forget your *cultural* calendar. Is this a national holiday, for instance? Or what special season is this in the *Christian* calendar? If it is Advent or Lent, you want to address appropriate issues or you will be "out of touch" with reality and where your congregation really "lives." (I once heard, for instance, an eloquent sermon on Jesus' triumphant entry into Jerusalem, but it was at a community Thanksgiving service and had little to do with Thanksgiving!)

3. AWARENESS OF GLOBAL ISSUES

There are additional broader concerns that should occupy your preaching from time to time, like world hunger, the active persecution of Christians, or war that is always present in the world, destroying life and property. Some of your listeners are compassionate about these issues, not to mention that they are essential concerns to preach about for a maturing Christian theology.

Other kinds of *global issues* include human and/or animal rights, political corruption, slave and sex trafficking, and ecological concerns. They are important even if your listeners aren't aware of them. From time to time, you may have to *raise* these issues through your preaching, to lift their Christian consciousness and call them to bring about change in the world.

4. CULTURE

"Local culture" is another component of context analysis. Every congregation has its own personality, sense of humor, taboos, interests, worldview, divisive issues or concerns, traditions, and understanding of the topic about which you are preaching (for or against it). An awareness of these cultural expressions is extremely helpful in how you formulate every sermon.

5. EXISTENTIAL ISSUES

Sometimes it is important to address *existential questions,* those issues that are important to people, such as the meaning of life (what's it all about?), theological concerns (grace vs. law, or where is a loving God in a time of human pain?), broken relationships (in families or your own congregation), and crisis situations (rampaging floods or terrifying tornadoes). These are important "need" topics that always relate to your listeners when addressed adequately. Their "fallenness" is important, too, so you might choose a need or desire that is typical of *all human beings* (sin, salvation, or fear, for instance), any of which is a spiritual need that will be significant and relevant. Your listeners always face temptations and have most likely made decisions or have wandered into sinful practices.

Abraham Maslow (1970) is also helpful here. Maslow hypothesized that humans have different levels of need and desire. Only when the lower needs are met can those at the higher levels be satisfied. Maslow helps us realize that we can't expect people to respond to the assurance of salvation when they are hungry. Nor can we effectively motivate people to love others (self-actualization) if they have no self-esteem. An awareness of these needs and desires can be of great importance in knowing how to preach prophetically in a life-changing way. Maslow helps us know that there are "essential" needs that people have, and any of them are possible ways to orient our preaching.

6. WHEN YOU VISIT

Not all preaching is done by the pastor or other leadership of a local congregation. Sometimes, visiting preachers are invited to speak. Of course, if you are visiting another congregation, you can't know about the local culture or the needs or desires of the people. I remember a time when I preached to a small village congregation in northern Moldova. This group of mostly-older, isolated people had hardly ever heard stories in preaching, and I came loaded with them. They sat politely silent and staring, men on one side and head-covered women on the other, about 60 of them stuffed in a little converted house. All of them stared straight ahead, never at me, and didn't blink during the entire time I preached. It is possible that this was their usual demeanor during worship, but I felt like I never "connected" with them. In fact, my sense is that they were "put off" by my preaching. It was *potentially* a good sermon, but not in that culture. My guess is that my approach to preaching was incomprehensible to them. To my mind, the only good thing about that experience was that the sausage we ate for dinner afterward (in the pastor's home) was the best I've ever had! A sermon needs to be preached within the local culture. If not, it will probably miss its mark.

You can't always avoid the kind of situation I met in Moldova, but how do you get information if you are a "guest" preacher or a visiting evangelist? Sometimes, you will have the opportunity to ask the person who invites you what the need is. But often, there is no opportunity to assess a particular need of the congregation. What do you do then? Well, your topic is *already* relevant if you've been invited for a particular purpose, such as a local church revival, mass evangelistic campaign, or missionary emphasis. The subject matter or reason for your invitation will already be important to your listeners.

Other than that, remember that there are many levels of needs and desires that people have. If you want to preach a *relevant,* transformational sermon, it is only important that you address *one* of these needs or desires. Just make sure that you clearly identify it.

FOUR TENSIONS WHEN YOU START WITH NEEDS

Finally, there are four important issues that will help you make appropriate decisions when you "preach to an itch." That is, as you try to be listener-centered, there are certain *tensions* that must be resolved if you want to hit the target with your preaching.

TENSION 1: INDIVIDUAL VS. GROUP RELEVANCE

First, you must decide whether you will focus your attention on *the individual's* personal needs or those of the gathered *community.*

Some biblical texts speak most directly to individuals (as 1 Corinthians 11:28-29). When you meet a text like this, it is important that you identify what *personal* need or desire is important. Individuals must have the opportunity to respond to the gospel. People bring personal hurts, issues, questions, hopes, and dreams with them to worship, and these types of concerns must be addressed. Just be careful when you plan to preach to a particular person with a particular need—he or she will probably not be present that Sunday morning.

Other texts (like Psalm 133) speak directly to a *corporate* body. Of course, a corporate focus is important when you do run across one of these "corporate" texts. But there are other corporate needs you can address in your preaching. If the church is preparing for an all-congregational retreat or a new home Bible study program, you should be inspiring them as a corporate body through your preaching. Does your church need to express greater love or friendliness toward visitors? Preach about it. Are you starting a building program? Preach about it. Is a special spiritual life campaign starting? Preach about it. If these issues and events are important to you and your congregation, they are important enough to preach about.

The great majority of texts, of course, are neither individualistic nor corporate; they can be taken either way. Sometimes when you bring a *personal* need or desire to a text, you will see a new truth; sometimes bringing a need or desire of the *group* will reveal truth that you didn't otherwise see.

Let's look at an example. Suppose I'm going to preach on the story of Nehemiah's decision to rebuild the wall of Jerusalem (from Nehemiah 2:11-18). I could focus my sermon on several types of need. I could, for instance, direct it to *individual* church members who should be "constructing" their spiritual lives. This approach would bring particular textual elements to light. Or I could preach to a group of preachers about *rebuilding* the first draft of their sermons. And if my *congregation* is preparing for a building project, I might use the text to challenge them to give their prayer support and money.

Any of these needs will lift different insights and application from the text. Of course, I would not apply this text to *all* of these situations in the same sermon. That would, of course, confuse everybody. So try to approach the text and your sermon *either* from a *personal* or *corporate* response to biblical truth, but not both.

The general principle here is that there are needs and desires of *individuals* and *the church community.* Both offer important interpretive insights for the text's relevance, but you should orient your sermon to only *one* of these particular audiences.

TENSION 2: ACCIDENTAL VS. INTEGRAL AUDIENCE

Second, when we consider audience-oriented preaching, there are *two distinct audiences* that are present in most preaching situations, and it can be helpful to identify which one you intend to address. These audience types are identified by Richard Schechner (1988).

The first of these is what Schechner calls the *accidental audience.* These are the people who *want* to be there. These are visitors who come by choice and members who are always interested in what you have to say. They enjoy worship and will ordinarily be fully engaged with you in the "performance" of preaching. It is of great importance to them that they be present. They want to learn or be touched in some way by the presence of God. Often, the preaching event can be an emotional, spiritually-charged experience because of the *accidental audience* that is present.

The second group is the *integral audience.* This group of listeners is composed of those who are *required* to be present. (In fact, they are necessary for any ritual experience.) These are the people who "know each other, are involved with each other, support each other." For the most part, they are present because they *have* to be there. These are the deacons, ushers, and choir members whose presence is required because of their responsibility in leading or helping with worship. Of course, some choir members, deacons, and ushers, while helping lead worship, are still members of the accidental audience because they *want* to be there, but this isn't always the case.

The problem with the integral audience is that they see their *required* attendance as an excuse to disengage themselves from the experience. The father of the bride, for instance, is *required* to be at his daughter's wedding, but sometimes will go to sleep once he has given her away. And it isn't unusual to find ushers out in the narthex telling jokes or reading the morning newspaper while you are preaching. So realize that your integral audience doesn't *have to be* "engaged" in the preaching event, and you thus have to "earn" their interest over and over again, every week.

Further, audiences are not just "flat" recipients of your preaching. They undergo changes *during* worship and the preaching event. Generally, a larger integral congregation can influence a smaller accidental audience—or vice versa. The stronger group helps fashion the response of the weaker. With engaging preaching, your accidental audience members can *positively* influence individual members of the integral audience—I've seen it happen. And sometimes, in the same way, a large group of *disinterested* integral audience members can easily set a tone that *minimizes* the potential impact of your preaching on an accidental audience.

You may not be able to do much about these different audiences, but being aware of them might help you understand why church members behave as they do. And that knowledge might help you better prepare to meet their needs.

TENSION 3: FINDING A BEGINNING: NEED VS. TEXT

When you preach, you can find "sermon starters" anywhere. That is, you can start building a sermon with a story, a text, a need, a desire—with just about any idea (we'll talk about this more is Chapter 21). Audience-centered preaching does not necessarily suggest that you must *begin* the sermon construction process with a need or desire. Rather, from *wherever* you get a good idea to start the sermon process, you eventually want to identify a need or desire to which the biblical truth speaks. This is the reason for Step 3 in writing your thesis statement: if you can identify a need or desire, it will make your preaching much more relevant.

No matter where you begin, with a *text* or a *need,* sometime in the sermon-development process you want to get to both of these important elements of biblical preaching. Only then will the biblical truth, drawn from a particular text, really have relevance to your listeners.

TENSION 4: DEPTH OF NEED AND LIFE CONCERN

There are also different *levels* of engagement that can be addressed.

For instance, there are *obvious* or *observable needs,* concerns, or issues. Perhaps the congregation is meeting in a war zone, or its windows and doors are barred to protect the building from vandals. Perhaps the people are divided by race or gender as they sit in worship.

But there are also *mundane, everyday* life concerns that can be identified. For instance, people always have a need to get along with their neighbors. They may be wrestling with a gossip problem, sexual promiscuity, or how to be civil to family members in a Christian home. Topics of *general interest* to people yield important preaching material.

There are also *circumstantial* needs of which you are aware—those kinds of needs that are not readily apparent, but can be challenging for your listeners. For instance, I taught a seminar in Hungary once. Present were Hungarians living in the border countries of Romania, the Ukraine, and Serbia, (and, of course, those living in Hungary). They were all native Hungarian speakers who still speak only Hungarian (their native language), but because their borders have been drawn and redrawn by politicians, they are now living in different nations. What happens in these situations is that the Hungarians who live in Hungary are less strict or conservative than those living elsewhere. The reason is simple: Hungarian foreigners (living in other countries) naturally want to maintain their own traditions and keep their language "pure" when they are living in a foreign country, where they are surrounded by people of different language groups and cultures and traditions. So they tend to be *protective* of their culture and faith. In fact, they are more "Hungarian" than those who live in Hungary. This same phenomenon is also true in American neighborhoods where ethnic peoples are surrounded by "foreigners." South Philadelphia is like that. Ethnic neighborhoods are divided by particular streets, and everybody knows who lives where. Identifying this kind of need, particularly where the church is inclined to separate itself from the community, may need to hear a strong biblical message that calls Christians out into the world.

CONCERNS WITH NEED-CENTERED PREACHING

Finally, audience-centered preaching raises some important cautionary questions. If you will keep them in mind when preparing your sermons, it may help to minimize their negative impact on your preaching. What are they?

First, if you preach only to meet the needs or desires of your listeners, you can easily overlook a broader, transcendent perspective on life. God solves problems within *His* world of meaning, not ours. If you keep this in mind, it should keep you from too narrow a perspective in your preaching. God is not only imminent. He is a much greater God than One Who stoops to meet our meager issues of life. So you might want to allow space to broaden your view of the nature of a transcendent God Who cares for us, but Who is, nonetheless, transcendent and in charge of our universe.

Second, if you only preach to meet the needs or desires of your listeners, you may leave them with the impression that Jesus (or the Father or Holy Spirit) is a cosmic servant who is ready to respond to our smallest whim or whimper. But a more biblical theology says that Jesus is the ultimate *Questioner,* not the "Answer Man" who meets every urge or need that we bring him. When Jesus becomes the cosmic "answer man," he stops being the one who demands to be Lord of our lives.

Third, if you only preach to meet the needs or desires of your listeners, it lowers the status of the sacred Scripture to a position of a private answer-book, like a personal Ouija board. You have to be careful that you not allow the Bible to become a proof-text for the needs or desires of your listeners. It is a far more significant Book than that, with a far more important role in our lives. It presents us with life-stretching issues; it is not just a tool to meet our insecurities and petty needs. Ultimately, the Bible is not read *by us,* it *reads* us.

Fourth, if you only preach to meet the needs or desires of your listeners, it is easy to become occupied with preaching *irrelevant abstractions.* Not *all* needs or desires need to be addressed. Some are trivial and insignificant. So try to meet accurately-identified needs or desires that really relate to where people are living.

Fifth, if you only preach to meet the needs or desires of your listeners, you may be presenting a too-simplistic gospel that focuses only on our sometimes-insignificant lives. Rather, the gospel forces us to see the rest of the world. The kingdom that Jesus brings has ramifications for injustice, inequality, immorality, and unethical governmental practices that we see all around us. So balance your audience-centered preaching with the *whole* gospel to and for the *whole* world.

THE PRACTICE OF SERMON CONSTRUCTION

Now let's return to our practice sermon that we've been looking it through these chapters. Our text, again, is John 10:11-16. And we've already identified the need that we'll be addressing in our sermon, because it was important to our thesis statement. As a reminder, it concerns several young people in my Sunday morning worshiping congregation who are not Christians. I have identified their need as *being restless in their search for meaning.* They will be present on Sunday, but because they are not members, I know that they *want* to be there. Thus, I consider them members of my *accidental audience.* So I know that they will be open to hear what I have to say. I will also be touching a personal need that they have, because I will orient this sermon toward their existential search for purpose in life.

This earlier decision of identifying a need or desire, as we have seen, has already had implications for each of the first three principles of biblical preaching: choice of text and one identifiable truth from within it, writing a simple thesis statement, and taking that thesis back to the text for exegetical purposes. We now come to the fourth principle of biblical preaching, that of *applying* that biblical truth to the people to whom we have been called to preach.

CHAPTER 15
Principle Four: Truth Application

UNWRAPPING AND REWRAPPING

We got many gifts for our wedding that we opened once we got back from a quick honeymoon. We had already carefully unwrapped and unpacked a nice blender, and then unwrapped two others (they were a "hot item" for wedding gifts in those days). Without opening their boxes, we set them aside in a basement storage area.

Some months later, we were invited to a housewarming party for a new couple in town. We took one of the unopened blenders from the basement, rewrapped it in suitable paper, and took it to them. They seemed deeply appreciative (hopefully, it was the only blender they received!). The gift that had been *wrapped* in wedding paper and then *un*wrapped was finally *re*wrapped in a different paper.

The process of working with the biblical text is like that. *Exegesis* unwraps the truth that has been contextualized in the biblical situation. A particular writer penned those words to a particular people in a particular context, and it was written for a particular purpose. The preacher *unwraps* that truth from its contextualized package. But then comes the next step, that of *rewrapping* that truth for today's different context and crowd.

This is the art form we know as *hermeneutics*. It reframes biblical truth in the contemporary context, where it is applied to a different situation than the one in which it was initially "packaged." It is this phase of the sermon building process that now concerns us—applying the truth of Scripture to today's world.

A PERSPECTIVE ON THE BIBLE

Before we examine particular principles and issues related to hermeneutics, I want first to return to the Bible to discuss an "applicational" view of Scripture. This relates to the Bible's inspiration and authority, again, but it's important because how you view the Bible's *applicability* determines how you relate it to life today.

In my view, the following five general principles of biblical application provide an overview of how and why it is appropriate and necessary for the biblical preacher to *apply* biblical truth to contemporary listeners.

1. Eternal inspiration of Scripture

First, when I accept the Bible as a God-inspired and authoritative Scripture, I mean that it is as applicable today as it was at the time it was spoken and/or written. It is a living Book through which God spoke and through which He still speaks. That's why I claim it as authoritative for preaching. And because it is my final written authority for what to believe and how to live, it is *applicable* to life today. This single posture provides the basis of all other hermeneutical principles. Without the "eternal applicability" of Scripture, preaching has no responsibility, authority, or accountability.

2. Rational orientation

Second, I adopt a *rational* approach to biblical application. Historically, there have been two primary schools of hermeneutics. One was the school of *Alexandria*. It argued that Scripture speaks in *symbols* and *allegory*. In this view, every word and idea has meaning, but not the obvious one. So, for instance, Jonah spent three days in the belly of the fish, an *obvious* reference (at least to the Alexandrians) to the Trinitarian God. This is the approach of the new gnosticism that says the Bible is a batch of intricate secret codes. The *real* truth of Scripture, then, is not understandable to most readers. Only those who know the "secret key" can unlock the meaning of these codes. (This is also the approach taken by many "End Times" scholars.) It allows any reader to interpret the Scripture in any way he or she wants, with absolutely no need for consistency between those who interpret it.

The second school was the school of *Antioch,* which, thankfully, became the acceptable way in which the Bible would be interpreted. It upheld the *historic* reality of revelation. Nothing was "hidden" in Scripture, because God's intent was to provide truth that can be *rationally* understood by all who read it. Thus, God's oral and written revelation had *meaning* for those to whom it was originally exposed. This school led to the literal-historical interpretation of the text, which eventually became the main hermeneutical approach of the Christian church.

I adhere to this second school of thought. It means that the kinds of questions I ask about any text or truth has to do with *understandable* answers with a recognizably "plain" meaning. I try not to make crazy, disconnected, stream-of-consciousness applications of biblical truth.

3. The Bible as a handbook

Third, when it comes to applying Scripture to life, I accept the Bible as a *handbook* rather than a "holy Book." Its truths are profoundly *practical* for our lives. The Bible certainly has symbolic value, and it speaks of matters that are far above our finite ability to understand, but the real *power* of the Bible comes when it is *applied* to what I believe and how I live. This makes it ultimately authoritative for my preaching.

4. The Bible is for believers

Fourth, I accept the Bible as a Book *for believers,* for those who desire to know God's will and obey it. Its "kingdom guidelines" are for people "in the kingdom," not for people "in the world." That is, I generally don't apply biblical truth to just *any* domain of human life. I don't assume that just because Jesus says to turn the other cheek (Matthew 5:39), the neighborhood bully or the underworld criminal should be forced to obey it (unless they become disciples of Jesus). Rather, the Bible applies to those of us in the Christian community. Its message is for disciples—or those I want to become disciples; we can't expect people in the world to understand it apart from Spirit-inspired illumination.

5. 21st century orientation

Fifth, when I apply the Bible in my preaching, I take it with a "twenty-first century" view. This is a rational, personal decision. I want to interpret and apply the Bible to the lives of people *today,* in a language and worldview that people understand in their usual way of thinking. I want to know how this passage can best be interpreted, explained, and applied to people in *this* contemporary culture. That means that I might have to bypass the "nesting" of certain biblical stories in order to proclaim biblical truth within that text. For instance, I might either *reinterpret* angels and demons for a culture that doesn't accept this kind of spiritual reality, or make a decision not to *comment* on such references when preaching from a text that includes them. However, in every way, proclaimed biblical truth needs to be understood and applied in the context of its listeners.

APPLICATIONAL PRINCIPLES

With this general orientation to the Bible's applicability to life today, let's examine some of the hermeneutical principles I have adopted over many years. Again, I share these with you not so that you will embrace them, but so that you will have a beginning point to develop your own consistent hermeneutic.

1. The "there and then" for the "here and now"

First, I use the principle of the *here and now.* Biblical preaching moves beyond *understanding* (which is the task of exegesis and explanation) to *application.* My goal is to discover what this passage meant to those for whom it was originally spoken or written so that I can proclaim its message to my listeners today. *"So what?"* and *"Now what?"* are important questions that help preaching move beyond merely *understanding* the text to *applying* its *truth* in our contemporary situation.

2. Specific application

Second, I try to apply the truth of the text *"locally"* and *specifically.* By this I mean that the biblical text is most relevant when it is applied to a particular *concern, need, desire, issue,* or *circumstance.* Truth that leads to "spiritualized theology" or a more general application tends to have no power and little interest.

3. Contemporary confrontation

God is still active today and wants to deal with me. The *meaning* of the biblical truth eventually arises in the listener, but it emerges from how the listeners first understand the text's relationship to their own lives.

4. Guidelines not law

Fourth, I generally apply biblical imperatives as *guidelines rather than laws.* That is, I believe that the Bible offers *guidelines* for living rather than *rules* to be obeyed. These are *principles* for living that guide us to a more satisfying Christian life. This implies a "soft" rather than "harsh" application of Scripture to life.

5. Progressive optimism

I also practice *progressive optimism* in my preaching. The gospel is filled with optimism and hope, stressing positive aspects of the Christian experience. It moves us forward and upward to maturity and wholeness, and away from sin and darkness. It reaches toward a *perfect goal* rather than back toward a *completed past.* While both perspectives are certainly evident in Scripture, I tend to interpret biblical truth "positively" rather than "negatively."

6. Realistic tolerance

Sixth, I adhere to the principle of *realistic tolerance.* By this I mean that human experience and weakness are always taken into consideration. *People* are the objects of God's love and revelation, not *Law.* Identifying sin is important because Jesus *forgives* sin, not to use it as a weapon to humiliate people or coerce them to accept God's will. The Bible calls people to *new freedom* in Jesus.

7. Rule of salvation

Next, I follow the *rule of salvation.* I simply mean that, ultimately, the Bible points to Jesus Christ and the salvation message. This long-range plan of God typically guides how I will apply Scripture.

8. Love rule

Eighth, I follow the *love rule.* Whenever there is a choice, I opt for love over doctrinal adherence. Jesus' great command was that his people love each other (John 13:34-35), not that they conform to a certain doctrinal perspective.

9. *Dynamic analogy*

Ninth, there are two ways to approach the application of biblical stories, those of *direct analogy* and *dynamic analogy*. If I were oriented to "direct analogy," I would *state* or *explain* the truth of the text. I would mention it *directly* when I talk about it. I would specify it for my listeners. I would tell them plainly what the text means for them. Biblical truth is removed from its context and brought into the world of the listeners, and I tell them how it can change their lives.

I prefer, however, to *imply* or *inspire* the truth in my listeners. This is what I mean by *dynamic analogy*. I lead them *into* the biblical story through the characters and events. Their relationship with the story lets them feel, hear, and see the story, and, through the narrative, to be confronted by the truth and be transformed. Thus, "dynamic analogy" *implies* the application. Typically, I *hint at* or *inspire* the story's meaning rather than state it blatantly.

10. *Action or attitude*

As we saw in the process of developing the thesis statement, truth can apply to changed *behavior* (by persuading my listeners), where a particular action is required. It can also lead to a change of *attitude* (when I inspire my listeners), where it might challenge a well-preserved idea, or present a new idea from the text. While biblical truth can be applied in either of these ways, it is important that I have only one of them in mind for the anticipated response of my listeners.

11. *Evangelism or discipleship*

There is one other decision I must make about the way in which biblical truth is applied. That is, do I apply the text for *evangelism* or *discipleship?*

The first, the *evangelistic orientation,* means that I apply the truth to the non-believer. When I work with texts about Jesus, for instance, I appeal to my listeners as if Jesus is *coming to* them in the same way he approached the person or persons in the text. An evangelistic orientation focuses on the listener who needs to meet Jesus.

The second approach is preaching for *discipleship.* It orients truth toward the believer who is trying to *be like* Jesus, or whose life needs to reflect the Spirit or character of God. It asks how the listener can *be* or *act* like Jesus (or Father or Spirit) as seen in this text.

These are two distinct ways of applying a biblical text. For instance, when I preach about Jesus meeting the woman at the well, I can apply the message in one of two ways. If I am preaching to *nonbelievers* (the evangelistic orientation), I want them to hear the words of Jesus as if he were talking with them. People find forgiveness and new life when they meet Jesus. He treats people today in the same way he treated this woman at the well.

But if I am preaching about this story to *disciples* (the discipleship orientation), I want to inspire my listeners to *act like Jesus,* to treat outcasts in the same way that Jesus treated this woman. The listening congregation is different, and their need is different, so the application of the story is different.

Or when I preach on the story of the Wayward Son in Luke 15 to nonbelievers, I say that the Father loves the sinner like that. Realizing the love of his father, the son responds by repenting. And when my listeners know the love of the Father, they must also be invited to respond in the same way, in repentance.

But there's another way to approach this story. If I am preaching to disciples, I note that Jesus represents the father in the parable. The father *goes out* to the wayward son and the elder brother. Because Jesus treats people this way, so we, as his followers, should pattern our lives after his. We, too, *reach out* to those who have deliberately left the church (like the wayward son), or those faithful members who are angry (the elder brother).

And look at Mark 10:46-52. The Bartimaeus story can be preached for evangelism: Jesus comes to the one who is spiritually blind. That person is led to respond to Jesus in the same way that Bartimaeus did. But if the Bartimaeus story is preached to disciples, the emphasis is that we should be like Jesus by *ministering* to the "blind outcasts" of the world like Jesus did.

My applications of these examples, of course, are not the only way to understand or interpret these stories. But they do give us an idea of these two different orientations to applying biblical truth.

It is important, though, that any sermon be focused on only one approach, otherwise it will be confused and disoriented. The idea is to single out the listeners you want to address and apply relevant biblical truth to them.

12. Consistency

Finally, I want to develop a *consistent hermeneutic* that helps me understand and apply Scripture in a responsible way. Just as I appropriate consistent exegetical principles that help me *identify* biblical truth, I also want to develop an equally-consistent approach to *applying* that biblical truth. Otherwise the Bible can become whatever I want it to be. Consistent interpretive guidelines, in the long run, help me apply Scripture consistently, no matter what text I'm working with.

Having examined these basic hermeneutical principles, then, we now must confront a more difficult issue. It concerns whether or not we can really exegete truth from the biblical context in which it has been embedded and legitimately reapply that truth to a completely different context.

THE HERMENEUTICAL CHALLENGE

David Buttrick (1987) writes that when we "borrow" truth from one setting where it has been applied (the biblical text) and re-apply it to a different context, we must be extremely careful. Separating truth from its milieu *alters* or *changes* its meaning, because truth was initially revealed within that context and is fashioned by that context. That is, the *context* is *essential* to the meaning of truth, and any "conversion" of the truth to another context changes its meaning.

This is an important issue. How can we really interpret the truth of Scripture in a way that upholds the integrity of the biblical text, but also allows us to "remove" that truth to apply it to another context?

In my view, this danger is particularly present when we extract truth from its "nest" without taking that *biblical context* into consideration. The preacher who disregards the historical background of the text when reapplying a truth to a contemporary situation is compromising the integrity of the biblical text. Further, by ignoring the immediate context, that preacher is likely to miss what the original context really reveals about that truth. It is a practice that abandons biblical preaching for theological preaching, because biblical preaching implies the submission of biblical truth first of all to its biblical "nest" before it can be reapplied to the contemporary context.

The biblical record is not simply valuable because we can pillage its depths for applicable truth. As a historical document, the Bible is far richer than that. It *had* meaning to those to whom it was initially spoken or written. We are borrowers of the truth that was expressed initially in those ways, and we seek to *re-apply* what has already been demonstrated in a particular biblical text and/or context.

So how, then, do we maintain the integrity of biblical truth when we seek to apply it to the contemporary scene? I offer the following considerations.

1. Applicable truth

First, *truth is applicable.* Biblical truth is contained in a particular biblical context. I want to extract the truth as carefully as possible from the text while honoring the biblical context, and apply that *truth* but not its context. That's the foundational project of hermeneutics. I can do this because of the eternal inspiration of Scripture: I accept the Bible's *relevancy* for me today.

2. Exegete truth rather than theology

We return to the potential confusion between truth and theology. That is, how do I know I'm applying biblical truth rather than the theology of the writer? Let's look at a few examples.

    a.   Doesn't Ephesians 6:5-9 affirm my right to hold slaves?

    b.   Did Paul mean in 1 Timothy 2:12 that a woman should never teach men?

    c.   As I've said before, could I preach from Mark 14:51-52 that followers of Jesus should be nudists?

    d.   Does Matthew 27:3-5 demonstrate that sinners should hang themselves?

    e.   Is John 3:3 good biblical support for reincarnation?

When we identify and apply biblical truth, we are drawing upon our *systematic* theology. A more sophisticated and experienced theology, with its broader biblical knowledge and deeper understanding of doctrine, will be better able to *identify* "acceptable" biblical truth for my preaching. The same holds true for the *applicability* of biblical truth. It happens as my own theology matures. Of course, there is always new information (biblical and otherwise) that helps us grow and adapt. It's the nature of discipleship. The truth that is discovered and applied is dependent on how open and mature the preacher is.

The five examples above, for instance, can be answered from a broader biblical perspective that leads to a more mature biblical application:

a.   I recognize that slavery is a *sin* against human rights and the dignity of the individual's personhood, but that perspective comes through a broader awareness of the biblical message. Christians, of course, have supported slavery from their own restrictive understanding of Scripture, citing such texts as this. But we now understand that these slave-supporting texts only *reflect,* not *teach,* the day and cultures from which the Scriptures emerged. My personal understanding of the gospel is deeper than that. I don't preach in support of slavery, because slavery simply cannot be justified with the freedom that Jesus brings. As I mentioned earlier, we must be careful not to borrow the writer's *theology* as if it were truth, nor to take biblical texts to support our own theological position. The Bible keeps challenging our finite views.

b.   The same might be said of the role of women. There are many Christian groups that prevent women from leadership in the Church. They use a few selected (contextualized) texts to "prove" that women should be subservient to men. My broader understanding of Scripture (including Acts 18:24-26, where Priscilla seems to be the one who taught Apollos) leads me to conclude that both men and women should be required to fulfill all leadership positions in the Church.

c.   The young man's nakedness in Mark's Gospel was a detail that was included to help us recognize the commotion of Jesus' arrest, and, perhaps, to put young Mark on the scene as an eyewitness ("young man" is probably a self-reference that "proves" his story). Nudity is certainly *reflected* in the Bible (Adam and Eve before the Fall, for instance), but we cannot say that it is *taught*—either from this text or any other. Indeed, Genesis 3:7 may reflect our natural human *shame* over nudity.

d.   The death of Judas shows his ultimate *despair* at betraying Jesus to the authorities. Here is a sad event that indicates the *unrepentant* sinner's ultimate destiny. It does not call us to kill ourselves, nor to encourage the suicide of sinners. That, too, would violate the broader doctrinal sanctity of human life.

e.   It is clear that Jesus' conversation with Nicodemus in John's Gospel has to do with an eternal *quality* of life, not an eternal *reincarnation* of the soul into another human life. The problem here is that the biblical "nest" is ignored. Other biblical texts that are typically cited as "reincarnational" must, also, be examined in their own contexts.

3.   *"Meaning" is not in the text*

Third, we should remember that meaning ultimately resides with the *listener* rather than the *text. Truth* resides in the text, but its *meaning,* its *application,* is how that truth relates to the listener. Because of this, it is the *recontextualization* of truth that is the most important function of preaching. "Truth" lives quite apart from the text from which it is drawn, and it does have "applicational relevancy" to each listener. At the same time, we must be careful not to borrow truth for our own purposes; that's why we must honor the biblical text first and foremost.

4. Contextual attribution

In order to keep truth contextualized within its own biblical "nest," it is important to *explain* the particular biblical context in the course of the sermon. That is, when listeners understand the *biblical* context, it makes it easier to make the application of its truth to their own lives. This approach keeps truth "contextualized" in its initial biblical "nest." Even the parables of Jesus that are *a-contextual* (as in Matthew 13) have a Middle Eastern flavor to them, and they can be related given that socio-economic and cultural milieu. So, for instance, a woman *sweeps* her house for a coin because Palestinian homes had dirt floors and no light. The sower sows seed but then doesn't plow it under, as is the customary farming technique in the Middle East (it's an interesting twist that should, in turn, help us understand the truth of this parable). And a wayward son who demands his inheritance is demonstrating a practice that is socially acceptable only *after* his father would be dead.

5. Contextual correlation

Drawing a *truth* from a text for reapplication implies abandoning the "nest" in which it was initially revealed. That can be problematic, but the practice can be sound if there is at least one *evident identification* of *equivalent* or *similar correlation* between the truth or context of Scripture and a need in the contemporary context. This links truth from context to context. The biblical truth can legitimately "live again" if this kind of equivalency can be shown. This may either be a *direct* or *analogical application.*

a. Direct application with exposition. With *expositional* Scripture, truth is *directly* applied. When contextual correlation can be demonstrated, truth can be immediately and directly related to our lives. For instance, Jesus commands us to love each other (John 13:34-35), and Paul writes that there must be order in the church (1 Corinthians 14:40). A philosophical question is asked of Jesus: "What is the greatest commandment?" (Matthew 22:36), and that same philosophical question, or one like it, could be asked today. We thus immediately recognize the applicability of the biblical truth to us because there is exact correlation between the biblical context and ours. Because these kinds of truth are obvious, there is little question about their application.

b. Analogical application with narrative. With *narrative,* such as a Gospel story or one of Jesus' parables, we apply biblical truth through *dynamic analogy.* It is a process that happens naturally when we read biblical stories, but there are two steps involved. First, as we read the story, we *exegete* it, thinking about which elements or actions might have *meaning.* Then we automatically, and usually simultaneously, *apply* those meaningful details of the story to our lives today.

This is what I call "dynamic spiritual analogy." It is the "spiritualization" of the practical details of a story or experience. We borrow from one domain (of biblical narrative, for instance) and make the truth applicable to another domain (in our case, that of the contemporary context). This *dynamic equivalency,* however, implies following the correlation principle so that there is at least one point of contact between the two contexts.

In the text about rebuilding the wall of Jerusalem (Nehemiah 2:17-20), for instance, the biblical truth can be applied either to building a new addition to the church facilities or building a new life (the correlation has to do with physical or spiritual *construction).* If the text is about a storm (Mark 4:35-41), it can be applied to the storms of life.

Sometimes contextual correlation emerges only when I bring a current need of my listeners into relationship with the text. If some correlation doesn't emerge from this basic relationship, I've either got the wrong text or have identified the wrong need. It is inappropriate to make the application without some kind of correlation.

These, then, are considerations in applying truth from one context to another. Again, I'm not asking you to agree with my interpretation of any of these texts. What I am saying is that your personal systematic theology will help you understand and apply these texts, but that we must be careful to identify truth from within its own milieu first of all, and then apply that truth to similar circumstances today.

Here, again, though, we see the art form of preaching. There are no simple or single answers to these questions or concerns. You must decide for yourself how truth applies, based on your own growing personal theology that emerges from the continued study of and incorporation of Scripture. As a biblical preacher, your integrity emerges from your desire to "correctly handle the word of truth" (2 Timothy 2:15). At the same time, you want to apply that truth as relevantly as you can to the particular situation or need to which you are preaching.

These principles, then, help us make the connection between the biblical world and that of today, and they help us maintain the integrity of biblical truth and the biblical text, as well as that of our contemporary context.

FEEDING THE SPIRITUALLY HUNGRY

The art form of hermeneutics seeks to apply a relevant Scripture to a hungry listener.

Let's now engage in a more dynamic discussion of how these principles of hermeneutics apply to a particular text and thesis. For that, let's return to Mark 6:32-44 (Mark's version of the Feeding of the 5,000), this time with hermeneutics in mind. That is, we will now "flesh out" the third step of developing a thesis statement: that of identifying a need or desire in the listener.

When I think about the application of this sermon, I begin with the contemporary need to which I will relate this story. I am casting my mind over my congregation and think about some visitors who have been attending regularly. In brief conversations with them, I have discovered that they seem to be searching for something, a place to belong or a philosophy to adopt. I perceive them as lost and lonely, in the world without Jesus, and they need to hear a positive word about Jesus who might be attractive to them.

As I look at the text, I see that those in the biblical crowd are lost (without guidance) and lonely (like sheep without a shepherd). This immediate connection with my own listeners is suitable, so I go back through the text and see the following truths that apply to this need:

Jesus is the shepherd for this crowd. Indeed, Jesus is compassionate. He sees them like sheep without a shepherd. (I make the direct application that my listeners are also like sheep without a shepherd.)

Jesus sees the need of these people. They are hungry, and he wants to feed them. (Jesus wants to feed my listeners, too.)

Jesus responds to the need—he provides an abundance of food—more than they can eat. (Jesus is able to provide spiritual food that fully satisfies my listeners.)

But now a new insight comes to me. These people in the text are both hungry and in need of guidance, and Jesus comes to feed them. And as I keep thinking about my listeners, and as I contemplate the text, it occurs to me that the people in Mark's story are both spiritually and physically "hungry." Suddenly, I see that my own listeners might also be *hungry* for Jesus. This gives me an even stronger focus. But when I bring these two ideas together, I now recognize a new thought, that my listeners are actually *hungry* for leadership. This gives me a different "slant" on the needs of my listeners, and I sharpen my preaching truth:

Jesus satisfies those who hunger *for leadership or meaning in their lives.*

And, then, too, I sharpen my thesis:

I want to inspire my "existentially lost" listeners to follow Jesus as their Shepherd.

These two statements, then, provide my guiding focus for the sermon: I now know that I will preach to my listeners (and fashion them) as those who are *hungering* for guidance. And my purpose in preaching this sermon is to inspire them that Jesus is a Shepherd who satisfied that need once and can satisfy it in their lives today.

THE PRACTICE OF SERMON CONSTRUCTION

We come finally to the last principle in the example we've been following from chapter to chapter. Now I want to see how I can apply my thesis to the needs of my listeners. Again, the text is John 10:11-16, and the thesis statement is: *"I want to inspire my restless, non-believing listeners to follow Jesus as their Good Shepherd."* We have also exegeted the text for the following "points":

1. he lays down his life for the sheep (vv. 11, 15)
2. he "owns" the sheep (v. 12)
3. he knows the sheep (v. 14)
4. the sheep know him (v. 14)
5. there is one flock and one shepherd (v. 16)

We now come to the fourth, hermeneutical, step of biblical preaching.

STEP 4: TRUTH APPLICATION

As you remember, I am addressing a group of young people who are not believers, but whom I also know are restless in their search for meaning. We just saw how Jesus as the Shepherd of Mark 6 might apply to their need, but now we want to see how Jesus as the Good Shepherd of John 10 might provide the same ministry.

For this particular target audience, I look over the text and decide to save the first "point" of biblical exegesis until the end of the sermon, because I want my listeners to see the depth of Jesus' love for them: as Jesus died for the sheep, so he dies for sheep today.

As I continue to bring my listeners and the text together, I reflect on the second, third, and fourth points I've identified above, and see that when Jesus calls people to follow or trust him, he demands to be Lord. This, then, may develop into one of the general "phases" of my sermon when I put it together, but there is clear evidence here that the "hard challenge" of Jesus' Lordship must be presented to non-believers: Jesus knows them and once they become disciples, they will know Jesus.

The fifth point above is that followers of Jesus are called into a large family of believers. I'll have to think about my listeners now, as to whether or not they will respond positively to "belonging" to the church family. I don't want to scare them away at this point.

When I apply the text in this way to this particular group, I want to be careful that I frame my contemporary context in a similar way that Jesus talks about the contextual setting in John's Gospel. I lift the biblical truth from that context and reinsert it into the context of my contemporary listeners. If I do it well, they'll be ready to commit their lives to Jesus.

I then might want to try the following phases, or steps, of this sermon:

1. Characteristics of the Good Shepherd. (As I was looking over the text, I realized that I hadn't identified any characteristics of the Good Shepherd, but my thesis requires that I talk about who Jesus is. So I added this first step even after I'd thought about the other phases.)

2. The Good Shepherd demands to be Lord.

3. The Good Shepherd dies for the sheep.

This is only a "rough" direction at this point, but it at least gives me a starting point from which to develop the sermon and thesis.

Section II:
Part B:
Narrative Content of the Sermon

When we talk about the content of a biblical sermon, the basic "substance" of the sermon emerges from the Scriptures: a single truth drawn from a single text. But there's a second component of the sermon's content that is equally important for preaching, that of story (it isn't necessarily necessary for a written essay, but it is for preaching). That is, we must remember that when we preach, we are shaping biblical truth *to impact our listeners.* For this reason, biblical preaching involves far more than just explaining the text accurately and/or in detail. It requires *actual communication* with our listeners. Otherwise, preaching is nothing more than a lecture on a subject related to the Christian faith. In my view, though (as I've been saying throughout this book), preaching is far more than that: if I don't "connect" with my listeners, I'm simply not completing the task to which I've been called.

It is for this reason that we now turn our attention to the second important component of the biblical sermon, that of *story.*

CHAPTER 16
Actualizing Resources

DEFINING THE SERMON'S CONTENT

As we have moved through the sermon-construction process in these past few chapters, we have talked about identifying a general preaching theme, isolating a text, specifying a truth and thesis, and exegeting and applying the text. We are now at the place where we must start to think about putting the sermon together.

We know that a sermon has many components, such as the nature and flow of the *argument,* the way the preacher *perceives* the text, how truth is *formulated* in the text and in this particular sermon, and relevant *exegetical information.* These are all important. But all of them also very naturally lead to *exposition.* That is, they have to do with *explaining* what the text means and the way a "followable" *argument* is constructed.

But a sermon is not a teaching lecture. It is a form of communication through which you confront your listeners with an important message from God. You *expound,* of course, but that's only half of communication. You also want the biblical truth to be *received.* You can *talk* all you want, and have the most important *information* in the universe to share, but if you can't *communicate* it in a way that your listeners will "hear" it, you're wasting your time. Good explanations and rational arguments may be fine for writing, but when left to themselves, they are poor transmitters of *oral* truth.

A sermon is a rhetorical *document.* Preaching, on the other hand, is a rhetorical *presentation.* They are two different methods of communication. This distinction is important, because written texts (like sermon manuscripts) are for *reading;* preaching is for *listening.* The components of a sermon are valuable only in so far as they contribute to how the sermon *sounds* after it is constructed; if the sermon isn't "hearable," it will have little impact on the lives of listeners. That's why stories are necessary.

Preaching, then, must first engage the listener's *ear* if it is to connect with the listener's *heart* and *mind. Proclamation* means capturing the attention of listeners in such a way that they are confronted with biblical truth and challenged to *act* on it or *respond* to it. That hardly ever happens when the pulpit is used to report fine biblical discoveries (no matter how insightful they may be). Again, a sermon is not mere *explanation*—it is *persuasive* rhetoric. It is only when we capture the attention of our listeners that there is even the slightest chance that they will be impacted by the truth of Scripture.

Many homileticians talk about these extra-expositional materials as *"illustrations,"* and, for the sake of consistency, I will keep that designation through the beginning of this chapter. Ultimately, these are the resources that help our listeners *hear* and *respond* to biblical truth. They include *stories, examples, metaphor, spiritual analogy,* and other similar kinds of resources.

We're going to look at four important issues in using "illustrations" in sermons: 1. why they are important, 2. their "power function" in communicating truth, 3. what kinds are usable and where you find them, and 4. the natural process by which we isolate and integrate them.

I. WHY ILLUSTRATIONS ARE IMPORTANT

We live in a story-telling world. Television sitcoms, best-selling novels, and motion pictures interest people because they are *stories.* Have you ever heard of anybody who went to the neighborhood Blockbuster to rent a *lecture?* We are *attracted* to stories; they *captivate* our attention. That's why they are important for our preaching.

Stories, though, have greater value than simply for entertainment purposes. They also give us *information.* They help us *understand* life. And, as rhetorical scholar, Walter Fisher argues, we naturally *think* in narrative forms and comprehend oral information most fully through *stories.*

AT THE VERY LEAST

Those who discuss the value of illustrations provide at least the following 10 reasons why they are important for our preaching:

1. *Illustrations* communicate *truth*

Because heavy explanation and exposition are not easily "heard" in oral communication, *stories* have the capability of "carrying" the message. Buttrick (1987) says that illustrations *communicate.* Indeed, in my estimation, they communicate truth *more powerfully* than *explanation.* Exposition does a good job of *explaining* truth for the mind, but story has the potential of *interpreting, challenging,* and/or *confronting* the listener's heart with that truth. People *naturally* listen to stories, and those narratives often lead them to a point of *conviction.*

2. *Illustrations* support biblical *"points"*

In a similar way, illustrations provide *support* for the sermon. Buttrick (1987) suggests two categories of resource materials: *illustrations* ("imported analogies") and *examples* ("slices of life"). Both *illuminate* the preacher's theme or the "points" he or she is making from the text. Thus, stories both *communicate* and *support*. They *convey* truth, but they also *strengthen* the points the preacher is making. The former is a *proactive* use of illustrations, the latter *reactive*. The former is related to *truth;* the latter to the *preacher*.

3.   *Illustrations* clarify *what is being said*

Illustrations not only communicate and support truth, they also *clarify*. They help explain the point the preacher is making in a way that exposition cannot. They bring clarity because they root truth in real life experience.

4.   *Illustrations offer* relief

Stories and examples offer *relief* from exposition. Many homileticians understand the sermon to be an *explanatory* discourse. Given that perspective, it is natural that they recognize one of the values of story as providing *relief* from the required intensive listening effort. That is, stories help the listener take *refreshment breaks* from the barrage of exposition that comes with most preaching. Again, it is easier for people to *listen to* stories than exposition or explanation.

5.   *Illustrations* re-establish attention

It has been clearly shown that listeners regularly practice *selective inattention* by taking "mini-breaks" from intensive concentration. After these short "aural rests," listeners rejoin the monologue, but only if it's of interest to them. Stories provide doorways through which this reentry is made—they help *recapture* attention.

6.   *Illustrations add* human interest *to explanation*

Illustrations make sermons *interesting*. When preaching becomes a "distant" theological or spiritual exercise, stories help apply that information to human life. They "ground" doctrine. They teach, but in a non-didactic way. They motivate, encourage, and inspire, but, at the same time, help the listener understand ways in which that inspirational truth works itself out in practical Christian living.

7.   *Illustrations provide* repetition

Stories give listeners an opportunity to re-hear the same truth or "point" in a different way. They provide a necessary *repetition* of the sermon's ideas. When listeners hear the same idea expressed in different ways, they are more apt to remember and make sense of the discourse. Stories *reinforce* truth.

8.   *Illustrations* minister

By "overhearing" the gospel in stories, hurting congregational members are able to relate their own lives to stories of other people who have faced the same kinds of questions or pain. When story characters find resolution to trouble or conflict, listeners also find resolution. In that way, stories *minister* to the lives of people. And when people *remember* stories (which they naturally do), the Holy Spirit continues to minister to them after the preaching event is over.

9.   *Illustrations* break down resistance. Skeptical listeners are sometimes ready to argue with the preacher's theology even before the sermon begins. But because people are captivated by stories, their resistance is broken down even when they are harboring doubt. In a way that exposition cannot do, stories offer a way to prepare listeners to be impacted with the gospel. By softening mental resistance, stories *minimize the struggle.*

10. *Illustrations* intensify the emotions
Finally, stories are effective communicative tools for *inspiration and persuasion;* they *prepare* people to respond. They work on peoples' *hearts* rather than their minds. Exposition stimulates *thinking,* but stories prick the *hearts* and *imaginations* of listeners, and, thus, bring them to a place of emotional involvement with the truth of Scripture.

All of these are good reasons why we should use stories in our preaching, and all are legitimate *effects* of stories. As such, they *accompany* "points" in the sermon. They *illustrate.* They *illuminate.*

However, this whole approach to illustrations presumes that a sermon is basically *expositional* and *propositional.* Illustrations, in this sense, *illustrate* a "point" the preacher is making. If you look back through the list, you'll note that in all but the first, the basic assumption is that the preacher *explains* and then *illustrates* what is being talked about. Here again is the old informational model.

Unfortunately, that terminology doesn't reflect what actually happens with "illustrations" in human communication. Stories, it turns out, are much more than *support materials* for the "points" we make in our sermons. They don't merely "illustrate" or "illuminate" truth; they actually *do the work* of communicating and constructing that truth within listeners. That is why I call them *actualizing resources,* and it to this subject that we now turn.

II. THE "ACTUALIZING" POWER-FUNCTION OF STORIES
"Actualizing resources" are those rhetorical materials that you bring into the sermon to *construct* the biblical truth you are proclaiming. They work together with your exegetical discoveries to bring the truth alive in the listener.

THE RHETORICAL CONSTRUCTION OF THE THESIS
"Rhetorical constructionism" says that people develop a worldview by the ways that *language* expresses reality and truth for them. Stories are good at that. It is simply not possible to tell a story without *adding* information or *framing* reality in a particular way.

Actualizing resources, then, *convey* and *extend* meaning. They *bring about* the thesis, and *create* the emerging message. They *isolate* and *confirm* biblical truth, and then *impact* your listeners with that biblical truth. They *actively* teach and develop that truth in the minds and hearts of your listeners. They *formulate* and *extend* your explanations. All the stories and examples and humor you use in your sermon actively *construct meaning.* They *help create the idea* of the sermon, and, thus, they *fashion truth* for the listener in a particular way.

Further, narrative both communicates truth and impacts the listener with truth. In that way, stories help shape reality for the listener. When your sermon engages stories, personal examples, analogies, and even jokes, the biblical truth is brought into clear focus for your listeners. Stories used in preaching are as much the *substance* of the sermon as is the exegesis. Indeed, *everything* in the sermon, everything *spoken* from the pulpit, each story and experience and example, contributes to the *creation* and *development* of the truth that is being proclaimed.

THE WHOLE SERMON AS THE "WORD OF GOD"

Here, then, is a very different understanding of sermon content. Your *whole sermon* actually fashions a theology and a framework in which your listeners understand biblical truth. All your chosen materials work together to *define* that biblical truth. This means that it isn't only the biblical text, or your exacting exegesis, or all the passionate arguments you present that shape the truth. All of these components certainly *contribute* to the truth, but it is the sermon *as a whole* that defines that truth in your listener's ear and heart. It is up to you, as the preacher-constructionist, to orient your entire sermon in a way your listener will respond to the biblical truth you are proclaiming.

For your listeners, then, biblical truth is "brought into being" through the sermon's *entire content and structure.* Biblical truth is defined and comprehended through the *whole* sermon, from beginning to end, not simply from the kernel of truth you extract from the biblical text or from the way you structure your sermon. We cannot divorce the thesis from the content. Listeners are brought along step by step through the process of *hearing* the discourse. They are *led to* truth. By the time you finish preaching, they should have come to a *new* experience, a *new* point of understanding, a *new* awareness of the Christian faith, a *new* attitude. *Everything* in the sermon will bring them to that point: every story, metaphor, and analogy. *Everything* works together to accomplish your thesis. That's when God speaks. That's when transformation happens. And that's why the "word of God" is *more* than the simple single biblical *truth:* it is the whole of the sermon.

When preaching is *transactional,* your listeners begin at one place in their spiritual pilgrimage, understanding, or worldview. Through a single text, carefully-defined rhetorical steps, and convicting stories, they end up someplace else. In that process, they are confronted with biblical truth. And you, as the preacher, hand in hand with the Holy Spirit, are guiding them through that experience.

III. USABLE RESOURCES

Let's imagine that you have already chosen a text and theme, fashioned a thesis statement, and exegeted several "points" from the text. At this stage, you want to collect various types of additional materials that will help you construct the sermon. What kinds are suitable? And where do you find them?

There are many different types of these resources that can be useful for preaching. Indeed, you can "baptize" just about any resource that might help you accomplish your thesis. And you can find these materials just about anywhere.

What follows is a beginning "resource catalog" to help get you started:

1. **Bible stories:** The Bible contains many stories that have the potential of establishing, identifying, and highlighting the truth you are proclaiming, quite apart from the central text you are using in your sermon. While I do not advocate building the thesis around more than one text, there are many stories in other parts of Scripture that can *support* your thesis and its development.

2. **Humor:** jokes and/or stories, either fictional or real

3. **Poetry:** especially poems that are easy to "hear"

4. **History:** stories from national history and traditions

5. **Culture** (such as theatre, the arts, music, literature, and dance): What are some of the great novels or short stories you or your people know?

6. **Geography:** land masses, mountain ranges, rivers, oceans—all can provide rich analogical resources for preaching

7. **Biography and testimonies:** whose lives best illustrate this biblical truth?

8. **Science and nature:** all branches, from astronomy to zoology, anatomy to physics, biology to meteorology, archeology to anthropology—the list is almost endless for useful domains of information

9. **Local traditions:** does your community celebrate special local, regional, or national holidays? Use them.

10. **Hobbies** (stamp and coin collecting, for instance) and **sporting events** can provide excellent resources to support biblical themes.

11. **Folklore and fables:** what traditional children's or folk tales do you know that highlight this biblical truth?

12. **Anecdotes:** what little stories have you read or overheard?

13. **Parables:** you can use the stories of Jesus, but don't be afraid to design your own.

14. **Your own family stories** or **personal experiences**

15. **Object lessons** by which you make *comparisons* between what you see in the world and biblical truth. Here's a flower growing through the pavement (an illustration of Christian persistence). There's a particularly bright star (a new biblical truth to seek). A dying tree, a muddy street, a pile of refuse—all can provide useful metaphors that bring biblical truth alive.

Any of these resources (and others) can provide important support for your thesis. In many cases, your listeners may already know many of the biblical, historical, and/or local culture stories you will use, but these become very helpful for preaching, because, by calling upon this already-known "community knowledge," your listeners will more easily grasp the biblical truth because they can relate it to information they already know.

RESOURCE SOURCES

There are many sources from which you can collect these materials, too. Among them are the following five:

1. Reference sources

Try to find *reference books* or *CD-ROMs* of stories, quotations, and anecdotes that are designed especially for preaching. Books tend to be arranged topically; *search keys* help you find materials on CD-ROM. There are also invaluable collections of *hymn stories.* And *commentaries* often contain useful information (such as Barclay's *Daily Study Bible Series).*

2. Memory

Don't discount your personal memory, reflection, and observation. You might want to take a few minutes from time to time to recall your own experiences and how they illustrate biblical truth. They can include object lessons, personal experiences you've had, events around you, people you've met, and bits of news you remember.

3. Imagination

There is no evidence that Jesus borrowed his parables from other people or sources. It is most likely that he developed them himself, and he was a master at it. There isn't any reason why you, too, can't design your own stories or illustrations. Just be ethical about it; don't try to *trick* your listeners. But if you have a creative mind, you might try your hand at creating a story that highlights the biblical truth you are proclaiming. Creative stories often convey truth in a way that explanation does not.

4. Spiritual analogy

There is great power in creating *spiritual analogies* for your listeners, and you can train your mind for it. Truth that is seen in an object, person, or one domain is brought to bear on another domain.

This principle is one that Jesus used regularly. In John's Gospel, for instance, there are no miracles of Jesus. They are "signs." That is, the miraculous events are not as important as the *person* to whom they point. On seven occasions, Jesus turned an *experience* into a "spiritual analogy" by making a statement about himself. These, of course, are the seven "I am" statements of John. Jesus shared bread with 5,000 because he is the "Bread of Life" (John 6:35). He was present at the candle lighting ceremony at the Festival of Booths, and announced that he is the "Light of the World," and then talked about different kinds of darkness (John 8:12-59). And when he raised Lazarus from the dead, he identified himself as the "Resurrection and the Life," and talked about those who are spiritually dead (John 11:1-53). For John, these miracle stories are "signs" with deeper spiritual significance than the mere display of a miracle. They aim beyond themselves. The *events* are minimized for the sake of the "point," and miraculous experiences are "spiritualized."

Many of Jesus' parables are like that, too. He took seemingly *ordinary* events and people and told stories about them that had spiritual power. He talked about a woman losing her coin, sheep and their caring shepherd, pigs and dogs and oxen falling into a ditch. He used wheat farming, and grapevines, and towers. These were ordinary features of life, but he used them to apply spiritual truth.

We do the same thing when we preach. We draw spiritual inference from particular biblical events or truths. We discover truth in the text and then see how it applies to the contemporary scene.

But we also move beyond that. Every time we talk about the "Body of Christ," we are drawing a truth from one domain (the human body) and applying it to another (the church). When we talk about the Christian life as a pilgrimage (as did John Bunyan in his *Pilgrim's Progress),* we are drawing a truth from one domain (a journey) and applying it to another (discipleship).

That's what I mean by *spiritual analogy.* It happens when "truth" is seen in one place, realm, domain, or object and applied to another. It can be a powerful way to convey biblical truth.

For example, suppose you are preaching from Romans 12:13: *"Share with God's people who are in need."* You want to impress on your listeners that Christians have a responsibility to empower one another. So a strong Christian stands alongside one who is weak, like a car's "jumper cable," you say, which provides a necessary "boost" from a strong battery to a weak one. Like that jumper cable, the Christian with extra spiritual energy "boosts" a weaker member's faith. We thus rely on each other in the Christian community.

You can train your mind to seek illustrative material like this. You might want to carry a notebook or pad with you: these kinds of inspirational insights occur when you least expect them, and if you learn how to think *analogically* like this, you will be on your way to a powerful preaching ministry.

5.   *Filing system*

I keep a set of resource folders that I have arranged by topic (such as "church," "despair," "humanity," and "salvation"). Early in my ministry, if I didn't already have a particular topical folder, I would add a new one whenever I found a story or advertisement, or if I remembered a personal experience I wanted to keep. I now have over 100 of these topical folders. My file developed over a period of years, but it is my most valuable resource for collecting and finding what I might need for my preaching.

What do I put in there? I clip articles from magazines, preaching journals, devotional booklets, and newspapers (including cartoons, photos, topical informational series, and news stories). I make notes from novels and short stories (I don't read fiction just to get materials, but I find useful stories from time to time). Sometimes I discover stories on television or in films that provide contemporary examples for what I might preach about, so I write them down. And I include those fresh analogies that come to me from time to time.

You, too, can train your mind to seek these kinds of useful resources for your preaching. I recommend that you carry a notebook or pad with you. An inspirational thought or experience will happen when you least expect it and you will want to write it down. I can never get enough of these kinds of useful resource materials—they are invaluable when it comes time to putting a sermon together!

IV. ISOLATING AND INTEGRATING USABLE STORIES

So you have a long catalog of possible sources for actualizing materials. But how do you know what stories are usable in a particular sermon? And where will you insert them? I now introduce a wonderful little brain function that helps you answer these questions.

RETICULAR ACTIVATING SYSTEM

Scientists tell us that at the base of the human brain there is an important "filtering" mechanism called the "Reticular Activating System." It takes all the sensory messages that enter your brain and decides which information is most important to you. That is, out of all the "data" you are receiving right now (through taste, touch, sight, sound, smell, and memory), your "Reticular Activating System" is eliminating whatever isn't necessary for you. For instance, if you are concentrating on this chapter, your *RAS* may be filtering out the discomfort in your shoe, that lunchtime conversation about where you'll vacation this summer, or the noise of traffic outside. All of that incoming data would be distracting to what is most important for you right now, and your *RAS* helps you focus on what *is* important to you.

Davor Peterlin, one of my good friends from Prague, purchased a Renault Laguna one year, an automobile that he really loved. Every time we'd go anywhere, he'd spot (and point out to us) every Laguna on the road or parked in a Czech village. His *RAS* focused his attention on the Laguna and filtered out his ability to notice other makes of car. I, on the other hand, could never spot a Laguna. I couldn't even *describe* what one looked like. But I would *always* notice other Honda Civic Hatchbacks, because that was the car I was driving at the time.

Or consider this. On the Charles Bridge in Prague, there are many artists and some wonderful watercolors of the city's skyline. One warm evening, I was standing on the bridge and I started to compare the *actual* skyline with the paintings I saw around me. I noticed that a lot of detail was missing from the artists' prints. Then I realized that some of the buildings on the skyline seemed to *clutter up* the "clean view" which the paintings portrayed. The artists, in actuality, were doing what the *RAS* does in our brains. For the sake of good art, they were filtering out bits of the skyline that didn't contribute to the impression they wanted to create of the beauty of Prague.

That's how the *RAS* behaves. When your attention is focused on a particular issue or concern, your *RAS* sorts through all incoming data and calls attention to what is relevant to you at the time.

What's this got to do with preaching? There are actually two applications. First, if you're working on a sermon, and you have defined your thesis statement so you have an idea of what you want to accomplish, your *RAS* helps you "see" the kinds of resources that will help you accomplish that purpose. It also filters out irrelevant data that doesn't contribute to your purpose.

Let's suppose, for instance, that you are planning to preach a sermon about the importance of *koinonia* (fellowship) in the local church. Once you make that decision, you see a television advertisement with joyous, laughing friends sitting around a dinner table. When you drive to a church meeting, you notice a family walking together on the sidewalk. A grove of trees comes to your attention. You stop to watch a scurrying cluster of ants carrying a crumb of bread. You begin to think of your church members as sheep in a sheepfold. And you remember warming stories about the time you were in a children's choir. Your *RAS* helps you identify relevant sermon possibilities.

But you must learn how to capture these opportunities, frame them appropriately for your particular thesis, and include them in your preaching. Defining a thesis early in the sermon-construction process helps you do this: your *RAS* will help you perceive life and discover analogies from nature and remember stories in a way that will help you bring about that thesis. It's why your thesis statement is so valuable: it focuses your exegesis, but it also helps you decide what *other actualizing resources* you will add to your sermon.

But there's a second benefit of the "Reticular Activating System." Your sermon actually becomes an *RAS,* a selective listening device, *for your listeners.* What you *include* in your sermon, and what you *eliminate* from your sermon, helps your listeners understand what you are saying. Relevant detail in the biblical text can focus your listener's understanding of the biblical truth you are proclaiming. The exegetical points, your sermon's phases, and the stories you tell, all should help bring about your thesis. So you *include* significant factors that support your thesis and *exclude* extraneous details. When everything works as it should, your sermon *focuses* your listener's thinking, like their *RAS* would do.

Of course, if you use a story that doesn't "fit" your thesis, or you tell a joke for its own sake, or you include information from the text that doesn't support your thesis, you only confuse your listeners. Extraneous detail can clutter, pollute, and confuse your message. The thesis provides the framework around which you build your sermon. It forces you to decide if *all* the bits of the sermon, all the textual "points," all the stories, and the particular beginning and ending, are helping you accomplish what you've set out to do.

INTEGRATING ACTUALIZING RESOURCES

Content materials in a sermon, of course, include elements of the biblical text. Indeed, biblical preaching demands that the text itself provide the main orientation for the thesis. The text *guides* what you legitimately can and cannot say about your thesis, otherwise it is not biblical preaching. So, you identify elements of the biblical text that make the sermon *biblical,* draw the truth from the text, and discover particular phases of the sermon through your exegesis. Your *argument* will be structured with these *truth-traits* of the text, which serve as the guiding phases for how the sermon will eventually come together.

But you also start to include the actualizing resources you've identified. At this stage of sermon construction, you bring all your textual "points" and all of the actualizing resources together. Lay them all out. Sift through them. Consider the traditional structural forms we will look at in Chapter 18 and see how everything fits together. Your actualizing resources fill in behind, through, before, and within these main phases of the text's movement. I generally try to find an exceptional story or example to begin and end the sermon (as we'll see in Chapter 19). And most of the time, in order to balance the sermon, I try to include at least one actualizing resource for every phase of the sermon.

And then, when it all comes together, all of it works together to bring the truth of Scripture to reality for your listeners. Of course, the biblical text must guide and restrict the use of the actualizing resources. The thesis must be *supportable by* the biblical text and other resources, but eventually, everything, working together, develops and carries out your thesis, and your listeners are confronted by biblical truth.

GUIDELINES FOR USE OF ACTUALIZING RESOURCES

Finally, there are several important issues when we think about the role of actualizing resources in our preaching.

1.   *Actualizing resources* construct *biblical truth*

As I've said earlier, the stories I use *support* and *carry out* my thesis. Standing alongside and among the biblical materials, actualizing resources *construct* truth when they are used. They aren't simply for entertainment or illustration or relief; they work together with the biblical text so that my listeners come to a point of *response.* For instance, one phase of my sermon is that God calls us to a new future. When I add a story, it serves as more than a *support mechanism:* it actually helps *construct* my listeners' understanding of God's saving, loving call. The story will *define* how my listeners understand the call of God—a different story would present Him differently.

2.   *An actualizing resource for* every phase *of the sermon*

I often use a story to help interpret and actualize a phase of my sermon. When I do that, I try to balance my sermon by including an actualizing resource for *every* phase. Sermons are awkward when they include a story for the first and third "points," but none for the second and fourth. We'll come back to this issue later, but the internal structure of a sermon is extremely important. Thus, I suggest that every phase of the sermon be brought to light through at least one actualizing resource.

3. Humor *lightens but it also teaches*

The use of humor in the pulpit is acceptable in some cultures and unacceptable in others. However, humor can be important. It adds sparkle to your preaching and reminds your listeners of your own humanity, particularly if you use yourself as the object of the joke. Humor can also be a good teaching mechanism when it helps construct truth. However, it is important never to use humor for its own sake; it should always be relevant to your thesis.

4. A specific *is more powerful than a general*

I find it helpful to use a "specific" incident rather than a general "type" or group. People relate to and are motivated by hearing a single story that serves as a "type" more than when they hear general information. For example, the story of one single starving child is far more challenging and convicting than a list of impressive statistics about all the starving children in the world. Similarly, I try to be *as specific as possible* in my language, by narrowing a "they" to a "he" or "she." I find that using *one* item rather than a list is more engaging ("battle-axe," for example, rather than "weapon"). And rather than saying *"people* in that place treat their Bibles with great gentleness," I might say "an elderly man carefully lifted his old worn Bible from its place on the table, ran his hand over its cover, and gently turned open its pages."

5. *Identify sources*

It is important to attribute sources, whenever possible. I do so because it keeps me honest and adds more "believable" support to my preaching. Just a quick reference to a source can make a difference. For instance, if I say, "John Temple tells the story of . . .," my listeners get an idea that this incident happened to somebody else, even though they don't know who John Temple is.

6. *Hardly enough!*

Finally, I use actualizing resources liberally! I never step into the pulpit without them, and I encourage you to do the same. People who listen to your preaching are bombarded with stories and experiences almost every moment of their days, Monday through Saturday, and to imagine that they don't "need" stories in your biblical exposition on Sunday is to miss the point. They *naturally* listen to stories. Since the goal of preaching is to *communicate* in the best possible way, your message demands it. *Never* preach without using stories and personal experiences, everywhere and always. The lives of your listeners may depend on it!

THE PRACTICE OF SERMON CONSTRUCTION

Let's see how the collection of actualizing resources works in actual practice with the example we've been following through the past five chapters. Just as a reminder, the text, again, is John 10:11-16, and our thesis is: *"I want to inspire my restless, non-believing listeners to follow Jesus as their Good*

Shepherd." We have also done some preliminary "thesis exegesis," and identified the following "trial phases" for this sermon:
1. Characteristics of the Good Shepherd.
2. The Good Shepherd demands to be Lord.
3. The Good Shepherd dies for the sheep.

These phases, initially, are supported by information from the text.

THE NEXT STEP: FINDING ACTUALIZING RESOURCES

By "trial phases," I mean that these are *possible* phases by which my sermon may come together. They may change later, depending on a changing need, a new awareness of the text, or the kinds of stories and analogies I am able to pull together. But by now my "Reticular Activating System" has started to work for me. As the week passes, I begin to identify some "sheep" stories or jokes that I remember. I also have two books about the 23rd Psalm on my shelf, so I pick them up and leaf through them for particular stories or examples that I might want to use. I look in my file folder on "evangelism," "pastoral care," and "church" to see if anything might be suitable. I'm not at the place where I want to think about structuring my sermon yet; I'm only collecting possible resources I *might* use. However, as I think about my exegetical points, I do want to pinpoint some *specific* stories or examples that might apply to each phase. Some of these might not have to do with sheep or shepherds; they might be "pastoral" stories that demonstrate these phases. Possible materials come in many types: full stories, sentences, or, even, metaphor or an entire metaphoric orientation to the sermon (such as the sheep and shepherd motif).

Once I identify potential actualizing resources, I collect them all and throw them into the mix of this sermon. But for now, this is all we need to do. But now we want to talk about the actual art of storytelling, since it is essential to good communication from the pulpit, and then we'll look at how to put the sermon together.

CHAPTER 17
Story Telling in Preaching

THE PRACTICE OF STORY TELLING

On July 6, 1974, a journalist, short story writer, and morning radio show host by the name of Garrison Keillor faced eight adults and four children for his first live broadcast of an old-fashioned radio program. On that day, Minnesota Public Radio launched its new series "A Prairie Home Companion." Three *recorded* shows had already been broadcast that summer, but this was the first *live* broadcast, and, almost overnight, it became a national phenomenon. On March 4, 1978 it found a home at the World Theatre in St. Paul, Minnesota, and on February 17, 1979, the *Prairie Home Companion* had its first national broadcast. By May 3, 1980, it became the first *series* program on National Public Radio.

The mainstay of that two-hour live broadcast was Keillor's homespun tales of the mythical Minnesotan village of Lake Wobegon. A masterful storyteller, millions of faithful listeners still tune in (as of this writing) every Saturday evening to hear about the lives of the residents of Lake Wobegon "where all the women are strong, all the men are good looking, and all the children are above average."

Keillor's *Prairie Home Companion* was just one more evidence of a national interest in story telling, which, within the past few decades, has resulted in a "society" of professional storytellers. Annual festivals are held where storytellers share their own original mesmerizing folk tales that have been told and retold and honed over time. If nothing else, the movement indicates the power of a good story.

Of course, the preacher who meets the same congregation week after week doesn't have the privilege of the professional storyteller who can "work over" the story each time it is told. Sometimes, of course, an evangelist will preach the same sermon over and over again and can "finely tune" his or her stories with each recital. But most of us work at *principles* of story telling week by week rather than the *stories* themselves, because only infrequently are we able to use the same story a second or third time. For this reason, we should examine some of the issues related to the telling of stories in our sermons.

NARRATIVE, STORY, AND EXPOSITION

We're going to look at a few *principles* of story telling later, but first, it will be helpful to distinguish between *story, narrative,* and *exposition.* Generally, a story involves people or objects as its main subjects. It has a beginning and an end. There is some kind of action that takes place. Sometimes there is a need, conflict, or problem that needs resolving: something "happens" in a story that reflects the kind of lives we lead.

The category of *narrative,* on the other hand, refers to "story" in its broadest sense. It *includes* stories, but it also consists of other types of *relatable accounts,* such as jokes, statistics, and other kinds of information that come to us *narratively* rather than through *explanation* (like a "story problem" in mathematics). But *narrative* also refers to any "happening" with a beginning, middle, and end, such as sequences of thought, a series of events, or a line of reasoning that are not really "stories." For instance, a sermon is a *narrative form.* Its movement "tells a story" from beginning to end, sometimes with a *reversal* in the plot, or a "developmental argument" that takes us from one place in our lives to another.

Thus, a *story* is what we might call an "example," while *narrative* is a way of perceiving life.

This brings us to a third term, *exposition,* which essentially means "explanation." Exposition is *orderly.* It presents cogent *arguments* and *rationale.* It imparts ideas in *lists.* It *tells* its listener or reader what something is. It isolates values by *exploring* and *explaining* them rather than *depicting* how they work out in experience, as a story would do.

In general, narrative follows a *story line* or gradual progression, while exposition provides *explanation* or logical reasoning. Exposition *summarizes* a text or *tells* its listeners what the text means.

Having said that, however, it is clear that humans *learn* most naturally through *narrative.* Truth invades our lives by *story* more than by *exposition.* As Bruce Salmon (1988) writes, "Stories can be powerful vehicles of truth." We don't generally appropriate or understand information by exposition with the same impact that we do with story. For this reason, transformational preaching seeks to minimize exposition and maximize the use of narrative forms.

PRINCIPLES OF STORY TELLING

Since story is so critical to how we think, we come to a few guidelines of good story telling that we should keep in mind when using stories. There are two types of stories that relate to preaching: the first is the ordinary *supportive* story that is told *within* the sermon. The second is when the story *is* the sermon (as, for instance, the *first-person narrative).* Many of the same principles apply to both, so the following discussion, for the most part, relates to either.

ELEMENTS OF A STORY

There are five basic components of a good story: character, scene, plot, "props" (what I call "contextualizing components"), and theme. When you tell a story, you should be mindful of all five elements.

Character

In some ways, character is the most interesting ingredient of any story for a listener. People are *attracted* to people. So let your listener see the *personality* of your characters. Identify *looks* and *actions.* A one word *description* or movement can tell a lot about a person. I could, for instance, tell a long story about a homeless man who had a heartbreaking history with his job and friends and who was finally abandoned by his wife and children. That can take a lot of time. Or I can paint a quick picture of him sitting, huddled over a flickering, oil-drum fire, deep sad lines etched in his face, his eyes distant and teary, contemplating the mistakes of his past.

Further, because of the powerful *identity* your listeners have with characters who are like them, when people *in your stories* confront the reality of biblical truth and *change,* your listeners want to do the same.

Scene

The setting in which the story happens is important. It not only sets the stage for the experience, but it can add to the image and impact. The topography, weather, and political environment are all important elements of story. A story that takes place in the rain, for instance, sets a particular mood or tone. A story that is set in a courtroom creates an immediate image for your listeners. A camping trip, a mugging in the city, a visit to grandmother's house for dinner—all are important settings in which action takes place and truth comes to bear on real life.

Plot

The sequence of events in a story provides structural coherence for your listeners. What characters do, what is done to them, where they go, how they talk, the challenges they meet—all keep interest and help carry your message. Often, a *tension* that is *resolved* in a story can be a cathartic experience for the listener. This, for Eugene Lowry (1980), is how change comes about.

Contextualizing Components

Contextualizing components are those details or objects in a story that give the story a *context.* They make the story "happen" and lend plausibility. Trees and toys and thunder are contextualizing components, but only when they are used in the story. Sometimes contextualizing components are insignificant and sometimes they provide important clues to the story (a path, for instance, can be a minor detail or it can be crucial if it leads a character somewhere). People can be contextualizing components when they don't serve any other function than "background" information (as the crowd in the Zaccheus story). Often, contextualizing components help us identify and unpack meaning, such as the green grass in Mark's story of the 5,000.

Theme

What's the message of the story? Why are you telling it? This component of every story is important for preaching, of course, because it keeps your story related to your thesis or to this phase of your argument. The sermon's purpose should determine what details you include in the story, in such a way that the theme of the story coincides with that of the sermon. Without that coherence, your listeners might be confused about the function of the story in the sermon.

POINTS OF VIEW

As you develop your story telling ability, it is important that you maintain the same *point of view* throughout. That is, as the story's narrator, you want to present a consistent perspective from which to tell the story. Not only does this "frame of reference" provide a *way* to tell the story, but it also adds *interest* to the story.

There are basically three points of view in every story.

Third person omniscient

The most used perspective in story telling is *3rd person omniscient.* Here, the narrator knows everything that has happened, is happening, and will happen, and chooses particular elements that support the theme for which he or she is telling the story. Most of the time, sloppy story telling means that the narrator simply tells whatever details occur to him or her at the time rather than including only those that are *helpful* to the thesis and eliminating those that are *not.*

The omniscient point of view is the easiest, of course, but the one with the least story tension. For instance, in telling the story of the widow of Nain (Luke 7:11-17), you talk about where Jesus was coming from and where he's going and what's going to happen next. And you fill in whatever theological information helps you fulfill your thesis. Unfortunately, because you know and *tell* all the events and details, the listener isn't very engaged in the story and can easily lose interest. So you might try one of the other approaches.

Third person limited

A second perspective is called *3rd person limited.* In this case, the story is told from one character's perspective, as a "he" or "she." Now you talk about the widow of Nain, but you give only those details of the story that the widow would know from her limited perspective. This grieving mother sees Jesus only when he approaches her. She may not know much about him. Nor does she know that her son is soon going to be raised. The narrator who tells a story in this way does *not* know everything that is going on. The perspective is limited. But listeners will be actively engaged in this kind of story because they will be busy filling in their own details and knowledge of the story.

First person limited

Finally, you can tell the story using the 1st person. The *1st person* narrator most often has a *limited perspective* on what happens in the story (the *"first-person"* or *"dramatic narrative"* that I previously mentioned is an example). If you tell the story of the widow of Nain (Luke 7:11-17) from her point of view, by assuming her character, you see the story as she would see it, and tell it as she would tell it. This is similar to the *3rd person limited,* except that you tell the story as if you were living it, *as that character.* This kind of restrictive perspective adds interest to the story, because your listeners know more about Jesus than the widow does. As with *3rd person limited,* your listeners are able to fill in details that the widow doesn't know. They understand what will occur next, and, by their own mental engagement with the story, they actually make the story "happen" in their own minds.

Playing with points of view

Let's say that you want to tell the biblical story from Mark 2:1-12, about the paralytic whose friends let him down through the roof. Suppose you decide to tell the story just as you read it from the text, as a *3rd person omniscient* narrator. You follow the biblical story line and describe everything you know about everything. It is, of course, repetitive because the story has already been read from the pulpit, and thus helpful for your listeners to remember it. But, at the same time, it is likely to be boring because your listeners just heard the same story told in almost the same way.

Another option is to tell the story from a *limited* perspective (either 1st or 3rd person). In any multi-character story, many different viewpoints could be chosen. In this text, for instance, you could tell the story from the perspective of Jesus, any one of the disciples, one of the four friends, the paralytic himself, or a woman in the crowd listening to Jesus inside the house. For any of these perspectives, you would tell the story in a limited way about the character (3rd person), or, with the possible exception of Jesus, from the 1st person perspective. Each perspective would present a different "slant" on the story.

Let's think, for instance, about the woman sitting inside the house. She would not see the four men carrying their friend up the outside stairs. As she listens to Jesus talk, she would hear scratching on the roof, feel bits of caked mud and branches falling on her, be startled by the sudden sunshine pouring through a hole in the roof, and see the paralytic being jerkily lowered down into the dimness of the room, and hear his cries of fright.

Of course, if the story were told from the point of view of that paralytic, he would hear his friends express their faith in Jesus, get his head and bottom bumped along as they struggle with him up the outside staircase, be embarrassed as he watches his friends tear the roof apart (and worry about who was going to repair it or pay for it), and feel himself getting lowered jerkily into the cool room below, all eyes on him.

By choosing a limited perspective, you, as narrator, can build tension in the story and make it more interesting to your listeners than if you use the 3rd person omniscient perspective. This is not to suggest that 3rd person omniscient isn't valuable or interesting. But it is to say that most of your listeners already know the biblical story, and when you repeat the story in the same way it was read, you allow your listeners the option of skipping the narrative, and, thus, potentially missing your message.

This discussion on "point of view" brings us to a discussion about when the story *is* the sermon, in what is called "first-person preaching" or "dramatic narrative."

THE FIRST-PERSON SERMON

When we tell *biblical* stories, there are certain details that must be included to "fill in" the story, and some that must be excluded. Many preachers who try the first-person narrative form are uncomfortable adding extra-biblical information to the story; they want to include *only* those details that the biblical writer has identified. But there are so few details that it makes for an uninteresting story. So what do you do? This raises the question of whether adding details *changes* the biblical story or not. How do you know *what* details to add to the biblical record?

First, we must remember that a first-person sermon is, first and foremost, *preaching.* It is *more* than telling a biblical story from the perspective of one of its characters. As with any sermon, the dramatic narrative must have a *purpose* wherein you are making a particular point. You are telling the story in a *particular* way, with a *particular* thesis. So you *include* those details that will help your listeners come to that point of decision. But as with any biblical sermon, you also *eliminate* any detail that is included in the text but isn't relevant to your thesis. The dramatic narrative, in this way, isn't different than any other kind of biblical preaching: you are simply adding illustrative material from outside the biblical record so your listeners will respond.

We also know that all stories, even biblical ones, include and exclude certain details (what I have called "contextualizing components"). That is, there are an unlimited number of contextual elements that can be identified in any story: weather, type of soil under foot, the thoughts of the story's characters, their eye color, all kinds of sensory influences, history, culture, personal relationships—the list is endless. In biblical stories, for instance, there are an infinite number of details that are omitted by the biblical writers so that their stories will convey meaning. In fact, *most* of these elements must be eliminated in order for the story to be focused and comprehensible. The biblical writers had to do this to meet their purpose, and so do you.

Every time you tell a story from the pulpit, then, you have the right to choose those details that help you tell it for a purpose. Just because the story was initially told with other details doesn't mean that they were the only contextual elements when the event happened. So you are simply re-inserting other details and eliminating some of the evident details in order to use the story for the communication of truth.

This is not a license to reject any story detail or add any other as you please. But it does bring us back to what I mean by *biblical* preaching, particularly with a narrative text: you are developing biblical truth that has been drawn from that story. That truth, in turn, is submitted back to the story, and, when you do that, additional details are necessary that help identify and flesh out that truth. For instance, in Jesus' confrontation with the rich young synagogue ruler from Luke 18:18-30, I can legitimately include details about how the young man got rich (from investments, real estate purchases, stealing, etc.). The main issue is not *how* he got his riches; the biblical truth is that his riches were keeping him from "selling out" to Jesus. The point is that I want my listeners to respond to *the biblical truth,* not *the details of the sermon or story.* My guideline is this: when biblical truth is drawn from and narrowed by the text, the "character" through whose eyes the story is told is no different than the preacher who constructs a sermon from other resources. Details must be added that help *actualize* the thesis. Thus, the guiding rule for me is that if the "imagined" details of the story help proclaim the *truth* of the story, they are acceptable.

Narrative approaches

There's one more issue related to 1st person story telling, which has to do with basic approaches to these kinds of sermons. There are three:

1. Invasion. The first brings the biblical story into the listener's contemporary world. I call it *invasion.* For instance, you could retell the story of the wayward son by setting the scene in suburban New Jersey. The younger brother goes to New York City and spends all his money. The biblical character "visits" the contemporary congregation and tells the story that happens *in the world of the listener* rather than the biblical world of the character.

2. Visitation. The second approach is when the biblical character comes out of his or her world and tells the story in the contemporary world. I call this *visitation.* In this case, the character knows the contemporary scene and recent political and technological history (and may refer to it). The story actually takes place in the *biblical* world, but the narrator introduces it and interprets it for contemporary listeners. That is, the story is made relevant to the world in which the listeners live. If you used this approach, you might say something like this: "I came from the pig pen. You don't even live on a farm here in Detroit, but let me tell you what it's like."

3. Infusion. The third approach is to bring the listener into the *biblical* story and *world,* what I call *infusion.* Now the *listener* is transported back into time, back into the political and economic domain of the character. The listener now becomes part of the biblical scene. The listener is in the crowd that experiences the story, either during the story or afterward. Now the story is told only with biblical details of the social context in which the story takes place. Now we hear the story of the wayward son. It includes family relationships, farming, dress, social customs, and other elements of the biblical context. No mention is made of the world in which the listener lives.

Best of the three. The problem with the first approach is that it weakens the importance of the historical story and, thus, the integrity of the Bible. The original context becomes meaningless, or, at the very least, *insignificant.* When we remake the biblical story in our own world's image (called "pastiche" by postmodern scholars), the past is brought into the present, and the time and place of the historic event becomes important only for the sake of *our* time and place. History and culture are essentially irrelevant.

The second approach also keeps the listeners in their own context. They are not transported to, nor do they become actors in, the biblical story. They "hear" the story as if it happened to someone else in another time and culture. Now the Bible becomes *allegorical.* We can *adapt* or obey its message only because we are *like* the people in the story, but it is *similistic;* it does not *force* comparison or involvement. There is no reason for the listener to be drawn into the story. It becomes an interesting *report* to a contemporary crowd, but is essentially non-confrontational.

The third approach commands the greatest impact. The listener becomes part of the *biblical* story in the *biblical* world. The listener *experiences* the story as the biblical character experiences it, and through that experience, the truth of Scripture comes alive in him or her.

Thus, while each of these approaches has some value, when the listener is transported into the biblical story, the greatest possibility of confrontation occurs.

Having examined the particular nature of first-person preaching, we now want to look at principles that are important for story telling, whether *biblical* stories, *whole-sermon* stories, or *any* story.

GUIDELINES FOR STORY TELLING

Telling a story *in a sermon* is, by far, the most common way you will use narrative in your preaching. Specific stories are mixed with sermonic exposition and are used to help "construct" your thesis.

Let's look, then, at some guidelines for story telling. I have gleaned these guidelines from various sources over the years, as well as from my own experimentation (and failure) at telling stories properly. The guidelines are suitable whether you are telling a story *within* a sermon or if the story *is* the sermon. I offer them as a *beginning place* for your own story-telling ability.

Rehearse

First, practice story telling. Try to spend time thinking through and telling your stories to yourself. Try different ways of expressing them. Use unusual words. Include action whenever possible. If you want to be a good storyteller, you need to *practice* these principles.

Risk

Second, take *risks* in telling stories. Sometimes you have to try something different to see if it will work. If you aren't used to writing stories or telling stories, start by working with a familiar Bible story. But grow from there and try other story forms in your sermons as well.

Tell it

The most important guideline for story telling is to *tell* a story, don't just *talk about* it. If you summarize the story or fill it with explanation, you aren't *telling* it, and it has little interest. Instead, think about what it means to *tell* a story. Provide details of sight and sound. Help your listeners see, hear, and feel what the characters see, hear, and feel. Lead your listeners chronologically through the story. Help them "live" it for themselves so they can *experience* the story, not just *hear about* it. So paint a picture—don't just *report on it* for them.

By-product

You have the power to combat your listener's personal and social *myths* through your stories. Because stories *transmit* truth, there are many "by-products" of story telling: you can change the values and foundational myths of your listeners through stories. So, for instance, when possible, use members of minority groups as your *best examples*. Include women in leadership positions in your stories. And don't promote unchristian principles through the details of your stories. I have an old book of good evangelistic stories, for example, but many of them are unintentionally racist and others are blatantly sexist. Instead of abandoning them altogether, though, I use them cautiously and eliminate offensive implications.

Details

Small *details* ("contextualizing components") add reality to a story, such as minor "human interest" events, colorful people, and interesting settings. Use as many *senses* as possible: sight (colors, images), sounds (including dialog), smells, textures, and taste. But don't let these minor details get the story off track. And don't "detail" a story to death. Provide only enough information to set the listener's imagination free. And keep your thesis in mind—it will help you know what details may or may not be helpful.

Action

Orient your story toward *action* rather than *"being"* ("the colorful leaves were swirling" rather than "it was autumn"). Use *action verbs* whenever possible—they help your listener stay interested in what you're saying.

Suitability

Don't just tell a story for its own sake. Make sure it helps you actualize your sermon's purpose. That's why it is important that you have a clear thesis in mind before you tell the story. Only with a clear purpose, only when you know what you're trying to accomplish in this sermon, will you know which parts of the story are essential and which are not important.

Remember that in the biblical narrative, certain details of the "event" are *included* but that other details are *excluded*. So keep your story focused, even if it was originally written or told in a different way. *Emphasize* certain elements that clarify your thesis and *eliminate* details that confuse your thesis. *Submit the story to your thesis.* It helps you know *how* to tell the story so that everything works together to actualize your thesis.

Ambiguity

It is extremely helpful, especially for the first story in your sermon, to *begin with ambiguity and gradually develop the story's focus*. This establishes and keeps the interest of your listeners, who will want to find out what you're talking about and what will happen.

ENDING A STORY

Sometimes questions arise about how to end a story. There are at least three ways.

First, if a story is used at the beginning or in the middle of your sermon, you can end it with a *pause*. This signals that you have completed the story and are ready to move on to the next phase of your presentation, without any transitional commentary.

Second, you can *summarize* the story's point or end it with a "moral," explanation, or exposition. This interprets the story immediately following its telling, and helps your listeners understand how it fits in to this particular part of the sermon.

Or third, you can *transition* immediately to another story, such as when you are developing this phase of your sermon with two or three examples.

KEEPING STORIES

Finally, let's think about how to find and store your stories. In Jeremiah 32:10-12, God told the prophet to buy his cousin's field, which Jeremiah did in a public ceremony. The problem is that the field is worthless and everybody knows it. It is a "shell" of land that will soon belong to the Babylonians who are besieging Jerusalem. Jeremiah is wasting his money.

But there's a "moral" to the story. The Lord says that the value of the land is *yet to come* (see verses 13-15). It has no value now, but one day it will. Thus, when Jeremiah buys the land, he is demonstrating hope in the ultimate return of God's people to Jerusalem.

Sometimes, a story is like that. It has value, but maybe not just yet. Sometimes a good story doesn't quite "fit" the sermon's purpose. Sometimes you get an idea for a sermon from a good story, but when you locate a text and collect other resources, develop your thesis, do your exegesis, and put the thing together, you discover that the initial story no longer fits. You have to discard it! Unfortunately, some preachers keep the story no matter what. They were committed to it from the beginning and think they *have* to include it. But it becomes distractive to the way the sermon has developed and it no longer has anything to do with the thesis.

At other times, you are searching for a good story, *any* story, to include in a sermon. You finally find one and you think, "There's something *good* about that story. It probably has a valuable *preaching point* to it, but I don't know what it is." That story, too, isn't quite ready to be preached. Like Jeremiah's field, it has truth, even though the time isn't "right" for it. Sometimes a different context or need will identify its value. Sometimes a biblical text will expose its significance. Sometimes your own frame of mind will be different enough to clarify its purpose. And sometimes a different thesis will help the story "live."

The point? Find a place to preserve these stories—a file folder or envelop or desk drawer or computer disk. From time to time, sift through your collection because only much later will these stories reveal their truth to you and be useable.

Section III:
The Structure of the Sermon

We have now wrestled with human communication theory and its importance for the preaching "event." And we have talked about the sermon in terms of its biblical and narrative content. We now turn to the third primary component of preaching, which is the *structure* of the sermon. Every sermon requires content (both biblical and narrative), but that content must be put in some kind of order that will help its listeners "hear" it. The sermon must be "listenable," and that brings us to the topic of *organizing* the material so it can have the impact you want.

In this section, there are three chapters (18, 19, and 20) that will help you work through a *listenable* way to present your message. After all, the sermon you've worked so hard to construct is only valuable if your listeners can "hear" it. If they don't, your message, no matter how consequential to the kingdom of God, can hardly be transformational. It's what we call *listener-centered preaching,* and we turn now to look at what that means.

CHAPTER 18

The Form and Structures of Preaching

GETTING ORGANIZED

If you are (or will be) employed as the pastor of a local congregation, one of your responsibilities will be to preach consistently, probably once or twice a week. In some parts of Eastern Europe, the pastor preaches two or three times on Sunday, and then two or three times during the week, often while holding down a fulltime secular job. But here in the West, you will probably be called upon to preach just *once* (or maybe twice) a week. If so, and you want to do it with excellence, it is important that you discipline yourself. That implies learning to manage your time and taking a consistent approach to sermon development.

We are at the stage of the sermon construction process where we have identified a theme, found a text, designed a thesis, exegeted the biblical text, and collected actualizing materials in the form of stories, metaphors, personal experiences, and spiritual analogies. Now it is time to put the sermon together into the kind of coherent structure that will be easy for listeners to follow. This is the *narrative argument* that we talked about in the last chapter. It gives "shape" to the sermon.

This and the next two chapters will introduce information that will help put the pieces of the sermon together. Here we'll find the classic *form* of public address, as well as its traditional organizational *models*. We'll then talk about ways to begin and end your sermons, and how to streamline the process.

A lot of this information comes after centuries of use. There's a reason for that: it's because these ideas and structures are "followable." That is, we preach to *listeners* who must grasp only what they *hear*. To preach effectively means that we must organize our thoughts in ways that are easily *heard*, not read.

Aristotle identified particular strategies of public discourse as "audience-centered" when he divided public address into *deliberative* (political), *forensic* (legal), and *epideictic* (ceremonial) styles. The type of speech depended on the *purpose* of the address, which he said helped the audience know what to *expect.* That's one of the functions of genre: *our* listeners, for the most part, already know what to expect because preaching is its own genre. But the models we'll look at in this chapter enable them to *follow* what we are saying. That is, when we design sermons that are audience-centered, we aren't only talking about meeting their needs. We're also talking about structuring our sermons in such a way that they will be *"listenable."* It only makes sense: unless our listeners *hear* us, they won't respond to the truth of Scripture or our persuasive intent, and there will be no transformation.

This approach is in keeping with Chapter 5, that a transactional understanding of preaching leads us to a relational *engagement* with our listeners and the use of oral language as that which is most "hearable" (Chapter 6). And in Chapter 7, we talked about extemporaneous *preaching without notes* as the preferable method of bringing about that transaction. Further, Chapter 14 suggested that preaching must be oriented to the *needs* of our listeners. Similarly, this chapter also focuses on listeners, but now our concern is with the sermonic *form.* However, when we structure our preaching in a way that is *hearable* for our listeners, we also discover that our sermons are *"rememberable."*[1] It's an added bonus.

When we start to think about sermon construction, we immediately start to think about the construction of buildings, so let's begin there.

AN ARCHITECTURAL TRIP TO PRAGUE

Let's assume you're an architect, and you've been invited to design an office building. You have already been given the purpose for the building, and you've thought about its functions. Your next step is to make a decision about the particular architectural *style* you will follow. Will it be an unusual English Tudor or Colonial building, or a contemporary glass and steel structure? Will it blend in with its surroundings or will it stand out in harsh contrast to its environment?

In Prague, St. Martin's in the Wall was one of the original four Roman Catholic churches in the early 15th century in which the Eucharist was served in "both kinds" (where both bread and wine were given to the communicants. All four priests, including Jan Hus, were martyred for that act). Today, a Czech Brethren congregation meets in St. Martin's. If you stand outside and peer up at the building, you notice that it's a hodgepodge. The chapel was originally built in a Romanesque style in the 12th century (joined to the Old Town wall), but a Baroque addition was added after a fire in the 17th century. And then a neo-Renaissance tower was added early in the 20th century. Today,

---

[1] "Memorable," of course, is the ability to *recall later.* But I am using the word *"rememberable"* to refer to structure that is easy for the *preacher* to remember.

it is a composite of these three major architectural styles from different eras—an odd assortment put together for functional purposes.

Let's head from here toward Old Town Square. Now we come upon the *Karolinum* of Charles University. This meeting hall (where graduation ceremonies are still held) also includes three different architectural styles. Its oldest Gothic "Oriel" window dates from the time of the University's founding in 1348 (the oldest in Central Europe). But a Baroque addition was added in 1718, and then a brick extension in the mid-twentieth century. If you glance along the walls of the *Karolinum,* you notice that they don't really match.

Unfortunately, a lot of sermons are just like these two buildings. There's no unity to them. They may have a cohesive and/or functional *purpose,* but their structures start out in one way, with one "look," but then head off in completely different directions. Those who orient their sermons in that way have no understanding of the importance of structure. Many of these preachers aren't even aware of the problem, because the sermon has been under construction all week long and it isn't confusing to the architect. But we're thinking now about our *listeners.* Without a coherent style, the sermon is difficult to follow. And when it is not followable, preaching is confusing and impotent.

This chapter, then, will help you preach *transformationally.* Not only will these traditional models make it easier for your listeners to follow what you are saying, but they make your sermons much easier to put together, and, as I have said, easier to remember. However, keep in mind that these models only provide the *structure* or *form* for a sermon. It is still your own persuasive intent that provides the passion and the confrontative call for change!

THE CLASSIC FORM

Before we examine *models* of sermon structure, we must first understand the classic *form* of public address. It has been around since the time of Plato, who wrote that "every discourse, like a living creature, should be so put together that it has its own body and lacks neither head nor feet, middle nor extremities, all composed in such a way that they suit both each other and the whole." But it was Aristotle, later, who first defined this "living creature" academically. His classic organizational form is a three-part structure consisting of an *Introduction, Body,* and *Conclusion.*

Briefly, the *Body* of the speech is where you *develop* your thesis (and it is here that we will focus our attention in this chapter). The *Introduction,* then, gets the listener interested in the subject, while the *Conclusion* provides closure. (We'll look more closely at the functions of these two forms in the next chapter.) Understanding the *role* of each of these three parts of public discourse is essential for every sermon.

But we *begin* by examining how to structure the *Body* of the sermon, since the Body is where we begin to *develop* the sermon. Granted, this may seem like an illogical starting place. You might have thought the best place to start is with the Introduction, from which you move right through your sermon. That, of course, is how you will *preach* your sermon, but your construction should actually begin with the Body. It is in the Body where all your *important information* is found. It is where your thesis (or claim) is *worked out.*

THE BODY

The Body of any public speech (or, in our case, a sermon) should bring *coherence* to your subject and thesis. That is, your listeners should be able to *follow* and *understand* the development of the claim you are making. They don't have the luxury of having worked through your biblical text all during the week, as you have. They haven't spent time contemplating your subject, as you have. They must rely only on what they *hear* as you talk to them. They won't grasp a rambling or wandering discourse, but they *will* be able to follow a *logically-constructed, listenable* form.

Your *listeners,* after all, are the reason that you are preaching this sermon. If you don't *communicate,* if your listeners don't *hear* what you're saying, if you don't *make contact* with them, you're wasting their time, and yours. Preaching is not just *explaining* your position on, or insights about, a particular biblical text. To adequately communicate, you need to use a form that your *listeners* will be able to follow.

TRADITIONAL ORGANIZATIONAL MODELS

Plato argued that structure is necessary to help listeners hear the message, of which there are six main forms. These prototypes provide you with good possible designs for how you will say what you want to say: they help you know how to put your sermon together.

Let's look at each one.

1. Topical

Topical organization presents your ideas or insights on a particular subject, such as reasons why people don't attend worship, three types of people who follow Jesus, or the meaning of Greek words for "love." The order of these "points" doesn't matter—they could be rearranged with hardly any change to the sermon. This type of preaching (also called "faceting") is the most popular kind for the old "three points and a poem" paradigm: three "topics" about a biblical text are defined and discussed.

If you are going to use this strategy, your job is to discover insights about a particular biblical text, and if you are really clever, you will start each point with the same letter of the alphabet. For instance, a topical sermon from Luke 13:10-17 might include the three points: "Jesus cares, Jesus cures, Jesus confronts." Or you could preach a doctrinal sermon from different texts by showing that "God is holy, God is just, and God is merciful."

The problem with topical organization. Before we go on, we must first confront topical organization, since it is the most problematic structural pattern for transformational preaching. In the "new paradigm" I am presenting, the *topical approach* should be avoided. Topical ordering has no persuasive purpose. It doesn't lead your listener to a new place in his or her Christian life.

It is a form you use when you want to *share information,* or when you have doctrinal or textual insights you want to identify, or when you are *explaining* points in a text. Topical organization doesn't encourage *preaching,* because it is fundamentally *teaching.* It is *informative* speech. Its only interest is in the *dissemination* of information or offering brilliant insights about the text. Preaching, on the other hand, is *motivational* and *challenging,* not informative.

I have listed this form here, however, because it is so widely used. I also refer to it so you will know it as the very *worst* structural model for preaching. Instead, I encourage you to use one of the other five patterns; they offer more promise for transformational proclamation.

2. Chronological

In *chronological* order, the subject is organized in a time sequence. Using this strategy, you might take a historical look at church unity, describe how a person becomes a disciple, or follow the events of a story as they unfold. When you use this structural strategy, one "point" or "step" must happen before the next, like following directions for putting a bicycle together.

For instance, in James 1:2-4, we see a naturally-developing four-step chronology from *trials* to *testing* to *perseverance* to *maturity.* One step must take place before the next. James 1:15, too, has a nice three-part chronological development, where *desire* leads to *sin,* which leads to *spiritual death.* One step is required before the next can be taken.

When you preach using this structure, it is important to keep your phases clean and in sequence, because you want to make it as easy as possible for your listeners to follow what you are saying.

3. Spatial

Spatial arrangement means organizing the sermon around particular locations or places, such as a "tour" of the church building that begins (or ends) at the baptistry, or the differences between the wilderness and the Promised Land. In ordering your sermon *spatially,* you will be helping your listeners "see" where these places are (to the right or left of the pulpit, for instance), or by making a clear distinction between one location and another, sometimes by pointing or gesturing. Using this organizational model will spatially locate Hades, where the rich man ends up, and Abraham's side where Lazarus resides (Luke 16:19-31). These are two distinct spatial domains, and each has its own characteristics. Using this strategy in your preaching helps your listeners keep these domains clearly identified and defined.

4. Cause-effect (or cause-effect-response)

With *causal* organization, the material is presented in a cause-effect relationship. Here, your thoughts are organized around two very clear ideas: here's the cause; here's the effect. For instance, you could talk about the results of revivalism (here's a revival—the *cause;* here's what happened afterward—the *effect),* or this is what salvation is (the *cause)* and here's how your life will be changed (the *effect).*

This model might also follow an *effect-cause* structure. So, for example, if you are preaching on Colossians 3:16-17, you might make the claim that if we want to worship in a right frame of mind (singing, praise, etc.)—that's the *effect*—then we must first let the "word of Christ" dwell in us—the *cause.*

It is also possible to offer a *solution* to an effect (the structure would then be *cause—effect—solution),* as in "your sin (cause) put Jesus to death (effect), so you must repent (solution/response)." Or, drawing from Luke 13:10-17 (the story of the bent-over woman), you might argue that systemic structures create problems for people *(cause),* which kept the woman bent over *(effect).* But Jesus healed her by *challenging* the laws of the Pharisees *(response).*

5. Problem-solution (or need-plan)

Problem-solution order (also called "need-plan") is a simple one, and similar to the two-step causal sermon. First you present the problem (or need) and then its solution (or plan), such as: "Here is sin *(problem);* Jesus died for it *(solution),"* or "This is the tragedy of world hunger *(problem);* here is a Christian response *(solution),"* or "Lost sheep *(problem)* need a Good Shepherd *(solution)."* If I am preaching on Psalm 22:6-10, I might follow this pattern: "When I feel like a worm—scorned, despised, mocked, and insulted *(problem),* I turn my thoughts to a trustworthy God as I have done since birth *(solution)."*

When either the *problem-solution* or *need-plan* arrangement is followed, it is important that the problem be discussed fully first, and then the solution (or vice-versa). The greatest difficulty with this structure is that it is very easy to "pollute" this simple two-phase approach, either by inserting solutions when you are still talking about the problem, or continuing to talk about the problem when you are offering the solution. Keep these points distinct *for your listeners' sake.*

6. Developmental

Finally, the *developmental* strategy builds from one phase to the next, one step to another. Somewhat like chronological development, this form, though, demonstrates progress in *thought* or *theme.* It follows a logical progression from one phase to the next. With it, you are gently moving your listeners from one position to another to another, thus building an argument that leads to personal conviction.

For example, I want to get my congregational members to invite their friends to a series of revival meetings, and I preach from Luke 5:17-26 (the healing of the paralytic). Phase 1 of my sermon is that there is something so attractive about Jesus that people overflow the house to see him. (It's the same attraction that draws the paralytic and his friends to Jesus.) Phase 2 suggests that these are *ordinary people* who are finding hope and new life in him. But (Phase 3), what is it that is attractive about Jesus? Well, from the text, we see that Jesus teaches, forgives sins, and heals. Phase 4, then, is that, in our world, people are also attracted to Jesus for the same reasons, and will respond to an invitation to our meetings.

Typically, with a developmental structure we are building just one step of a staircase at a time, but then we add another and another, bit by bit, one by one, until we get our listeners to where we want them to be.

STRUCTURAL ISSUES FOR PREACHING

These, then, are the five predominant ways to structure a sermon (if we omit the *topical* model). With them come a few particularly important issues for our preaching.

Moving beyond the informational

First, I have said that *topical organization* always leads to a teaching approach. But these other traditional organizational patterns can *also* be merely informational. You *could* use the cause-effect or problem-solution structure simply to *talk about* problems or issues or evidences of spiritual degeneration in the world. You *could* utilize the developmental format just to *share information.* Using these patterns does not ensure that you will be "persuasive" in your preaching. That's why your *rhetorical intent* is so important. And your carefully-defined *thesis.* And when you bring all your *actualizing resources* together, and add your own *passionate, persuasive ability,* and *streamline everything* according to the structure we'll examine in Chapter 20, you will change a merely informational sermon into a *transformational* one.

Phases

Second, the specific "moves" of each of these traditional models are what constitute the "grounds" of your argument. They, in turn, support the claim (or thesis) you are making. These main "points" of your sermon are the *phases* (or what David Buttrick [1987] calls "moves").

But where do these *phases* come from? Their discovery emerges from two sources. The first is the text itself. Once you have identified the biblical truth and have fashioned a thesis statement, you take that thesis back to the text to see how the text supports or informs the thesis. The "points" that you discover in the text, then, become the building blocks for your sermon's phases.

The second source of your phases is the organizational structure you adopt for this particular sermon. When you examine your textual "points," and bring them to one of these major traditional models, the structure will help you decide which of the "points" becomes a *phase.*

The phases, in turn, lead to the fulfillment of your thesis. Each phase is developed in its own way, with information from the biblical text and your own stories that bring that particular phase to life. But one phase should naturally lead to the next, so that, together, the phases, and their transitions, build your narrative argument according to one of these traditional models.

Internal structure

Next, it is important to develop each phase in a similar way, so there will be *internal balance* in your sermon. So, for instance, if you follow a pattern of "text, explanation, story" for the first phase of your sermon, keep that same internal structure for all the other phases. This principle not only makes it much easier for your listeners to *follow* you, but it also helps *you* remember the sermon (especially when you are preaching without notes).

Let's look at an example. Suppose I have decided to preach a sermon on the Geresene demoniac (Mark 5:1-20). My thesis is: "I want to inspire my listeners to go home and tell their family members about new life in Jesus." In taking that thesis back to my text, I decide I will follow a chronological order. The "phases" for my sermon, then, are:

1. *The man meets Jesus*
2. *Jesus heals him*
3. *The man goes home*

In order to provide internal consistency in the sermon, I will now develop each of these *phases* by using the same internal pattern for each (these are what I call *steps*). So in the first phase *("The man meets Jesus")*, I first retell the biblical story, and then briefly explain what it means for us (we meet Jesus today), and then conclude with a story that *actualizes* that point (a skeptic hears about Jesus).

This, then, is the internal structure I will follow for the next phase *("Jesus heals him")*, and the last *("The man goes home")*. I develop these three phases identically, then, using the same *steps* in each: the story of the text, explanation/application, and a contemporary story. Figure 18.1 (on the next page) shows what it might look like.

Doctrinal preaching

While most transformational preaching is persuasive, action-oriented discourse, we must also recognize that some preaching must be *doctrinal*. The Scripture is inspired, writes Paul, to correct, teach, rebuke, and train for righteousness (2 Timothy 3:16-17). That is, the Bible is inspired not only for *behavior,* for what we *do,* but also for what we *believe.* So biblical preaching often means presenting biblical truth that affirms and/or clarifies doctrine.

However, it seems that the five structures lend themselves to persuasion or inspiration, but not to *teaching* doctrine. That ordinarily comes through the topical pattern, which I have rejected. So how do we preach doctrine, where we convey some of the great truths of our faith?

Unfortunately, too many preachers fall into the bad habit of *informing* their congregations of all the important doctrinal points they want them to believe, with full theological explanation. As I have been saying, though, providing information hardly ever *transforms* people—it only barrages them with *theological thoughts.*

So when those Sundays come when you are led to *teach doctrine,* I encourage you not to do it! At least, don't do it as *teaching,* and don't do it *informationally.* And don't use "theological" preaching—keep it *biblical.*

How, then, should you preach doctrine and maintain your conviction to preach transformationally? Well, realize that doctrine is relevant only when it *applies* to people's lives, when it affects their *actions* and *attitudes.* In that way, doctrine, as with any biblical truth, can be very *transformational.*

Figure 18.1

Internal structure: Mark 5:1-20

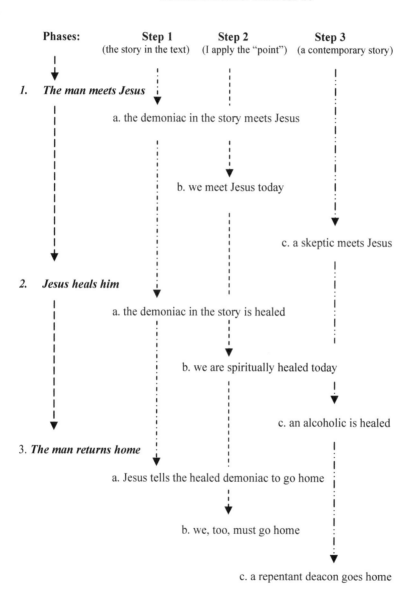

So, as with any other biblical sermon, approach your doctrinal text with an *inspirational* or *persuasive* thesis statement. *Doctrine* is really just biblical truth, which you can easily identify in a single text. You can also pinpoint a clear need or desire for which that doctrinal truth is convictingly relevant. And you can challenge your listeners to *respond* to that doctrinal truth as to any other, by *inspiring* an attitude change or *persuading* them to change behavior. That's doctrinal *preaching.*

The principal focus of doctrinal *teaching,* though, is that doctrine is fully *explained,* with all the nuances of what it means. But, again, that is meaningless rhetoric for your listeners. You will be much better off if you stick to *one* particular facet of the doctrine and make it relevant.

Doctrinal preaching for transformation can change your listeners' *attitudes* by a deeper understanding of biblical truth: *because God loves us, we have reason to* experience *His comfort; Jesus gave his life for us so that we might become disciples; because God is Creator, He helps us cope with our fears and circumstances.* And transformational preaching of good biblical doctrine should influence *behavior: the inspiration of the Bible leads us to* read it *devotionally; the separation of Church and State convicts us of political responsibility.*

So, when you preach *doctrine,* make it *inspirational* or *persuasive* rather than just *didactic.* Stay away from the topical approach, and stay away from theological preaching. You can develop a legitimate, biblical, action-oriented thesis around the doctrinal truth, use inspirational stories and examples to develop it, and adopt one of these structural patterns, just as you would when preaching any other kind of biblical truth.

Structural variety

Finally, the value of these classic patterns is that they provide *options* for how to organize your sermons. If you think of a sermon as a bridge, you are leading your listeners from one side of the river to the other. The structural pattern provides the stanchions; they help you recognize which parts of the sermon go where so your thesis will have a better chance of being *actualized.* In turn, because these structures help your listeners more easily follow what you are saying, the chance that they will be impacted by biblical truth is far greater.

These patterns can also lead you to a host of possibilities for different *kinds* of sermons. Some texts, of course, lend themselves to particular structural patterns (as we saw in the two James passages, for instance). But most texts are usually not laid out in these "neat packages," as we might expect. In fact, most of the time, a text does *not* follow logical "aural orderings." This is not to suggest that Scripture doesn't argue logically or rationally, but the structure of written and oral communication is very different (as we saw in Chapter 6). Oral communication needs *listenable progression* for the sake of the hearer. Written language is organized differently, because the reader can approach the material at his or her own pace, and re-read and reflect on it as necessary. It means that biblical texts are hardly ever structured according to these traditional organizational patterns.

For instance, when the Apostle Paul wrote his letter to the Romans, he was not contemplating how each little bit of his letter would be *preached*. He structured his argument for a *reading* audience. He was *writing* to them, not *talking* to them, so he was using a different kind of language, one that would accomplish his intended purposes from a distance. Thus, when we use Paul's (or any other) written text for oral preaching, we sometimes must rearrange and reorganize the text's order or subject matter for a *listening* audience. Again, these traditional ways of structuring *oral* discourse enable *your listeners* to be better able to grasp and respond to the truth of the text.

The art of the preacher comes, then, in recognizing that in the great majority of texts, there is *no single organizational pattern*. For most preaching, a single thesis drawn from a single text could lead to several different organizational patterns (depending, of course, on the thesis). Drawing on the text for the basic phases in the sermon, then, the preacher discovers that different *structures* lead to different *sermons*. Let's look at a few examples of what I mean.

A First Testament "test case"

To see how different organizational patterns can lead us to different insights and approaches to the text, let's look at the story of the fall of Jericho in Joshua 6. This story could be told using any of the six organizational patterns we have seen above. Of course, different thesis statements and congregational needs would apply, and the exegetical details of the text would be different for each. But let's work through this exercise to demonstrate the possibilities that might occur.

1. Topical. Here, the phases of the sermon are informational and they don't necessarily call for action. Nonetheless, for instance, we could preach the following: *(Phase 1): People who live in Jericho will falter. (Phase 2): People who live in Jericho will fail. (Phase 3): People who live in Jericho will ultimately fall.* (Application: people who are outside God's will are like those who lived in Jericho; they will also falter, fail, and fall if they don't come to Jesus.)

Of course, the phases of this sermon are *informational* and don't necessarily call for action. They could be moved around without hurting the thematic development. There is no convicting *movement* in the sermon. Thus, because it is not transformational, I urge you *not* to use this form. I offer it only to demonstrate an example (and a good one) of what a topical arrangement looks like.

2. Chronological. As one chronological option, we could preach the text in this way: *(Phase 1): God's people had a history up to this point, (Phase 2): the time East of the Jordan is a time of preparation, and (Phase 3): the people of God overcame obstacles when they entered the Promised Land.* (Application: our church has a wonderful history. Now we are preparing ourselves for our future. There are obstacles we must meet in order to be where God wants us, but He is directing us and is with us.)

3. Spatial. The spatial arrangement of the story helps us "see" the plan of God: *(Phase 1): East of the Jordan is the place of incompleteness; (Phase 2): the Promised Land is the place of fulfillment.* (Application: there are two domains of life: a place of incompleteness and dreams East of the Jordan, and a place of fulfillment in the Promised Land.)

4. Cause-effect. The cause-effect strategy can also be arranged by effect-cause (and, in this case, adding a response), which I'll attempt with this story: *(Phase 1: the effect): Our cities are in a lawless and hopeless state which gives rise to prostitution; (Phase 2: the cause): Cities are places in which people are walled away from God. (Phase 3: the response): The wall is obliterated by the action of God's people and Rahab is released.* (Application: Cities today are breeding grounds for prostitution because cities separate people from God. Christians are called to break down those walls so prostitutes will be able to respond to the love of God.)

5. Problem-solution-response. Here's one possible problem-solution approach: *(Phase 1: the problem): God's people need to inhabit their Promised Land, but it is occupied. (Phase 2: the solution): God helps His people overcome the enemy. (Phase 3: the response): God's people take the risk to accomplish His solution.* (Application: our church has a problem: we aren't getting enough offerings. But God will help us overcome our lack of resources [solution]. We must take risks as we fulfill the mission to which God has called us [response].)

6. Developmental. The developmental form generally leads to any number of ways the story could be preached. Here's one: *(Phase 1): God's people have a leader in Joshua. (Phase 2): Joshua leads God's people to knock down the walls of Jericho.* (Application: God has given us an evangelist who will help us knock down walls that keep people from Jesus.)

These patterns, then, provide examples of how one text can be developed in any number of ways. Now let's move on to the Second Testament.

Second Testament examples

Instead of exploring all six patterns from one text, let's look at one narrative and one expositional passage, and look at three possible structural arrangements in each. In so doing, we will again see how different structural patterns help us "discover" information for a sermon. (The topical form is not used in either of these examples.)

Easter story. The first text is from Luke 24:1-12, one of the narratives of Easter morning. Ordinarily, this text would be handled *chronologically* (told as the events unfolded on that first Easter morning). So let's try three *different* approaches, and see what kind of insight we gain into the text using these organizational patterns.

3. Spatial. If we look at the passage from a spatial pattern, for instance, we might see a "here" and a "there." *(Phase 1): The "here" is the Upper Room, filled with confusion, despair, hopelessness, and grief. (Phase 2): The "there"* of Easter morning is the empty tomb. *(Phase 3): We see Peter's movement from the "here" of the Upper Room to the "there" where Jesus finds him (see verse 34).* In this instance, Peter becomes a "type" for the confused listener who is now in a position to be found by Jesus.

4. Cause-Effect-Response. If we approach the passage causally, we might relate the story through the eyes of the women. *(Phase 1: the cause): An empty tomb . . . (Phase 2: the effect): . . . leads the women to tell the disciples. (Phase 3: the response): Their testimony drives Peter to the tomb to see for himself.* So we might persuade our listeners to give witness to the living Jesus so others will find him for themselves.

5. Problem-Solution. If we looked at the passage from a problem-solution perspective, we might focus on verse 11. *(Phase 1: the problem): The disciples don't believe the women who have reported the resurrection. (Phase 2: the solution): Peter ran to see for himself.* Here, we would persuade our listeners not to believe in Jesus just because of somebody else's testimony. Rather, they can come for themselves to see and experience the risen Jesus.

The difference between this and the prior example is the focus of attention is on the *disciples* in this instance, but on the *women* in the former. Thus, the phases of the sermon would be developed differently, and different elements of the text would be employed. In the former example of the women, we might focus on the *positive* perspective of an immediate response; in the latter (unbelief), we might challenge the *negative* perspective of unbelief.

A Roamin' Christian? Now let's look at another familiar text that also has several structural possibilities: Romans 12:1-2.

2. Chronological. Following a chronological strategy might present us with a problem, because Paul doesn't write the text in what we ordinarily think of as a chronological sequence. That is, we can't *offer our bodies* until we are *transformed,* and we can't be transformed until we *change our minds.* This brings us to one possible chronological approach: *(Phase 1): Let the Holy Spirit change our minds. (Phase 2): Then we will be transformed. (Phase 3): That will result in specific sacrificial action (offering our bodies).*

But there may be a different chronological pattern in this text. That is, in certain preaching situations, it could be that Paul does have the chronology right. Perhaps he means to imply that we *act* first and then our *attitude* follows. So, adopting a behavioral model, we might preach this text chronologically in this way: *(Phase 1): We offer our bodies (Phase 2): In that action, we are transformed by the renewal of our minds. (Phase 3): We then know the perfect will of God.* That is, we act first, taking necessary risks. Then we feel *right* about it. Then our heart follows.

3. Spatial. When we approach the text *spatially,* we might notice: *(Phase 1): There is a "secular world" out there. (Phase 2): There is a "sacred world" in here.* Thus, we are either conformed to the "secular" world or transformed mentally toward the "sacred" world. The sermon is arranged, then, with a "here" and a "there."

6. Developmental. If we follow a *developmental* pattern, we could understand the text as concerned with spiritual transformation. As we think of the Christian experience, we re-organize the text in this way: *(Phase 1): We are naturally conformed to the world, (Phase 2): but we must be transformed by a renewed mind. (Phase 3): Then we will know the perfect will of God, which, in turn, (Phase 4): leads us to offer our bodies as a living sacrifice (which is only possible once our minds have been transformed).* In that sense, we might perceive a step-by-step development of changing our minds about the world, then seeking God's perfect will, then offering our bodies. One by one, step by step, we are gradually transformed spiritually.

These examples, of course, have only presented certain possible organizational patterns for each text; there are several other options in each. Further, looking at the phases of each in this written form suggests *informational* sermons. Indeed, the basic structure of a sermon can easily lead you to an informational-style of preaching. But it is your intent, thesis, and persuasive strategy that would transform each of these sermons into *transformational* preaching.

These, then, are the traditional ways in which the "Body" of a sermon can be constructed. In these organizational models, all the biblical information you want to proclaim is found here, in the "Body" of your sermon. But now you must look at how you get your listeners from what they are thinking about when you step into the pulpit to this important biblical message. And how do you end the sermon?

We must not miss the importance of these critical components of the classic form of public address, what are called the "introduction" and "conclusion." Listeners require preparation time in the sermon that gets them ready to hear this important "word of God," and then a time of encapsulating the truth of the message that gets them ready for their lives in the world. The next chapter then asks the questions: how do we get our listeners interested in this biblical truth, and how do we end?

CHAPTER 19
The Alpha and Omega of Preaching

PREACHING AS PROCESS

The Bible, of course, doesn't report every word of every sermon preached by its characters. What *is* recorded are often *summations* of the high points or a description of the thrust of the sermon. And sermons also tend to be contextualized within the biblical narrative (though, of course, some prophetic proclamations are not contextualized for the reader). But the sermons that are included are there to carry the theme or intent, or help complete the structure of the book in which they are included. This is why Stephen's lengthy sermon is important: Luke uses it to support his developing thesis in his book.

But in other places in the Acts, we get only snippets of longer sermons. Such may be the case in Acts 14:8-18, for instance, where Paul is preaching to the god-worshipers in Lystra. His whole proclamation recorded by Luke is that God is a great "Crop Producer." We don't know if there was more to the sermon or not. Paul begins pretty close to the end of that sermon—there just isn't much to it at all.

So we probably cannot argue that all the sermons we find in the Bible are *complete* texts. That is, we can't use the preaching evidence in the Bible to support shorter sermons in our own ministries! If you begin too close to the end, it might be that there is too little content in the Body of the sermon, and, thus, you didn't spend enough time *developing* your thesis.

But when we look at preaching from the listener's point of view, we realize that a sermon evolves from the first utterance you make until you leave the pulpit. For them, it is one long progressive narrative form, and it needs to make sense to them, opening to closing. For a listener, "content" doesn't merely refer to the way the theme is carried out in the Body of the sermon; "content" refers to the whole business.

This is why the *Introduction* and *Conclusion* of the sermon are so important. Indeed, the beginnings and endings may be the *most* important parts of your sermons, both for the content and how your sermon comes together structurally.

In the classical form of fashioning public address, we now begin to think about how to start your sermon. This most appropriately happens *after* you know what you want to say in the Body.

THE INTRODUCTION

Every sermon begins with an utterance of some kind. Sometimes it is an excuse. Sometimes it is a joke. Sometimes it is an announcement about the topic on which you're going to preach. And sometimes, even, it will be captivating! But in today's world, with its easily-distracted listeners, an interesting Introduction is essential.

According to Aristotle, the Introduction has three basic purposes. We'll look at these three purposes, and then come back to talk more about the first.

1. CAPTURE ATTENTION

The Introduction's first, and most important, function is to *capture the attention of your listeners*. Your listeners come to worship, but that doesn't automatically mean that they will be attentive to your sermon. It isn't uncommon for listeners today to "tune you out" before you even start preaching. That's why the very first words out of your mouth are important. From the outset, you have to *earn* the right to be heard. It is helpful to envision your listeners, for the most part, as being a *passive* community, and it is *your* responsibility to engage their attention.

2. FOCUS ATTENTION

A second purpose of the Introduction is to *focus the attention* of your listeners. From the outset, you want them to start thinking about the subject and purpose of your sermon, and you need to start doing this from the moment you open your mouth. In the Introduction, you will lead them from what they *were* thinking about to what you *want* them to be thinking about.

3. PREVIEW

The third purpose of the classic Introduction is *to preview what is coming in the sermon*. Traditionalists say that you, as the speaker, should tell your listeners what they can expect to hear in the coming speech. That is, you should define carefully and exactly what is coming so your listeners will be better able to "hear" it when it comes.

Actually, Aristotle's advice was to provide your listeners with the subject of your speech three times. The Introduction is the time to tell your listeners what you are *going* to tell them, then you *tell* them in the Body of the speech, and, finally, in the Epilogue, you remind them what you *told* them.

While that advice has lasted for centuries, and is important for Aristotle's categories of public address, telling listeners exactly what to expect can make your preaching predictable and trite. For this reason, I don't advocate the use of this third purpose in your Introductions.

But if we accept at least the first two purposes of the Introduction, it is valuable to establish and focus our listeners' attention. How do we do that?

HOW NOT *TO GET ATTENTION*

From the very first utterance of your sermon, you either start capturing the attention of your listeners or you start losing them. If you're wise, you'll think strategically about how to win and focus their attention, because, by far, capturing the attention of your listeners is the most important aspect of the Introduction. There are many ways you *could* do that.

Interest

First, you could start with what your listeners are *already thinking about.* This means that you must know what is grabbing their immediate attention. When they enter the worship center, what is occupying their thoughts? With 100 people in a congregation, how many different subjects are on their minds? Well, some are thinking about where they were last night. Some are envisioning upcoming vacation plans. For others, it is Sunday dinner, ways to snag the cute boy at school, job stress, life questions, broken, healed, and/or ongoing relationships in the church, illness of family members, favorite food, a ball game that afternoon, the bluish tint in a particular woman's hair—the list is endless. How can you know the subjects in which people are interested every Sunday? The answer is quite simple: you can't!

Needs

There's a second strategy, then, which is to try to *meet needs* that people bring with them. Surely there are common needs that everybody has. But how can you possibly meet *everybody's* needs in a single sermon? Yes, it is possible to meet one person's need, but there are a whole *batch* of needs that every person brings to the worship experience. If Abraham Maslow is right, we can't escape our needs or desires, but, unfortunately, they are different for every listener. Again, it's foolish to try to meet every need right at the start. Of course, the most effective sermons are those that *do* meet needs, but most listeners aren't even aware of their needs before you start preaching. Thus, trying to meet everybody's countless needs at the outset is a hopeless cause.

Preacher's choice

You might try to *ignore* their needs and preach what you *want* to preach, what is good for you and interesting to you. Unfortunately, then preaching quickly degenerates into irrelevancy to your listeners. Your sermons will have meaning only for you, and that's dangerous for a public speaker.

Worship

So you try something that happens in many churches. You spend a lot of time pepping people up through music and praise, and, by so doing, use *worship* to *establish their interest.* You design your worship, praise, prayer, music, readings, and everything else in the service to *focus* their attention. Your hope is that when there is a unified worship theme, your listeners will get in the right "frame of mind" for preaching.

While this approach sounds good, there are at least four problems with it. First, not everybody is "moved" by worship in same way. Some participants worship most fully in chorus singing; others only through the old comfortable hymns. Some worship most fully through deeply intense prayer, while for some it comes through Bible reading. Some are moved most fully because of the fellowship that comes in corporate worship, through the reminders that they are not alone (for them, the introductions to worship and announcements are significant). Some people worship most fully when they can listen to choral music, others only with the loud thumping rhythms of a Christian rock band. This simply means that you can never be sure everybody is "primed" for preaching through the same worship experience.

Second, this view leads to the erroneous notion that worship is important only as it "prepares" the worshiper for your sermon. Worship, then, doesn't happen except when it is "connected" to preaching, and it's only valuable when it gets people ready to hear your sermon. There is little value in worship for the sake of worship.

Third, preaching is often a time for worshipers to "rest." The beginning of the sermon provides the opportunity for many of them to "disengage" worship, to practice "selective inattention." If worshipers know what to expect, they tune you out before you even start preaching. Minds wander. We can't hope to keep everyone interested through a whole worship experience.

And finally, sometimes the worship readings, music, and rhetoric "fall flat." The songs are sung, the Scripture is read, the choir sings, but there is no "experience." When worship is rote, and you needed it to get your listeners ready for your sermon, you're in trouble!

Theme announcement

Now you try something else. When you step into the pulpit, you *announce your topic*. Surely that will get people interested in what you have to say! So, after reading the Scripture, you say, "Today I've decided to preach about repentance," or, "As you just heard, this text is about the judgment of God."

In my experience, this is by far the most popular beginning to sermons, but is also one of the surest ways to *lose* your audience. There's a simple explanation for this. When you let your listeners know your topic right at the start (what *you* are interested in), that gives them the *option* of listening or not. (Imagine yourself as a teenage boy thinking about a cute girl you met the night before. The preacher announces the subject of the sermon: the "Abrahamic covenant and its relationship to Adamic sin," or the very first comment is: "When we read this Scripture, we immediately see that Paul is addressing the problem of unity in the church." Guess what is more interesting to that boy?)

So when you begin with a rhetorical *question* or by *announcing your topic*, your listeners will often begin thinking about their own concerns. In actuality, you will hardly *ever* interest a congregation through a declaration of your subject or posing an uninteresting question. It can happen, but usually only if it is a highly controversial subject or very clearly directed toward a particular need or issue the congregation is facing. In fact, the opposite is generally the case: the sermon starts out as a "lost cause" when the topic is announced in the first utterance. (This is a problem with a lot of sermon titles, too. If they give away too much, the topic is already "announced.")

Greater interest

O.k., so you try one more option. You pick a topic that's *more interesting* than what your listeners are thinking about! While this approach sounds good, there are difficulties with it, including whether or not you can really do it. (Can you always come up with a topic that is more interesting than sex? Or the latest movie? Probably not.)

A second objection is that you will end up preaching only on highly interesting or controversial topics. It limits what you can preach about: sex, violence, money, power, aggression, violence, and, maybe, dieting (or whatever is the latest fad in your own context). And, of course, it means that you end up neglecting some of the most valuable truths of Scripture.

Having rejected these options for ways to capture the attention of your listeners, then, let me posit a more significant way to begin your sermons.

CHANGE THEIR INTEREST

It seems clear that capturing attention is problematic. Here's my suggestion: *don't* try to meet your listeners where you think they are, or according to what they're already thinking about, or what already interests them. Rather, get them interested in your topic by *changing their interest!* How? Here are a few guidelines.

Preach to the disinterested

First, as you begin to fashion your sermon and its Introduction, design it for someone whom you imagine would *not* be interested (the lowest common denominator). Reaching the most potentially *disinterested* person means that you will also capture the attention of those who are ordinarily interested.

Earn *their interest*

Second, *generate their interest* in your topic. Rather than trying to *compete* with what they are thinking about, *change* what might be on their minds. How? Well, it is helpful to think about what has the power to change *your* interest. There are at least three possible ways to do this:

Story. You can begin with a *story* or *personal experience*. People will almost always tune out *exposition,* but they can hardly ever stop themselves from listening to a *good story.* Walter Fisher argues that human beings are *homo narrans,* that we are creatures who are captivated by and learn most fully through *story.* So consider a personal experience, newspaper account, or story you got from the Internet. Just make sure it relates to your topic, because you can't abruptly switch from theme to theme to theme in the same sermon and hope to keep your listeners engaged. But you *can* use a story as a way to *focus attention* on your subject. It doesn't take much effort to find one that is relevant to your theme, or to rhetorically construct a story or metaphoric image in a way that relates to the biblical truth you are proclaiming. Return to Chapter 17 and think again about how to tell stories.

Collective interest. Second, you can start with the *collective interest* of your congregation and lead them from there to where you want them to be. For instance, if a new baby has just been born in the church family, or there is a special church event, or if it is a holiday season, begin there, and find a way that this interest links up with your message. A major crisis or tragedy in the community will naturally be on the minds of your listeners. There are many concerns, ideas, or images that are common to the people in your congregation. Tapping one of them will automatically be of interest to them.

Surprise. Third, try beginning with the kind of orienting *surprise* that will startle your congregation into listening. When I introduced this idea to my students in Brjansk, one of them preached that night at a Prayer Meeting. He stepped into the pulpit, gazed at the congregation for a moment and then said, "I'm glad there are no cannibals in here tonight!" The listeners actually leaned forward—they had never before heard a statement like this from their pulpit!

I began one Christmas sermon with a loud sneeze. There were startled expressions, and a lady in the choir shouted, "God bless you!" That led me to explain what "God bless you" means in our culture, and took me to Tiny Tim's comment, "God bless us everyone!" (from Charles Dickens' *Christmas Carol).* It was a message about the blessing of Christmas.

On another Christmas, there was a popular television commercial for "Whisper" perfume, which said, "If you want to capture someone's attention, Whisper!" I began by *whispering* this line, an opening, again, which was unexpected, and those who had already gotten comfortable for the sermon sat upright to make sure they heard me right. They were startled into listening. (This led to the message that God "whispered" into our world in Jesus' birth.)

All three of these introductions were attempts to provide a surprising beginning to a sermon. If you try this tactic, be sure it relates to your thesis and the sermon that follows.

The value of starting with story

Of these three options, a *story* of some kind[1] provides the greatest "control" over your listeners for the longest period of time. When told well, your listeners are engaged in your story until you get to the Body of the sermon. Their attention is *captured,* and they usually can't help it. Stories are powerful rhetorical tools, because listeners are compelled to "stay with you" to find out what happens. Here are a few guidelines that might be helpful.

Be specific. The most captivating stories are those that are *specific,* that deal with one person or one incident rather than a summation of information. So, for instance, rather than talking about the *world's* problems or summing up *sins* of commission or omission, try starting with a *single* experience, episode, or example.

---

[1] There are many options here: a personal experience, joke, fable, news story, anecdote, fairy tale, short story, biographical incident, Bible story—the list is almost endless.

After that, you can use your startling statistics or summary, but use a single, specific story to get their attention first.

Relevancy. As I've already said, make sure that your opening is relevant to your topic. That is, however you begin, every utterance in your sermon, from opening to closure, should work to bring about your thesis. Some preachers will tell jokes to "warm up their audience" first. When that happens, they must then expend energy to *redirect* their listeners' attention to the subject of the sermon once the joke is over. What usually happens at that moment is that the "real" topic is announced, and then the listeners tune out the sermon because it isn't of any interest. In most cultures, jokes or funny stories are perfectly appropriate to use in preaching (and I encourage them!), but only when they are relevant in some way to the theme.

Ambiguity. Finally, try to *begin with some kind of ambiguity* in the story. That will perk up the ears of your listeners and make them wonder what's going on. This very naturally keeps them with you through the rest of the story. Ambiguity means that your listeners are *forced* into finding out what you're talking about, and by the time their interest is satisfied, you have focused their attention on your topic, text, and toward your thesis. Of course, *keeping* their attention through the rest of the sermon is the function of good organization and the kinds of actualizing resources you've included in the sermon's Body, but a good Introduction will get them ready for it.

Having examined your sermon *openings,* let's now turn to its *endings.*

IN CONCLUSION

During the six years that I was doing my doctoral work, I taught public speaking at five different campuses in the Philadelphia area. Because public speaking is perpetually one of the most fear-producing experiences for people, first speeches tended to elicit a lot of nervousness. Often, this anxiety relates to the *end* of the speech. On one occasion, a bright young student completed her self-introduction, but hesitatingly apologized for such a short speech, and then added, "Well, that's all I have to say about that. I guess, er, that I'll just sit down, thank you very much, I think that's about all . . . Well, I hope you like what I said, but I guess I'm done now, and, ah, I just . . ." As she said this, she shrugged her shoulders, looked toward the ceiling, flushed, and, keeping one hand on the lectern as long as she could, slowly made her way to her seat. It was a fairly common experience, and I hardly ever commented on it—for many, this was a first time in front of a group. As time went on and these students got more training and experience, their endings became much more strategic and succinct.

It remains true, however, that some public speakers just don't know how to *finish,* especially a lot of preachers. If you haven't thought through a good ending, this can become one of the most dreadful parts of preaching, particularly when you go on and on without being sure how to put a stop to it.

The conclusion, of course, can be one of the most important parts of any sermon you might preach. It can stimulate and excite your listeners, or it can bring an insightful, stimulating, motivational sermon to a deadly, screeching halt! So, let's think about *endings.*

The *Conclusion* of your sermon, in the classic formulation, has two basic purposes. First, it provides a *summary* either of what you've said or your thesis. The summary reminds your listeners what they heard. Sometimes it also includes a summation of the theme and all the "points" that you developed in the sermon.

But secondly, the Conclusion should also offer *closure* to your preaching. That is, you have followed a process of development through the whole sermon, and now you want to end it with something that "wraps it up." (As David Buttrick [1987] says, "conclusions are designed to conclude.") But the closure also ought to *naturally* bring your listeners to a point of hope or decision, fulfillment, inspiration, or challenge.

It's important to include both of these closing elements: *summation* and *closure.* Sometimes a preacher will end with one *or* the other, and that's problematic. And this brings us to reflect on weak endings.

THREE BAD WAYS TO END IT ALL

There are three particularly awkward ways to conclude a sermon (and I've heard them all). The first is to end just with the *summary* without any *closure* afterwards. You tell your listeners, again, everything you just told them—point by point. Or you refresh their understanding of the theme of the sermon, or its text, by summarizing it in an encapsulated way. In so doing, you lay a speed bump out on the highway. Generally, it stops the listener's thinking process because it offers no challenge. Everything is now completed and summarized, and what might have been convicting now becomes "teaching." A potentially good message degenerates into *explanation.*

A second problem is in using the last phase of the sermon as *closure,* which, in turn, leaves the sermon unfulfilled. The last point *can* serve as an ending (as we'll see in the next chapter), but this strategy ought to be used only if the *developmental* model is used. When a sermon follows one of the other four traditional forms, the last phase only serves as the final part *of the Body* of the sermon; the Conclusion must come after this. When there is no Conclusion segment to the sermon, when the classic form is not completed, there is a significant problem with the sermon, because its structure includes only an Introduction and Body.

Finally, some preachers will read a *quotation* or *poetry* at the end of the sermon, either as summation or closure. The problem is that this kind of ending is difficult for your listeners to "hear," because these are *written* language forms. (However, in Eastern Europe, *poetry* tends to be highly engaging, stimulating, and inspiring for its listeners. In that context, ending with poetry can be an excellent choice for an inspiring, uplifting sermon.) In general, though, written language is not motivational, because it isn't *transactional.* So the sermon falls flat, just when you want it to be inspiring or persuasive. Further, any reading at the end of a sermon tends to be *explanatory* rather than challenging, because it stops the thinking process.

BETTER WAYS TO END

There are better strategies to end your sermon than the three we've just looked at. Of course, you want your Conclusion to be a *natural follow-through* from the sermon, so let's think about some better options.

First, in the *developmental* strategy, the last *phase* of the sermon may become your Conclusion, particularly if the last *phase* brings everything together to a single focus. All the other phases, step by step, will have been leading your listeners to this point. For instance, 1 Peter 1:22 includes a beautiful three-phase developmental form: 1.) obeying the truth 2.) leads to a pure faith, which, in turn, 3.) leads to a love for all Christians. Preaching the text as it stands means that the sermon would end up at a place of action: loving each other. In this case, you might bring things to closure with a convicting story, but it would serve as the final step in this third phase of the sermon. (We'll be addressing this option more fully in the next chapter.)

But what if you are preaching a Problem-Solution, Cause-effect, Spatial, or Chronological order? How do you end your sermon then?

First, use your strongest and most inspiring or convicting illustration for closure. It should bring everything to a point of conviction or decision, and there isn't any better way to do that than with a story. It, more than anything else, will best re-capture the attention of your listeners. They are, by now, tired of listening. I don't mean that they are tired of listening *to you*, but even the most imaginative and interesting and powerful sermons take energy for listening, and by the time you're getting toward the end (and your listeners should have a pretty good idea that you're finishing up), they will be tired. It is here that a story most naturally reengages their interest and attention. That's why I recommend that you use your strongest or most convicting story here, the one that best captures and "drives home" your thesis.

It is also helpful to remember that the best and most clever endings are those that refer back to the opening. If you can complete a story you started in the Introduction, or can "fulfill" your opening here at the ending, that often provides nice "bookends" to your message. You might tell part of the story in the Introduction, and use the rest of it at the very end, particularly when it completes or wraps up the entire force of your argument. Or you might start with a metaphoric approach at the beginning (a pilgrimage or bridge, for instance), leave it behind during the Body of your sermon, and re-introduce it again at the very end as you bring the whole sermon together.

Second, sometimes it is helpful to briefly *summarize* for your listeners where you've brought them. What message or biblical truth did you want them to experience? A quick statement may suffice, or you may summarize the phases you've developed in the sermon to arrive here. But try to be sensitive to your listeners: in some cases, a summary will be counter-productive.

A third possible ending is with a question or statement that will encourage further reflection. "What would the Lord have us do?" is that kind of question. Or, "As the Holy Spirit spoke to disciples in the past, so He speaks to us today. What response will you make as you continue to contemplate what this means for your life?"

Fourth, in a few instances, the *text* itself may serve as a fitting "conclusion." Sometimes it can be reread or retold with an emphasis on your thesis, particularly if a return to the text will suddenly bring it to sharp focus. But I would urge you to avoid the temptation to offer an *expositional* summary of the text (or of everything you've said)—that becomes repetitive and boring.

Fifth, an expositional "call to action," such as an invitation or way to act on the biblical truth, provides a worthy ending. If so, give your listeners a specific behavior that will help them respond to this biblical truth in a tangible way. This, of course, should be part of the Body of the sermon, but at its closure you can re-introduce it as a "call to action."

Finally, your conclusion should be consistent with your tradition. Is it your congregation's custom to end with a prayer, recite "The Lord's Prayer," hear a simple "Amen," or sing a hymn? Any of these endings are appropriate. If your tradition doesn't encourage an opportunity for public decision, you might want to provide time for a non-threatening silent response or private prayer. Or, if it's appropriate, try reciting one of the Creeds. If you want to be more daring, open up a time for public prayer from the congregation. (It is customary for Eastern Europe congregations to stand or kneel after the first and third sermons to voice individual prayer-responses.)

The point is that the closure of your sermon should naturally lead to whatever type of ending is appropriate. For instance, I typically end my preaching with a hymn of commitment, and try to lead from the sermon closure to the hymn. In this way, my listeners "hear" the hymn as a follow-up to the message. If the transition is adequate, the hymn will also create the opportunity for personal response to the message.

The most common type of ending in evangelical circles, however, is the invitation, so it may be valuable to reflect on some issues related to this kind of ending to the preaching event.

THE INVITATION

At the conclusion of many sermons, an invitation is given by the preacher for the listener to become a Christian, rededicate his or her life to Christ, or become a member of the local congregation (whether the sermon was on any of those themes or not). When I was pastoring, I found that this kind of invitation-ending was *expected* of me, so it had become meaningless to everybody, including "insiders." Is there a role for the invitation, then? I believe there is, but with these guidelines:

First, know *why* you are offering an invitation. Is there a purpose beyond tradition? If you only do it because church members expect it and it is as good a way to end as any, then it may be an ineffective way to conclude.

Second, if you do offer an invitation, it should be *a response to the sermon,* not just a call for salvation. An invitation that calls for salvation after you have stirred your listeners to tithe misses the mark.

Third, the invitation should encourage *private* decision, one that is between that listener and his or her Lord. Only privately-made decisions that are shared publicly will really stick. A *coerced* public decision does not very often lead to long-term commitment. So invitations that ask people to make a *public profession* of faith, rather than a public profession of their *private commitment,* may only result in short-lived responses.

Fourth, *public decision* is valuable in that it activates a consistency principle. People tend to behave according to those things to which they commit themselves publicly. So if a public profession is a *follow through* to a private response, it becomes significant.

Finally, extended invitations are counter-productive. If the Holy Spirit hasn't dealt with a person through the course of the sermon, *tormenting* probably won't help. Remember that the *Holy Spirit* does the convicting and converting, not you as the preacher. Provide the *opportunity* for listeners to respond, but don't coerce them.

We have now examined the Classic Form of public address, which has served speakers well for centuries. But this form and its six organizational models can become ordinary and expected if used consistently, especially for a congregation that listens to your preaching week after week. I'd thus like to suggest a way to streamline this Classic Form for preaching, in a way that honors the principles but provides much greater freedom for you as the preacher. We turn now to Chapter 20 for this discussion.

CHAPTER 20
The Red Arrow

COMMUNICATION "CONNECTS"

The goal of preaching is to *communicate*. If your listeners don't understand your message, your preaching is a waste of time. That's why the traditional organizational patterns are helpful. They say that *listening* is easiest when it follows a naturally flowing "narrative"—from one step to the next in logical progression. The traditional models have served us well over the centuries because listeners most easily *comprehend* oral input in these ways. The most understandable sermons are those where the ideas naturally move from one step to the next in a well-organized pattern.

However, a regimented adherence to the "Introduction, Body, and Conclusion" form is sometimes not only too *predictable,* but it tends to be *boring* for a consistent audience. The preacher who vigorously maintains the *Introduction* (with a clearly stated purpose and preview), *Body* (with clearly laid out organizational principles and exactingly-defined steps), and *Conclusion* (with summation and closure) will get tedious week after week. So we want to *adapt* this classic pattern.

Jesus said that he came not to do away with the Law but to fulfill it (Matthew 5:17). In the same way, we want to *fulfill* the classical form and traditional models. But the Law must be *understood* first; only then can we understand what Jesus meant to *fulfill* it (by which he probably meant practicing the *spirit* of the Law). That's why we examined both the form and the traditional models so thoroughly in the last two chapters. But now that we *understand* them, we can *transform* them.

Our purpose now, then, is to *replace* the *rules* and *legalities* of what we have learned with the *spirit* (or principles) for which they were designed. We *exchange* a strict adherence to regulations with *freedom.* To do this, it was important to understand the classic *form* and its rationale, and the traditional *models* of public discourse. We aren't going to *abandon* these structures and their principles, only *modify* or *streamline* them. Now we stop thinking of *three* identifiable parts of a sermon, with its *five* somewhat confining models, and envision only *one* approach. Now we start to conceive of a sermon as *a single* flowing discourse, because that's how our listeners *hear* it.

So we abandon the procedures we've learned so far. Now we see the *form* from a different perspective, one that moves us beyond knowledge, beyond sharing information, beyond a *rules-oriented* approach. Now we fix our heart on *persuasion.* Now we see the sermon as a vehicle through which we bring our listeners to a point of decision. Now we *preach.*

This change in orientation brings all the argumentation and structure and stories together and forces us to rethink how our listeners will *hear* our preaching. We want them to comprehend the sermon as a smooth, singly-directed discourse from beginning to end, to *follow* and *grasp* our progression of thought easily. We want our preaching to wing its way like a singly-pointed arrow that will shoot them right in the heart. We don't want them to get a lot of ideas or go off in many different directions. Instead, we want them to naturally *hear* what we are saying so they will be confronted with biblical truth. This is what makes a sermon "followable." And this idea, again, calls us back to oral discourse and informal conversation. It's a side trip that will help us grasp the nature of the kind of *formal* discourse our listeners most easily *hear* (and should expect) when they listen to our preaching.

HOW CONVERSATIONAL STORIES WORK

Here's a listening exercise you can actually try sometime, but for now we'll just imagine it. Suppose you and I are standing around at the mall with a small group of friends, and we begin to tell personal stories. In this kind of ordinary, folksy, informal conversation, we are engaged in a social process of what discourse scholars call "turn taking."

Here, in an exaggerated manner, is how it works. I begin by telling a story or joke, such as an interesting event that happened to a friend or a personal experience. Because it's near Thanksgiving, I decide to tell about my most memorable Thanksgiving meal. I was in college, and, because I couldn't get home for Thanksgiving that year, I was invited to our pastor's home with 20 others from the university community who were in the same situation. Instead of the usual turkey dinner with all the fixings, we ate rice. The money the family would have spent to feed us was then used to send a CARE package to India.

Now, my "turn" is completed and you jump into the conversation. According to the way our social discourse is organized, you are free to pick up on *any detail* of my story. Coherence in informal conversation comes not by subject or theme, but by a *detail* from the prior story. So, for instance, you are not restricted to tell a *Thanksgiving* story, but it can be about an event that is triggered by *any* detail from my story. In this instance, you tell about the first time you ate rice and shrimp at the home of a *Chinese* friend. When you are finished, somebody else remembers a joke about a *Chinese* restaurant, and the next remembers the conclusion to the Jean Shepherd movie, *A Christmas Story,* which takes place in a Chinese restaurant. And someone else remembers the prize *leg lamp* from that movie, and the next tells about a crystal *chandelier* she bought in Prague. The conversation, then, goes off in several directions, depending on what element of a prior story "triggers" the next story for a member of the group. I've tried to depict this pattern in Figure 20.1. The whole "event" has coherence not because there is a common *theme,* but because one *detail* from the previous story "triggers" the next. Often, the conversation *will* follow the same theme, but that isn't required in informal conversation. And sometimes, a group member who wasn't fast enough to take a turn at the appropriate time will jump back in later, a move which often forces the conversation to return to an earlier point, creates an awkward intrusion, and stops the flow of conversation.

Figure 20.1

How informal conversation works

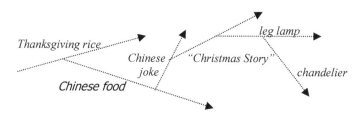

Actually, this makes a good story-telling party game. The first person begins a story in any way he or she wants. At a given signal, the next person takes over. This continues until everyone has a chance to contribute. The story has coherence through its *transitions,* but it heads off in many twists and turns that lead it far away from where it started. However, each part of the story still links directly with what has just been said.

Preaching, of course, is not *informal* conversation, but some preachers exhibit this same tendency in their sermons. An idea from one verse reminds the preacher of another text, which, in turn, triggers another, and that text leads in a different direction altogether. It's a kind of "Thompson chain reference" sermon, without much coherence except for transitions between *ideas.* Certainly, it never leads to change in the listener. It may be "followable," but, because there is no pointed argument, it never confronts the listener with anything specific.

To preach effectively, then, we want to *formalize* this "connected triggering" process. How do we use this same principle but bring it to usefulness in our formal preaching experiences? How can we make our sermons "followable" at the same time that they are *pointed?* To answer this question, we return to the subject of "narrative."

THE SERMON AS *NARRATIVE MOVEMENT*

"Narrative" isn't just about telling stories. When we think about a *formal* oral presentation such as a sermon, we realize that it follows a *narrative* type of structure: it begins, has a middle, and it ends. That is, the sermon is a *narrative form*. It follows a "story pattern," and listeners "hear" sermons as *movement*.

This understanding of "sermon" should be helpful for your preaching. If you perceive a sermon as a *developing story,* you begin to think of *progress* within it. You create a narrative that your listeners will be able to follow easily. You lead them from one place in their thought process to another. But *coherence* in formal discourse, particularly if you want to be transformational, comes by its *thesis connectedness* rather than by its *details*. When that happens, your *listeners* undergo movement as your *sermon* undergoes movement.

This is what I mean by *"narrative" movement* for each sermon. A good sermon moves the listener along from thought to thought, *phase* to *phase,* in a logical, easy-to-follow progression of ideas. This means that there is both narrative structure *within the stories* you use in the sermon, and a narrative structure to the *whole preaching event*. It is a much more helpful way of viewing the sermon than the archaic structures that come with the classic model. Otherwise, as I said earlier, preaching too easily becomes static and informational.

Let's take an example. If you organize your sermon as *problem-solution,* for instance, think of it as *following a plot*. You first establish a problem so that your listeners *recognize* that problem. Then you offer the solution through which you help *them* reach resolution. Through the sermon structure, you have created a sense of movement, that something is *happening*. Something isn't right. They are uncomfortable. But then you move them to *satisfaction*. They come face to face with biblical truth that helps them grow through the tension and discover how that truth is applicable. But it happens in one long flowing progression of ideas.

This, in part, is what Walter Fisher's "narrative paradigm" helps us realize: people most naturally *perceive* life through narrative. So a sermon, from beginning word to ending word, is "heard" as a single narrative process in which something *happens*. It is, for our listeners, a *movement* of ideas that progresses from one thought to the next.

This streamlined *narrative* understanding should change the way we put our sermons together. We should think of the whole sermon structure as a *narrative form*. This is Buttrick's (1987) idea of "moves," which provide structural development that the listener can follow naturally from one thought to the next. And it is MacArthur's (1992) point, that "proper communication in preaching involves taking people through a logical, systematic, and compelling process."

The classic form and traditional models of public speech provide this kind of *"listenability"* for those who hear us preach. But we are now about smoothing it all out. Now we bring together the topic, the thesis, the particular text and its relevant exegesis, the actualizing resources, the listeners and their needs, the preaching environment and contexts, and the sermonic structure. We know the biblical truth we will proclaim, and we know *how* we want our listeners to respond. Now we *preach.*

In so doing, we move beyond the rules. We exchange what we have learned for a new, more streamlined approach. And so we come to the model of the *Red Arrow.*

THE RED ARROW

The Red Arrow is a simple thing to look at, but it provides a powerful image of what transformational preaching should *sound like* to the listener:

Figure 20.2

The Red Arrow

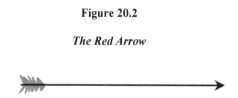

You can't tell from this black and white image, but only the arrow's *feathers* are a flaming, brilliant red; the rest is black. (The arrow on the front cover is a better image.) We'll look at its *description* later in the chapter, but it is the overall design that concerns us now.

The *Red Arrow* is a single coherent whole, and the sermon is constructed with that in mind. *All* elements of the sermon, its exegetical points, exposition, and actualizing resources work together from the beginning to the end of the sermon, from the first utterance to the last, from one phase to the next and one step to the next. The sermon is heard just as smoothly and pointedly as the shaft of an arrow.

But first, we must revisit the most critical and essential component of preaching.

TASMITTRAP

What would you say is *The Absolute, Single, Most Important Thing To Remember About Preaching?* Is it the biblical truth? The structure of the sermon? Is it the beginning? Or the preacher? No. All of these are important. But there is only one *most important* aspect of preaching: it is your *purpose,* or *thesis.* This answer assumes, of course, that you've got all the other pieces together, but if you don't know *why* you want to preach this sermon, all of the rest matters little.

If you don't learn anything else from this book, or from all your years of preaching, remember your *thesis,* your commanding idea. Haddon Robinson (1980) calls it the "idea." Bryson and Taylor (1980) identify it as the "essence of the sermon in a sentence" (the ESS). Bill Thompson (1981) calls it your "central controlling idea." Homileticians agree that the preacher needs a specific idea or purpose around which to orient the proclamation. Whatever you call it, if you want your preaching to be *transformational,* you must know *what* you are preaching about and *why* you are preaching it! Otherwise you are simply following a meaningless ritual.

However, as I've already said, developing a thesis statement may not happen immediately. Sometimes it comes to light only after you bring the biblical material into contact with the need. It may come only after several attempts to exegete the text or follow various paths that don't lead you anywhere. But if you keep returning to ask *why* you are preaching the sermon (the great *"So what?"*), to find a narrow, single-pointed thesis, your hard efforts and *stick-to-it-iveness* will eventually pay off—for you and your listeners.

And once you discover it, don't get side-tracked! You will find other interesting information, stories, examples, or points of exegesis as you continue to put your sermon together. Just make sure that your biblical information and other resources ultimately work toward a clear and cohesive thesis by the time you step into the pulpit.

The answer to why you want to preach this particular sermon lies in your thesis. Think of your sermon in its totality: exegesis, hermeneutics, actualizing resources, and structural form—all work together toward the single goal that is identified in your thesis. This is what I call *aimed* preaching, and it is symbolized by the *Red Arrow.*

AIMING THE SERMON

When we talk about a single focus or aim to a sermon, we are, of course, talking about the sermon's *structure,* not its content (though we can't easily separate the two). The idea moves us one step away from the classic *form* and the five (or six) traditional *models.* We now take everything and very *singly* and *simply* orient it all into a cohesive discourse. Now we develop an argument (even though we may not be arguing). Now we are *building a case* about how the truth of Scripture meets the need of our listeners. Now we are preparing to *tell the story that is the sermon.*

Everything we've done so far is critical and *not to be neglected!* But now it's time to put the mechanics aside so we can fashion a clear argument and build that argument *narratively,* so our listeners will be able to follow the whole discussion as it moves in a logical, "followable" presentation. We put all the materials together in a way that brings our listeners to a point of decision. In this respect, a sermon is directive; it is focused in one way; it is *aimed* and *streamlined.*

When we talk about streamlining the sermon, it's a matter of re-focusing (or *fulfilling)* the classic form and traditional organizational models. The *Red Arrow* helps to move us in that direction. It has three phases of development, as does the classic form of public address, but the three parts of the arrow are the *feathers,* the *shaft,* and the *point.* They reflect the same functions as the

Introduction, Body, and *Conclusion,* but in a more cohesive way. With the *Red Arrow,* we keep in mind the purposes of the classic form, but we now submit that approach to an even-more "listenable" model for preaching.

ARROW FUNCTIONS

The *whole arrow* is brought to bear on the development of the thesis, from the feathers to the tip. This makes the sermon more coherent than the classic model where the main idea is developed only in the "Body." With the *Red Arrow,* when we are thinking about how our listeners *hear* our sermons, all materials, biblical exegesis, and insights gently lead them from one phase to another, in logical and listenable progression, from the very first utterance to the last.

But while there is a streamlined orientation to the whole sermon, there are also specific purposes of each of the three parts of the arrow. Let's look at those functions now.

Feathers

The most interesting and attractive part of the arrow is the feathers. They are bright red, and they are the only part of the arrow that is red. There's a reason for that. The bright red color *captures* the interest of your listeners, *orients* that interest, and then *focuses* it down the shaft of the arrow.

The feathers, then, are where the sermon begins. The "eye" (for preaching, of course, we are actually talking about the "ear") catches the red feathers first. They are the "hook," the interesting part of the arrow. They attract attention, but their underlying purpose is to get the listener started along the shaft to the point.

Note that the red feathers are attached to the shaft in a narrowing fashion. From the start of the sermon, they begin to focus attention toward and along the shaft and, subsequently, to the "point" of the discourse. This is how beginnings are "connected" to the shaft. When you capture the attention of your listeners, do it in a way that is connected to the rest of your sermon and your thesis. An arrow with disconnected feathers just won't fly! So tell a story or personal experience, or use an analogy from nature that will command the attention of your listeners, but use it in such a way that it starts focusing that attention toward the "point" of the arrow.

Shaft

The purpose of the shaft is to carry the listener from the feathers to the point. The shaft is straight, not bent. It is aimed according to your thesis, which, of course, helps keep you on the "straight and narrow."

This doesn't mean, however, that everything in the sermon is predictable and falls into a straight-line pattern. Eugene Lowry's (1980) "homiletical plot" structure, for instance, is designed in the form of a downward-facing fish. The discourse reaches a point of tension and then undergoes a reversal. But the reversing argument suggested by Lowry is still coherent and *unidirectional* to the listener. It moves *temporally* from one step to the next, from tension to resolution. Sometimes, contradictions are presented and then refuted in a sermon. Sometimes there is a continual ebb and flow in a sermon, from one posited idea and its rejection to another. But all keep "pointing" in the same direction. When you preach, you want your sermon's structure to direct your *listener's perception* toward the "point."

Thus, the arrow is not meant to suggest that every sermon is *linear* in composition. On the contrary—sermons vary in structure (according to the traditional models) and in the ways the biblical material is dealt with (determined by the thesis). The development of the thesis can follow many, many different patterns (as we'll see shortly), but the idea of the *Red Arrow* is that this particular sermon is going in *one single* direction from beginning to end, no matter how the internal *phases* are constructed. The shaft, in this sense, is *temporal* rather than linear.

The 'point"

The ending place for the sermon is the tip of the arrow—its point. Here at the "business end" is a reminder that the arrow is *pointed,* and that it has *one point.* It has a single direction, a single thesis. It is not a "forked arrow" (with two points), a "trident" (with three), nor a "Gatling-gun arrow" (with nine or ten). Any of these structures might be suitable for teaching, but for transformational *preaching,* there must be one singly-developed point (determined by your *thesis).* You want everything in the sermon to contribute to the "point," and everything you say keeps directing your listener's attention toward that "point."

That is to say that your thesis already identifies the anticipated response, so you should move your hearers toward this response from the very beginning of the sermon. The "point" is evident on the arrow from the very beginning, but when the sermon reaches the end of the shaft, it is time to "bring it home." The purpose of the *point,* after all your argument, is to strike your listeners in the heart with biblical truth, to bring them to a time of decision, challenge, inspiration, and/or commitment. But the whole discourse, from feathers to shaft to arrowhead, should lead them there. Don't tack your "point" on at the end by suddenly arguing for a particular commitment or response. You should have your point in mind and in your design all the way through.

The arrowhead is also *noticeable.* It is not simply an extension of the arrow's shaft, as with a target arrow. This is a hunter's arrow with a defined point. It suggests that the "closure" of the sermon is distinctly recognizable for decision or commitment or final inspiration.

The tip of the arrow also reminds us that it is important that you learn how to *terminate* the preaching event. Arrows are of a particular length: longer or shorter ones don't fly very well. The length of a sermon depends a great deal on the local tradition, but the preacher has to know when to stop. The *arrow* ends at a particular place—it does not extend indefinitely. Concluding the preaching transaction should not happen apologetically or by trying to force another "point." It should end in a convicting, startling way that is in keeping with the entire presentation. At some point in the process, as the classic form reminds us, you must *stop*.

At the same time, however, the *point* of the arrow indicates a *continuation*, not a *conclusion*. The verb "to conclude" means "to shut." That indicates a blunt end or rubber tip on the arrow rather than a point. But the *Red Arrow* uses an *arrowhead* instead of a flat end, because the most transformational sermons are those where the word of God, by the Spirit's urging, *continues* in the heart and mind of the listener. A skillfully constructed sermon will so stimulate the listener that the word of God continues to be preached in life-changing ways. That's when the Holy Spirit takes over the direct preaching function.

KEYS TO STRUCTURE

In order to effectively organize your sermon *narratively,* we now return to the concept of *phases* and *steps*. We have seen that every sermon is a "narrative form" with a beginning, middle, and end. It moves from thought to thought, in logical, *listenable* order. *Phases* and *steps* are rhetorical constructs that help you organize and fashion your sermon in this way. As a reminder, *phases* are big sections of the sermon, while *steps* are minor divisions within these phases. But rather than seeing them as distinct "blocks" of material, we now want to orient them to the *narrative, "Red Arrow" movement* of the sermon.

THE *PHASES*

A sermon is a series of phases, or points, or, again, what Buttrick (1987) calls "moves." Each of these "blocks" of material in the sermon is a step in its development. Each is a major portion of a sermon.

Aristotle used the term "period" to refer to these major divisions of a public address. (The Introduction, for instance, is a *period.)* We can thus think about a sermon like a hockey game, which has three periods. But so you won't get the idea that your sermon must have *three* periods, a baseball game has *nine* periods (called *innings),* and an American football game has *four* (which we call *quarters).*

I've borrowed this idea from Aristotle, but "period" has a finite quality about it. It begins succinctly and ends succinctly. Rather, we should think of *Red Arrow* sermons as developing by *idea* rather than *time* boundaries. Each phase contributes to the advancement of the thesis. These are successive sections or stages or parts of the argument, each of which plays a role in the whole sermon. Each phase helps your listeners move in logical progression from where you start with them until you finish. All phases *cohere* around the thesis, and all create the sermon's narrative argument in a *connected* way.

The *feathers* constitute the first phase of the sermon, and the *arrowhead* the last. These phases are unlike the shaft-phases in that the *feathers* provide the attention-capturing opening that begins to focus attention toward the shaft (the internal development of the thesis), and the *arrowhead* brings the entire sermonic movement to closure. These are specialty phases; the others, along the shaft, will be internally developed by *steps,* which we'll see shortly.

Structuring a sermon in phases has advantages: it helps you *construct* your sermon, makes *transitions* much easier (particularly when your phases are distinct), and makes it much easier *to remember* the sermon for a noteless transaction.

Further, a phasic approach will help you *contain ideas*—to eliminate *pollution* (when a foreign idea "invades" a phase) or *overlap* (when an idea that belongs to another phase erroneously enters this one). At the same time, it helps you see how different components of the sermon *interrelate* with each other. They help you *balance* your sermon, both by structure and time.

Phasic options

When we free up the traditional models by relating them to the *Red Arrow* image, the possibilities for sermon structure become almost endless. As an example, let's look at some additional "shaft" structures offered by Fred Craddock (1985). Each of the following lines provides a different narrative argument that could be used within the shaft (or Body) of any sermon. Each provides a distinct method of organization. Together, they help us see that there is almost no limit to how a sermon can be organized:

- What is it? What is it worth? How does one get it?
- Explore, explain, apply
- The problem, the solution
- What it is not, what it is
- Either/or
- Both/and
- Promise, fulfillment
- Ambiguity, clarity
- Major premise, minor premise, conclusion
- Not this, nor this, nor this, nor this, but this
- The flashback (from present to past to present)
- From the lesser to the greater.

Certainly, these forms *could* lead to informational preaching, but the *Red Arrow* structure helps us think about them in terms of narrative movement that is aimed toward a point. While Craddock argues that form should follow the text, I find that that approach too often leads to *predictable* sermons, exposition, and a *teaching* style rather than single-truth proclamation.

What I am suggesting instead is that, while structural development is *essential,* your sermons don't have to be *restricted* by the classic form or traditional models (though, as we've seen, they certainly *can* be shaped by them). Organizational patterns are *narrative arguments* that help you say what you want to say. Ultimately, they depend on the text you use, the need you are addressing, and the thesis you develop.

THE *STEPS*

While *phases* help you organize your sermon into big parts, there are also developments within each phase that I call *steps*. These are *minor segments,* or what we might call *internal* sections of each phase.

For instance, you may be preaching from the story of the woman who anoints Jesus' feet with her hair (Luke 7:37-50). Let's say that the first shaft-phase (after the feather-phase) is that Jesus makes "outsiders" feel welcome. Within this phase, I want to talk about the story, particularly that part of the text where Jesus is making the woman feel comfortable. This is my first *step* of this phase. I then expositionally relate that truth to us today, that we, too, should make outsiders feel welcome in worship (the second *step*). Finally, I tell a story about a friend of mine who made a stranger feel welcome in her restaurant. This, then, becomes the third *step* in this phase. These three steps, then, are sub-portions that develop the idea that Jesus makes outsiders welcome. Together, they complete this phase of the sermon, and they get me to the next one: that Simon, the host, learns from Jesus.

In general, then, the *phases* create the overall *narrative argument* in the sermon, while the *steps* bring each phase to life.

Internal balance

The identification of steps also helps you *balance* the internal structure of your sermon (as I showed in Figure 18.1). Thus, if your first phase includes a reference to the *biblical story,* then an *explanation* of a biblical "point" from the text, followed by a supporting *story,* then *each* phase should follow the same *step* arrangement: *text, explanation,* and *story.* Apart from the *feather* and *arrowhead* phases, the shaft-phases should develop in the same way. This strategy will help you *design* your sermon as well as *remember* it.

Let's return to our sermon about Jesus and the sinful woman, and to the second phase: *Simon, the host, learns from Jesus.* I will develop this phase in the same way as the first: step 1: I tell the story from the text, orienting it only to Simon's response and to what Jesus is teaching him. Then, in keeping with the same step-pattern from the first phase, I explain what this means for us, that we, too, must learn the same lesson from Jesus (step 2). I then tell a contemporary story about a Christian martyr who learned from Jesus and sacrificed his life for another (step 3). In this way, the internal steps of my second phase match those of the first. I would do the same with the next phase.

TRANSITIONS

A sermon that has movement *carries* the listener from one place to another, phase by phase, in such a way that content, form, and function come together. While your thesis determines that flow, it is essential that your listeners be *guided* through the experience, from one phase and step to the next, so that everything is coherently aligned. That implies adequate *transitions,* that you create relationships *between* each part and from each part to the whole. There are three basic ways to manage transitions.

First, a transition can be a verbal link between a new phase or step and the previous one. You do it by summarizing what you just said and preview what's coming. This strategy helps the listeners follow your reasoning easily. (You might say, for instance, "We have just seen how Jesus confronted the Pharisees. Now let's see their response.")

A *pause* is a form of oral punctuation that can also be a useful transition. By pausing between phases or steps, you send a signal to your listeners that you are now providing a break and will be starting a different portion of your presentation.

Third, because different genres start in different ways, you will be directly *informing* your listeners that you are starting a new phase or step by using familiar openings. For instance, a letter starts: "Dear So-and-so." Listeners know I am reading a letter—I don't have to *tell* them. And a story begins in a recognizable way. When I say, "One day, I was walking across a meadow with my sons," my listeners know that I am telling a story without my having to *announce* it to them.

The greatest problem preachers have with transitions is that they mistake *steps* for transitions. Sometimes they think that an *explanation* or a *story* or a metaphoric *image* is a transition. No! *Phases* and *steps* carry the narrative argument; transitions are tools that get your listeners from one of these portions to the next. Don't use new information to *link* phases—that is extremely confusing to a *listening* audience.

So your *steps* build *phases,* and your *phases* build your *argument,* and everything comes together in a coherent way to fulfill your *thesis.*

ADVANTAGES IN USING PHASES AND STEPS

There are at least six advantages in the *phase and step* approach.

First, outlining a sermon by phases gives you a *quick overview* of the development of your argument. That rough outline helps you identify *steps within phases,* and you can see where you have too much or too little *information* or where you lack actualizing resources.

Second, it is easy to move these "blocks" of material when you are thinking about the final structure of your sermon. Once you define them, it is easier to see how they might work together differently.

Third, this conceptual scheme helps you *link* each part to the previous one and to the whole, from step to step (story-telling to exposition to actualizing material), and phase to phase (each contributing a distinct part to actualizing the thesis).

Fourth, when you use a story (or spiritual analogy or metaphor), this phase-and-step structure helps you *introduce* or *move into* that unit of speech without explaining to your listeners what you are doing. And you'll naturally know when those parts are to be inserted.

Fifth, it makes your sermon *easy to remember* for noteless preaching. When you perceive your *narrative argument* as a system of phases and steps, you naturally see yourself *moving from phase to phase,* and, within each phase, *step to step.* It simplifies your preaching for you.

Finally, this phasic structure helps your listeners *follow* what you're saying. They will stay with you because the *narrative movement,* to their ears, *sounds* like you are taking them somewhere. At the same time, because you are preaching without notes, you will be using *natural oral language* that is much easier for them to *hear* than written language.

Using phases and steps is a *perceptual* issue, actually. Initially, this approach helps you understand the *purpose* of your sermon and how you will bring it about. But, in the end, it helps your listeners better grasp your message and, in turn, be confronted with biblical truth.

Epilogue:
Before and After

Now that we have completed our survey of the three components of all preaching (with a particular focus on *transformational* preaching), we arrive at one final (but important) aspect of this practice, that of how we *get ready* to preach (the source of our ideas) and a few remarks related to when we're *done.* The following four chapters, then, are designed to help you discover ideas for sermons, how to organize your time and establish a preaching plan, and develop "completion strategies" that become important *after* you've stepped out of the pulpit.

CHAPTER 21
Jump Starting Your Sermons

THE PRESSURE IS ON!

It's starting to get late in the week, and you are thrashing around looking for a sermon idea. Perhaps you are lying awake at night. Or you are pacing around your office with an open Bible in your hand. Or you are spending an inordinate, anxious amount of time on your knees.

After reading the next two chapters, this shouldn't be a problem, but assume now you're trying to find a good preaching idea. Where do you begin?

There is one simple guideline that is important to keep in mind. A sermon has many components: the theme or idea, a text, a congregational or listener's need, exegetical information, a local, regional, national, or global concern, stories, metaphors, your own interests or what has captivated your attention recently—everything we've looked at in this book. Here's the principle: a sermon can begin *at any one of these points*. There is simply no restriction on the *origin* of an idea for a sermon. If you don't use a lectionary, you, as the preacher have great freedom in picking an idea or choosing a text and what exactly you want to say about it. Even if you do use a lectionary, there are elements of any sermon that provide inroads to what you'll say. Let's, then, explore some of the possible sources for sermon ideas.

SERMON SEEDS

The tiniest little mustard seed grows into a big tree, Jesus says (Matthew 13:31-32). Sermons are just like that. A seed, from any source, gets planted, and it germinates and sprouts and then bursts into full boom. Those seeds provide *beginning* places for sermons, and there are many of these starting points from which idea-seeds can originate.

As you become a disciplined preacher, you will start to do some deliberate and strategic thinking about the origin of your sermon ideas instead of waiting for a suitable thought late every week. What I've listed here are only some of these starting points, but they should give you a glimpse of the wide range of possible sources for preaching ideas.

1.   SCRIPTURE

There are many ways that Scripture can provide sermon ideas.

First, in the free church tradition (where the preacher has complete choice over the text and sermon topic), *a passage of Scripture* might be of particular interest. Maybe you have been leafing through, or actively studying, your Bible, reading a devotional booklet, or looking at a commentary, and a text seems to grab you by the heart or mind. These kinds of texts provide passionate and interesting sermons because they have first *interested* you.

Another way to stimulate Scripture origins is by preaching a biblical *theme* that you develop over the course of several weeks. These kinds of thematic *sermon series* are usually established by subject matter (different passages about "grace," "biblical pilgrimages," or "characters from the Bible," for instance). Here, in successive sermons, you move from text to text on that theme. Series like these provide preaching topics for several weeks, and are often interesting to preach because you have been attracted to these texts and/or the theme itself.

And, of course, you can also preach one sermon or a series of sermons from one book of the Bible, or a particular theme in one book.

2. PERSONAL INTERESTS

Second, your sermon can begin with *your own concerns or interests*. Perhaps you have an idea that is intriguing (the mustard seed image in Matthew's Gospel, for instance), a global issue that you want to develop (like feeding the poor), or a special theme about which you feel called to preach (such as missions or tithing). Often one of these personal themes or ideas will "grab" you. They come from your personal Bible study (keep a notepad handy!), commentary reading, Christian literature, or a journal entry. Take a walk in the forest from time to time to reflect on *objects in nature.* These analogical insights can stimulate good sermon ideas. Find a way to collect these ideas in a folder, box, or computer file so you can locate them when you need to.

Again, sermons you preach from these ideas will tend to be energetic because they are of interest to you. But use caution here: personal interests can also become *petty* or *dogmatic* as you focus on concerns that are relevant only to *you.* Sometimes, your personal issues have little or no interest to your listeners.

3. CALENDAR

Another great source of sermon ideas is *the Christian calendar.* The Advent season (four weeks before Christmas) is a time to reflect on the coming of Jesus. The Lenten season (the six Sundays before Easter) provides tremendous opportunities to consider who Jesus is and what it means to follow him. From Easter until Pentecost (a seven week period) is a great time to preach about the Holy Spirit's presence in the life of the disciple or congregation. These traditional Christian holy days and seasons are important because they cover a wide range of issues that are important for the Church.

But don't forget *national holidays* or *special historical celebrations.* In America, for instance, Martin Luther King, Jr. or Independence Day are holidays on which people's attention will be naturally focused already. The Sunday before Women's Day in many places in Europe (March 8) provides a great opportunity to honor the significant ministries of women in the church. Holidays can be excellent opportunities to preach about Christian values, God's providential care, or political issues.

4. NEEDS

We've talked a lot about needs or interests as essential components in developing your thesis statement. Often this is the source from which your sermon will emerge. When you start here, your preaching becomes immediately *relevant,* because it relates the gospel to a particular concern or issue faced by your listeners. With this kind of *prophetic preaching,* your proclamation centers on a word from God for this people in this time and place. There is no question that this kind of sermon is the most effective and direct way to free the Holy Spirit to transform lives. *Need-driven preaching,* then, orients biblical truth to the particular group and situation you are addressing.

Of course, as I've already argued, transformational preaching *requires* this "connection" in every sermon. If you follow this practice, you want to learn as much as you can about your listeners. You should *know* them well. It helps even more if you love them!

Apart from the issues we discussed in Chapter 14, there are two primary ways to *discover* what would interest your listeners.

First, through personal observation, you can *perceive* certain *needs* of the congregation. These are the needs or desires that *you* notice or you get through informal discussions with your members—at Board meetings, in Bible Study groups, or at the Sunday School picnic. But there are also the *universal* needs of your people, of sin, fellowship, and maturing in discipleship. New Christians need to be grounded in the Christian faith and in how to participate in the life of the congregation. Infighting or power struggles among church leadership, the need for teacher training, a building program, or a crisis situation are all legitimate beginning points for sermons. You will notice them if you pay attention. These are the kinds of needs you *observe.*

A second way to discover congregational needs is through their *voiced needs.* Perhaps a church member has asked a question. Or, as many preachers do, you may solicit ideas from the congregation. Some preachers make available a little card for written questions or concerns. Others gather a group of parishioners together to reflect on the needs of the congregation. Sermon talkback sessions provide another forum, where the discussion of one sermon may reveal other issues that are relevant and important. This approach will help you become even more aware of your congregation and preach relevant sermons that meet them where they are actually living.

5. TRADITIONS

Local church traditions or *programs* provide preaching themes, too. Your congregation might have an annual evangelism thrust, a Memorial Service that honors faithful church members who have died during the past year, or a "Homecoming" event. Or your church may be engaged in a building program. Another approach is to try a comprehensive church-wide curriculum (as a series during Lent or Advent, for instance), where the mid-week Bible study, home study groups, Sunday School classes, and weekly sermons all follow the same theme or text.

6. CHRISTIAN MATERIALS

And what about your own reading of *Christian literature?* There are many resources from which to draw ideas: books, magazine articles, and web sites are only a few. Especially notable is *a sermon or story you have heard or read.* Most of the time when I have the opportunity to *listen* to good preaching, one or more sermons are often generated (I always try to have something to write on). *Hymns* or *songs,* the *stained glass windows* in your worship center, or a small group Bible study session may lead to a sermon idea. And if you have access to them, don't neglect other kinds of preaching resources, such as *books of sermon outlines,* the *lectionary,* or your own files of *actualizing resources.* And if your local newspaper prints titles of sermons in its Saturday edition, you might develop your own sermons from the *titles* that other preachers advertise.

7. WORLD

Finally, in an increasingly secularized culture, you should keep "contact" with the "world out there" if you want to stay relevant to your listeners. Include "secular" books in your personal reading schedule, such as biographies, historical novels, how-to books, and poetry. Find out the kinds of *fiction* your members are reading. And don't forget the *humanities;* inspirational art, lectures, poetry, music, and history can all offer rich materials and ideas for your sermons. Or subscribe to a magazine or two that you know your members enjoy reading. And find out what contemporary sociologists and psychologists are saying. These resources provide "escape opportunities" from the ordinary routines of ministry, but they also help you better understand the mind-set of the people with whom you worship week after week.

BEWARE OF "DOCTRINAL" PREACHING

Sometimes, generating a sermon idea from any of these sources can lead to an emphasis on *doctrinal* preaching. That is, you may want your listeners to *understand* biblical truth because you think your theological insights and advice are brilliant and relevant. You may be more inclined to want them to *know* the Bible and what it means rather than calling them to action on its truths. Again, that will lead you to informative and *explanatory* sermons, which result in teaching discourses, which, again, aren't very transformational.

COMPLETING THE SERMON

It's worth asking now which of the above approaches uses the Bible? Well, of course, if you are a biblical preacher, they all do! Which of these beginnings leads to the best convicting, inspirational, persuasive, or motivational sermons? Clearly, they all can. How? Well, when a sermon idea *starts* with any of these sources, that doesn't mean that it ends here. The *beginning point* only gets you rolling. You now develop a sermon with all the elements we've talked about: a congregational need, a text and biblical truth, stories, and a specific thesis. The seed only *begins* the process: the mustard *tree* looks very different from the mustard *seed.* Like that, all the elements of good preaching that we've talked about must eventually be brought into the sermon construction process.

But there's another *artistic* view on constructing sermons: you will probably discover, as I have, that most sermons develop *as you put them together.* As you engage in sermon construction, *everything* can change from start to finish: the thesis, text, biblical truth, exegesis, structure, and actualizing resources. Sometimes your original idea will lead you to a *better* preaching idea, and sometimes your stories or text will *not* support the original idea you had. So, in the process, you find that you have to *change* something (the original idea, text, or stories you use). In any case, don't be afraid to abandon your original idea.

PREACHING PRINCIPLES, AT THE END

This brings us to four helpful, important principles of preaching.

1. A sermon isn't a sermon until it is preached

Only when a sermon is *being preached* does it really count. None of your listeners is aware of the work you put into developing your sermon. They don't know what you might have intended to say. They don't know the great flash of insight you had last Tuesday that got intentionally omitted in the final version. All they know is what they *hear.* They are recipients only of the final product.

2. No sermon is ever perfect

Don't expect any sermon ever to be *perfect.* There is no single, ideal way to preach any text, any biblical truth, or any sermon. A sermon grows out of the materials you have in hand at this particular moment. It includes the stories you have collected, the text and the exegetical insights you have drawn from it, the congregational need you have identified, any of the particular environmental influences that have impressed you, and whatever else occurs to you. When you are under the time limitations of *having* to preach, you are restricted by what you have been able to gather at the time. Those "pieces" of the sermon will be sufficient to fashion that sermon in a particular way. So if you keep praying about what you have and let the Spirit of God hover over the chaos for a short period of time, a sermon will generally emerge. Sometimes it comes with a brilliant flash of insight, and other times with the deep frustration of hard work and agonizing thinking.

3. Just decide

Your problem may not be that there are too *few* ideas on which to preach, but that *you must settle on one of them for this particular sermon.* You may sometimes feel like the captain of an ocean liner looking over the whole ocean and not knowing in which direction to steer your ship. The issue for you, rather than one of *lack* of possibilities, is, in reality, one of *indecision.*

That is, sometimes you will cast about looking for just the right sermon or perfect idea. It is frustrating when you can't find it, and you may be inclined to give up hope. But the reality of taking on a disciplined approach to preaching means that sometimes you must *decide.* You just have to make a choice, given the information you have at hand. You might miss a real target (this happens even to the best archers from time to time!), but you can still fashion a listenable and challenging sermon, even if it doesn't hit your listeners as powerfully as you'd like.

4. You won't ever run out of ideas!

When you are a biblical preacher, you should always have more ideas than time to preach them! Remember that each text has many preaching themes, each congregation and situation is different and requires different biblical insights, and you as a preacher keep changing. In such a changing environment, there should never be a lack of preaching subjects. To illustrate what I mean, let's look at a configuration of preaching possibilities that I've identified in Figure 21.1 on the next page.

How many times does 1 go into 192? From all the *potential* beginnings for sermon ideas we looked at in this chapter, I've decided to start with a *congregational need.* That is, I narrowed down all *possible* ideas to a single theme, and finally chose "unity in the church," though I could have settled on any other. I have labeled this theme as Level I in the diagram.

Second, I now identify some *potential texts* from which I might preach this sermon (Level II). I've found four without much thought, and probably could have found many more if I used my concordance or other resources. But let's assume that these four are my "finalists." This gives me *four* potential sermons—one from each text.

From these choices, I now will pick only *one* of them, since I want to orient my sermon around just one text. *Any* could be used and would lead to a perfectly good sermon, but for various reasons I choose the text from John 17:20-23.

Third, I now isolate and define a *single* biblical truth from that text (Level III). So, for the John 17 text, I might identify the following three biblical truths:

- *Truth 1:* Being right with God creates unity in the church (verses 1-5).
- *Truth 2*: Unity emerges when we work in a new community (verses 6-12).
- *Truth 3:* Jesus prays for the unity of his future followers (verses 20-21).

I am also assuming that I could find *three* biblical truths in each of the four texts. That now gives me a possibility of *12* potential sermons on the same theme (four texts with three truths in each).

Figure 21.1

The potential wealth of sermon possibilities

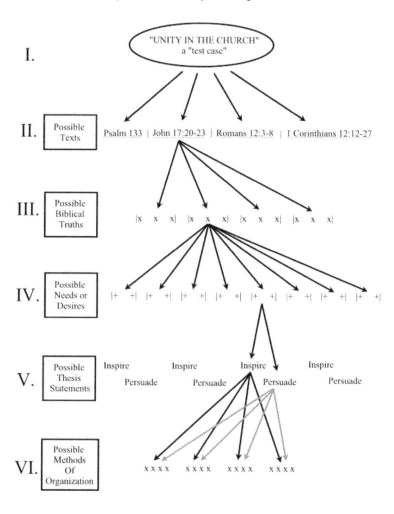

Of course, I'm not finished yet. I now want to talk about a specific orientation for this truth: a need or desire, as a *lack* of something needed or something to *reach* for (Level IV). I might adopt a *need*-approach if there is continual fighting between church officers. Or I might preach a *desire*-oriented sermon if I want to inspire my congregation to dream about the benefits and support that happens when Christians work together. So, if we suppose there is just *one* need and *one* desire around which I could orient any of these sermons, we are now up to *24* options.

I now must design a thesis statement (Level V). With each preaching *truth,* I could either *inspire* my congregational members to unity or *persuade* them to *do something* about unity. These statements, of course, depend on the particular need or desire I want to address. We've had practice designing thesis statements, so we don't need to do that now, but let's assume that we could develop at least one thesis statement for each rhetorical intent (either *inspire* or *persuade).* That gives us *two* approaches to each need or desire, and brings us to *48* possible sermons, using the same theme.

Finally, I think about ways to *structure* the sermon. To the five usable *traditional* models for preaching, Fred Craddock adds the 12 that we saw on page 300. (This is not to mention a host of other possibilities.) However, let's say that I could organize each of these two thesis statements in only *four* ways, depending on my exegesis, the actualizing resources, and particular need in my congregation (Level VI). Now I have *192* potential sermons, again using only *one theme.* If I preached only once a week, that's about four years of sermons!

Of course, I'm not encouraging you to do this. Your congregation would stop coming if they had to hear four years of sermons on unity! I only use this chart to illustrate the great number of sermons you *could* develop from only one theme. This is to say that you have a wealth of preaching material at your fingertips. Compound this by the tremendous, almost uncountable number of preaching themes and possible texts for each, the possible needs or desires of your listeners, and the almost infinite possibility of stories and personal examples, and you have many, many lifetimes of sermon possibilities!

KEEPING IDEAS

Finally, it is important that you find a way to keep all your good ideas so that you can sort through them from time to time or find a particular idea when you need it. This keeps fresh sermon ideas in front of you—ideas that are of interest to you. Drawing from these ideas keeps your preaching relevant and exciting, if you don't allow most of them to escape through neglect. To do that, I use a simple file folder labeled "Sermon Ideas" that I feed regularly with little notes on Bible texts, magazine articles I find stimulating, and references I hear other preachers use. However, I'll talk more about this in Chapter 23, so there's no need to pursue it more fully now.

CHAPTER 22
The Preparation Process

MAPLE SYRUP AND PREACHING

Putting a sermon together from idea to "amen" is a *distillation process.* It comes when the preacher, a simple theme, a text, actualizing resources, a congregational need, and local circumstances all come together. Everything contributes to the *meaning* of the text for this time and place. It all distills down to one singly-focused event that has transformation written all over it. It's rather like making maple syrup.

Those who produce maple syrup first draw the sap from the maple trees. It is collected bucketful by bucketful, sloshed in a large vat, and then boiled down to get the wonderful stuff that I put on waffles on a cold winter morning. There's nothing quite like it! It takes 40 gallons of maple sap to get one gallon of maple syrup. That's a lot of boiling!

In preaching, all the elements of the sermon have to be boiled down just like that. It involves the distillation of a biblical text to discover its driving or orienting purpose and main sense of order. That produces a thesis that enables the truth to emerge. But then we throw in the preacher's personality, the congregational need, the actualizing materials, and the immediate circumstances. We study it all and think it through, and "Holy Spirit heat" provides the fire that finally boils it all down and distills it into a wonderfully powerful sermon. And then you step into the pulpit and "serve it up." The waffles are ready!

Like that distillation, we will now follow a process of sermon construction from beginning to end.

THE CONSTRUCTION PROCESS IN 16 EASY STEPS

Through this book, we've examined theory and the practical application of many elements of preaching, as well as issues related to constructing sermons. Content, structure, communication, the preacher's role—all are critical. But now it's time to put it together.

So I want to take you through a "typical process" of sermon development, from idea to completed sermon. Of course, this is only *one* way to do it, but I offer it so you can see how I process everything for one sermon. I don't expect you to adopt my strategy, but I do encourage you to develop your own routine.

Before we begin, though, there are two important matters to discuss. First, these "steps" are presented in *one* logical order in this chapter. But, unfortunately, the sermon construction process doesn't always fall neatly into this kind of chronological pattern. Because preaching is an art form, there are many different ways that a sermon comes to birth. It might begin with Step 4 or 5 or 2, and sometimes you have to return to a prior step. But eventually all the components should come together in some fashion. These steps will remind us, at least, of the elements that are important.

Second, there is one component of the distillation process that can't be stipulated in a procedure like this. It is that Spirit-generated *passion* that empowers you to bring something transformational to life. The 16 steps that follow will distill a *sermon* out of the syrup-producing vat, but it is your own *zeal* and *persuasive ability* and *orienting focus* that will ultimately transform a mere "sermon" into "transformational preaching." The radical difference between "delivering a sermon" and "preaching" is monumental, but no one can tell you how to make the jump from one to the other.

Let's turn, then, to examine the 16 steps in this "sample" process. As we go, we'll develop an actual sermon using the same theme we looked at in Figure 21.1 of the last chapter, that of local church unity.

1. IDENTIFY A GENERAL TOPIC

This initial step answers the question, "What will I preach about?" Its answer may emerge from a congregational need, season of the year, or an interesting revelation from my personal devotions. I'm beginning with a single *theme.* That is, when I think about my congregation, I realize that there are members of different social groups who aren't comfortable together, so I decide to preach on "unity in the church."

2. CHOOSE A TEXT

Because I began with a topic, I must now locate a specific passage of Scripture that will orient my sermon. I could, of course, have begun with the text, and then my second step would be to find the general theme from within it. But when I start with a topic, I usually try to identify several different texts so I have some options. From memory, then, I narrow the possibilities to four: Psalm 133, John 17:20-23, Romans 12:3-8, and 1 Corinthians 12:12-27.

Now I must pick *one* of them. They are all potentially good texts, but I want to choose one that has the greatest bearing on the need I will be addressing. So I return to each of the texts and read them through and decide, given my particular congregation, the recent experiences that raised this need to my attention, and my first thoughts about the text, that John 17:20-23 seems to be the best choice.

3. WRITE A SINGLE THESIS: 5 STEPS

I now follow the five steps that we discussed in Chapter 12 that help me arrive at my preaching thesis. This step may take me some time, but it's well worth the energy I spend on it, because a clear thesis here will make the rest of the process much easier.

1.) One theme

Because I started this process with a theme, I don't need to re-discover it. If I were starting with a text or season, it would be important now to find a general theme for this sermon.

2.) One biblical truth

Because every text has many preaching themes and biblical truths in it, I could identify several. Each one would shape the sermon in a different way. So I now look through my text and locate the following three biblical truths in the passage:

> *Truth 1:* Being right with God creates unity in the church (verses 1-5).
> *Truth 2:* Unity emerges when we work in a new community (verses 6-12).
> *Truth 3:* Jesus prays for the unity of his future followers (verses 20-21).

This step in developing the thesis, though, means that I must narrow my choice to just one. As I reflect on my local situation again, I decide that I will affirm that Jesus prays for disciples today. But I also become aware that, in this prayer, Jesus seems to actively support the ecumenical movement. And, too, I think I should encourage my congregation to be united because Jesus *loves* people of all kinds.

I now realize that I can't include all of these ideas or my sermon will become explanatory and informational. I must eliminate as much as I keep. So I work hard to settle on *one* biblical truth, and finally decide it will relate to the unity of believers because that's what Jesus *prayed for*. This rough statement helps me get closer to the biblical truth I want to isolate. As I rethink my listener needs and the text, I want to write my biblical truth as clearly and succinctly as I can, as a full sentence in which there is action. Eventually I arrive at the following: "Jesus prays for unity among his disciples today."

3). A need

A sermon brings together a text and a need and lets them inform one another. When I think about my congregation in light of this text, it becomes even clearer to me that I must address divisions and factions in our church, but, for now, I will simply identify the discomfort of my members with those of other social classes in the congregation.

4). My rhetorical intent

I now decide whether I am going to *inspire* my listeners to *think* differently about each other or *persuade* them to *behave* differently. Because the need is a *visible* one, I decide that I will try to get them to change their behavior: this, then, will be a *persuasive* sermon.

5). The working thesis

It is time now to bring these four steps together into a "working thesis." This thesis will guide my later choice of actualizing resources, the text and its exegetical points, the need of my congregation, and my own reflections on the text. I call this a "working thesis" because it will probably change as I develop the sermon. Indeed, I hardly *ever* have a well-developed or finalized thesis at this early stage, but I need to start somewhere to put my sermon together.

I don't necessarily call attention to the biblical truth in my thesis, because that's stated above. The thesis tells me my ultimate goal: what I want to accomplish by proclaiming the biblical truth.

There are *many* different thesis statements that could be fashioned from the biblical truth that I've identified. So I look at everything I've got so far and think again about my congregation and the text. I have already decided to orient the sermon toward a *practical* demonstration of unity, so, after some fussing with it, I arrive at the following: "I want to persuade my listeners to *demonstrate* their love for one another." I will base my sermon on the text from John 17:20-23, and will focus it on Jesus' prayer for the unity of his future disciples. But, when my preaching is done, I want my listeners to *behave* differently toward each other, though I'm not yet sure in what way. This thesis statement, at least, gives me a place to start.

4. THESIS EXEGESIS

I now want to exegete the text for my thesis, so I bring the biblical truth and thesis back to my text and "draw out" those insights and biblical truths that will help me accomplish that thesis. I don't want to exegete every detail of the text (which would take a lot of time), but I *do* want my sermon to *reflect* biblical truth and *channel* that truth for my listeners. This step also implies that I will *not* include certain elements of the text in this sermon.

When I come back to the text in John 17:20-23, I am now able to identify the following exegetical points that support my thesis:

> *v. 20: Jesus prays for all future disciples*
> *v. 21: Jesus' prayer is specific: that future disciples will be united in will*
> *v. 21: unity emerges from our relationship with God. That is, when God is our Father, we are common children*
> *vv. 22-23: unity demonstrates that Jesus comes from the Father and loves the whole world*
> *v. 22: disciples have the glory of Jesus, and it is this glory that unites us*

I then think about a rough "narrative structure" for these elements of the text, as follows: my church members should *demonstrate* unity because: unity extends from God through Jesus to us, Jesus prays for us, and our unity provides a clear witness to Jesus' love for the world.

5. APPLY THE TRUTH

This step is a natural follow-up to the process so far. I want to be sure to *apply* the truth to the need I am addressing. This is the hermeneutical step. The contexts are similar between those in the early church and my own congregation. Jesus' prayer for unity among early believers was relevant for them, and it is relevant for us. Our *practice* of unity will demonstrate Jesus' unity with the Father, his love for the world, and his glory in us that unites us.

But because this is a persuasive sermon, I also want to give a *practical way* that unity can be seen. As I think about this issue, I suddenly decide that I will work with the deacons to organize small Lenten home groups for four weeks. At those home meetings, we will mix the social classes together. We'll study a curriculum on the nature of the Church. This initiative will bring my people together in a way that will demonstrate our unity in Christ. So now I change my thesis statement to read: "I want to persuade my listeners to attend a small home Bible study group." This, in my mind, will be a good demonstration of Jesus' love for them, and a good way the community will see our unity. After all, that's what Jesus prayed for.

6. COLLECT ACTUALIZING RESOURCES

Knowing that people "hear" stories and anecdotes more powerfully than they hear exposition and explanation, I now spend time seeking the right kinds of stories, examples, metaphors, and/or analogies that will help me accomplish my thesis. There are many different kinds of these support materials I can find, so I spend time searching out my database, file folders, and books of illustrative materials. I also remember other biblical texts that might be useful in actualizing my thesis, particularly biblical stories.

I always want to collect *more* actualizing resources than I will need, because I know that I'll discard more than I use. I may start with 10 or 12, but end up with only 5 or so. But they give me options. And what I collect will help determine how the final sermon will be fashioned. For now, just a few will help me get started, though I won't make the decision about which of them I will actually use until later.

After thinking and researching a bit, I now collect the following: James 2:1-7 (and the problem with rich and poor). I also remember the Corinthian church that was having a major problem with unity (I find a particularly helpful text in 1 Corinthians 1:10-17). And I remember a story from my childhood when I felt isolated from the other kids at school because I was "different." Here's a newspaper clipping about a congregation that split over a petty doctrinal issue and a magazine article that concerns a major denominational split. And I looked through my computer CD-ROM on various subjects related to "church" and isolated three good stories about local church unity. Finally, I remember an old "Parable of the Tools" that I dig out of my files.

7. BRING IT ALL TOGETHER

Now comes the actual business of putting everything together for the first time. To do that, I gather it all in front of me—all my data, my exegetical notes, my thesis, my own thoughts on the text, and all the actualizing resources I've collected. I usually just list everything on a piece of paper, or I take all the bits of paper on which I've written notes to myself and spread them out. When I do that, here's what I get:

> James 2:1-7: rich and poor
> 1 Corinthians 1:10-17: factions
> childhood story: personal isolation
> newspaper clipping: local church division
> magazine article: denominational split
> geese: unity in flying
> sheep: respond to danger together
> Text: John 17:20-23:
> > 20: Jesus prays for all future disciples
> > 21: Jesus prays that future disciples may be united in will
> > 21: unity emerges from our relationship with God
> > 22/23: unity shows that Jesus comes from the Father,
> > > Who loves the whole world
> > 22: disciples have the glory of Jesus; this glory unites us

There it is, in a way that I can see it all together. I again reflect on whether or not the *theme* or *text* is right for the *need*. I reflect again on my listeners (as well as I know them), and remind myself of limiting factors, such as time, place, season of the year, or Christian calendar.

But, mostly, I want to examine all the "pieces" I've collected and think about them. I try to see how my narrative argument will come together from the textual points I've identified. I try to see if there is a noticeable "gap" in my argument or whether I need additional stories or actualizing resources. I might have to add additional ideas. I might return to the text and give it another look. If I haven't yet specified a thesis, I try to work one out now: this will give me an idea of how to pull the materials together. (Sometimes, my thesis emerges only after I bring all these components of the sermon together. Or a particular story may help frame it for me, or one point from the text, or the need.) Again, the thesis doesn't have to be exact yet, but I am seeking a way to bring order to all the ideas and bits of information I've collected.

8. IDENTIFY THE SERMON'S STRUCTURE

It's now time to roughly organize these materials into a coherent *narrative argument.* I do this by working back and forth between the five traditional models (leaving out *topical),* the Red Arrow and other structural options, and the exegetical "points" I've identified. To be a faithful biblical preacher, I want to organize the sermon according to the textual points I have found, as they work together in a logical kind of argument that will support my thesis.

But I also want to settle on *one* form that will bring together what I've collected, and organize it in a way that will help my listeners understand and respond to the biblical truth (that Jesus prays for *demonstrated* unity among his disciples).

At this phase of sermon development, I generally just push the little papers around on my desk, or draw arrows, or number and re-number the items on my page. I try to "see" what a problem-solution order might look like, or a chronological or developmental structure.

After I've looked over what I have, I decide a cause-effect model might suit the materials. At this point in my understanding of the text, I see that v. 21 says that because we are commonly related to the Father (cause), we are united in will (effect), and, further, in vv. 22-23, that our unity demonstrates our Christian faith to the world (an effect).

This is a bit awkward (cause-effect-effect), and doesn't suit a clean cause-effect structure, so I adjust it to a *progressive* structure:

Phase 1: we are commonly related to the Father
Phase 2: we are united in will
Phase 3: our unity is demonstrated
Phase 4: for a witness to the world

I remember again that my ultimate goal is to get my listeners to *demonstrate* unity by attending the small group meetings. When our unity is visible and noticeable, our neighbors will see Jesus in us.

9. PREPARE A ROUGH OUTLINE

Once I have identified the structure, it is now time to put everything together for the first time. So I do a rough outline or sketch. I must decide what I want to keep and what might not fit. I try to think how I will get from the opening story to the text and the phases of the sermon. I start "playing with" the information in front of me. I try to see how the stories and other actualizing resources might fit into the structure. What stories or analogies do I have that will support each of these phases as I've defined them? I try to think about which story would offer the most engaging opening, and which I might use for closure. Now I think of the *Red Arrow* as a very directive, pointed kind of narrative argument that I want to make in this sermon.

This, then, leads me to my rough outline. Here, I put on paper just what I have envisioned up to this point. I do it very simply: I take a sheet of paper and list the *phases* and *steps* of the sermon as I see them coming together. I try to keep the same *internal pattern* for the *steps:* if I first explain a particular idea, follow it with a discussion of the text, and use a story, I will keep that same pattern: explanation, text, story—until I've exhausted all the phases. I think of my sermon as a singly-focused "narrative" that will move my listeners from the attracting "feather phase" to the "phase by phase" development of the shaft of the arrow, until I conclude at the "arrowhead phase." Now I want to check my general argument to see if this approach will really lead my listeners to recognize and act on the biblical truth I am proclaiming.

I do not try to make the sermon perfect at this stage. I only want to establish *some kind of order* in which to put everything together.

Story issues

Before we move on in the process, though, there are three issues that I often confront when it comes to including stories in the structure.

1. What if I have two stories that support the same phase? There are times when this happens, and I have two choices. Either I save one of the stories for another sermon, or I try to use one of the stories for the beginning or the ending of the sermon. When I choose the second option, I might have to adjust the story in a way that makes a better fit either at the opening or closing: if I use it at the beginning, it will have to be told in a *captivating* way; if at the end, it will have to *encapsulate* the thesis and bring my listeners to a point of decision.

2. What if I need additional resource materials? I sometimes find that I need additional resources to help "fill in the gaps" of my outline. That is, I just don't have enough resources to develop each phase with a story. What do I do?

First, I might spend an hour or two tracking down additional potential stories or thinking about relevant experiences from my own life. That's o.k. It's part of the sermon development process, and the more time I spend here, the better my sermon will be. I simply go back to my sources for this (as we discussed in Chapter 16).

Second, I try to remember that *narrative movement* is important for my listeners, not the *structure* of my sermon. I want to design a "followable" organizational pattern from start to end, but there are many, many options for how to do that. I don't want to get "stuck" on just that one model that I might have started with.

For instance, suppose I am following a good, four-phase developmental model, and I have a good story for all phases except the third, but there is just not enough time to find the "right" story for that phase. One option is to abandon the four-phase developmental structure in favor of the following *deductive* pattern:

- Opening story
- Explain the "point" of the text according to my thesis
- Actualize that thesis with another story
- End with my most powerful and relevant story.

Or I might try this *inductive* approach:

- Story followed by a second story, which
- leads directly to what the text says;
- End with my concluding story.

This is simply to suggest that there are other ways to approach the sermon when I think *narratively* (and in *phases* and *steps)* rather than rigidly trying to adhere to a pre-formed model.

3. What do I do when I have a great story that doesn't fit? There are times when I will have started the whole sermon process with a great story, but, by the time I've come to this point, I realize that it no longer fits anywhere. What do I do? Well, there are some options (these options should be considered both here and in Step 12).

1.) I can eliminate the story if it doesn't fit. I'll just save it and use it in another sermon later.

2.) If I have a story that I absolutely *want* to use, I might have to *change my thesis* to reflect that story. The thesis isn't sacred, and *everything* is changeable in the sermon development process (because a sermon isn't a sermon until it is preached). Or I might want to develop another *phase* for my sermon that best utilizes it—if the biblical text supports it. If I take either of these approaches, though, I try to make sure that I still maintain a clearly focused thesis so I don't head off in a lot of different directions. When I find that I am pursuing *two* ideas, I also might consider dividing the material into two different sermons, and preach the second one next week, as a two part series.

3.) I can *change* the story slightly, if that helps it conform to my theme or metaphor. Remember that the *way* a story is told doesn't necessarily alter the *events* of the story. Sometimes I put it in a slightly different context, or eliminate some otherwise-distracting details so it fits a particular *phase* of my sermon. This doesn't mean that I change the *intent* of the story, but I find that I can usually adapt the story in a way that helps me fulfill my thesis.

The rough outline

Now let's look at where we are. All of my work so far, before I even start writing, has provided an overview of what I want to do with my sermon and how I want my listeners to respond. This is my initial rough outline, and, up till now, it looks like this:

Phase 1: Opening story: I saw geese flying together yesterday.
     This is the way Jesus intended for us to live as his followers.
     We see this in John 17: 20, where he prayed for *our* unity.
Phase 2: We are related to the Father in unity (verse 21)
     Actualizing resource: *James 2:1-7:* rich and poor didn't get
          along until they realized that God was their common Father.
Phase 3: we are united in will (verse 21)
     Actualizing resource: *sheep* respond to danger together
Phase 4: our unity is *demonstrated* (verses 22/23)
     Actualizing resource: *Parable of the Tools*
Phase 5: for a witness to the world (verse 23)
     Actualizing resource: *1 Corinthians 1:10-17:* church factions
     Actualizing resource: newspaper clipping about a local church division
Phase 6: Closure: a neighboring church that tried small groups

You may notice that I have an extra actualizing resource in the fifth phase: the newspaper clipping about a local church division. I don't right now know where to put it, but I definitely want to try to use it in the sermon, so I've inserted it here. When I start writing my first manuscript (in the next step), I'll get a better of idea of where it might fit.

10. WRITE A ROUGH MANUSCRIPT

Now I actually write a manuscript. This is a "rough draft" that I develop from the rough outline. Sometimes, this is the most difficult part of the process, but it depends on how carefully I've thought it out, how clear the outline is to me, and how disciplined I am to "get it done." I find that it is important to write out, *in full,* just what I want to say, word for word. There are at least four good reasons for this.

First, it gives me the opportunity to get all the material down on paper and see how it *feels* when I'm writing it out.

Second, it helps me check the approximate length of my sermon from how many pages of rough manuscript I write. I will know immediately whether I need to edit it or add to it in the final version.

Third, this rough manuscript gives me the chance to check the *flow* of my sermon: what fits and what doesn't. I'm checking to sense whether or not there is any *narrative movement* in the sermon. My outline may seem fine, but when I write it out, I notice that the pieces don't exactly fit where I initially thought they would.

And, fourth, it helps me see large gaps in my reasoning or places where I need additional resources, narrative, or exposition.

There are three additional issues related to the rough manuscript. First, when I write the rough draft, I ignore grammatical rules (this makes the writing more fun than if I am nitpicky about how I write). This rough manuscript isn't for anyone else to see—I'll destroy it when I do the final manuscript, anyway. It's only for my own use, a preview that helps me get ready for the final manuscript. So I don't worry about spelling or punctuation—I just get as much as I can on paper!

Second, as I write the rough manuscript, I experience a phenomenon that used to frighten me. That is, I discovered, as I wrote, that my sermon was going in a very *different* direction than I had envisioned up to that point. I learned after several such experiences to relax—it is part of the creative process of an emerging sermon. My sermon isn't completed until I finish *preaching* it, and my listeners have no idea beforehand what I'm going to say or how I'm going to develop the text. So I let the Spirit-led creative process work for me during the writing of the rough draft, and I am free to make changes from the original rough outline *as I go.* There isn't anything sacred about my original idea, the actualizing resources I have collected, the way I have understood my text, or my rough outline. I am just trying to make sensible order out of what I've collected so far. This is a chance to put things together in as coherent a way as possible.

Finally, because this is a rough manuscript, new ideas come to me as I am writing it. So sometimes, I make **bold** or *italicized* notations right on my rough draft while I'm typing it in my computer, or sometimes I write on the hard copy by hand as soon as it comes out of the printer. It's still very rough, because I'm only starting to think through everything I've got.

(Because of the length of rough and final drafts, I have decided not to develop our example further. If I did, you would notice a great difference between these two manuscripts. I can already see places in my rough outline where I don't think this sermon, as it is, will "preach" very convictingly, but you can work that out for yourself.)

Let's return, then, to the next steps.

11. LET IT COOK

Now is the time to let the rough draft "cook" for a while. I've spent some exhaustive time working on this sermon. Now I leave it for a day or two. This helps me get a fresh perspective on it when I return to it, even if I haven't thought about it at all while I've been "away" from it.

We'll talk about a weekly schedule in the next chapter, but it is clear that you can't leave your sermon for two days if you start working on it on Saturday morning! Start earlier in the week.

12. RETURN AND REFLECT

After my time away, I return to the rough draft and look it over. I look on the pages for notes, arrows, additions, or changes I made during the time I was writing it. (These, of course, are obvious changes that I already know I want to make.) But now that the whole idea of the sermon has *cooked* in the back of my mind, I come back with fresh eyes. And there are many things I will change about it.

I now ask myself some of the following reflective questions:

1. I look at my thesis. *Why* am I preaching this sermon? What *specifically* do I want to say? How do I want my listeners to respond?

2. In my rough manuscript, did I end up at a different place than I started? This is the most consistent issue I face in my sermon construction process. When I start writing, I have a particular idea in mind, but by the time I finish writing the rough draft, I have discovered new points from the text, thought of other stories, or found my manuscript veering off in a different direction because of a different need that occurred to me when I was writing. This means that I did not maintain a consistent thesis through the whole rough draft. That's o.k. But now I either need to change my thesis or the way my sermon flows.

3. Is there any *narrative movement* in the sermon? A natural flow? How will it *sound* to my listeners: will they be able to *follow* my thoughts easily and naturally? If some of the movement is not natural or easy, then I need to work on the organization and/or transitions.

4.   It is also the time to look for *balance* in the sermon structure. If one *phase* of my sermon has a story that follows it or "brings it home," does every phase?

5.   Does the beginning and ending grab me? How can I tell the opening story with greater ambiguity and more concrete images that will better capture my listeners' attention? Will my concluding strategy bring things to adequate closure and provide ongoing challenge?

6.   What do I need to *eliminate?* What gets me off the thesis?

7.   Is the manuscript too long or too short? Do I need to add or eliminate stories, or should I eliminate one of my *phases?*

8.   Have I organized *similar* thoughts in the same phases of the sermon? I want to keep each phase distinct from the others, so are all my comments grouped where they belong in each *phase* of the sermon?

9.   Is there too much *explanation?* I sometimes find that it is best to interpret and/or explain the biblical truth during *one* phase of the sermon rather than in many places. Sometimes, of course, I restate my biblical truth over and over again as a mnemonic device, but, sometimes, trying to include it in different ways at different places in the sermon makes the sermon difficult to remember and difficult for my listeners to "hear."

10. Are my written sentences too long? Generally, if I use short sentences in my manuscript, my oral language structure will automatically lengthen them when I'm in the pulpit.

13. DEVELOP A SECOND OUTLINE

I remind myself again that *everything* is changeable: my thesis, structure, phases, exegetical points, biblical truth, and other resources. So after having given my rough draft a careful examination, I now re-outline the sermon. This often requires a major reorganization in the structure, or a reassessment of my thesis, any of my actualizing resources, my opening and closing, and, maybe even, my textual points. I might have to add new transitions between the phases of my sermon, or rethink and reframe the biblical truth. The phases may need to be reconfigured into a more-listenable pattern.

With my new "awareness" of what this sermon could be, I now attack my rough draft and rearrange it. At this stage, I mark up my rough manuscript, sometimes a great deal. This, then, brings me to a *second outline* of the sermon. This second outline comes from the worked-over rough draft. In this "final" outline, I again simply want to list each *phase* and *step* of the sermon, from beginning to end, just as I did with my rough outline. This one, though, has more coherence to it, and helps prepare me for the final manuscript. Here's the final outline:

Phase 1: Opening Story: The drama of the Corinthian congregation
Phase 2: Problem: Danger in the church!
        Actualizing resources: denominational split
                              local church division

Phase 3: Solution: Jesus prays for us
             Text development: Jesus prays for our unity
                     Jesus prays that our unity be visible
          Actualizing resources: sheep huddle together in danger
                       geese fly together against the wind
Phase 4: Our response: Small group study!
          Actualizing resources: success of church with small groups
Phase 5: Closure: story of a multi-racial church that learned to get along

14. WRITE A FINAL MANUSCRIPT

When I come to my final rewrite, I pay attention not only to the *organization* of the whole sermon, but to its *wording.* So if I have repeated a particular word often, I try to insert synonyms. This may not make much difference when I am preaching without a manuscript or notes, but it helps me *think through* different ways of saying the same thing. When I write these things down, it helps me remember them.

Or I might find that many of my sentences begin in the same way, such as "I think . . ." or "It was a good thing . . . " So I try to rewrite them. If all my sentences are in the active voice, I may intersperse a few passive sentences (but only a few!). If there are only *statements,* I might want to add a few *questions.* If I am using an old cliché or trite phrase, I want to add colorful language. If I am mixing conceptual metaphors, I want to reorganize things to follow a single metaphor (such as a bridge, tree, or an athletic theme). I want to eliminate anything that might *distract* my listeners from my thesis. I am simply trying to add *variety* to the final manuscript, not because the manuscript will be read from the pulpit, but because it forces me to think through what I am going to say and how I am going to say it.

Now I take a deep breath and write my final draft. With my computer, I move *phases* and *steps* as necessary. I delete what doesn't fit and insert new materials that do. And I "fine tune" my language.

There are now two questions that you might be thinking about.

1. Why a second manuscript?

There are four good responses to this important question:

First, *organizing* and *reorganizing* my sermon helps *clarify* and *settle* the message in my mind. It gets more firmly rooted for the pulpit transaction.

Second, I usually don't get it right the first time. It doesn't take long to discover that the first attempt needs rethinking. Further, there is deep satisfaction that comes with "perfecting" a manuscript. When I radically shift the content the second time through, I realize how disorganized the sermon was on the first attempt. Once through doesn't create as much *coherence* as the second time.

Third, working through this entire process and writing a second manuscript helps me see what *doesn't* fit in this sermon. That is, some issues or stories didn't occur to me when I first put my ideas down on paper. Writing a rough manuscript, spending time reflecting on it, and then rewriting it helps me better decide what I *will* preach.

Fourth, a second time through creates a *better manuscript.* I now have a copy of a well thought-through sermon. There will be times in the future when I may want to preach the same sermon to a different congregation. A well-done manuscript provides a much more significant resource for the future, especially if I want to preach on the same text later but have no ideas. It is also useful as an exegetical resource for other sermons on the same text (for this reason, I usually keep my exegetical notes attached to the manuscript), and is valuable, especially, for *background information* on the text.

2. Why all this trouble when I am preaching without notes?

This is another good question. Again, I have a few responses:

First, preaching without notes does not mean preaching without preparation. It simply means that I go into the pulpit without any notes to rely on. When I begin my sermon construction process knowing I will preach without notes, it helps me know how to prepare more simply and effectively. Going through the manuscript a second time engages my "preaching mind" more deliberately.

Second, working through my manuscript twice helps me get the *flow* of my sermon fixed in my mind, in a way that once through doesn't provide. It forces me to get a *clear idea* of what I want to say.

Third, undergoing the process twice helps me *remember* the sermon for preaching without notes. It creates images or pictures in my mind of what I want to express in my sermon. If I short-circuit this process, the images aren't as sharp or crisp, and are more easily forgotten. I am writing so I *can* preach without notes, and two times through provides a way of reflecting again on the sermon's flow.

Fourth, working through a sermon twice helps me *write like I speak,* so the sermon will *sound* better to my listeners. I try to write for *hearing* rather than reading. The structure of oral language dictates that I think about "speaking my manuscript" as I write it. This helps me prepare to preach while I am still working through the writing process.

Fifth, this process enables my oral language to be more *formal* rather than *informal.* Informal conversation isn't appropriate in a formal speaking situation, so I think about vocabulary and grammar that is respectable, but is, at the same time, *listenable.* I want my words to reflect a broader vocabulary than I can think of "on my feet." Writing forces me to use *simpler words and more concrete images* that communicate better with my listeners. That is, writing helps develop useable *extemporaneous* vocabulary. The more I "correct' myself on paper, the better I become at keeping my speech clear and simple.

Sixth, it helps me sharpen my *story-telling skill.* When I think through *sensate* images and vocabulary, suitable ambiguity, and final resolution, it creates sharper and more engaging stories.

Finally, it forces me to think about the *transitions* I will use between phases of the sermon. Sometimes I don't have a very clear idea of how to get from one phase to the next, and going through the manuscript twice helps me think through my ideas more effectively and clearly, and to get from one to the other. I rarely understand this the first time through, so this process prepares me to preach without notes.

15. DRAFT A "PREACHING OUTLINE"

Once my second ("final") manuscript has been written, I now write a brief "preaching outline" from this document. I simply list the *phases* and *steps* one by one. I might jot statistics or dates down that I want to remember, because this is the outline I use for my final preparation.

This final outline is the *only* document with which I rehearse my sermon. I have written the manuscript twice, but now is the time to clarify the *sermon* and streamline it in my mind for *preaching*. A simple outline serves this purpose most efficiently, because it forces me to encapsulate the sermon in my mind. So I leave my manuscript behind and, as risky as it is, do my final preparation without it.

16. REHEARSE FOR THE MAIN EVENT

Finally, I prayerfully practice preaching the sermon from the outline. I have "thought it through" at least twice now, and have written it through twice. I know the flow of the sermon, but when I do my final preparation, I want to get a feel for the *narrative argument* and the stories. So, using only the outline, I "preach it through" twice by myself, until all *phases* and *steps* are satisfactorily "linked" to each other and to my thesis.

There's one more secret I have discovered. It is that every practice run is different. The sermon takes on a slightly different emphasis or flow each time I "preach it through" in my mind. I've learned to celebrate this phenomenon. I do it only to get the flow of the sermon firmly embedded in my mind, but it means that a sermon is a living experience when I actually preach it. It's not a worn out, tightly written essay that was meaningful in my study, but is a living transaction between my listeners, the biblical text, and the Spirit of God, and I am at the heart of it. Preaching comes alive because it's a *unique* experience when I step into the pulpit, unlike anything that has happened up to this point. *A sermon is not a sermon until it is preached,* and when I do finally preach it, it is a very different experience than it was in its rehearsal. It is *only* what happens in the preaching *transaction* that really matters. All the rest is "prologue."

So all my preparation, especially this final rehearsal time, is simply the opportunity for me to get myself ready for that grand moment when I step into the pulpit and engage in a living transaction with real people in a real context and bring the living word of God to bear on that relationship. That's transformation!

ONE FINAL PRAYER

You might be wondering where the Holy Spirit is in this process. In my experience, it is essential that you bathe the entire practice of sermon construction in prayer—from the inception of the idea to the choice and exegesis of your text, from seeking appropriate stories that will help bring about your thesis to the thesis itself. Only when the Holy Spirit has control of your mind and insights, from the beginning of the envisioning process to the final "amen," will you be flexible enough to fashion the kind of sermon that will transform people's lives. So pray often and long about your preaching ministry. Pray sincerely about this particular sermon. Pray for your listeners before and during the preaching event itself. And pray for yourself as you engage your listeners in the transaction of transformational preaching.

Just before I step into the pulpit, I breathe a quick prayer, too. Sometimes it's a prayer for my memory, sometimes for my listeners, and sometimes I am a bit upset with God for leading me to preach this particular message. Sometimes I don't feel I'm ready for it. But when I mix all of the anxiety with the live event of preaching, when the Holy Spirit says, "Go!" something extraordinary happens! Preaching is ministry, even when I don't feel adequately prepared for it.

So Charles Allen (1978) cites Dean Inge, who prays:

> *Dear Lord, this sermon of mine isn't much, but I've worked honestly on it, and it's the best that I can do, at least at the moment. I know that any good which comes from this sermon will be Your doing and not mine. Please help me so to live that I may become an increasingly uncluttered channel of Your grace. To that end, may I think Your thoughts after You, and speak Your word. I love You, and I love these people among whom I serve. That's that, God, amen.*

CHAPTER 23
Planning Your Preaching Ministry

SPIRITUAL ARROGANCE

There are some interesting customs among Baptists in Eastern Europe. When I taught in Siberia, for instance, I found out that the most promising young men who have been Christians for six months are designated "brothers" by the pastor. It means that they are expected to start preaching. It is customary to include three sermons at every worship service (including Sunday morning, evening, and, usually, during three or four week night meetings), and the pastor determines which brothers will preach during that service. Some pastors let them know just before worship begins, while others simply point to the poor brother at the time he is expected to preach. (All the brothers sit with the pastor on the platform throughout the service.) He must then "prepare" between the time he leaves his seat and gets to the pulpit. Those who are particularly alert think about sermon possibilities ahead of time.

Except in a few traditions, we usually don't preach in that spontaneous way in the West. Most of us know ahead of time that we are going to preach on Sunday, and we typically have adequate time to prepare—if we take it. The preacher who steps into the pulpit without prayerful *preparation* may be demonstrating spiritual arrogance, unwittingly claiming a better "connection" with the Holy Spirit than others in the congregation. Those who work under this assumption, of course, determine *when* and *how* the Spirit will inspire a sermon. And when the Spirit inspires according to the *preacher's* timing or the relentless worship schedule, the impression is that he (the Holy Spirit) is "immediately-tappable" and at the beck and call of the preacher. Those who confine the Spirit's movement to the *moment,* then, are guilty of boxing him in according to their own whims. When this happens, the *preacher,* not Jesus and not the Holy Spirit, becomes Lord of the pulpit.

Mark 13:11 is sometimes used to support this approach. Jesus says, "Do not worry beforehand about what to say. Just say whatever is given you at the time, for it not you speaking, but the Holy Spirit." In its context, he is clearly referring to arrested Christians who are taken to trial. He is talking about a day when there is no opportunity to know ahead of time what charges or accusations will be made against the disciple. That is, there is absolutely no indication that Jesus was establishing a principle for a *consistent preaching ministry* here, and it may be time to revisit the idea of preparation time for pulpit ministry.

GOD, THE ADVANCE PLANNER

It is clear from a study of Scripture that God has a *long view* of human history and the amount of time we spend in our lives. It begins in Genesis 12:1-3, when God promises a future to Abram. Here is an "advance plan" of God, one that took centuries to bring to completion.

And Psalm 139:16 reminds us that *before we were born,* God knew us. The Psalmist fully believed that God worked in advance of his birth. The prophet Jeremiah tells us that God has *plans* for us (29:11), and Jesus included *future* believers in his priestly prayer in John 17:20-21.

In 2 Thessalonians 2:13, the Apostle Paul presents God's long-term "plan" of salvation, and, in Romans 8:28-30, he reports that we are included in it. In 2 Timothy 1:9, he writes that salvation in Christ Jesus was given "before the beginning of time," an idea that is repeated in Ephesians 1:4-12, one of the great "predestination" passages. There, it is clear that God decided on the *plan* of salvation even before *time* was created. (This text does not necessarily lead to the doctrine of *personal* predestination, though that doctrinal point, as well, indicates long-term planning.) Later in the Ephesian letter (3:10-11), *the church* becomes a central factor in God's plan and salvation process.

And let's not forget Hebrews 11 and the roll call of faith of these heroic individuals who trusted God to lead them to a new future. They clearly relied not on what was *immediately* ahead, but on the *distant fulfillment* of a promise. All of these texts remind us that God is an Advance Planner.

TAKING CHARGE OF YOUR LIFE

If we are to tap the resources of a God Who acts by design, we must learn to be prayerfully open and submissive to Him. For that, we turn to the beginning of Jesus' ministry in the first Gospel, where we note Mark's theology about Jesus' *preparation* for his work. In Mark 1:12, Jesus is sent to the desert *(ερημος)* after his baptism. (This word is variously translated as "desert," "wilderness," or "solitary place.") There his faith is tested, much like fire tests and refines gold.

Then, in Mark 1:35, Jesus again heads out to "a solitary place" for prayer early in the morning. "Solitary place" is the same word Mark uses for "desert" in verse 12. Again, out there, Jesus is being "proven."

Finally, in Mark 1:45, we are told that Jesus "stayed" out in "lonely places" (again, the same Greek word is used). With this desert metaphor, then,

Mark is telling us, at the beginning of his Gospel, that Jesus gradually "came into" and finally resided completely in the will of God. That is, after his baptism, Jesus was taking charge of his life and destiny through times of *regular* prayer in which he *recognized* his Father's will, and, finally, lived *completely* in his Father's will.

When we as preachers, too, come into the presence and control of God's creative energy, we recognize the importance of *submissive discipline.* The most important fruit of the Holy Spirit is *self-control,* which stands at the end and most respected place on the list (Galatians 5:23; see also 2 Peter 1:6). *Discipleship* means *discipline,* and when the Holy Spirit empowers us, he enables *us* to manage our own lives and relationships and routines. And when we come to Jesus as *preachers,* we ask him to be our commanding Lord and submit ourselves to his resident Spirit. Then we should become *self-controlled,* too, especially in our preaching ministry.

That's a very different approach than being a *reactive* disciple who is always *responding* to the demands and needs of other people. When that happens, it is *other people* who determine how I carry out my Christian life; their *emergencies* characterize my ministry. Of course, the Holy Spirit *may* lead me to adopt this life-orientation, but being available to the whims of everybody around me is usually just an excuse for poor self-discipline and a sign that the Holy Spirit really is *not* in control after all. And that can destroy the possibility of a preaching ministry that is truly strategic and transformational.

What follows, then, is my own approach to personal discipleship for preaching, principles that I have found to be helpful for my life and sermon preparation. My prayer is that this discussion will help you find your *own* disciplines of life, so that you will satisfactorily manage your life for more powerful preaching.

PLANNING YOUR PREACHING MINISTRY

As I grew in my own understanding of what it meant to be a disciple who relies on Jesus as Lord and his Spirit as Guide, I gradually discovered the importance of disciplines in my maturing process. I found it to be even more important as I realized the awesome responsibility I had in proclaiming the gospel.

One of the most significant continuing education courses I attended after seminary was a two-day time management seminar, in which Ed Dayton and Ted Engstrom of *World Vision* argued that there are four "spheres" in which to think about how we use time. Their book, *Strategy for living* (1976), is adaptable to preaching, so let's examine these four "spheres" of time with an eye to sermon construction. They include an examination of your life's *purpose, long-range* planning, a *weekly* routine, and, finally, the *daily* schedule.

I. LIFE ORIENTATION

We begin with an understanding of your overarching rationale for living. It has four components.

1. Purpose

For what purpose do you exist? What's your aim in life?

I decided early that my guiding purpose in life is to *serve Jesus,* no matter how or where he wants to use me. I would not only follow his leading as closely as I can, but will take every opportunity to serve him even if I am not sure if this particular action or decision is in his fullest will for me or not.

This guiding purpose, in turn, determines how I spend my time, decisions I make about my personal, family, and professional life, and the effort and energy I give to preaching and teaching. So I preach because Jesus is my Lord, and because I know that when I preach I am serving him. I also know that he has gifted me to preach and teach, and that I am only truly satisfied when I am exercising the gifts he has given me. Of course, these gifts are present but not yet perfected, so I continue to develop and hone my skills every time I practice them.

So, what's *your* reason for living, *your* general orienting purpose in life? Once you decide this, the rest begins to fall into place.

2. Goals

The second step is to set specific *goals* that help you accomplish your purpose. "Behavioral" goals are those that are specific, time-bound, and measurable. They are important so you can tell if and when you accomplish them. It's a simple system: when you meet the goal, it helps you fulfill your purpose. Thus, every time I prepare for and then preach, it is a *goal* that helps me fulfill my purpose of serving Jesus.

3. Steps

Third, specific steps help you meet whatever goals you identify. This brings us to weekly and daily strategies, which we'll examine later in this chapter.

4. Priorities

The last part of the process is to organize steps in priority fashion. This is a call to be *proactive* in ministry. I found that a lot of my time was spent "fighting fires" in pastoral ministry, and if I was to take my preaching and teaching ministries seriously, I would have to be more disciplined. Establishing priorities helped with that. It meant I was able to determine for *myself* my own life's purpose and calling rather than relying on what others wanted me to do or be. It also helped me take quality (and non-guilt producing) time with my family.

Setting preaching priorities simply meant that each sermon (a goal) was important to help me fulfill my purpose (of serving Jesus). Thus, I had to set aside the routine responsibilities of weekly and daily time to do it well (steps). These time slots became *priorities* for my ministry.

This overall life management approach, then, prepares the way for the following *long-range planning* and *weekly* and *daily* routines.

II. LONG-RANGE PREPARATION

Preaching was a consistent discipline of ministry for me when I was pastoring. This implicated all aspects of pastoral ministry. My understanding of pastoral ministry, as it is reflected in the Second Testament, is that there are six major pastoral responsibilities that must be balanced in the course of ministry. If these duties are to be adequately managed, it essentially leaves only 8 – 10 hours for preaching preparation. Since this responsibility came relentlessly, week after week, I quickly learned that certain routines would help me get my preaching schedule organized properly, in a way that would help me maximize these few hours for preaching. I realized that I had to be able to *see ahead* quickly and *keep* advance information at my fingertips. That, in turn, required time-saving measures. One of those was to do as much long-range preparation for my preaching as possible. Eventually, I discovered four principles that helped me meet this objective.

1. Collect immediate ideas

The greatest need I had when I started preaching was for relevant stories to help construct my sermons. So I had to find a way to collect inspirational ideas that came to me. To do that, I got into the habit of carrying a small pocket notebook with me wherever I went (sometimes it was just a scrap of paper). Why? I found that good sermon ideas did not wait until I was at a convenient place or time. Ideas flow freely when I am stopped at a traffic light, sitting in a neighborhood café, or on the golf course. Some of the very best ideas have come at other times than when I was *preparing* a sermon. So I had to capture those challenging, convicting ideas that I couldn't wait to preach.

When I jot down an idea, it is not necessarily well developed, but I try to provide enough information so I won't lose the momentary inspiration that comes with it. Unfortunately, I have lost more ideas than I retained simply because I didn't write enough details in my notebook when the idea came to me.

If you haven't yet begun to work on an idea-collection process, start now. You might want to recopy your little messages on note cards, or enter them in your computer, as soon afterward as you can.

2. Sort and keep ideas

Second, I had to find a way to *keep* those ideas. For this, I used an ordinary file folder that became a "catch-all" into which I tossed my preaching ideas: the notes I'd written, spiritual analogies, magazine articles, news clippings, advertisements, Xeroxed book pages (with bibliography written on them), devotional booklet pages, stories, jokes, etc.—anything that stimulated sermon possibilities. Most of these ideas were never used, but at least I had a place to collect them. Just the act of writing and storing ideas kept those ideas flowing, so I have never run out of good ideas for my preaching. (You might want to look at the structured system Ilion T. Jones [1956] suggests, but in the end, you must design or adapt whatever procedure works best for you.)

You should also work out your own disciplined way of *finding* these ideas. I never developed a very fancy retrieval system, so my temporary folder became their home. It meant rummaging through the whole batch of little pieces of paper every time I looked in there, and that was an unwieldy system. With the sophistication of computers these days, you can probably start now to develop a system that will be usable for many years in the future.

3. *Planning retreats*

Early in my ministry, I spent hours at the beginning of each week trying to think up a good sermon topic for the next Sunday. This practice not only made it extremely difficult to start on next Sunday's sermon at the beginning of each week, but it created serious problems with the use of my time. Knowing that a preaching opportunity was always coming, I was spending extra time for sermon preparation that should have been spent on other responsibilities of pastoral ministry, and I found myself getting more and more frustrated.

After my time management seminar, then, I took a proactive posture about sermon preparation, but it took a radical change in my schedule. I set aside a three-day planning retreat three or four times a year. I started by camping, but was then offered the use of a church member's cabin. (You might find another location where you can be out of your usual routine of ministry, away from the telephone and drop-in visitors.) When I took these retreats, I counted them as "ministry time" rather than vacation, announced it to my Board, and took everything I needed to do sermon and church planning: different translations of the Bible, a concordance, a calendar with holidays and special church dates on it, my sermon idea folder, our hymnal and a hymn concordance, and my files of stories, cartoons, jokes, and personal experiences that I had been saving. At this retreat, along with strategizing for general church ministry, I would plan the next four months of preaching themes, titles, hymns, and sermon texts. When I had finished with this four-month worship schedule, I had an advance list of topics for the choir director and worship leader, who could plan music to coincide with the worship theme for each Sunday.

I started with a sheet on which I had written all the Sunday dates. I would note holidays or seasons (Lent, Advent, and communion Sundays), or special days such as a choral cantata, special Sunday School program, or baptism. This gave me an overview of how to "fill in" these dates with the good ideas I had collected since the last retreat.

During this time, I would also think about balancing "heavy" preaching topics with lighter ones, prophetic preaching with humorous, and doctrinal issues with practical applications, to keep my preaching fresh and relevant. Figure 23.1 on the next page provides one sample section of an actual preaching schedule I used.

Figure 23.1

Preaching and Worship Schedule
September 13 – October 11, 1988

Sep 13:   Theme: Renewal of our priorities
           Call to Worship: Hebrews 12:2
           Meditation Hymn: "'Tis So Sweet To Trust in Jesus"
           Scripture: 1 Kings 20:37-42
           Sermon Title: BUSY WITH OTHER THINGS
           Commitment Hymn: "Take My Life"
           Benediction: Psalm 26:2-3

Sep 20:   Theme: Sharing our faith
           Call to Worship: Matthew 28:19-20
           Meditation Hymn: "Pass It On"
           Scripture: Acts 26:28-31
           Sermon Title: GOING PUBLIC
           Commitment Hymn: "I'll Go Where You Want Me to Go"
           Benediction: Mark 5:19

Sep 27:   Theme: Growing as a Christian
           Call to Worship: 1 Corinthians 3:10-11
           Meditation Hymn: "More About Jesus"
           Scripture: 1 Peter 2:4-5
           Sermon Title: ONLY BECOMING
           Commitment Hymn: "Higher Ground"
           Benediction: Mark 1:17

Oct 04:   Theme: Renewal of our faith
           Call to Worship: Psalm 26:2-3
           Meditation Hymn: "May the Mind of Christ My Savior"
           Scripture: Ezekiel 37:1-14
           Sermon Title: BRITTLE BONES AND NEW BLOOD
           Commitment Hymn: "My Eyes are Dry"
           Benediction: Psalm 51:10
                        Note: Communion

Oct 11:   Theme: Missions
           Call to Worship: Psalm 72:19
           Meditation Hymn: "Jesus Shall Reign"
           Scripture: Psalm 67
           Sermon Title: EXTENDED LIFE
           Commitment Hymn: "Send the Light"
           Benediction: Psalm 67:7
                        Note: World Mission Offering

4.   *Weekly folders*

Finally, I developed a weekly file folder system for each Sunday of the year. I labeled one folder for every week, labeled with the month and week number: "January 1," "January 2," etc. I also labeled four folders with the number "5" to account for the fifth Sundays that come every three months.

When I was pastoring fulltime, I kept about three months of these file folders in my desk where they were readily available. In each, I would collect information for the sermon I intended to preach on that particular Sunday. I started filling these folders at my planning retreat, and discovered that my *Reticular Activating System* was on alert when I used this system, so that my eye and ear were attuned to pick up any resource materials that helped actualize that particular theme in a later sermon. When I found a story that potentially suited a particular sermon, I would toss it in the folder for that Sunday.

Then, when it came time to write the sermon each week, I would just go through what I had already collected. This provided me with a lot of *potential* directions for that sermon. Of course, many of the stories related to the general theme, but they weren't necessarily relevant to the text or thesis I eventually developed. However, it always meant that when it came time to start working on that week's sermon, I already had several options available.

By following this system, I had a pretty good idea at the beginning of each week what my sermon topic, text, and theme would be, and I had already collected some actualizing resources. It freed up a lot of sermon preparation time, because I found that I no longer had to spend long hours at the beginning of every week thinking up a good topic, finding a text, locating suitable hymns, and seeking good stories.

I encourage you to begin your own system as soon as possible—perhaps even before you have to start preaching consistently. You will be astounded at how much time these planning principles will save you.

III. WEEKLY PREPARATION ROUTINES

This brings us, then, to a *weekly routine* in ministry. I found that my sermon preparation routine was easily manageable in eight to ten hours per week. This was the schedule that developed gradually over a period of almost 15 years of pastoral ministry when I was responsible to preach at least once a week. My schedule was based on one preaching service each week. You, of course, will have to adapt this routine according to your own context of ministry, particularly if you are responsible for two, three, or four sermons a week, as is the case for many pastors in Eastern Europe. You'll have to find a weekly routine that works best for you, but *my* typical weekly routine looked like this:

Monday

On Monday, I would file away yesterday's sermon manuscript, outline, and bulletin. This seemed to provide a "jump start" to working on the next sermon, so I would get out the sermon folder for the coming Sunday, look over its contents, but not spend much effort on it. On most Mondays, I looked at the theme and thought about what current need or issue I should address. Steps 1, 2, and 3 (from the 16 steps in the last chapter) were predetermined at the Planning Retreat, though often a congregational need or immediate circumstance in the community would focus the text or topic for that week.

Tuesday

Both churches I pastored printed a weekly bulletin, and Tuesday was the day in which I would compile that information. I often found myself making changes to what I had pre-determined at my planning retreat. Sometimes, for instance, a previously chosen hymn no longer fit the sermon, or the prior text did not suit the current situation. I felt free to change these things in the more immediate context of ministry.

Wednesday

On Wednesday, I would spend about an hour on sermon preparation. I again looked through the file folder for the next Sunday, examined the materials I had already collected, took a look at the biblical text, and jotted down a few additional ideas or notes (Steps 4, 5, and 6). Sometimes I checked commentaries. Often, I would search for additional actualizing resources (Step 7), and sometimes outline the sermon that was already emerging in my mind (Steps 8, 9, and 10).

Thursday

Thursday was my main preparation day, the day in which I organized the ideas I had in front of me (Step 10). I would then write a rough draft of the sermon (Step 11). Work on this phase of sermon preparation took half of Thursday morning, generally about two hours. This was my first opportunity to get things down on paper. I would change, edit, and adapt these ideas as I worked through this draft. I also found that I had to find more stories, or crystallize the thesis. My main purpose, though, was to get the information written down and printed out, and often I would make notes right on the printout.

Friday

Friday was my day away from the office and the immediate work with church issues or church people. It was not only a great opportunity to spend time with Ellen and the boys, but to let the sermon "cook" (Step 12). As I indicated in the last chapter, this was one of the most indispensable steps in the creative process. I would leave the rough manuscript in my office and would not think about it during this day.

Saturday

On Saturday morning, I returned to the sermon and examined what I had previously written in the rough draft, but now with a fresh mind. I would go through the manuscript, re-read the text, finalize the thesis, and move my actualizing materials to better fit this new focus. If I needed to, I would find new materials, exegetical support, or stories. I also eliminated a lot of what I had written (Step 13). Then I reoutlined (Step 14) and rewrote a final draft from the new outline (Step 15), and then wrote a "final" outline from the finished manuscript (Step 16). This portion of the preparation generally took about two hours, and the resultant outline was usually in detail. I would take *only* this outline home with me.

Saturday night, then, was my time for personal sacrifice. From 9:00 until 11:00 was final preparation time. (Preaching effectively requires sacrifice, and this was mine.) I studied the outline I brought home with me, saturated my mind with it, read it over, checked its flow, adjusted it, added to it, and preached it through (to myself).

After that came the first real "test" of the sermon: I preached it twice to myself on Saturday night *without the outline*. This, I found, was the most critical time of sermon preparation, when I found out where the sermon didn't flow naturally or where it was too complicated to remember. I found particular places between phases where I stumbled. I had trouble with a transition or two. Sometimes, I found that, even after two written manuscripts, the ideas still didn't *naturally* flow from one to the next. So, even at this late hour, I was still adjusting the outline, rearranging it, and adding other stories. I frequently reminded myself that "it isn't a sermon until it is preached!"

Thus, I rehearsed the sermon once with the outline and twice without it. Each time through was different, but the process of preaching through it helped prepare me for the actual preaching event the next morning.

Sunday

Finally, Sunday is at hand! During my last pastorate, I got into the habit of walking to our church building on Sunday morning (we were fortunate to live about 30 minutes away). On this journey, I took *no* outline, but preached through the sermon once more (in my head), and once more made mental adjustments. Final preparation just before worship meant engulfing myself with the message, reminding myself of the thesis and intent of the sermon, its beginning and sometimes its ending, and its general order.

This, then, provided my usual weekly routine for sermon preparation, generally taking between eight and ten hours.

Your own routine will probably not work out like this, of course. You will have your own family obligations, restrictions, and local context and culture to work with. (When I explained this process to my Russian students, one of my students, with a look of horror, exclaimed, "On Sunday morning, I've got a cow to milk and four children to get ready, and we have to drive 30 kilometers!" I assured him that this is not the only way to do it, but he would have to find his *own* way of putting a sermon together.)

However you do it, start now on your own weekly routine. The more quickly you settle into a *pattern,* the more quickly you'll start saving time in sermon preparation.

IV. A DAILY SCHEDULE

Finally, from the earliest time in my ministry, I found it important to establish a *daily* routine, as well. A daily schedule keeps me more focused and better able to accomplish what needs to be done. This was true in pastoral ministry, but is applicable to *any* kingdom work.

As a pastor, it was my custom to spend mornings in my office. I then visited or planned administrative details in the afternoon, and used evenings for meetings or other visitation. There weren't any hard and fast rules for this, but developing this kind of *routine* helped me to work adequately and make necessary adjustments when I had to.

Typically, I started each morning with 45 to 60 minutes of devotions while still at home (I still follow this routine). I read Scripture and other devotional literature for my own growth as a Christian, which often leads to valuable preaching ideas. However, my intent is not to spend this time looking for preaching material—it's a quiet Bible, devotional, and prayer time—a time for me to meet with my Lord.

My typical day got me to the office by 8:00 or 8:30 every morning. In my daily routine, I found out that a *schedule-orientation* (planning *specific* times each day for various tasks, appointments, or meetings) didn't work well for sermon preparation. That is, I couldn't schedule specific times for reading, writing, exegeting, or contemplating for the sermon, because I couldn't easily control appointments or interruptions. So I started using a *task-oriented* approach, where there were specific duties I wanted to accomplish each day. If one of these tasks was interrupted, or I didn't get to it when I planned to, I was able to do it at another time during the day. I simply wrote a *"to do" list* each morning, noting the things I wanted to get done, but without assigning specific times to complete them. (I also found that it was easy to intersperse specific appointments or meetings into this kind of routine.) Generally I would work at the most important jobs first, and scratch them off my list when I completed them.

These principles, then, in these four "spheres" of life management, have been extremely useful for me in accomplishing an effective preaching ministry. But, again, *you* should establish your own schedule and routines for ministry rather than try to follow my pattern. The important thing is that you start a schedule that *works for you.* The word *disciple,* after all, implies *discipline,* and, most of the time, we cannot get much proactive ministry done without these routines of life.

CHAPTER 24
After Words for Afterwards

APPROPRIATE ENDINGS

Perhaps you've heard of the woman who was leaving worship one Sunday morning. She greeted the pastor and said: "I liked your sermon so much! It was like water to a person who is drowning!"

The next week, she tried to improve on that: "I liked your sermon so much! Whenever you preach, your sermon is always so much better than your next one!"

Well, whether she intended it or not, she mixed up her images. In actuality, transformational preaching suggests that your sermon be like water to a *parched wanderer* in the desert. And each sermon should be better than the *previous* one. When all is said and done, preaching that has no "punch" is preaching that will hardly ever be transformational. You won't always preach like that, but you always have the opportunity to improve. Jesus points us forward, not back (Luke 9:62).

So let's think about that day when you finally get it right, when you're comfortable with your preaching style. It's Sunday afternoon. You've worked hard all week, and put together a great sermon. You stepped into the pulpit and the ensuing transaction fully engaged your people, who were moved to respond. Now the preaching event is over.

After the words of the sermon have been uttered, after the transaction of preaching has brought your listeners to confront and respond to biblical truth, you still aren't finished with this sermon. There are four additional components of the preaching ministry that are important "after words" for afterwards. We'll look at them now: 1.) the natural depression that follows good preaching; 2.) storing your sermons in a retrievable way; 3.) what to do if you get a chance to re-preach a particular sermon, and 4.) how you spend a lifetime changing and growing as an artist.

Let's start, then, on these "after-preaching" issues.

I. DEPRESSION

When Jonah visited Nineveh, he was a very effective preacher. The whole city repented. But Jonah wasn't happy. He knew from the very beginning that God would save those terrible sinners, and he was boiling about it! In Jonah 4:2-3, he had a chat with God,

> *"I knew that You are a gracious and compassionate God, slow to anger and abounding in love, a God Who relents from sending calamity. Now, O Lord, take away my life, for it is better for me to die than to live."*

Jonah went out of the city and built a little booth and watched the city, probably to see if God would destroy it after his little temper tantrum. He stewed in his own depression and wallowed in self-pity.

Jonah was an unhappy preacher! He didn't want to preach when he was commanded to do it, and after he preached, he didn't like the response of the people. He wanted them to *reject* his message so God would wipe them out. He was depressed.

When you preach as exhaustively as Jonah did, you, too, will probably experience this kind of *depression.* Expect it, because it's part of the preaching experience.

Archibald Hart (1995) tells us that adrenaline is an important chemical in the makeup of our bodies. Whenever a person faces an anxious time or threatening situation, adrenaline immediately starts pumping through the body, creating a natural "fight or flight" response. The usual physical pattern is "alarm, activation, and recovery." That is, God created your body in such a way that after you expend yourself in a fearful or passionate experience (such as preaching), your adrenalin courses through your body in its *alarm* mode and gets you ready to do battle *(activation).* But when it's all over, your body needs time to settle back to a "normal level" of existence (the *recovery* period).

It is this recovery stage that is important to keep in mind when we are done preaching. Recovery is natural, and it happens through physical depression. It is the way that our body responds and recuperates.

Unfortunately, many of us interpret the *physical* reaction as an *emotional* one. Often after preaching, my first thought is, "How stupid! I can't believe I forgot that part!" or "I wonder why nobody responded today?" or "So-and-so didn't say anything this morning—I must not have preached as well as I thought." Almost every time I am finished preaching, I feel as if I haven't done my best.

Hart's discussion is helpful, because I learned that that's the *depression* talking. Now that I *expect* this kind of reaction, I let it sweep over me for the hour or two that it takes my body to get back to normal. I heard Hart speak once. He said that, after a long weekend of speaking engagements, he tries to return to the airport two or three hours early. He slumps in the corner and lets the depression take over. By the time the flight is ready to leave, his body is back to normal and he arrives home in good mental shape.

If you have done your best and preached your heart out, it's a legitimate adrenalin experience, and you should expect a time of depression. This does *not* mean that you failed in your preaching responsibility. It only means that your body was so "alive" during the event that it experienced an adrenalin rush, and now it is getting back to normal.

So don't "second guess" yourself. Remind yourself that you had been commissioned by the Holy Spirit to preach this sermon. If you were exhilarated during and immediately after the preaching event, if you felt during the experience that you were "connecting," then let the doubts engulf you on Sunday afternoon. (If you don't feel the depression, chances are that you didn't adequately engage your preaching.) Don't deny this natural "recovery" period that God provides through the aftermath of the adrenalin rush. You did your Spirit-directed best, given the time and energy and resources you had available. Now it's time to move on.

II. FILING

It is now Monday morning. While the sermon is still fresh in your mind, you should find a way to store it. Why? There are three good reasons.

First, it's helpful to have a final manuscript of this sermon in case you want to preach it again.

Second, it helps you keep a catalogue of the stories you've used in this sermon. If, in a few years, you're preaching on the same theme and need an appropriate story, you might be able to find it in an old sermon (even when you don't preach from the same text or preach the same sermon).

And third, you have spent some time exegeting the text. In case you want to preach from this text again, you'll have your notes available to see your prior insights into the text.

So if you decide to file your sermons for any or all of these reasons, there are two issues to consider: 1. final adjustments to your manuscript, and 2. developing a filing system for retrieval purposes.

Final adjustments

Before you tuck your sermon away, you ought to consider making "late adjustments" to it. That is, during the last minute preparation for the sermon, or during the preaching experience itself, you probably made changes to the sermon: the stories you used, the structure, the order, or, even, exegetical points you made. Or, between Sunday and Monday, after you've had a day to think about it, you might find that you *should have changed* something to make your preaching more effective. So, while you are filing the sermon away, you have one last opportunity to think it through and reflect on how it was received by your listeners. Sometimes you might jot a note on the manuscript that will help you restructure the sermon the next time, or you will be reminded of a different story that would have been useful.

So on Monday morning, during the ten minutes it takes to file away the old sermon, take one last opportunity to strengthen your future preaching ministry. Make this "used" sermon better, just in case you pull it out again for re-use.

Filing system

It is also important to develop a filing system for your sermons so you can easily retrieve them. Because I started preaching before computers were readily available, I file away my *hard* copies. I've now got two file drawers filled with my sermons, numbered chronologically. It's an awkward system, but it has been useful for me. You might consider keeping your sermon manuscripts on computer disks after you have preached them. However you do it, it's important that you do.

For retrieval purposes, I developed three lists by which I keep track of my sermons. Again, these are hard copies, but you might be able to develop a similar kind of computer system that will work well.

1. Title index. First, I number my sermons consecutively, and the first index is for sermon *Titles*. On these sheets, I keep the number of the sermon (in chronological order), its title, text, the date on which I preached it, and a grade for it. (The grade helps me quickly pick a "good" sermon if I'm looking for one later.) Figure 24.1 on the next page provides a sample "Title" sheet.

2. Topical index. Second, I have a *thematic* list for my sermons. I include almost 200 different categories in this file, and use a half sheet for each. (I've listed the topics in Figure 24.2 on pages 348-349 to serve as a beginning point for your own list.) I find that I don't use many of these topics, and from time to time I add a new one. But at least they give me some options.

After each sermon, I take time to categorize it, usually in at least three different ways under three different topics. For instance, the John 17 sermon we worked through in Chapter 21 could be topically identified by "unity," "church," or "ecumenism." Any one of those topics would help me find it later. This topical index also helps me find already-preached sermons when I want to preach on that same topic later. It also helps me find texts and stories I have already used. In this file, I list the sermon number, title, and the date I preached it.

3. Textual index. The third index is used to keep track of the biblical texts I have used. If I have a choice of texts for a particular sermon, I can use one from which I haven't yet preached. I keep this information in two ways. First, I keep a list with every book of the Bible and every chapter on it, and I put a check mark against the chapter. This list gives me a quick overview of which books or chapters of the Bible I have been overusing or avoiding.

But I also keep a "text box," in which I place business-card sized records. On each one, I identify the biblical text in the upper left corner, the sermon number in the upper right corner, its title in the center, and, below that, the date(s) on which I preached this sermon. This card helps me more easily find the sermons I have preached on a particular text. This is especially helpful if I am doing a biblical series. A sample card is in Figure 24.3 on page 350.

Figure 24.1

Sermon Title Index

Sermon #	Title	Text	Date	Grade
600	Book People	2 Chron. 34:29-33	22 Feb 87	B
601	The Salvation Process	Phil. 2:12b-13	01 Mar 87	A-
602	Where Were You?	Mark 14:27-31	08 Mar 87	A-
603	God and the Soap Business	Malachi 3:10	15 Mar 87	A
604	The Great Giveaway!	2 Kings 7:3-11	22 Mar 87	B
605	The Satanic Objection	Ephesians 6:10-18	29 Mar 87	A

Figure 24.2

Topical Index

ACCEPTANCE	DEVOTIONAL LIFE	INTEGRITY	RESPONSIBILITY
ACCIDENTS	DISCIPLINE	INVOLVEMENT	RESURRECTION
ADVERSITY	DISCIPLESHIP	JESUS	RIGHTEOUSNESS
ADVENT	DISCOURAGEMENT	JOY	SABBATH
AGE	DOUBT	JUSTICE	SACRIFICE
ALIENATION	EASTER	JUDGMENT	SALVATION
ANGELS	ENCOURAGEMENT	KINDNESS	SATAN
ANGER	ESCAPE	KINGDOM OF GOD	SCIENCE
ANXIETY	EVANGELISM	LABOR	SECOND COMING
APATHY	EVIL	LAW	SECURITY
BAPTISM	FAILURE	LEADERSHIP	SELF-EXAMINATION
BAPTISTS	FAITH	LEISURE	SELFISHNESS
BEATITUDES	FAMILY	LIFE	SERVICE
BELIEF	FATHERS	LONELINESS	SEX
BIBLE	FEAR	LORDSHIP	SIN
BROTHERHOOD	FELLOWSHIP	LOVE	SINGLES
BUILDING	FORGIVENESS	MAN, MEN	SOCIAL PROBLEMS
CHANGE	FREEDOM	MARRIAGE	SPIRITUALITY
CHARACTER	FRIENDSHIP	MENTAL HEALTH	STEWARDSHIP
CHARACTERS, BIBLE	FRUSTRATION	MINISTRY	SUFFERING
CHILDREN	FUTURE	MIRACLES	SUICIDE
CHRISTIANITY	GIFTS	MISSIONS	SURRENDER
CHRISTMAS	GIVING	MORALITY	TEMPTATION

CHURCH
CHURCH AND STATE
CHURCH GROWTH
CHURCH UNITY
CITY
COMFORT
COMMITMENT
COMMUNION
COMMUNICATION
COMPASSION
CONCERN
CONFORMITY
CONSCIENCE
CONSECRATION
CONVERSION
CONVICTION
COURAGE
CREATION
CREATIVITY
CREED
CRIME
CRISIS
CROSS
CULTS
DEATH
DECISIONS
DEDICATION
DESPAIR

GOD
GOOD FRIDAY
GOSPEL
GOSSIP
GRACE
GRIEF
GROWTH
GUIDANCE
GUILT
HAPPINESS
HATE
HEALING
HEALTH
HEAVEN
HELL
HISTORY
HOLINESS
HOLY SPIRIT
HOME
HOPE
HUMAN NATURE
HUMILITY
HUNGER
IMMORTALITY
INCARNATION
INFLUENCE
INSIGHT
INSPIRATION

MOTHERS
NATION
NEW BIRTH
NEW YEAR
OBEDIENCE
OPPORTUNITY
PALM SUNDAY
PASTOR
PATIENCE
PEACE
PENTECOST
PERSEVERANCE
PILGRIMAGE
POVERTY
POWER
PRAYER
PREJUDICE
PRIDE
PROTESTANTISM
PROVIDENCE
PURPOSE
QUESTIONS
RACE
REDEDICATION
REDEMPTION
REFORMATION
RENEWAL
REPENTANCE

TEN COMMANDMENTS
THANKSGIVING
TIME
TITHING
TRINITY
TRUST
VICTORY
VALUES
VIOLENCE
VOCATION
WAR
WILL OF GOD
WISDOM
WITNESSING
WOMEN
WORK
WORRY
WORSHIP
YOUTH

Figure 24.3

Text card

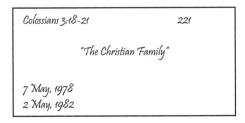

Colossians 3:18-21   221

"The Christian Family"

7 May, 1978
2 May, 1982

III. RE-PREACHING

You will notice in Figure 24.3 that I preached this sermon on two occasions (once in each of my pastorates). From time to time, you will have the opportunity to preach a sermon a second or third time. Don't be concerned about this—Ellen makes a wonderful potato soup that is better on the second and third day than when she first serves it. Sometimes you will have the opportunity to take a sermon "on the road" (as when I preach the same "mission sermon" in several churches), or when you are invited to fill a friend's pulpit as a guest preacher, or when you have the privilege of preaching at an ordination service or ecumenical worship experience or other special local church occasion (such as an anniversary or homecoming Sunday). In fact, when you preach an old sermon again, chances are that you will choose one that seemed particularly good in its first incarnation. (This is why I "grade" my sermons in the *Title* index.) If you made "after notes" on the manuscript, you already have thought about a new focus for it, so it should be an even more powerful sermon that it was the first time through. With a new *need* for this sermon, or a new thesis statement, the sermon will easily be "reborn."

However, I have never preached the same sermon to the same congregation. I only re-use a sermon when I will be in a different preaching environment. The greatest problem with re-preached sermons is the strong temptation to use the old sermon "as is." You might think it is just as suitable to the new preaching opportunity as it was when you first preached it, but spend some time reworking it for the particular situation in which you are now going to preach it. You might want to juggle around some of its stories to better fit the current context, need, or your own frame of mind. Or you might want to develop a slightly different thesis.

Keep in mind, though, that whenever you preach an old sermon, you preach it in a different context. Every preaching situation is different because the *congregation* is different—even if most of the people are the same. Because every listening audience has different needs and a different personality, a transactional preaching experience is always different—even when the *content* is essentially the same.

So if you preach a sermon again, think about all the steps involved in constructing a sermon, and remember the important role that congregational *need* played in its development and final design. The arrow was aimed somewhere specific. To take an old sermon that was suited for a very different context and congregation and try to hit a different target with it means your arrow will probably miss the new target altogether. So be sure to refashion an old sermon to fit its new environment.

And don't forget that every preaching situation is different because *you* as the preacher are different, too. Because of this, you never really re-preach the same sermon anyway. You bring with you a very different perspective on the text, and you might come with fresh actualizing materials. Just be ready and willing to make those changes when you prepare.

If you can keep in mind that *each* preaching experience is unique and different, your use of a former sermon can be just as fresh as it was when you preached it the first time.

IV. LIFETIME CHANGE

One of the real joys I discovered during my days in seminary was that I always had boxfuls of exciting sermon ideas from my biblical studies courses, other classes, and hallway discussions. This doesn't mean that I preached everything I heard, because not everything was adaptable to a sermon. But I loved to engage the new and exciting insights I was learning—my early sermons seemed to be filled with original thoughts and were always stimulating. I found, in the academic environment, that there was always a new idea or conversation that would inspire a creative idea for my preaching.

But once I left seminary, I didn't have that same stimulation. So I had to learn some other ways to be challenged for good preaching ideas. What did I learn about how to keep those ideas coming? Here are some final "after words" for the time when you leave formal theological education. I pray that these recommendations will help keep your preaching fresh and exciting.

1. An art form

First, remember that, as a preacher, you are an artist. As such, you are only allowed to *practice* your art. You never perfect it. So keep at it. Take risks in your preaching. Be encouraged by the things you got right in last week's sermon, and work hard to change the things that didn't work. There's always *another* opportunity to practice (and hone) your preaching.

That means you have to "learn as you go." Keep *developing* your skill. Keep *working* at it. Your relationship with Jesus Christ will grow, mature, and develop just as any relationship does. And you'll find that your preaching will reflect that growing relationship and understanding of your own theology. Let your preaching reflect your own "growing edge." That will keep it alive and fresh and interesting for your people.

And be yourself! Reread Chapter 8 from time to time. Remember that if God wanted *somebody else* to be in your place, to preach *this* particular message, He wouldn't have put *you* here! God wants you as you are, and He will use the gifts and inspiration and skills you have. As a result, the sermon you are preaching is the one that God intends to be preached, because He wants it to be incarnated *through you!*

2. Go to it!

This book is designed to *prepare* the way for you to preach. Hopefully, this introduction has provided enough tools to use when you preach regularly. But you'll only learn how to preach, how it all goes together, when you start preaching consistently. Learning happens through disciplined practice, week after week, month after month, year after year. Even then, it should take a long time to feel comfortable with your own style. So I encourage you to keep *growing* in its practice every time you step into your pulpit. The only real way to tell if your education was any good is to see how you're doing ten or twenty years later. Use this book as a resource and refer to it from time to time.

But you'll want to develop your own plans and procedures for preaching. The suggestions I've made in this book give you some ideas of what worked for me, but you will have to arrive at your own style and theory for your own ministry. Of course, what works best for *you* might not work for anybody else. So adapt and apply everything in this book (and anything else you read), because your unique preaching environment has a culture of its own.

3. Find a routine

As I have said here, experiment so you can find your own best schedule, organization, and style of presentation. What suits *you* best? I encourage you to settle in to a *routine* during your first year or two. Ultimately, *you* have to wrestle with texts, needs, and ideas that will be relevant to your local situation.

4. Daily devotions

Keep your own faith alive with Bible study and prayer. Don't let sermon or Bible study preparation take the place of your own growing relationship with Jesus Christ. Spend time *contemplating. Study* the Scripture in all its contextual beauty, and let its personal power for your life overwhelm you from time to time. Think through and reorient your own theology. And keep giving the Holy Spirit more control over your mind, heart, personality, and preaching.

5. Continuing education

When asked why people stop turning to pastors when they face deep questions of life, Bishop M. Simpson is quoted as saying:

> One reason is, I believe, the neglect of study on the part of many aged ministers. They lose that stimulus which belongs to other professions . . . To the physician every case is a new study. New remedies are discovered and recommended. He must keep abreast of the times, or some intruder will take away his practice. The attorney finds some new element in almost every case. New decisions are given by the Supreme Court, and he must study them. In statesmanship new complications are constantly arising. The

connections of nations are so numerous, the questions involved are so various and something so vast as to require the utmost comprehension to grasp them and the constant attention to the least minutiae and detail. The statesman has no old sermon that he can pick up and apply. He must think and study and write, and thus keep his mind ever active and fresh. There is no time for him to nod or sleep. But the old minister sits down under his vine or fig-tree, and there is no one to molest him or to make him afraid . . . He is pressed for time, and brings before his congregation of today a discourse which he had made twenty years ago, on an issue then living, but now almost forgotten. His thoughts are of the past; his sermons are of the past; and the generation of today feels that he is scarcely one of them."

The challenge is that you keep growing in your faith and your ability to preach, especially after your formal theological education is completed. Keep learning and growing after seminary. There are two kinds of continuing education you should be looking for.

Formal. *Formal* continuing education opportunities include both degree and non-degree study opportunities, such as seminars, evening or Saturday courses offered at a nearby seminary or your denominational office, or small voluntary study groups with neighboring pastors. It includes continuing your education through advanced degree programs. It involves learning new information from those who are called to teach. It happens in every area of life and ministry, but especially in preaching. Any opportunity to study the discipline of preaching from others, even poorly designed or taught courses or seminars, will be to your benefit (sometimes you learn how *not* to preach from these experiences)! And if you have the opportunity to take a short study leave or a sabbatical, find a program where your preaching can be challenged and encouraged and strengthened.

Further, attend seminars or evening courses at your community's high school adult evening program or local library (if they are offered). You don't have to restrict yourself to courses that challenge your growth as a *Christian* or *preacher. Any* subject matter can be useful for your own personal development, and can have an impact on your preaching ministry. (I once took an evening course in oil painting, and once I joined a short-term literature discussion group at the local library. I have no idea how these courses influenced my preaching ministry, but they were wonderful self-growing experiences for *me* as a preacher.)

Informal. The second kind of continuing education is *informal.* By informal, I mean that the study is not guided by someone outside yourself, as in a formal program. It may involve reading books, periodicals, or newspapers of any kind—actually just about *anything* you can get your hands on. Almost every month, new preaching books are on the market, and you should read them with consistency. Apply and/or process what you read (and hear) about preaching. If you find it useful, learn from it; if not, reflect on it and reject it. Listen to tapes of other preachers (always with pencil handy!), and if you have the chance from time to time, visit other worship services where you can hear other men and women preach.

Remember that preaching is a growing discipline that takes a lifetime of study. Keep at it, and be encouraged!

Finally, and ultimately, may the words of the Apostle Paul to his young friend, the preacher, be your watchwords as you continue to practice, for the rest of your life, the art of *transformational preaching!:*

> ***"Do your best to present yourself to God as one approved, a workman who does not have to be ashamed and who correctly handles the word of truth."*** (2 Timothy 2:15)

Appendix
Five Sermons

This Appendix includes five sermons that I've preached. All serve as examples of what I've been talking about in this book. They are certainly not perfect, nor will they necessarily be suitable for your own preaching. But I've included them so you could see the kind of sermons I'm talking about in this book.

These sermons are in "final manuscript" form, which means that many adjustments were made *after I wrote them* but before I preached them. That is, as I prepared each of these messages with a particular congregation in mind, as I worked through my outlines, and as I rehearsed the manuscript using *oral* language, these messages would have undergone slight changes, in both language and organization, and the final "product" (in the transaction of preaching) would have been different than any prior "rehearsals" I'd done. Thus, these five examples are *sermons,* not *preaching.* They provided *content* for the actual preaching event, which took place in a particular environment with a particular congregation and its needs, and my own final assessment of how these messages "sounded" with the flow of oral language. I do not have those adjusted "transacted" sermons on hand (nor their recordings), but these examples, at least, will give you an idea of what transformational sermons might look like in their final written draft. I trust that they will be helpful to that end.

The sermons are *"What's Your Name," "When Grace Happens," "The Pain of Jesus," "The Spoken Word,"* and *"Backward Communion."*

WHAT'S YOUR NAME?
Judges 6:11-16

Somewhere back in the 1740s, a group of Methodists gathered for their weekly worship in a barn. A troublemaker wanted to disrupt the meeting, but knew that the doors would be locked once the meting started, so he climbed into a hidden burlap sack and waited until the meeting would start before he started his hooliganism. As soon as the worshipers gathered, they began to sing one of Wesley's great hymns. In those days, the hymns spoke powerfully of biblical images and salvation, and the congregation sang so lustily that the troublemaker stayed quiet until the singing would be finished. But as he lay there in the darkness of his burlap sack, the words of the hymn spoke powerfully to him, and the Holy Spirit began to speak to him. It was almost as if he heard the Lord calling him by a new name, and when the singing was done, he emerged from the sack, repented of his sins, and became a follower of Jesus.

A call to follow Jesus is a powerful thing. He speaks into the restlessness of our lives, into the broken places, into the vacuum, into the fears and sins that we harbor internally, and he touches us with grace and calls us by a new name, a name that we "own" for the rest of our lives in this world. Having a new name means that Jesus needs you for a special purpose, perhaps in church leadership, to speak a kind word to a neighbor, or to introduce someone to Jesus. He gives you a new name.

They'd gone up there on a retreat, Jesus and his 12. They were far away from their usual territory of ministry, down in Galilee, now up in the hills of Mount Hermon, up toward where Caesarea Philippi was—almost 30 miles from the coastline of the Sea of Galilee. It would have taken them a couple of days to get up there, time for them to get away from the pressures of ministry.

Jesus went to spend time with his disciples. They'd been sent out to the villages all throughout the region of Galilee, preaching and teaching and healing and casting out demons. Now they are heading off to a debriefing session. They've been engaged in ministry already, but now Jesus wants to help them understand a bit more clearly what it means to follow him.

When they arrive, he asks them, "As you've been going about, who did people think I am?" One disciple responded, "Someone said you are John the Baptist come back to life." Another said, "I heard somebody say you were Elijah."

And then Jesus looked intently at these 12 who knew him the best and asked, "But who do YOU say I am?"

At that point, Simon, one of the faithful fishermen of the group, one of the first called, impulsively blurted out: "You are the Messiah, Son of the living God!"

And Jesus says, "Blessed are you, Simon. This did not come to you by flesh and blood. And because of this revelation, your name is now going to be

Peter, the Rock, and on this Rock I will build my Church, and not even the Gates of Hades will prevail against it."

It was here, in this setting and on this revelatory occasion, that Simon received a new name. He still fumbled along, still made errors in judgment, would even deny knowing Jesus. But he began living by a new name. And later, when he wrote his first letter to the church, he talked about an inheritance that we receive when we receive a new name, even though we pass through difficulties in appropriating it (1 Peter 1:3-9).

By what name is Jesus calling you? More specifically, is it a name you haven't yet envisioned for yourself? It is a call to fulfillment, purpose, and completion.

Times were extraordinarily difficult for the Jewish nation, as we discover in our story from Judges 6. They had settled in the Promised Land, but they were in trouble. On every hand, the Midianites were oppressing them. They lived in fear. They lived in shelters in the clefts of the mountains, and in fortresses, and in caves—any place they could find where they could hide from the enemy. From time to time, they would sneak out and plant crops— they had to eat! And they would watch the crops grow, and just then, the Midianites and Amalekites invaded the land, brought their camping gear, and ravaged the crops, until nothing was left. The land was destitute and without any growing thing. They did the same with livestock—they swept away or slaughtered the cattle, sheep, and donkeys. Nothing was left alive. The nation was in peril, and impoverished.

So how did God respond? Our text opens in the midst of all the trouble, where we find Gideon hiding in a winepress, threshing wheat. One does not thresh wheat in a winepress! He's hiding. He's a coward. He doesn't want to be discovered by the Midianites, or, perhaps, the Lord.

But an angel comes to him and says, "The Lord is with you, Mighty Warrior!" Did you hear that? The Lord does not accept Gideon's fear. It's as if He doesn't know that Gideon is a coward. Gideon perceives that he is not ready to work for the Lord, but the Lord calls him by a new name, "Mighty Warrior!" It's a call and a charge.

It doesn't matter how young or old you might be. The Lord calls those who are ready. Maybe the Lord is calling you to fill a tremendous need in church leadership, calling you who are still early in your education in school. Maybe you are wandering around, threshing wheat, trying to find your way in life, fighting fires. But the Lord is stirring something new inside you, giving you a new name, a new future, a new identity, a new call.

If you sense the Lord calling you, giving you a new name, maybe you've got your objections. Gideon did. Look at his response to his new name.

First, he says, "Pardon me, Lord, but if You are really in charge, why all this trouble? Where are all the miracles? You've abandoned us and given us into the hands of the Midianites!" And the Lord says, "Go in the strength you have and save Israel from the Midianites! I'm sending you!"

Then Gideon says, "That's great, Lord, but if you'll excuse me, you've got the wrong guy. I come from the weakest clan of Israel, and I'm the very weakest of all of them!" And the Lord says, "But I will be with you!"

When the Lord calls, we might have the same kind of objections: "I'm not the right person. I'm not good enough to be a pastor (or a missionary)." Or, "I'm just a woman and there's no place for me in leadership." Or, "I don't have the right gifts to do what you're asking." Or, "Our church is too small to make much of a difference in our community."

I was counseling at one of our Senior High camps in Southern California back in the 80s. The counseling staff arrived at camp the day before camp was to start, so we could get organized. After we got there, the camp director came into the room where we had gathered for a prayer meeting and said, "I just got a phone call from our speaker for the week. As you know, he's a pastor in Houston, Texas, and a hurricane just ripped through the city. Many of the homes of his members were destroyed and he cannot leave them." We then talked about what we were going to do for the morning chapel services, and then we went to prayer.

From the moment the prayer time started, the Holy Spirit grabbed hold of my heart and was shaking it. I knew that he wanted me to volunteer to preach, but I resisted. I said, "But Lord, I didn't come prepared for that." My heart just kept shaking. I said, "Lord, I don't have any resources to put a sermon together, not even my jokebook" (high school kids need jokes). My heart just kept shaking. Only when I said, "O.k., I'll do whatever you want. I'm ready!" Then my heart stopped shaking. After the prayer time, I said to the camp director, "I'm willing to speak on any one morning or all week long, whatever you need." The Lord had been speaking to others during that prayer time, too, so I only did one session. Altogether, that week of camp was the most dynamic and meaningful week for our campers.

So what is the Lord saying to you? "I am with you. I will prepare you. You don't have to worry about anything if you are obedient to my call." That is, the Lord calls *ordinary people* to give themselves to Him, and He'll take it from there. He only needs those who are willing, willing to respond to His call, willing to say "I'll do what you want, even though I don't think you've got the right person."

Finally, after arguing with the Lord, Gideon relents, and we see his obedience as one of the strongest of the judges of Israel. You can read about his exploits in the next two chapters, up until the end of Chapter 8. You, too, when you are obedient, may discover the wonders of the call of God.

It was 1996, and a Hungarian Baptist by the name of Šandor Szenczy was watching a report on television about children in North Korea who were suffering due to extreme poverty. Šandor's story goes something like this. While he was watching that television program, he sensed the Lord calling him to do something about it, as if he was being given a new name. But he wasn't sure what he could do. He had lots of excuses: he was only one man, he was in a little Baptist church in a little Baptist Union tucked away in Europe. But the Lord kept calling him by a new name: "Do something about it!"

So Šandor determined to do something. But what? He remembered Peter getting a new name and later on stepping out of the boat to walk on the water, with his eyes fixed on Jesus. Šandor felt that he should act with that same kind of faith.

He decided that maybe the best place to start would be to head to the North Korean embassy, so he went down to Budapest and knocked on the thick wooden door. It was opened a crack for him; behind it was a guard who asked him what he wanted. He said he wanted to speak with the ambassador. The door remained open only a crack. So he told the man his name. The door remained open only a crack. For the next few minutes Šandor stumbled through an explanation of who he was and that he wanted to help the children in North Korea. The door didn't open any further. Finally, after 15 minutes of talking, in desperation, he said, "I have a million dollars that I want to take to North Korea to help the starving children!" He doesn't know why he said that, but suddenly the door flew open. He was ushered into the private quarters of the ambassador. Pretty soon, the ambassador himself entered, along with his wife, two children, the ambassador's secretary, the doorman, the driver, the cleaner, the cook, the dog, the cat, and (as Šandor says) three blind mice. They looked at Šandor. Šandor looked back. There was an embarrassed silence. Then the ambassador spoke, "I understand you have a million dollars you wish to give to North Korea?" "Er, no." said Šandor. The Ambassador flushed, embarrassed, and said, "Ah, I misunderstood. You have brought a million dollars' worth of supplies, food, and clothing for our children?" "Er, no." Suddenly the ambassador grew impatient. "Then what do you have?" he shouted. "Er, I have faith," said Šandor, "and I would like to pray for you." So he raised his hands and prayed for fifteen minutes. When he opened his eyes, only the driver was still standing there. The man grabbed Šandor by the arm and threw him out of the building. Outside, he picked himself up off the street, danced around in a circle, and sang and shouted praise to God. For the first time in his life, he acted on faith in the living God. He had been given a new name, and he trusted that God would honor this small step of faith for His glory.

Well, Šandor went home and said to his wife, "Honey, I'm going to take one million dollars to North Korea!" "Fantastic," she said, "Praise the Lord! But where are you going to get the money?" Šandor said, "I guess the Lord will provide it." He then announced his mission to his church. They said, "That's wonderful! Praise the Lord!" But they said, "Where's the money?" They prayed about it. Šandor took to heart his new name and went to work. He knocked on office doors and contacted businesses and hospitals and spoke to individuals, and one month later, he was able to deliver one million dollars' worth of aid to North Korea!

Soon afterward, Šandor established Hungarian Baptist Aid, which, at the time, was the only humanitarian aid organization that has access to North Korea. They were the only agency that had access to the Chechnyan Muslims who had settled in the Pankizi Gorge in Georgia. They work in many countries around the world, sharing the love of Jesus through humanitarian acts. Often they are the first to send rescue teams into areas suffering from natural disasters. Their budget is runs into many millions of dollars every year. They employ 20 full time staff. They are working against child trafficking and have organized world conferences on this and many other issues.

Šandor heard God calling him by a new name, took a leap of faith, and started working on the new direction that God chose for him. Yes, he had questions and concerns. Yes, he had good excuses. But when it came right down to it, he acted obediently and has been used of God in tremendous ways.

What of you? Is God calling you by a new name? What is it? Where is He leading you? Will it perhaps be to professional Christian service, as a pastor or missionary or Christian counselor? Or is He calling you to be the very best witness you can be where you teach school or in the office building in which you work? You have a new name. Now it's time to take it seriously.

Hey, what's *your* name?

WHEN GRACE HAPPENS
Ephesians 2:8-10

Genevieve Topping was an American Baptist missionary to Japan in the 1930s. One year when she and her husband were home on furlough, a wealthy family invited them to stay at their house in southern California while they were out of town.

Genevieve and her husband had just moved into the house when, one afternoon, two masked men forced open the front door, and, at gunpoint, demanded all their money. Genevieve said, "We are American Baptist missionaries and don't have much money. But we've just been paid, and you are welcome to it, if you'll allow me to get it from the bedroom." The gunmen agreed and allowed her to leave the room. There she collected their salary packet from the top of the dresser and some extra cash that was in there, and brought it out to where the men were still pointing their guns at her husband. Graciously, she gave it to them, and then said, "There. You have all our money. Now let's sit down and talk!"

The men were dumbfounded, but did as she asked. She said, "You are welcomed to take our money, and I want you to know that we harbor no resentment. We forgive you, because we serve a God Who knows who you are and He loves you." They talked together that afternoon, and at last those two gunmen said, "We want to know your God, too." They became followers of Jesus that day and later both became pastors. Genevieve understood what *grace* is all about, and that grace can really make a difference in our world.

That's what can happen when *grace* happens. It is here, in grace, that the Christian understanding of the nature of God lies. Grace is God's unmerited, undeserved love for us. He knows us inside and out, better than we know ourselves. In spite of our sin and inclination not to do what He wants, to make our own lives as best we can, in our imperfection, God still loves us. In spite of willful and deliberate turning our backs on God, still God loves us. We know that love in Jesus Christ who died for us while we were yet sinners, and that there is nothing we can do to earn the love of God.

That's what this text in Ephesians 2 is all about. It is the heart of the gospel of Jesus Christ. It is a message that needs to be communicated to the world and put into practice. Our salvation comes not because we are good people, not because we've established a good reputation, not because we belong to a church, but only because God has first loved us, in our sin. Jesus came to die for my sin and your sin so we never have to die a spiritual death, so that we can be new people here and now who are able to extend the grace of God to others. That's what salvation means. It is an uncanny, counter-intuitive understanding of God, but it's what the Bible teaches us about God.

I have found that this is the single most difficult Christian concept to understand. This foundational piece of the gospel is more misunderstood than anything else. We think that we're going to heaven because we're good people. Nonsense! We might be better than those who live around us. We might be better than just about everybody else who ever lived. But if we think we have no sin, we are badly mistaken. The Christian Gospel says that only in Jesus can we know salvation—only through his cross—only because salvation is a free and undeserved gift. There's nothing we can do to earn it.

Pastor Marjorie Kitchell tells about her attempt to illustrate the grace of God one Christmas in worship, so she announced, "Whoever wants this beautiful Christmas poinsettia may have it. All you have to do is come up here and take it." Everybody stared at her. She waited. And waited. Finally a mother timidly raised her hand and said, "I'll take it."

"Great!" said Marjorie, "It's all yours." That's what she wanted—a quick and easy acceptance so she could get on with the application in her sermon. But the mother said to her son, "Go get it for me."

Marjorie said, "No! If you want this gift, you must come and get it personally. You can't send a substitute."

The mother shook her head. So Marjorie waited again. It was a gorgeous flower, unusually large, wrapped in red cellophane with a gold satin ribbon. It was set in front of the pulpit to brighten their small sanctuary during the holiday season. Several people had commented on how beautiful the plant was. Now it was free for the taking.

Someone snickered, "What's the catch?"

"No catch," she replied. "It's free!" But no one moved.

A college student asked, "Is it glued to the altar?" Everyone laughed.

"It is not glued to the altar. Nor are there any strings attached. It's yours for the taking."

"Well," asked a pretty teenager, "can I take it after the service?"

Marjorie shook her head, though she was tempted to give in. "You must come and get it now."

She was now wishing she'd never started the whole thing, when a woman she had never seen before stood up in the back. Quickly, as if she were afraid she'd change her mind, she strode to the altar and picked up the plant. "I'll take it," she said.

As she returned to her seat carrying the free gift, Marjorie launched with enthusiasm into her text on Romans 6:23: "The gift of God is eternal life. Believe it. Receive it. It's free!"

When the service had ended and most of the people had gone home, the woman who claimed the poinsettia came to the platform, where Marjorie was picking up her Bible.

"Here!" she said, holding out her hand. "This flower is too pretty to just take home for free. I couldn't do that with a clear conscience." Marjorie looked down at the crumpled paper she stuffed into her hand. It was a ten dollar bill.

Grace is incomprehensible for us, too. We just don't get it. We think we have to do something to earn God's love. But Jesus died for us. Salvation is a free gift, and there's nothing we can do to earn it. That's the good news.

One afternoon at my first pastorate, I was sitting at my desk and got a call from an elderly woman who said she lived just down the street from the church. She asked me to come and talk with her husband who was dying of cancer. I hung up and walked the three blocks down to her house.

When I rang the doorbell, the door opened, and there she stood with a cigarette hanging out of the corner of her mouth, in a housecoat, her hair disheveled. She led me through a cluttered living room into a side room where her husband was lying on a daybed. She said, "Walter, this is Pastor Brown from the church up the street," and then she went and got a kitchen chair for me to sit on. She closed the door behind her.

Walter Denman thanked me for coming. His face was pale and drawn and his teeth didn't fit very well. There was the smell of death in the room. He told me that he'd had a dream the night before. His best friend had died six months ago, he said, and in this dream, his friend was standing on a sunny, country lane waving to him, beckoning for Walter to come with him. Walter woke up with a start and realized that he didn't know how to get where his friend was. He said, "I've not been a bad person, but I never attended church or been a religious man. I just don't know what to do."

I said, "Walter, there's a very simple answer to the question you're asking." I then explained the love of God that is not dependent on anything we do in this life, but just because we are His creations. I read John 3:16 and Romans 3:23 (that all of us are sinners), and Romans 6:23 (that sin leads to spiritual death, but eternal life is a free gift in Christ Jesus our Lord). We talked about what that meant, and then I read Romans 10:9, that "if you confess with your lips that Jesus is Lord and believe in your heart that God raised him from the dead, you will be saved." That's all. There's nothing we have to do. It's a free gift.

I remember that Walter turned toward the wall. Tears were streaming down his cheeks, and he whispered, "It's too simple. It's just too darned simple!" I said, "Yes—you're right. That's why it's such good news." And then I asked him if he wanted to invite Jesus to be his Savior and come into his life. He nodded and I led him in a simple prayer of salvation.

For the next two weeks, I went every day and read to Walter from the Gospel of Mark, and then he died and joined his friend.

Walter's wife, Lillian, began coming to church and soon became a Christian. A few months after that, I was leading a Bible study and asked how these members knew they were Christians. Lillian spoke right up. She said that she had always been a horrendous driver on the road. She was speed crazy and if anyone came up and started to tailgate her in the left lane, she would put her lights on so that the car behind her would think she had put on her brakes. More than once, she said, she saw the car behind swerve so it wouldn't plow into her. "But now," she said, "I'm a very courteous driver. I obey the speed limits. I let people out of their driveways in front of me. I wave and smile a lot. That's how I know Jesus is transforming me!"

That's the transforming power of grace. Once we understand grace as a free gift, once we allow God's love to touch us deeply, He begins to work in us to transform us.

But there is a catch: grace demands that we respond. Once we fully appropriate the good news of Jesus and his love for us, then we no longer want to continue our old ways of doing things. Grace changes us, from the inside, so we are no longer the people we were before God's grace captured us.

Paul writes here that because we are "graced" by God, He has created good works for us to do. That is, once we know grace, we are able to extend that uncanny grace to others. Once grace changes us, it then can flow out of us, if we dare. Once we "get" it, everything changes. We are free and unhindered to become who God created us to be. We are free to live differently from the world. Once we are exposed to and accept the grace of God, then we can, in turn, offer grace to others around us. There certainly isn't anything human about it.

Between 1997 and 2004, Baptists in the Republic of Georgia had been victims of a campaign of violence instigated by a renegade Orthodox priest named Basil Makalavishvili. He and his followers stole and burned non-Orthodox religious books in 1997. In February 2002, he led a mob that looted the Baptist Union's warehouse in Tblisi where he burned Bibles. In 2003, he led a mob that beat up some Baptist pastors. Then they attacked the Cathedral Baptist church in Tblisi, and on the day before Easter of 2003, his followers burned down one of the Baptist churches in eastern Georgia. The situation had been tense for many years and President Shevardnadze came to the Cathedral Baptist Church to apologize for religious violence in the country. And then in March of 2004, Makalavishvili and nine of his followers were arrested and thrown in jail, where they remained until their trial in November of 2005.

Malkhaz Songulashvili, pastor of the Cathedral Baptist Church, was called to testify against Makalavishvili, and when he arrived at the courthouse, the room was already filled with Makalavishvili's supporters. For three hours, Malkhaz, on the witness stand, spoke about Christian values, the ecumenical movement and religious liberty for everyone. The judge, prosecutor and visitors were very attentive and asked questions about differences among Christians and specifically about Baptist distinctives.

Then the judge asked what Malkhaz wanted. He responded, "I demand that these people be pardoned and released." Everyone was shocked! Makalavishvili's lawyers said, "Do you really want to forgive them? Everything? Including material losses?" "Yes," replied Malkhaz, and then said that he was demanding absolution without conditions, since that's the nature of Christian grace. The defense attorneys didn't think they heard him right, so they asked again, "Without conditions?" And Malkhaz said, "Well, the only condition is that they bring the red wine for the Communion we will share after they are released." There was laughter and cheering. And then, ignoring the rules of the court, Malkhaz rushed to the cage where the prisoners were sitting and shook hands with all of them. People were crying and clapping their hands, and as Malkhaz was leaving the courtroom, a small boy grabbed the sleeve of his robe and said, "Thank you, Bishop!" He later found out that this was Basil's grandson.

That evening, Malkhaz received a message from the prisoners saying, "Even if we are not released, we will be ever grateful to you." And a few days later, at the anniversary of Malkhaz's ordination, Makalavishvili sent two small icons as gifts to Malkhaz, along with a huge decorated anniversary cake.

That's what grace is and what grace does. Once we have been touched by the grace of God, and fully comprehend it, it changes everything about us—how we behave, how we carry on our relationships, how we do our jobs, and how we live out our faith in our homes, communities, schools, and church.

Paul writes here is that grace is a free gift. There's nothing we can do to earn it. We are loved and accepted by God. But He also wants to use us to extend His grace into our world. And we can do it. We don't have to be perfect. We don't have to understand it. We just need to practice it in our relationships and in the world around us. We can make a difference, if we but dare to follow Jesus.

Grace, the undeserved love of God, can transform our lives and our world, if we would only believe it.

THE PAIN OF JESUS
Mark 14:32-42, 15:33-37

Precisely at three o'clock in the afternoon, three long trumpet blasts went bouncing off the marble walls of the Temple precincts, and the milling thousands came to life; the ritual slaying of Passover lambs has begun. At one side, a group of priests begin singing the *Hallel,* praises for God's great deeds in the Exodus, while other priests stood at the front of long lines that snaked their way out of the Temple. The head of every household stood with his sacrificial lamb, and waited in line until he was at the front, where he would slit the lamb's throat. The blood was let into a gold or silver basin that was passed along the line of priests and flung against the altar. This was the heart of the ritual, signifying that the sins of that family were atoned for and the people of God were forgiven. Other priests flayed and dressed the lambs that were taken home and prepared for the Seder meal that evening.

30 years after Jesus was in Jerusalem for the Passover, Josephus tells us that there were 256,000 lambs sacrificed. There is no reason to believe there would have been many less than that on this occasion. The blood from the lambs was splashed against the altar. If there was only a pint of blood per lamb (a minimal amount from each animal), that means that there were between 40,000 and 42,000 gallons of blood flung against the altar! William Barclay tells us that the blood from the altar ran down a little channel and emptied into the Kidron brook outside the walls of the city.

Jesus is in Jerusalem for the last time. He has sent two of his disciples into the city to prepare the Passover meal, and they have done so. Perhaps one of them purchased the sacrificial lamb and waited in one of these lines, and then hustled off to the house to begin the roasting. Later, Jesus and his apostles arrived and climbed the steps to the Upper Room where they shared the Seder meal. In its course, Jesus took one of the cups of that meal and said, "This cup is God's new covenant, sealed with my blood." And they went out after the meal, and through the streets of Jerusalem and out one of the eastern gates to go over to the Garden of Gethsemane. On their way, they would have crossed a little footbridge over the Kidron brook. The water ran red from the blood of the lambs, and its sweet smell was heavy in the air. Perhaps then Jesus remembered his baptism and the words that came from heaven, "This is my beloved Son in whom I am well pleased," words from the 42nd chapter of Isaiah, the text about the Suffering Servant of God, the one who was to come, the Lamb of God who was to be slain for the sin of the world.

Jesus has been to this Garden many times before, but this is his last. This night is different. It is a night of agony with a difficult choice to make. He took his disciples with him for companionship. He did not ask them to pray for him. He didn't teach them anything. He just asked them to sit and watch with him because he was facing a very lonely battle and needed their support. But they had been with Jesus here before and knew this could be a long night, so they just sat down and dozed off. They left Jesus alone to fight this battle by himself.

Indeed, Jesus is in a battle for his very identity soul and for our souls. Mark tells us that he is in *agony.* The Greek word means a deep, shuddering awe, the greatest degree of horror and suffering imaginable, a sorrow so great that death is preferable.

And he cannot pray as he usually does. The typical posture for prayer is to stand before God with your hands raised toward heaven, but Mark tells us that Jesus cast himself face down on the ground. He has no energy to stand before God. He is agonizing over this prayer.

Notice how he addresses God: "Abba!" Jesus uses this word only here in all the Gospels. It is not his usual way to address his heavenly Father. The word "Abba" is a unique term that means something like "Heavenly Daddy." It is evidence of how deeply troubled Jesus is: he casts himself into the welcoming, trembling arms of his Dad, at this most difficult hour of his life. His emotional pain is great, because he knows that he is facing the cross.

Jesus would have seen crucifixions before, seen victims carry the 100-pound cross-beam out to that place of death, their backs torn open by the lash of the Roman execution squads. He has seen the iron spikes driven into warm human flesh, the shuddering thud of the cross as it is dropped into its hole on Golgotha. He has seen the unbearable pain and torture and suffocation of those who have been hung there, baking in the hot afternoon sun and dying of thirst. He has seen their naked humiliation and heard the ridicule of passers-by. He has seen these victims push themselves up onto the little knob of wood on the upright, the *sedile,* to relieve the suffocation (that afternoon, you'll remember that the Roman soldiers came to break the legs of the victims—that's so they can no longer push themselves up on that seat so that death comes more quickly).

But let's leave Jesus in his agony in the Garden for just a moment and take a little detour to sometime in the middle of the second century, at 2 pm on February 23. An old man has been led to the arena. His name is Polycarp and he is a follower of Jesus. He was hiding in a small upper room when they came for him. He could have escaped and gone elsewhere, but he said, "May the will of God be done," and he walked down the stairs to meet his captors. Then he ordered a meal for them and went off to pray for two hours. When he returned, they were so surprised at his composure that his captors said, "Polycarp, all we want is for you to say, 'Caesar is Lord.' You don't even have to mean it." But he refused, and they took him out to the amphitheatre. The Governor asked him to curse his Christ, and Polycarp replied, "For 86 years I've been his servant and he has done me no wrong. How can I now blaspheme my Lord and Savior?"

The Governor said, "I have wild animals and I'll send them on you." The old man replied, "Call for them! It is no worse than any other kind of death."

The Governor said, "Better yet—I will put you to death by fire!" Polycarp replied, "Why do you hesitate? That is preferable than the fires of hell."

Finally, after more discussion, the Governor realized that there was nothing he could do or say that would break Polycarp's resolve, and growing tired of the game, he decided that Polycarp would die by fire. The brushwood was piled up and logs thrown on and Polycarp removed his clothing. They asked him if he wanted them to nail him to the stake on which he would be burned alive, but he refused, asking that they only tie his hands behind him. He held his head high and stepped into the pile of wood, and as the flames licked up around him, he prayed, "O Lord, I bless You because you have thought me worthy of this day and hour." Polycarp died singing.

Not only Polycarp—he was merely one of thousands by that time. Stephen was stoned to death. All the Apostles were martyred except John. Early Christians were crucified, subject to the humiliation of public dismemberment. Some were thrown to wild animals for the pleasure of the blood-thirsty citizenry. Some were drawn and quartered, where each hand and foot was tied with ropes to four different horses that were sent in different directions. Nero impaled Christians on poles, covered them in tar, and set them afire to light up his garden parties. Even today, our Christian brothers and sisters are being persecuted and put to death for their faith all over the world. And most of them are dying joyously with the same composure and grace as Polycarp.

So my question is: what's wrong with Jesus? Why do we have a public record of his agony when these others faced their deaths with grace that borders on joy?

Well, perhaps Jesus wasn't agonizing over the physical pain he was facing. Something else may have been going on. Perhaps Jesus is agonizing over his existential pain. Let's think: he is of the same Essence as his heavenly Father. He has never been separated from that deepest and closest intimacy with his Father. They are One, of the very same nature and will. But Jesus is going to the cross as the Lamb of God, to take there the weight of all the sin of the world, your sin and my sin. Because God is a holy God who cannot stand sin in His presence, Jesus knows that if he goes to the cross, he will be utterly separated from his Father. He will be taking a risk of being completely and hopelessly abandoned by God. The physical pain is of little concern—that will be over in a few short hours. It is the private pain of his heart over which he is battling. The tension Jesus faces is maintaining his intimacy with his Father or acting on his love for us.

Three times Jesus prays that the cup will be taken away from him: if there is any other way, make it so! Three times the answer comes: the cross. It is the only way to do it. It is the only way that salvation can be won, in his own loneliness, and he is the only One is all the world's history who can do it. Three times he wrestled with the question. Three times he found himself alone because his disciples were sleeping. Here in the Garden, the real battle was fought. Here our salvation was won.

Yes, after the third season of prayer here in the Garden, Jesus accepts the cross as the only way. He will risk it. He will risk torturous separation from his heavenly Father for an eternity if need be, because that's how much he loves us. Yes, he will go. He will allow himself to be arrested and bound and led away, out of the Garden, to his trial and crucifixion. He will allow himself to be slapped up against a crude, splintery cross, impaled there and left desperately alone, hanging halfway between heaven and earth, knowing only sin. And the sky will turn black and the wind will kick up and the rain will beat upon him and the earth will tremble and all of creation will rebel at the injustice of it all, and Jesus will cry out, *"Eloi! Eloi! Lama sabacthani!"*

It is done. The battle has been won. The only way for our salvation to be secured is if Jesus goes all the way to the cross, if he dies with our sin and the sin of the world, if he alone bears that heavy burden of sin pressing down upon him. He will die so we will never have to risk that eternal abandonment of God. His love for us wins out!

Taking a deep breath, the battle is over. Getting to his feet, he raises the sleeping disciples once more. Voices can be heard; yellow torchlight can be seen flickering through the olive trees. The crowd is coming to arrest him, led by a traitor. Calvary is ahead.

And the Lamb of God is bound and pushed back across the Kidron brook into the city for his trial. Perhaps, just perhaps, there, on the little bridge, the bright moonlight glistens off the crimson water. The sweet scent of the sacrificed Passover lambs' blood is still in the air. Jesus stands here as another Passover lamb. But something is different about him. These other lambs had no choice in the matter, but Jesus goes willingly so that we won't ever have to face the real pain of eternal isolation and separation from God.

How much does Jesus' love you? This much? (Hold your hands apart in front of your body about a foot from each other, palms facing each other.)

This much? (Move your hands outward approximately another two feet.)

This much? (Stretch your hands out to arms' length, palms still facing each other.)

No—Jesus loves you *this much!* (Turn your palms out, to a position of crucifixion. Hold them here until the end.)

And he stretched out his arms and died.

"Behold! The Lamb of God who takes away the sin of the world."

"Behold! The Lamb of God who risks eternal separation from his Father because of his love for us."

"Behold! The Lamb of God who takes away my sin and your sin."

What, then, will be your response? What *must* be your response?

THE SPOKEN WORD
Mark 5:18-20

When Will Whitman was first appointed an American Baptist missionary, he was assigned to work in humanitarian aid in Bangladesh, alongside an Australian Baptist missionary named Manny Lane. When Will first arrived in the country, he came in at the port city in the south, and Manny was in the north. They planned to meet halfway on the long highway that stretches from north to south.

I heard this story from Manny himself in an Australian Baptist church. He said the highway is a simple two-laned road in the middle of the country. On both sides, the road slopes directly down to rice bogs, and they stretch as far as the eye can see, from horizon to horizon. Every once in a while, you pass through a little village and the people come out, but almost immediately you are again on the open road with not a soul in sight.

Manny first met Will here, on this long stretch of lonely road. When they saw each other, Manny pulled his jeep over to the side of the road and watched Will stop his jeep and get out, and, with long strides, he came over with his hand extended. He said, "Hi, I'm Will Whitman!" He and Manny shook hands, and Manny said that immediately there were about 100 people standing there with them, having come up from the rice fields. While he and Will talked, these people were standing watching them. All of a sudden, Will turned, walked over to his jeep, reached inside, pulled out his big black Bible, and came back. He then announced in a loud voice, "It is no accident that we are here today. God has brought us together." He then preached a gospel message for the next 20 minutes. When he was done, Manny and Will shook hands, Will got in his jeep going north, Manny got in his jeep heading south, and they went on their way. They wouldn't see each other for another few weeks.

After the worship service in which Manny shared this story, I asked him, "Hey, Manny, when Will first preached in Bangladesh, did you interpret for him?" He said, "No." I said, "Who did then?" He said, "No one." I said, "You mean Will knew enough Bengali when he first arrived to be able to preach? That's amazing!" And Manny said, "Oh, no—you've got it wrong. Will preached in English!" So here were all these Bengali peoples standing there on the highway, blinking in the hot sun and listening to a foreigner preach to them in a language they didn't know!

That was o.k., as far as Will was concerned. He believed that the Word of God in its spoken form has power. It takes shape and extends out and brings results. That's why Jesus is identified by John as the *Word* of God who has become flesh. It's the way God communicates with the world, and it's the way we are called upon to communicate. The spoken word has power.

Here is Alek Flek, a Czech who had studied at Charles University in Prague. He was an atheist, as are most Czech students, but he'd been witnessed to by a couple of his Christian friends. They told him a lot of stories about Jesus, but it all sounded preposterous to him.

Alek saw his girlfriend one evening after that, and he started to tell her about these stories. He said, "They are ridiculous! I can't believe that anyone would believe this rubbish! This myth about Jesus being born in a stable, and Magi coming to bring gifts to him, has no factual basis. And when Jesus grew up, he taught people a new way of life—a lot of ethical teachings that obviously came from the writers who made all this stuff up. And there are stories about Jesus healing people and they claim he even fed 5,000 at one time. And then he was put to death on a cross, and they say he rose from the dead. It's astounding, all the lies these people believe!" Alek shared the stories with his girlfriend that night, and they left each other.

About two weeks later, Alek saw his girlfriend again. She said, "Oh, Alek, I'm so happy! I'm a Christian!" He said, "What?" She said, "Yes! I heard all those stories you told me about Jesus, and I talked with a Christian friend about it all and I believe them and now I'm a Christian!" It wasn't long after that that Alek also became a believer. His girlfriend became his wife, and several years later, he finished his Master's degree at the International Baptist Theological Seminary in Prague and became a dynamic, active Christian. The last time I saw him, Alek was translating the Old Testament into Czech, running a Christian bookstore in Prague, and pastoring a congregation. The spoken word, even though he didn't believe it, had power. It captivated his girlfriend in such a way that she believed.

Charles Spurgeon was to speak in an auditorium in London one evening, and he went there in the afternoon to test the acoustics (there were no microphones in those days). He went to the platform and shouted out, "Behold the Lamb of God who taketh away the sins of the world!" Satisfied, he immediately left. Unknown to him, there was a workman up in the rafters who heard those words, and, as a direct result, gave his life to Jesus Christ.

The spoken word has power, but it needs to be let loose in the world.

Our text is an interesting story from Mark 5. Jesus is coming to new territory, the land of the Geresenes, within the district known as the Decapolis, or the Ten Cities. These were foreign cities, Roman outposts. Each had its own marketplace, forum, theatres, local god or goddess, games, and colonnaded walkways.

Jesus went over there and landed right in a cemetery, where a strange, wild man lived. He would cut himself with stones, and people from the nearby village used to come out and chain him to a stone wall so he wouldn't hurt himself. But he would break the chains and cut himself, anyway.

This wild man came running down to Jesus, shouting, "What do you want with me, Jesus, Son of the most High God?" Jesus was speaking to the spirit in this man, "Come out, you evil spirit." And the man was saying, "Don't torture me!" When Jesus asked the man his name, he replied, "Legion, because there are so many spirits in me!" And he begged Jesus not to send them out of the region. There was a large herd of pigs there, and in a word, as Mark tells the story, Jesus sent the evil spirits into the pigs. They rushed down the slope and into the sea and drowned themselves. At that point, the pig keepers ran into town to tell the pig owners that their pigs had all been killed, and the whole town came running out to Jesus. To their surprise, there was the wild man, sitting there, clothed and in his right mind, but they asked Jesus to leave their territory because they were afraid.

It was then that the wild man asked Jesus if he could go with him. But Jesus refused, saying, "Go home instead to your own people and tell them what the Lord has done for you." And the man went not only to his home, but to the other villages around there. All the people were so amazed that when Jesus returned to that territory in Mark 7:31, there were 4,000 people who came to hear him speak, and he fed them, just as he had fed the 5,000 in Galilee. This changed man went out and shared what God had done for him, and the spoken word called and challenged and tickled his hearers so that they wanted to know Jesus for themselves.

That's what happened with the woman whom Jesus met at the well in John 4. He told her that he could give her living water, and she went into town and started telling others about this Jesus, and they came out because of her testimony. They met Jesus and believed, but they said to the woman, "We no longer believe just because of what you said. We have heard for ourselves— we know for ourselves that this man is the Savior of the world." That's the power of the spoken word.

It leads me to two questions. First, do you have anything to talk about? How has Jesus been working in your life, empowering you, touching you, moving in you, transforming you? If you don't have a story to tell, you can't know the power of your witness. Get right with Jesus Christ. Give your life to him if you've never done so. It's the most important decision you can make, and you will experience freedom and fullness like you've never known before.

The second question is if Jesus is working in your life in some exciting way, who are you talking to about it? We have a responsibility to tell the world what God is doing in your life and our church! You don't have to convince anybody about it—just get the word out!

I was on the overnight train from Brjansk to Moscow with a few of my students. The train left Brjansk at midnight to arrive in Moscow at 6 in the morning. There's also a train that leaves Moscow at the same time for Brjansk, and the two trains pass in the night about halfway there. I was in a sleeping compartment with four of my students. We were in our beds, sleeping, when the train slowed and stopped—this was the sidetrack, I knew, where we had to wait for about a half hour so the southbound train could pass by. As soon as we stopped, Igor hopped down out of his bunk and went out. I could hear voices outside the train, and my interpreter told me that there was a marketplace there—the townspeople came out every night and brought food and toys and souvenirs, and Igor was going to buy some things for his five children. In about 20 minutes, the door opened, and Igor came in with a large teddy bear in plastic wrap that he set on the floor, and then he went out again and closed the door behind him. I lay there in the dark wondering where he had gone. After about 15 minutes, the train started to move, and I was sure that Igor had gone back out to the marketplace and had now missed the train. I was worried. After 30 minutes, I was sure that's what had happened. I know that my Russians are pretty resourceful, but he didn't know where we were staying in Moscow, so it was unlikely that he could find us. But then, after another fifteen minutes, the door opened, Igor came in, hopped up into his upper bunk, and I finally got back to sleep.

The next morning, just as we were pulling into Moscow, I asked Igor where he had gone last night. Igor speaks a little English, and he said, "I was with train lady." I knew he meant the woman who served our car on the train—she's the one who brought our sheets and blankets and coffee in the morning. Igor said, "I was with train lady. We talk about God." He had a broad smile. Here was Igor, three time zones away from his home and church in Novosibirsk, witnessing to a train lady at 3 o'clock in the morning. He wasn't going to get a new member out of it, but he only wanted to talk with her about Jesus and to tell her what Jesus had done for him. That impressed me. We don't know what power his testimony had on that train lady—that wasn't our business. That's the work of the Holy Spirit. Igor was simply being faithful in getting the word out there.

Back in 1977, two of my students were young men in their youth group at their local church in a little Russian village named Kletnya. They had a new pastor and he wanted to do something with the young people in the church. So he started an orchestra. He got some instruments and gathered 12 young people together and taught them how to play. They learned quickly, and it wasn't long before they were playing in Sunday morning worship. And then there was an evangelistic campaign in the church up in Brjansk, and this little youth orchestra was invited to play on that Saturday night. So they went up there, about an hour's drive, and they played and they listened to the evangelist, and all 12 of them repented that night and gave their lives to Jesus! It was a powerful spoken word.

When they came back home to the church building late that Saturday evening, they decided to call the other members of their youth group. 35 came to the church that night, and the kids in the band told the others what had happened to them. That night, all 35 of these kids gave their lives to Jesus.

In March of 2002, that group had their 25th anniversary. Every one of them is still an active lay leader in that same local church, except three. One is now the pastor of that church. Another pastors a local Baptist church in a nearby village. And the third moved to northern Russia where he a pastor and vice-president of the Russian Baptist Union. It happened because of the power of the spoken word.

You may be the only link between someone and your Lord. You may have the spoken word that someone in your world needs, waiting.

Let's return to Will Whitman. A few years ago, he was in Bangladesh, and he and a Bengali evangelist were invited to visit an unbelieving village. Will had a touch of the flu and wasn't feeling well. And it was an extremely long trip and the weather was hot and sticky. They got there after dark and were fed a big meal, and then were taken to the patriarch's hut where several other villagers had gathered. Will was invited to speak, but the heat and illness and a full meal made him sleepy and he found it hard to keep his eyes open. As the conversation went on long into the night, Will kept nodding off, and the Patriarch became offended because they were talking about such an important subject. Finally, in disgust, the old man said, "Why did you come to Bangladesh anyway?" Will answered, "I didn't choose this place." That offended the Patriarch even more, but Will said, "I came because God called me. He brought me here to tell how you can know Him in a personal way."

The old man looked shocked, and then slowly said, "Do you know that for 20 years, in this house and in the house next door and that one across the field, our village has met together and called out to God: "God, Who are you? How can we know you?" And Will asked, "Did God ever answer?" The old man's chin dropped onto his chest and, with a deep sigh, he shook his head.

By now, the hut was jammed with more people, and one of the villagers said, "We will sing now." And they started a little song that said, "O Lord, we are sinners. Because of our sin, there is a big gap between us and You, a gap no one can cross. It's like a swift river that no one can swim. We need a boatman, someone to take us across the river." These were people who had tried their best to please God, but knew that they fell far short. And they started a second song: "O Lord, we have heard that someone can show us the way to You, someone who died and rose again, someone who can give life to the dead. Who is he? What is his name?"

Will was just ready to pick up his Bible to introduce them to Jesus, but the evangelist stopped him. The villagers started to sing a third song in which they cried out to God to send someone who could show them the way.

When they finished, Will asked where these songs came from. Someone said a wandering holy man taught them a long time ago. Another said they came from a holy Book, and one said they were just made up. Then Will took up his Bible and told them about Jesus who had died and risen, the one who came to show the way to God, as God's fullest revelation of Himself. When he asked them to trust Jesus, many came to faith.

Today there is a community of faithful, committed Christians in that village. It happened because of the power of the spoken word. Here was a village that was hungry to hear some good news from heaven. It was Will's spoken word that fulfilled their songs and brought them to Jesus. All they needed was someone to speak the word to them.

Your word about Jesus is important, and powerful. Maybe someone is waiting to hear that word of hope. Maybe someone needs it. Will you speak it?

Let it out! Give it freedom! Provide *something, anything,* so the Holy Spirit can do His work!

BACKWARD COMMUNION
Luke 22:14-19

Ellen and I used to be roller coaster aficionados. When we were living in southern California, one of our favorite adventures was to take our boys up to Magic Mountain, a wonderful amusement park about a half hour from our house. In that park, the Colossus sits next to the parking lot. In its time, it was the largest wooden roller coaster in the world. It has double tracks that give you one of those jerky, bumpy rides up and down and around. It goes hurtling along at 62 mph on first descent down 115 feet of track. If you get the very last car, it actually lifts off the track. What a great feeling!

Every once in a while, the Colossus staff runs one train the inside track forward, and a train on the outside track backward. I tried the backward-facing car once, from the very last seat. It was an interesting experience. I discovered that when you ride forward, you have something to lean back against, but when you ride backward, there isn't anything to keep your body from being thrashed around. Plus, you never know which way the train is going to go next, so your stomach gets a bit queasy and your neck gets wrenched and whiplashed. Once was enough!

In spite of that, when I was riding that last car backward, I saw where *we'd already been* rather than where we were going, and I learned some things in the process.

Sometimes when we do things backward, we get a new perspective, which can be a very healthy thing. Now, I don't suggest that we do things backward just to do things differently, but sometimes it helps us focus on what's important and helps us see better who we are, what we do, and how we do it. And for us as Christians, it can be important to learning more about how we understand and practice our faith.

When it comes to our communion service, we ordinarily follow the centuries-old pattern of the church, which comes from 1 Corinthians 11, the earliest written document in the New Testament that contains information about the Lord's Supper. Paul tells the Corinthians that Jesus took the bread, gave thanks, broke it, passed it to his disciples, and said, "This is my body which is broken for you." And, in like manner, Jesus took the cup after supper, saying, "This cup is God's new covenant, a covenant of forgiveness, sealed with my blood. This is my blood shed for the forgiveness of your sins." This same pattern is written down later by Mark, the first Gospel, and then Matthew. When John writes his Gospel, the latest of all of them, he has no communion service in the Upper Room. Instead, the actual communion elements come in John 6, after Jesus feeds the 5,000.

But now we come to Luke's Gospel, written after Mark and Matthew but before John. Did you hear what Luke writes there about the Upper Room? "After taking the *cup,* Jesus gave thanks and said, "Take this and divide it among you. For I tell you I will not drink again of the fruit of the vine until the kingdom of God comes." And *then* he took bread, gave thanks and broke it, and gave it to them, saying, "This is my body given for you; do this in remembrance of me."

Hmm. First the cup and then the bread? What's going on here?

Well, you'll notice that there's a second cup in verse 20 (which I didn't read). In many of the earliest manuscripts of Luke's Gospel, that second cup is omitted, so there's still only one cup and one loaf, but in reverse order.

We should know that this isn't a contradiction among the Gospel accounts. In the Passover meal, there are actually 4 cups, and Luke is talking about either the first or second cup, then the bread, and if he did include another cup, it would have been the fourth cup.

But if we take only one cup and one bread in Luke and do it in the order in which he suggests—that is, if we do communion backward—what does that teach us? What kind of different perspective do we get on the communion service? What can we learn?

What I see is a very clear gospel presentation—the gospel explained in the Lord's Supper, which is exactly the definition of an ordinance.

Jesus first took the cup in Luke's account. Wwhat does the cup signify? As one of the first two cups in the Passover meal, the cup would have signified *the past* to these Jewish disciples: it was a reminder of the first Passover and the exodus. But Jesus also says (in the other Gospel accounts) that it is a cup of forgiveness. It's a cup of the new covenant of Jeremiah 31:31-34. Our garments are washed white by the blood of the lamb. The cup cleanses us, purifies us, sets us free from what is past. Our sins are forgiven through Jesus' blood.

Bruce Larson tells the story of a Catholic priest living in the Philippines, a much-loved man of God who carried a secret burden of a long-past sin buried deep in his heart. He had committed that sin once, many years before, during his time in seminary. No one knew of this sin. He had repented of it and had suffered years of remorse for it, but he still had no peace, no inner joy, no sense of God's forgiveness.

There was a woman in this priest's parish who deeply loved God, and who claimed to have visions in which she spoke with Jesus, and He with her. The priest, however, was skeptical of her claims, so to test her visions he said to her, "You say you actually speak directly with Christ in your visions. Let me ask you a favor. The next time you have one of these visions, I want you to ask Him what sin your priest committed while he was in seminary."

The woman agreed and went home. When she returned to the church a few days later, the priest said, "Well, did Jesus visit you in your dreams?"

She replied, "Yes, He did."

"And did you ask Him what sin I committed in seminary?"

"Yes, I asked Him."

"Well, what did He say?"

"He said, 'I don't remember.'"

That's the nature of the forgiveness that we know in Jesus Christ. 1 John 1:9 says, "If we confess our sins, God is faithful and just and will forgive our sins and cleanse us from all unrighteousness." We are set free from all that hinders us, from all that keeps us from being what God wants us to be, from the sin that separates us from God and each other. It comes in the cup. We are *forgiven,* and our sins are *forgotten!*

But then, in Luke's account, Jesus takes the bread and says, "This is my body which is broken for you." This is the bread of life. That is, Jesus did not come merely for forgiveness, but also to fill us with his living bread, with what is essential for life.

Do you remember the little parable Jesus told about the man who is cleansed of a demon who goes out and finds seven demons more terrible than he and brings them back (Luke 11:24-26)? When we are cleansed and forgiven by Jesus, the space needs to be refilled with the Bread of Life. Doing communion backward reminds us that we are forgiven and then we are filled with the new presence of Jesus.

In one of those great stone cathedrals in Europe there was a large, magnificent pipe organ. It was a Saturday afternoon, and the custodian was making one final check of the organ loft in the balcony. He heard footsteps echoing up the stone stairway, and turned to see a man in slightly tattered clothes coming up the steps. "Excuse me, sir," the stranger said. "I have come from quite a distance to see the great organ in this cathedral. Would you mind opening the console so that I might get a closer look at it?" The custodian at first refused, but the stranger seemed so eager and insistent that he finally gave in.

"May I sit on the bench?"

"Absolutely not!" came the reply. "What if the organist came in and found you sitting there?"

But the stranger looked so sad and was so persistent that the custodian gave in. "But only for a moment!" he said.

Well, the stranger seemed very much at home on the organ bench, and pretty soon he asked the custodian if he could *hear* what the organ sounded like. "No! Definitely not!" came the reply. "No one is allowed to play it except the cathedral organist."

The man's face fell, and his deep disappointment was obvious. He reminded the custodian how far he had come and assured him that no damage would be done. Finally he relented and the stranger pulled out some stops and began to play. Suddenly the cathedral was filled with the most beautiful music the custodian had ever heard: the music transported him heavenward.

In what seemed all too short a time, the disheveled stranger stopped playing and slid off the bench, and with joy on his face, started down the stairway. "That was the most beautiful music I have ever heard in the cathedral," said the custodian. "Would you mind telling me your name?" The stranger turned for just a moment and replied, "I am Felix, Felix Mendelssohn." Mendelssohn was one of the greatest organists and composers of the nineteenth century!

The custodian was alone and the beautiful music was still ringing in his ears. "Just think," he said softly, "I almost kept the master from playing his music in my cathedral!"

Jesus comes to us like that, as the Master Musician, to fill us with his presence and to play his music in and through us. That's the quality of life we know in him as the Bread of Life.

So, in the communion process, we are *forgiven* and then *refilled.* Life is new and wonderful. It's really what communion is all about.

During my third summer at college, I was invited to be the youth director at a church in a small Michigan town. I found out that during the first week I was there, the church was holding Vacation Bible School, so, as a new staff member, every morning that first week, I was present at the opening sessions.

At the time, the church had an interim pastor, an energetic 72-year-old man. During the opening session on Monday, he told the children that he was going to teach them a song that they would sing at the closing program on Friday night, a song that included all the books of the New Testament. He sang it for them that morning and had them try. Tuesday morning, they sang it again, and then on Wednesday, the kids knew it pretty well. That morning, he told them that they were going to play a trick on their Moms and Dads at the closing program on Friday night and he would tell them about it the next day. On Thursday morning, the kids sang the song correctly and loudly, and then he said, "Boys and girls! Tomorrow night we will have our closing program, and we're going to sing the song *backward.* Tomorrow morning I'll teach you how to do that!"

Well, the kids were all excited about this, and I thought, "It's taken him all week to teach them the song the right way. How in the world is he going to teach them to sing it backward in only one morning?" Well, Friday came, and the children came pouring into the sanctuary with great enthusiasm, talking about the joke they were going to play on their parents. It was the last day of Bible school and they knew they were going to learn how to sing the song backward! They were sitting in the first three rows of the sanctuary, and the pastor again led them in the song.

And then he said, "Now, boys and girls, tonight at the program, I'm going to say, 'Moms and Dads, your kids have learned to sing a song that has all the books of the New Testament in it,' and then you'll stand up and sing it, right where you are. And then I'm going to say to them, 'And now, we've got a very special surprise! The boys and girls not only learned how to sing this song forwards, but they also know how to sing it *backwards!'* Then you all just turn around in your seats and we'll sing it again, backwards!"

Well, the kids thought this was the greatest practical joke they'd ever heard! The pastor told them it was a big secret and they weren't to tell their parents or it would spoil the surprise! They sang it that morning and it went very well—the kids, giggling even louder, turned around in their seats and sang the song at the top of their lungs!

Evening came and the church was packed for the closing program. The children were all sitting in the front three rows and the pastor told the parents that the boys and girls had been learning a special song that week with all the books of the New Testament, and now they were going to sing it. The children, giggling, stood up and sang the song. And then the pastor said, "Moms and Dads, your children also learned how to sing this same song *backwards*. Let's sing it, boys and girls!" And the kids turned around, expressing all the fun that only kids have in those situations, but there was a great surprise waiting for them! That morning, they sanctuary had been empty. Now it was filled with faces watching them. They were in shock, but they recovered and sang the song well for the second time. Singing it backward gave them a different perspective, and it was surprising!

As we share first the cup and then the bread this morning, may our communion celebration give us new awareness of what the gospel means in our lives. May we, with great joy, be surprised again by the wonderful good news of Jesus and his love!

Subject Index

Lightning Source UK Ltd.
Milton Keynes UK
UKHW04f1029250718
326263UK00001B/151/P